ROOK & WARD
ON
SEXUAL OFFENCES
LAW AND PRACTICE

First Supplement to the

Third Edition

H.H. Judge Peter Rook, Q.C. M.A. (Cantab.),
of Gray's Inn, Barrister
and Robert Ward, C.B.E., M.A., LL.B. (Cantab.),
LL.M. (U.B.C.), of the Middle Temple, Barrister,
Formerly Fellow of Gonville and Caius College, Cambridge

with Chapter 19 – Medical Aspects of Sexual Assault by Dr Beata Cybulska,
Chapter 20 – DNA, Law and Statistics by Graham Cooke, of
Lincoln's Inn, Barrister,
Chapter 21 – Disclosure by Johannah Cutts and
Update to Appendix C to Main Work – A Guide to Prosecuting and Defending
Cases Involving Sexual Offences by Patricia Lees

LONDON
SWEET & MAXWELL
2008

First Edition

Second Edition

Third Edition

1990 by Peter Rook and
Robert Ward
1997 by Peter Rook and
Robert Ward
2004 by Peter Rook and
Robert Ward

Published in 2008 by
Sweet & Maxwell Limited, of
100 Avenue Road,
http://www.sweetandmaxwell.co.uk
Typeset by Interactive Sciences, Gloucester
Printed and bound in Great Britain by Athaenaem Press Ltd, Gateshead

No natural forests were destroyed to make this product; only farmed timber was used and replanted.

British Library Cataloguing in Publication Data

A CIP catalogue record for this book is available from the British Library.

ISBN 978–1–84703–171–6

HOW TO USE THIS SUPPLEMENT

This is the First Supplement to the Third Edition of *Rook and Ward on Sexual Offences Law & Practice* and has been compiled according to the structure of the main work.

At the beginning of each chapter of this Supplement the mini table of contents from the main work has been included.
Where a heading in this table of contents has been marked with a square pointer (■), this indicates that there is material that is new to the work in the Supplement to which the reader should refer.

Within each chapter, updating information is referenced to the relevant paragraph in the main work. New paragraphs which have been introduced in this Supplement have been identified as, e.g. 25.19A. This enables references contained within these paragraphs to be identified in the tables included in this Supplement.

Preface to Supplement to the 3rd Edition

It is now over three years since the Sexual Offences Act 2003 completely overhauled much of the law governing sexual offences. Our 3rd edition was written so as to coincide with this radical change in the legal landscape. Since the implementation of the new Act on May 1, 2004, there have been a series of significant developments on a number of fronts in respect of prosecutions of sexual offences. These have not been confined to Court of Appeal decisions dealing with key definitions in the new Act or legislation to solve problems stemming from the absence of transitional provisions,[1] but include the repercussions of the far-reaching new evidential and sentencing provisions in the Criminal Justice Act 2003 and the definitive guideline in respect of sentencing for sexual offences published by the Sentencing Guidelines Council (SGC) in April 2007. We have endeavoured to include all these developments, as far as it is practicable, within this Supplement. The evidential developments have warranted substantial coverage, as the "bad character" provisions are arising frequently in the trials of sexual offences. We have reproduced the SGC definitive guideline within the relevant chapters.

Whilst to some extent, the regime governing the admissibility of evidence of the previous sexual history of the complainant has bedded down following the House of Lords' decision in *R. v A (No.2)*, the last three years has seen the Court of Appeal continuing to wrestle on a fairly regular basis with the provisions of s.41 of the Youth Justice and Criminal Evidence Act 1999, and from time to time fresh points have arisen. We welcome the requirement now in the Criminal Procedure Rules that all s.41 applications must be in writing. It is essential that minds are concentrated upon what is truly relevant, and that the regime is applied rigorously. However, we do echo the warning given in our 3rd edition, that whatever the theoretical flaws in the provisions, now we have reached the present position in the aftermath of *R. v A (No.2)*, it would be unwise for Parliament to take any course that risks, in the pursuit of desirable goals, the legislative overkill that Lord Steyn referred to in his opinion in that case.

The prosecution of non-consensual sexual offences continues to be high on the political agenda as concerns persist as to how to improve the conviction rate. Whilst the new definition of consent in the 2003 Act represents a significant improvement over the previous law, it is imperative that the issue of the complainant's "capacity" is addressed properly by judges, lawyers and juries. Many cases are reaching the courts where the complainant has been very intoxicated at the time of the alleged rape or sexual assault. "Capacity" is, of course, an integral part of the definition of rape. Whilst a drunken consent is still a consent, if a complainant becomes so drunk that their understanding and

---

[1] See Ch.1. The deeming provision in s.55 of the Violent Crime Reduction Act 2006 is designed to solve the problem of complainants who cannot remember whether the rape or sexual assault was before or after May 1, 2004.

knowledge as to what is happening is non-existent or very limited, a properly directed jury may well decide that the complainant did not have the "capacity to agree by choice".

The issue has been under the spotlight following the *Dougal* case in Swansea, which involved the alleged rape of a very drunk Aberystwyth student, where it appears that the issue of capacity may not have been sufficiently addressed. The trial judge, at the invitation of the prosecution, stopped the case after cross-examination of the complainant. The following day, misleading headlines appeared in the press suggesting that drunk complainants could no longer be raped. The Home Office reacted to this by proposing that there should be a statutory definition of "incapacity through intoxication".[2] In fact, we already had the required law. This has now been confirmed by the President of the Queen's Bench Division in *Bree*,[3] a rape case where both parties had voluntarily consumed a great deal of alcohol. The Court of Appeal stated: (i) the 2003 Act, by defining "consent" for the purposes of the law of rape, and by defining it by reference to "capacity to make that choice", sufficiently addresses the issue of consent in the context of the voluntary consumption of alcohol by the complainant, and (ii) the issue of "capacity to make the choice whether to agree", in circumstances where the complainant may have been voluntarily intoxicated, does need to be properly addressed in a summing up. A mere recital of s.74 of the 2003 Act is not good enough. In *Bree*, the jury should have been given some assistance with the meaning of "capacity" in circumstances where the complainant was affected by her own voluntary intoxication, and also whether and to what extent they could take that into account in deciding whether she had consented.

Predictions that the evidential presumptions about consent listed in s.75 would arise very rarely in practice have proved entirely accurate. We frequently ask delegates at seminars whether they have ever encountered them, and so far there has been only one such case. The presumption would have arisen in that particular case because the complainant was so drunk he had no memory of events and the complainant was asleep. When questioned further, the delegate admitted that his client had pleaded guilty! So much for the grand statutory design, with the presumptions to bolster the new definition of consent. They have achieved the status of the proverbial damp squib. It is regrettable that such a long gestation period produced a wholly ineffective device. We suggest there is a case for revisiting the original proposals of the Sexual Offences Review in *Setting the Boundaries*, and having particular definitions of circumstances where, if proved, absence of consent would be established. The Scottish Law Commission,[4] having observed the Sexual Offences Act 2003 in operation, is now proposing seven particular definitions. If they become law in Scotland, they should be scrutinised

---

[2] Consultation Paper, *Convicting Rapists and Protecting Victims—Justice for Victims of Rape*, Office for Criminal Justice Reform, Spring 2006.

[3] [2007] 2 Cr. App. R. B [2007] Crim. L.R. 900. See also *R v H* EWCA Crim July 10, 2007.

[4] Scottish Law Commission Discussion Paper on Rape and Other Sexual Offences (No 131), published January 30, 2006. The final Report and Draft Bill are to be submitted to Ministers in late November 2007: lecture by Professor Gerry Maher QC of the Scottish Law Commission, *Reviewing Rape and Sexual Offences*, Edinburgh, October 8, 2007.

with care by those south of the border with responsibility for criminal law reform. One of the particular definitions relates to the situation where the only indication or expression of consent by the complainant to the conduct occurs at a time when the complainant is incapable, because of the effect of alcohol or any other substance, of consenting to it. Would this be not be a better way of catering for the ever-increasing number of cases where the complainant was heavily intoxicated at the relevant time? Other particular definitions are similar to the circumstances contained in our present evidential presumptions, for instance, where the complainant agrees or submits because of violence or the threat of violence. Also included is the situation where the only expression or indication of agreement to the conduct is from a person other than the complainant. Importantly, unlike the evidential presumptions in s.75, such a list would have a practical impact on the trial of sexual offences and send out signals to society as to what amounts to criminal sexual conduct.

Staying with the issue of consent in the prosecution of non–consensual offences, we consider that the relevance of evidence of a rape defendant being HIV positive or suffering from another STD deserves further consideration by Parliament. We acknowledge that delicate social policy issues are involved. In *R. v B.*,[4A] the Court of Appeal took a restrictive view, notwithstanding the new definition of consent in s.74 of the 2003 Act, and so the issue appears to have been settled for the time being where a rape defendant fails, without any express deception, to disclose his HIV positive status. However, many feel that the existence of that status fundamentally transforms the nature of the physical act of sexual intercourse, and the vast majority of sexual partners would not freely agree by choice to sex that involved running the risk of contracting the disease.

The issue of "capacity" is not the only one that has exercised those who feel that juries may not be approaching the critical issues in these trials in the appropriate way. Traditionally, defence counsel have made much of a complainant's apparently compliant behaviour, often accompanied by a lack of physical resistance or verbal protest, and then followed by late disclosure of the allegation and inconsistent accounts which are said to show untruthfulness and unreliability. However, research has shown the enormous impact of the trauma of rape upon rape victims.[5] Such conduct may in fact be unsurprising and not in any way suggestive of an untrue complaint. At the time of writing this Preface, we await with keen interest the results of Home Office proposals recommending that expert generic psychological evidence be admissible so that juries can hear of the acknowledged psychological reactions that occur after a prolonged relationship of abuse and/or after a deeply traumatic event.[6] The expert would be able to comment on why

---

[4A] [2007] 1 W.L.R. 1567.

[5] See the work of Dr. Fiona Mason, Consultant Forensic Psychiatrist at St. Andrews Hospital, Northampton. See also P. Frazier and E. Borgida, *Juror common understanding and the admissibility of the rape trauma syndrome in court*, (1998) Law and Human Behaviour 12, 101–122; G.C. Mezey GC and M. King, *Male Victims of Sexual Assault*, OUP (1992); J. Harris and S. Grace, *A question of evidence? Investigating and prosecuting rape in the 1990's*, Home Office (1999).

[6] *Convicting Rapists and Protecting Victims—Justice for Victims of Rape. A Consultation Paper* (2006) p.19; Home Office Report: Sexual Offences Act 2003—A Stocktake (2006).

victims often delay reporting, blame themselves, seek to minimise the events and their injuries, have incomplete and inconsistent memories of the incidents giving rise to the allegation, do not seek to resist, and do not take opportunities to escape. The expert would not comment on the behaviour of the particular complainant, but, for instance, in a case where the complainant is of systematic abuse during a protracted period, they would explain the popular misconception that leads us to fail to understand why the victim may still be reluctant to leave their abuser or willingly testify against him.

Juries may be expecting the impossible by evaluating the reliability of deeply traumatised victims simply on the basis of their ability to give coherent and consistent accounts of their experiences. Most of us are simply unaware of the common reactions of victims of rape, and so it makes no sense to assume that the average juror will have an understanding of them unless they hear generic psychological expert evidence of this nature. There is a real danger that jurors are currently assessing the evidence of complainants detrimentally because of power-ful myths and misconceptions that are held by many people. Research publicised by Amnesty International in 2005[7] reported[7A] that a third of the people in the UK believe that a woman is partially or totally responsible for being raped if she has behaved in a flirtatious manner. It is not for lawyers and judges to attempt to address rape myths in speeches and the summing up. Of course, the defence may wish to seek to contradict this evidence by calling their own expert, and this could prolong trials, but surely this is a price worth paying so that a balanced picture can be put before juries. In time, a broad consensus will emerge and such evidence will eradicate some of the public attitudes based on myths that may well be leading to fallacious lines of reasoning on critical issues in rape trials.

We are also still awaiting the results of the Home Office proposal in the same consultation paper that complaints of sexual offences should be admissible whenever they are made. We acknowledge that such complaints are now evidence of their truth under the Criminal Justice Act 2003, that s.120 of that Act as liberally interpreted in *O.* has, to some extent, loosened the previous common law restrictions, and that in many cases juries are currently hearing of them. It may well be that if a complaint is very late, the defence will wish to put it in evidence. However, we are firmly of the view that sexual complaints, including the nature and timing of them, are illuminating whenever they are made and should all be admissible. Such a reform would sit well with the admissibility of generic psychological evidence.

Many of the sentencing provisions of the Criminal Justice Act 2003 came into force in April 2005. In a series of decisions, the Court of Appeal has made the "dangerousness" provisions workable. These provisions are engaged by most sexual offences, and judges have to consider on a daily basis whether an offender represents a significant risk of serious harm to members of the public by the commission of further sexual offences. It is in the context of sexual offences that

---

[7] *Convicting Rapists and Protecting Victims*, last note, p.10.
[7A] Difficulties could, however, arise where a complainant has made inconsistent statements. See *Coates* [2007] Crim. L.R. 887.

the absence of the power to pass extended sentences in respect of all but the least serious sexual offences is at its most stark. Many feel that this is a legislative accident which was not detected during parliamentary scrutiny of the Criminal Justice Bill, almost certainly because of the complexity of the provisions. Sexual offences cover a wide range of culpability and, as a result, the maximum sentence for most sexual offences is 10 years or over and so they are "serious specified offences" for the purposes of the CJA 2003. It follows that an apparently unintended consequence of the dangerousness provisions is that extended sentences are not available for adult offenders who are considered to be a significant risk but have committed relatively minor sexual offences. We feel that this is an unfortunate omission which should be addressed as a matter of urgency.[8]

Again we have had enormous assistance from colleagues and friends. The complexity of the new sentencing provisions underlines the achievement of Tim Maloney in covering these developments by updating his three chapters, Ch.22—*Sentencing of Sex Offenders*, Ch.23—*Notification and Notification Orders* and Ch.24—*Sexual Offences Prevention Orders, Foreign Travel Orders and Risk of Serious Harm Orders*.

In her lectures, Johannah Cutts has that rare ability to make the subject of disclosure interesting, and her performance on paper is equally illuminating. She has provided a valuable update to her Ch.21—*Disclosure*. We are also indebted to Alexandra Ward for her excellent updating of two chapters, Ch.7—*Sexual Offences Against Those with a Mental Disorder* and Ch.17—*Vulnerable Witnesses, "Special Measures" and Related Matters*. David Campbell provided great assistance to us in respect of Ch.8—*Indecent Photographs of Children*.

As mere lawyers trying to continue to provide a comprehensive work we are most fortunate to have authoritative updates on subjects outside our expertise. Dr Beata Cybulska found time to escape from the pressures of running a busy sexual assault referral centre (SARC) to cover recent medical developments in Ch.19—*Medical Aspects of Sexual Assault*, whilst again we have had the benefit of Graham Cooke's grasp of different disciplines in his Ch.20—*DNA, Law and Statistics*.

Practitioners have told us that they have found Patricia Lees's guide (Appendix C) to prosecuting and defending in such cases of enormous value. We are extremely grateful to her for updating this.

We cannot underestimate the assistance we have received from Professor David Ormerod of Queen Mary's College, London University, who has always been ready to discuss problems as they arise, and invariably is able to shed immediate light upon them with his encyclopaedic and incisive mind. Neil Kibble of the University of Wales has continued to illuminate the darker recesses of the s.41 regime for us, whilst in respect of sentencing in sexual cases, we have gained enormously from constructive input from H.H. Judge Beatrice Bolton, H.H.

---

[8] See *Reynolds* [2007] 2 Cr. App. R. (7) 87 where the Court of Appeal had to deal with a number of cases where judges had passed extended sentences where they did not have the power to do so.

Judge Micheal Meattyear, Mohammed Fakrul Islam and Joanne Savage, secretary to the Sentencing Guidelines Council.

We would like to give a special mention to Mohammed Fakrul Islam, formerly librarian and now a pupil at 18 Red Lion Court. Over the last four years he has taken the time to provide us with a constant supply of new cases and/or publications which have a bearing on law and practice in this area. His careful vigilance has eased our task.

The contribution of Amanda Bowring of the Crown Prosecution Service also deserves to be highlighted. She has kept us abreast of significant new developments in respect of the prosecution of sexual offences.

Again we wish to thank our publishers for their forbearance. Nicky Penn has throughout provided us with full support and understanding, and as always we are deeply grateful to her. We would also like to thank Laura Cooper, our house editor, for her swift and efficient handling of the potentially fraught final pre-publication stages. We are most grateful that she was able to accommodate us by including a spate of significant cases including *Cartwright* where judgement was given on November 8, 2007.

P.R.

The Old Bailey

R.W.

Cambridge

November 2007

Supplement to "Rook and Ward on Sexual Offences: Law & Practice" 3rd Edition

Sexual Offences Act 2003: Commencement

The Sexual Offences Act 2003 was brought into force on May 1, 2004, by the Sexual Offences Act 2003 (Commencement Order) 2004 (SI 2004/874). Section 140 of the Act repealed or revoked much of the previous legislation on sexual offences, as listed in Sch.7 to the Act. Section 141 empowered the Secretary of State to make transitional provisions. However, no such provisions were made and the Court of Appeal felt unable to interpret the Act or the Commencement Order as providing a transitional regime.[1] It followed that, after commencement, where the prosecution could not establish whether a sexual offence was committed before or after the commencement date, the proceedings would fail because the prosecution would not have proved whether a statutory offence was committed under the old or the new law.

This lacuna in the law was filled by s.55 of the Violent Crime Reduction Act 2006, a deeming provision which came into force on February 12, 2007. It covers the situation where a defendant is charged in respect of the same conduct both with an offence under the 2003 Act and with an offence under the old law, and the only thing preventing him being found guilty of either offence is the fact that it has not been proved beyond a reasonable doubt that the time when the conduct took place was either after the coming into force of the 2003 Act offence or before the repeal of the old law, as the case may be. In such circumstances, for the purposes of determining guilt, it shall be conclusively presumed that the time when the conduct took place was when the old law applied, if the old offence attracted a lesser maximum penalty; otherwise, it will be presumed the conduct took place after the implementation of the new law. If the penalties are the same, then it will be conclusively presumed that the conduct took place after the commencement of the 2003 Act.

---

[1] *A (Prosecutor's Appeal)* [2006] 1 Cr. App. R. 433 sometimes referred to as *R v C* [2005] EWCA Crim 3533; and see *Newbon* [2005] Crim L.R. 738.

CONTENTS

Contents

TABLE OF CASES

TABLE OF STATUTES

TABLE OF STATUTORY INSTRUMENTS

CHAPTER 1

RAPE

SENTENCING

The sentencing guidelines

On April 30, 2007, the Sentencing Guidelines Council published definitive   1.18
guidelines on the sentencing of offenders convicted of offences under the Sexual
Offences Act 2003 Act. The guidelines apply to all offenders sentenced on or after
May 14, 2007, irrespective of the date of the offence. All offences under the 2003
Act are covered in the guidelines, along with the offences relating to indecent
photographs of children (see Ch.8). The courts are required to take the guidelines
into account[1] and they are therefore the first point of reference in sentencing for
any offence under the 2003 Act. The preparatory documents issued by the
Sentencing Advisory Panel and the Sentencing Guidelines Council should not be
treated as authoritative for sentencing purposes.

---

[1] See *Oosthuizen* [2005] EWCA Crim 1978; [2005] Crim. L.R. 979 as to the proper approach to SGC
guidelines. Whilst it is not open to a court to disregard such guidelines, this does not mean that they
must be followed slavishly. Section 174(2)(a) of the Criminal Justice Act 2003 recognizes that the
sentencing court may depart from a guideline where there is a reason to do so, albeit the reason must
be spelt out. A judge is not entitled to impose a higher sentence than would be appropriate by reference
to the national guidance for reasons of local deterrence, unless statistics are available to demonstrate
greater prevalence than that nationally of a particular offence.

The guidelines assume a first-time adult offender convicted after a not guilty plea. They set out starting points depending on the nature of the offence and also sentencing ranges. Aggravating and mitigating factors that are particularly relevant to the offence are listed separately. The list of aggravating factors is not exhaustive and the factors are not ranked in any particular order. Where harm is inflicted over and above that necessary to commit the offence, it will be an aggravating factor. Rape, along with most other sexual offences, is a specified offence for the purposes of public protection provisions in the Criminal Justice Act 2003 and the court must therefore determine whether there is a significant risk of serious harm by the commission of a further specified offence in accordance with the dangerousness provisions of that Act. In every case, the court should consider ordering the offender's disqualification from working with children or a sexual offences prevention order (SOPO).

In relation to starting points and sentencing ranges, the guidelines provide as follows[2]:

"2. As an aid to consistency of approach, the guidelines describe a number of types of activity which would fall within the broad definition of the offence. These are set out in a column headed 'Type/nature of activity'.

3. The expected approach is for a court to identify the description that most nearly matches the particular facts of the offence for which sentence is being imposed. This will identify a starting point from which the sentencer can depart to reflect aggravating or mitigating factors affecting the seriousness of the offence (beyond those contained within the column describing the type or nature of offence activity) to reach a provisional sentence.

4. The *sentencing range* is the bracket into which the provisional sentence will normally fall after having regard to factors which aggravate or mitigate the seriousness of the offence. The particular circumstances may, however, make it appropriate that the provisional sentence falls outside the range.

5. Where the offender has previous convictions which aggravate the seriousness of the current offence, that may take the provisional sentence beyond the range given, particularly where there are significant other aggravating factors present.

6. Once the provisional sentence has been identified by reference to those factors affecting the seriousness of the offence, the court will take into account any relevant factors of personal mitigation, which may take the sentence outside the range indicated in the guideline.

7. Where there has been a guilty plea, any reduction attributable to that plea will be applied to the sentence at this stage. This reduction may take the sentence below the range provided.

8. A court must give its reasons for imposing a sentence of a different kind or outside the range provided in the guidelines."

The guidelines state that the factors to be taken into consideration in relation to offences of rape are as follows[3]:

"1. The sentences for public protection *must* be considered in all cases of rape.
   a) As a result, imprisonment for life or an order of imprisonment for public protection will be imposed in some cases. Both sentences are designed to

[2] p.18.
[3] Pt 2A.

ensure that sexual offenders are not released into the community if they present a significant risk of serious harm.

b) Life imprisonment is the maximum for the offence. Such a sentence may be imposed either as a result of the offence itself where a number of aggravating factors are present, or because the offender meets the dangerousness criterion.

c) Within any indeterminate sentence, the minimum term will generally be half the appropriate determinate sentence. The starting points will be relevant, therefore, to the process of fixing any minimum term that may be necessary.

2. Rape includes penile penetration of the mouth.

3. There is no distinction in the starting points for penetration of the vagina, anus or mouth.

4. All the non-consensual offences involve a high level of culpability on the part of the offender, since that person will have acted either deliberately without the victim's consent or without giving due care to whether the victim was able to or did, in fact, consent.

5. The planning of an offence indicates a higher level of culpability than an opportunistic or impulsive offence.

6. An offender's culpability may be reduced if the offender and victim engaged in consensual sexual activity on the same occasion and immediately before the offence took place. Factors relevant to culpability in such circumstances include the type of consensual activity that occurred, similarity to what then occurs, and timing. However, the seriousness of the non-consensual act may overwhelm any other consideration.

7. The seriousness of the violation of the victim's sexual autonomy may depend on a number of factors, but the nature of the sexual behaviour will be the primary indicator of the degree of harm caused in the first instance.

8. The presence of any of the general aggravating factors identified in the Council guideline on seriousness or any of the additional factors identified in the guidelines will indicate a sentence above the normal starting point."

Court of Appeal decisions on sentencing under the 2003 Act that pre-date the guidelines may be instructive if they are compliant with it, in that they are likely to go into more detail and so may usefully supplement the guidelines. In relation to rape, the guideline adopts the starting points established in *Millberry and others*.[4] So five years is the starting point in the case of an adult victim raped by a single offender where there are no aggravating factors at all. Where any of the particular aggravating factors identified in the offence guidelines are involved, the suggested starting point is eight years.

The sentencing guidelines for the offences of rape and rape of a child under 13 (s.5 of the 2003 Act) are as follows:

Type/nature of activity	Starting points	Sentencing ranges
Repeated rape of same victim over a course of time or rape involving multiple victims	15 years custody	13–19 years custody

[4] [2003] 2 Cr. App. R.(S.) 31.

Type/nature of activity	Starting points	Sentencing ranges
Rape accompanied by any one of the following: abduction or detention; offender aware that he is suffering from a sexually transmitted infection; more than one offender acting together; abuse of trust; offence motivated by prejudice (race, religion, sexual orientation, physical disability); sustained attack	**13 years custody** if the victim is under 13 **10 years custody** if the victim is a child aged 13 or over but under 16 **8 years custody** if the victim is 16 or over	**11–17 years custody** **8–13 years custody** **6–11 years custody**
Single offence of rape by single offender	**10 years custody** if the victim is under 13 **8 years custody** if the victim is 13 or over but under 16 **5 years custody** if the victim is 16 or over	**8–13 years custody** **6–11 years custody** **4–8 years custody**

Additional aggravating factors	Additional mitigating factors
1. Offender ejaculated or caused victim to ejaculate 2. Background of intimidation or coercion 3. Use of drugs, alcohol or other substance to facilitate the offence 4. Threats to prevent victim reporting the incident 5. Abduction or detention 6. Offender aware that he is suffering from a sexually transmitted infection 7. Pregnancy or infection results	*Where the victim is aged 16 or over* Victim engaged in consensual sexual activity with the offender on the same occasion and immediately before the offence *Where the victim is under 16* ● Sexual activity between two children (one of whom is the offender) was mutually agreed and experimental ● Reasonable belief (by a young offender) that the victim was aged 16 or over

The guidelines stress that for sexual offences more than for many others, the sentencing process must allow for flexibility and variability. The suggested starting points and sentencing ranges are therefore not rigid, and movement within and between ranges will be dependent upon the circumstances of individual cases and, in particular, the aggravating and mitigating factors that are present.[5]

The guidelines also state that the extreme youth or old age of a victim should be an aggravating factor.[6] The aggravating and mitigating factors set out in the guidelines are additional to those in the Sentencing Guidelines Council's Guideline on *Seriousness* (issued in December 2004).[7]

A person convicted of rape[8] is automatically subject to notification requirements in accordance with the SOA 2003, s.80 and Sch.3.

Form of penetration

The guidelines state that it is impossible to say that any one form of non-   **1.18A** consensual penetration is inherently a more serious violation of the victim's sexual autonomy than another. The starting points established in *Millberry* are therefore applied to all non-consensual offences involving penetration of the anus or vagina or penile penetration of the mouth.[9] This is in line with the approach adopted by the Court of Appeal in *Ismail*,[10] a case of forcible oral sex where the Court observed that, although there is no risk of pregnancy associated with oral rape, there remains a danger of infection from sexually transmitted diseases and that amounts itself to an aggravating feature. In that case, a sentence of six years' detention in a young offender institution was upheld on the 18-year-old offender who raped a 16 year old girl in a public place at night. The offender had no previous convictions and pleaded guilty at the plea and directions hearing.

The relationship between the victim and the offender

The decision in *Millberry* established the principle that sentencers should adopt   **1.18B** the same starting point for "relationship rape" or "acquaintance rape" as for "stranger rape". The guidelines apply this principle to all non-consensual offences. Any rape is a traumatic and humiliating experience and, although the particular circumstances in which the rape takes place may affect the sentence imposed, the starting point for sentencing should be the same.[11]

---

[5] p.5.

[6] para.2.7. As to the youth of the victim, see *Cervi* [2007] 2 Cr. App. R.(S.) 60, where the Court of Appeal upheld a sentence of 7 years for the rape by a young man of previous good character of a girl aged 14 while she was asleep. The judge took the starting point as 5 years and then took into account the aggravating factors, being the age of the girl and the fact that the defendant persisted in addressing his attentions to her during the course of the offence.

[7] paras 1.20–1.24.

[8] Or found not guilty by reason of insanity, found to be under a disability and to have done the act charged, or cautioned: s.80(1) of the 2003 Act.

[9] para.2A.2.

[10] [2005] 2 Cr. App. R.(S.) 542.

[11] para.2.6.

Previous consensual activity between offender and victim

1.18C In limited circumstances, previous sexual activity between offender and victim may amount to mitigation. In *Millberry,* the Court of Appeal held that the offender's culpability in a case of rape would be "somewhat less" in cases where the victim had consented to sexual familiarity with the offender on the occasion in question than in cases where the offender had set out with the intention of committing rape. The definitive guidelines state:

> "An offender's culpability may be reduced if the offender and the victim engaged in consensual sexual activity on the same occasion and immediately before the offence took place. Factors relevant to culpability in such circumstances include the type of consensual activity that occurred, similarity to what then occurs, and timing. However, the seriousness of the non-consensual act may overwhelm any other considera-tion."[12]

Custodial sentence may not always be appropriate even for adult offenders

1.18D For a recent example, see *Attorney-General's Reference (No. 96 of 2006) (John William Miles),*[13] where the Court of Appeal held that a community sentence for attempted rape was not unduly lenient in the unusual circumstances of the case, though it stressed that such a sentence will rarely be justified as there needs to be an element of deterrence in sentencing such offences. The facts are instructive. The appellant, a young man aged 20 with no previous convictions, pleaded guilty at the earliest possible opportunity to attempted rape. He went to a public house with the victim, a girl aged 16, whom he had known for some time. They went to a car park and had consensual sexual intercourse. After some time, the victim said that she did not want the intercourse to continue and the appellant ceased. After talking for a while, the victim got up to leave. The appellant pulled her to the ground and pulled down her trousers. He attempted to penetrate her vagina with his penis but she prevented him from doing so. He put pressure on her neck so she had difficulty breathing. Eventually he released his grip on her throat and masturbated himself, ejaculating over her. He then phoned the police on his mobile phone telling them he had just practically raped someone. He was sentenced to a community order with an unpaid work requirement of 100 hours and a requirement to attend an accredited sex offender programme for 36 months.

The Court of Appeal stated that the sentencing judge had been right to conclude that the starting point was about five years, and acknowledged that the sentence would have to have been reduced to reflect the appellant's age, his plea and the particular expressions of remorse which arose out of his confession to the police immediately after the offence was committed. In those circumstances, taking into account the three month period the appellant had already served, the

---

[12] p.24, para.6. See also para.2.21.
[13] [2007] 2 Cr. App. R.(S.) 30.

sentence would have been a very short period of custody indeed; far shorter than would enable any assistance by way of education to be given to him. The Court felt that was a relevant consideration for the judge in concluding how to deal with the case in the ultimate interests of the public. It is submitted that the approach adopted in this case was wholly exceptional.

Young offenders

The youth and immaturity of the offender must be taken into account in each case.[14] Where the victim is under 16, mitigating factors include (i) sexual activity between two children (one of whom is the offender) which was mutually agreed and consensual and (ii) reasonable belief by a young offender that the victim was aged 16 or over. See *Corran*[15] for non-prescriptive guidance to sentencers in respect of young offenders and child victims. Where all mitigating factors converge in a case involving a young offender and a young victim, exceptional circumstances may justify a non-custodial sentence. See also *R. v G*,[16] a case of rape a child under 13 (s.5 of the 2003 Act) discussed in para.3.9 below.   **1.18E**

In *Millberry*, the Court of Appeal said that when sentencing young offenders for rape, the serious nature of the offence will mean that custody will normally be the appropriate disposal, but that the sentences should normally be significantly shorter than for an adult. However, this approach admits of exceptions and is not meant to be of invariable and inevitable application; where the facts of the case are particularly serious, the youth of the offender will not necessarily mitigate the appropriate sentence.[17]

In *R. v B*,[18] the Court of Appeal upheld an indeterminate sentence of detention for life in respect of the 15-year-old offender who, as a pupil, had forced a teacher to perform oral sex twice, having dragged her from the classroom and told her he would kill her. The sentencing judge fixed a notional sentence of nine years with a specific term of three years and eight months. The Court of Appeal held that the case was unique, that exceptional violence had been used and that the offender's young age had to be balanced against the seriousness of the offence. While the age of the offender was something a court had to take strongly into account, it could not be a matter that prevented an appropriate sentence on particular facts.

Cases more serious than envisaged in the definitive guidelines

The type/nature of activity attracting the highest suggested starting point is repeated rape of the same victim over a course of time or rape involving multiple offenders. The guidelines recommend a starting point of 15 years in such cases, with a sentencing range of 13 to 19 years.   **1.18F**

[14] Definitive guidelines, para.2.9.
[15] [2005] 2 Cr. App. R.(S.) 73; [2005] Crim. L.R. 404.
[16] [2006] Crim. L.R. 821.
[17] See *Asi-Akram* [2006] 1 Cr. App. R.(S.) 260; *Patrick M.* [2005] 1 Cr. App. R.(S.) 218.
[18] [2006] EWCA Crim 330.

In *Attorney-General's Reference (No. 14 and 15 of 2006) (Tanya French and Alan Webster)*,[19] the Court of Appeal agreed with the trial judge's remarks and the Attorney-General's submission that the case went beyond that envisaged by the guideline authorities. It combined the aggravating features of repeated rape of a victim over a period of time, breach of trust, and the most vulnerable victim possible—a tiny baby. The Court held that this last feature should be treated as an additional aggravating factor, and that the extraordinary and abhorrent features of the treatment of this victim called for a starting point of 24 years.

Life imprisonment or imprisonment for public protection?

1.18G   As rape is a "serious specified offence" under the dangerousness provisions of the Criminal Justice Act 2003, sentences of imprisonment for public protection must be considered in all cases. The definitive guidelines state that a life sentence "may be imposed either as a result of the offence itself where a number of aggravating factors are present, or because the offender meets the dangerousness criterion".[20] It follows that in an appropriate case, which is likely to be rare, the seriousness of the offence may itself justify a life sentence whether or not the defendant meets the dangerousness criterion.

This represents a different approach from that so far adopted by the Court of Appeal in sentencing under the dangerousness provisions. So in *Betteridge*,[21] the Court of Appeal substituted a sentence of imprisonment for public protection for one of life imprisonment in a very serious case of rape where the complainant, the 14-year-old friend of the appellant's daughter, had stayed over at the appellant's house. The appellant had tied up the complainant's ankles with a belt, made her drink a mug of absinthe and forced open her legs. He had subjected her to anal and vaginal rape, and attempted to force her to give him oral sex. The trial judge concluded that there was a significant risk to members of the public of serious harm occasioned by the commission by him of further specified offences. In reaching that conclusion, the judge took into account the very serious breach of trust, the element of force used and the fact that the appellant had diminished the complainant's resistance by forcing her to drink alcohol and by tying her up before committing the offences upon her. He indicated that the fact that the appellant had been capable of perpetrating these acts in these circumstances on a friend of his daughter satisfied him that the dangerousness criterion had been met, and went on to impose two life sentences.

The Court of Appeal stated[22]:

> "Having decided that there was a significant risk within the meaning of section 225(1)(b), the judge should then have proceeded to consider whether the seriousness of the offences was such as to justify the imposition of a sentence of imprisonment for life. Instead he proceeded immediately to impose a life sentence. The level of

---

[19] [2006] EWCA Crim 1335.
[20] p.24, para.1(b).
[21] [2006] EWCA Crim 400.
[22] At para.20, *per* Swift J.

seriousness required for the imposition of a life sentence is dealt with in *Lang* in paragraph 8, where the Vice President said:

'It is not clear whether, Parliament, when referring in sections 225(2)(b) and 226(2)(c) to the seriousness of an offence or offences being "such as to justify" imprisonment or detention for life, thereby making such a sentence mandatory, was intending to adopt this Court's criteria for the imposition of a discretionary life sentence (see *R v Chapman* [2000] 2 Cr.App.R.(S.) 77) or was seeking to introduce a new more restrictive criterion for seriousness relating it solely to the offence rather than, also, to the dangerousness of the offender. On the basis that Parliament is presumed to know the law, we incline to the former view. This construction is supported by section 143(1), which requires the court, when considering the seriousness of any offence, to consider the offender's culpability and "any harm which the offence caused, was intended to cause or might foreseeably have caused". This language clearly requires consideration of culpability of the culpability of the defendant as well as the seriousness of the offence and therefore involves consideration of dangerousness.' "

The Court of Appeal in *Betteridge* took the view that, serious though the offences were, they would not hitherto have been such as to justify a discretionary life sentence, and nor did they now. They quashed the life sentences and substituted for them sentences of imprisonment for public protection.

In *Martyn Frost*,[23] the Court of Appeal upheld the trial judge's decision to pass concurrent sentences of life imprisonment in respect of 10 counts of rape. Although the dangerousness provisions of the Criminal Justice Act 2003 did not apply to the rape counts, the case is a good illustration of where life imprisonment would be justified as opposed to a period of imprisonment for public protection or a determinate sentence. The case related to the abuse of three girls who were step-daughters of the applicant. A relationship had developed between him and the mother of the girls, and the applicant had moved in with the family. He was unemployed but the mother worked full-time at a hospital. During a period of over two years, the applicant sexually abused his three stepdaughters. He became increasingly obsessed with a computer, and made 28 films showing him sexually abusing the girls. Every form of sexual abuse imaginable was on the films: touching, digital penetration, anal rape, vaginal rape, oral sex both ways, the use of objects on the girls, anally and vaginally, and ejaculation on them. His voice could be heard on the films giving the girls instruction as to what to do. In all, about 4000 photographic images were found, 10 of which were at the highest level as defined in *Oliver*.[24]

In the Court of Appeal, the applicant challenged the life sentences for the offences of rape. The Court agreed with the trial judge's description of this catalogue of offending as "one of the worst and most horrifying cases of child abuse which has ever come before this court" and took the view that the offences were sufficiently serious to support a long sentence of imprisonment. It also felt that the scope, frequency and depth of offending rendered it impossible to say with any reliability when the applicant would no longer pose a significant risk of serious harm from further offending. The Court noted that when, due to the

[23] [2006] EWCA Crim 1798.
[24] See para.8.07 of the main work.

9

vention of the children's mother, that avenue for physical gratification was
d to him, the applicant, with some determination, pursued his taste for
ophilia on his computer and gained his gratification by acquiring and storing
voluminous fresh material of abused children, as well as by continuing to enjoy his
back-catalogue of the abuse he had personally inflicted on his step-daughters. The
court felt that the judge's description of the applicant as a devious and committed
paedophile was merited, and did not think it arguable that a life sentence was other
than both appropriate and necessary to meet the justice of the case.

Boys under the age of 14

*Allegations of historical sexual abuse where the defendant was or may have been
aged between 10 and 14 at the relevant time*

1.54   Section 1 of the Sexual Offences Act 1993 abolished the presumption that boys
under the age of 14 are incapable of vaginal or anal intercourse with effect from
September 20, 1993. The presumption still applies to allegations involving
penetration before that date. However, evidence of penetration can be adduced and
the case can therefore be dealt with as an indecent assault.

   At common law there was a rebuttable presumption that a child aged not less
than 10 but under 14 was *doli incapax*, i.e. incapable of committing a crime. The
presumption was rebutted only if the prosecution proved beyond reasonable
doubt, not only that the child committed the *actus reus* with *mens rea*, but also that
he knew that the particular act was "seriously wrong" and not merely naughty or
mischievous. This presumption was abolished by s.34 of the Crime and Disorder
Act 1998. The intention was to put children aged 10 and above on the same
footing as adults from the time of the implementation of s.34. The presumption
will still apply to pre-abolition historic abuse cases.[25]

ABSENCE OF CONSENT

Consent and "capacity" under the Sexual Offences Act 2003

1.88   "Capacity" is an integral part of the definition of consent. Whilst a drunken
consent is still a consent, if a complainant becomes so intoxicated that they no
longer have the capacity to agree, there can be no consent. ~ development on
                                                                              old case
   This issue was put under the spotlight following the case of *Dougal* at Swansea
Crown Court in November 2005. The defendant had been charged with the rape
of an Aberstwyth student, who had consumed a significant amount of alcohol.
Following cross-examination of the complainant, prosecution counsel informed
the judge that he did not propose to offer any further evidence, because the

---

[25] *Andrew N.* [2004] EWCA Crim 1236.

prosecution were unable to prove that the complainant had not given consent because of her level of alcohol consumption.[25A] The trial judge directed the jury to enter a "not guilty" verdict. The Home Office subsequently consulted on a proposal that there should be a statutory definition of "incapacity through intoxication",[26] although no steps have yet been taken to implement this proposal.

In *Bree*,[27] the complainant, a student, shared a flat with the appellant's brother. One weekend, the appellant visited and went out with a group of his brother's friends, which included the complainant. She drank to excess and on returning to the flat, kept being violently ill. She recalled being in bed and said that, when she was lying there, she became aware that the appellant's face was between her legs and he was placing his tongue in her vagina. She then remembered him coming towards her and inserting his penis into her vagina. She said she did not consent, but did not know how to stop the activity. She did and said nothing. She felt uncoordinated. She could remember being asked whether she had a condom and saying "ow" when the appellant penetrated her, but her recollection was "very patchy" because of her intoxication. The appellant was charged with rape and the issue at trial was consent. The prosecution put the case to the jury on the basis that the complainant had not consented and, so far as she could, had made that clear, but here severe intoxication had hampered her ability to resist. The appellant's case was that, though the complainant had been intoxicated, she was not so drunk as to be incapable of consenting and she had in fact consented. The judge directed the jury simply in terms of the definition of consent in s.74 of the 2003 Act. "Capacity" is not defined by the act and the judge did not direct the jury on its meaning or effect in the context of the case. The appellant was convicted and appealed on the basis that the judge had inadequately directed the jury.

The Court of Appeal quashed the conviction, and in doing so made a number of observations on the operation of the law on the issue of "capacity". In particular, the Court stated that some of the hugely critical discussion arising after *Dougal* missed the essential point. In that case neither counsel for the Crown, nor for that matter the judge, was saying that a complainant who through drink is incapable of consenting to intercourse must nevertheless be deemed to have consented to it. Nor were they saying that a man is at liberty to have sexual intercourse with a woman who happens to be drunk, on the basis that her drunkenness deprives her of her right to choose whether to have intercourse or not. Such ideas were wrong in law, and offensive.

The decision in *Bree* does not represent a fresh interpretation of the law governing this issue. Sir Igor Judge P., giving the judgment of the Court, pointed

---

[25A] In *Bree* [2007] 2 Cr. App. R. 13 para.32 the Court of Appeal observed that, without knowing all the details of the case, it would be open to question whether the inability of the complainant to remember whether she gave her consent or not might on further reflection be approached rather differently.

[26] See Consultation Paper, *Convicting Rapists and Protecting Victims—Justice for Victims of Rape*, Office for Criminal Justice Reform (Spring 2006).

[27] [2007] 2 Cr. App. R. 13.

out that the relevant principle was summarised in *Lang*[28] and stated: " . . . in our view the 2003 Act provides a clear definition of 'consent' for the purposes of the law of rape, and by defining it with reference to 'capacity to make that choice', sufficiently addresses the issue of consent in the context of voluntary consumption of alcohol by the complainant."

However, the Court of Appeal did stress that judges must give juries assistance about how properly to approach the meaning of "capacity" in circumstances where a complainant may have been affected by voluntarily induced intoxication, and also on whether, and to what extent, they can take it into account in deciding whether the complainant had consented.

Sir Igor Judge P. stated:

"In our judgment, the proper construction of section 74 of the 2003 Act, as applied to the problem now under discussion, leads to clear conclusions. If, through drink (or for any other reason) the complainant has temporarily lost her capacity to choose whether to have intercourse on the relevant occasion, she is not consenting, and subject to questions about the defendant's state of mind, if intercourse takes place, this would be rape. However, where the complainant has voluntarily consumed even substantial quantities of alcohol, but nevertheless remains capable of choosing whether or not to have intercourse, and in drink agrees to do so, this would not be rape. We should perhaps underline that, as a matter of practical reality, capacity to consent may well evaporate well before a complainant becomes unconscious. Whether this is so or not, however, is fact specific, or more accurately, depends on the actual state of mind of the individuals involved on the particular occasion."

It follows that in all cases where there is evidence upon which the jury could find that the complainant was voluntarily intoxicated by drink or drugs, they should be given directions as to the possibility that intoxication may have led him or her to behave differently from the way they would have done if entirely sober.[29] A drunken consent is still a consent. However, in cases where there is evidence upon which the jury might properly decide that the complainant did not have the capacity to agree by choice, the judge should direct the jury on the issue of "capacity".

Cases where one or frequently both parties are heavily voluntarily intoxicated are so fact specific, there are dangers in slavishly following a prescriptive specimen direction. However these points often arise in such cases and when they do, need to be addressed in the judge's summing up.

   (i) Consumption of alcohol or drugs may cause someone to become disinhibited and behave differently from the way they would normally behave. If they are aware what is happening, but the consumption of alcohol or drugs has caused them to consent to activity which they would ordinarily refuse, then they have consented no matter how much they may regret it later. A drunken consent is still a consent if a person has the capacity to make the decision whether to agree by choice.

---

[28] [1976] 62 Cr. App. R. 50, referred to in para.1.94 of the main work.
[29] See also *Coates* [2007] EWCA Crim 1471, at para.44, *per* Sir Igor Judge P. [2007] Crim. L.R. 887.

(ii) However a person may lose the capacity to consent through the consumption of drink or drugs. Clearly a complainant will not have the capacity to agree by choice where they were so intoxicated through drink or drugs, their understanding and knowledge were so limited that they were not in a position to decide whether or not to agree. Thus, if a complainant becomes so intoxicated that they no longer have the capacity to agree, there will be no consent.

(iii) A person may reach such a state without losing consciousness. For instance a person may be in a state where they know they do not want to take part in any sexual activity with someone, but they are incapable of saying so. Alternatively, they may have been affected to such a degree, that, whilst having some limited awareness of what is happening, they are incapable of making any decision at all.

(iv) If a person is asleep or has lost consciousness through drink or drugs, they cannot consent, and that is so even though their body responds to the defendant's advances.

Consent and capacity to consent—withdrawal of case from jury

Issues of consent and capacity to consent in cases of alleged rape should normally be left to the jury to determine. *R. v H*[29A] *(Application by the Crown Prosecution Service under s.58 of the Criminal Justice Act 2003)* is a highly instructive case where the Court of Appeal decided that it was not reasonable for the trial judge to have withdrawn the case from the jury and he had erred by withdrawing the case from them. It was for the jury, not the judge, to decide, on the basis of the evidence called, whether, on the facts, the complainant had the capacity to consent and/or in fact consented to intercourse or not.

   The complainant was a 16 year old girl who had come to London to celebrate the New Year. She got drunk, became separated from her friends and ended up at White City getting into a car with strangers. The car drove off. During the journey, a man in the front passenger seat "fingered" her, as in digital penetration. She said that she did not know when this started or how it happened. She told the jury that the unknown man must have undone her jeans without her knowledge. All she could say was that she saw his hand between her legs. She pulled it out, did up her trousers, and told him to get off. His response was to laugh. She said she did not consent to what the man did. The prosecution case was that ten minutes later the defendant asked her for sex. She described what happened in her video taped interview:

> " . . . I just remember the man in the back saying, 'Can I have sex?' but I can't remember what I said to him and all of a sudden my trousers were like yanked down and then he was like, he'd like pulled them down to my knees and then he just like pushed my legs forward and my like jeans were like covering my face and my nose, and he was just like having sex with me and I remember I couldn't breathe or anything . . . . I think I might have tried to say get off me but I don't think he could

1.88A

[29A] Court of Appeal, Tuesday July 10, 2007.

13

hear me because like the jeans was over my face and there was some music playing."

She confirmed in her evidence that she did not want to have sex with the man,
that she did not think that she did so willingly and she did not think that she
would have consented. She said she could not remember what she had said
because she was drunk. The prosecution argued that by using "consent" it was
clear that the complainant meant that she could not say whether she had actually
said "yes" or "no". The defence argued that she was unable to exclude the
possibility she had said "yes" to sex. A full DNA profile obtained from semen
found in the crotch area of the complainant's underwear matched the defendant.

The trial judge, in his ruling, observed that, at its highest, the complainant's
evidence was that she did not think she would have consented. He stated that the
prosecution accepted that the complainant could not say that she did not say
"yes". In respect of the issue as to whether she lacked the capacity to agree by
choice as a result of taking drink or drugs, he found that although there was
evidence of drunkenness, it was insufficient to allow a jury safely to conclude that
the complainant had lacked the capacity to consent.

This case serves as an important reminder of some fundamental principles in
respect of the appropriate approach to consent. (i) there is no requirement that
absence of consent has to be demonstrated or that it has to be communicated to
the defendant.[29B] It does not matter that the prosecution cannot establish that the
complainant did not say "no" or that the complainant was incapable of saying
"no". (ii) the fact that a complainant cannot remember if she consented or not is
not necessarily fatal to a prosecution and (iii) there is no requirement that the
complainant should be incapable of putting up some physical resistance or that
they did put up physical resistance.

The Court allowed the appeal against the trial judge's ruling and remitted the
case for trial at the Crown Court.[29C] The Court observed that it would be a rare
case indeed where it would be appropriate for a judge to stop a case in which, on
one view, a 16 year old girl, alone at night and vulnerable through drink, is picked
up by a stranger who has sex with her within minutes of meeting her and she says
repeatedly she would not have consented to sex in these circumstances.

Consent—withdrawal of issue from the jury

1.88B   In *R. v H*[30] the appellant had been charged with rape and his defence was that the
alleged conduct (oral penetration) had simply not happened at all. The judge
directed the jury properly as to the ingredients of the offence (including consent)
and then said: "You may think that the issue of consent does not arise in this case,
it being the defendant's case that it never happened at all. So you may think that

---

[29B] *Malone* [1998] 2 Cr. App. R. 447.
[29C] The defendant was subsequently convicted by the jury.
[30] [2006] EWCA Crim 853.

your task can be simplified by asking yourself [whether the defendant did the act alleged]. If the answer is yes, the defendant would be guilty. If the answer is no, he would be not guilty." While the Court of Appeal had some sympathy with the judge's natural wish to identify for the jury the central issue between the parties, it would have been better had he been less emphatic. However, it could not be said that the issue of consent had been withdrawn from the jury: the judge had left them to decide whether they could simplify their task, and they would only have done so if they were sure that consent was not an issue.

EVIDENTIAL PRESUMPTIONS AS TO CONSENT

Section 75 of the Sexual Offences Act 2003

The evidential presumptions in s.75 of the 2003 Act arise very rarely in practice. **1.99** In most cases, absence of consent, and the defendant's state of mind, will be proved without reference to evidential or conclusive presumptions. In any event, it is clear that they do not apply to inchoate offences.[31] The presumptions continue to require the prosecution to disprove consent if, in the circumstances defined in the section, there is sufficient evidence to raise the issue.[32] The defendant is usually in a position to point to sufficient evidence to raise an issue as to whether the complainant consented and/or whether the defendant reasonably believed that the complainant consented. However, in practical terms, the existence of s.75 may well mean that the defendant is obliged to enter the witness box to provide an explanation where one or more of the circumstances has been established without contradiction, and sufficient evidence to raise an issue has not emerged during cross-examination.

How will a defendant satisfy a judge that the presumption does not apply?　　　✗　　probs with Act.

The analysis in the main work as to how s.75 operates in the rare case where there **1.114** is insufficient evidence to raise an issue is supported by *Wang*,[33] where the House of Lords held that a judge may never direct a jury to convict.

CONCLUSIVE PRESUMPTIONS AS TO CONSENT

Deception

Sexual intercourse induced by a fraudulent promise

The conclusive presumption under s.76(2)(a) that the complainant did not consent **1.144** to the relevant act, and the defendant did not reasonably believe that the

---

[31] This problem is highlighted in H.H. J Rodwell QC, *Problems with the Sexual Offences Act 2003* [2005] Crim. L.R. 290.

[32] *Jheeta* [2007] 2 Cr. App. R. 34, at para.23, *per* Sir Igor Judge P.

[33] [2005] UKHL 9.

complainant consented to the act, did not arise in a case where the defendant deceived the complainant by creating a bizarre fantasy which led her into having sexual intercourse with him more often than she otherwise would have done. In *Jheeta*,[34] the complainant and appellant met while students and started a sexual relationship. To prevent the complainant from breaking off the relationship, the appellant sent her threatening text messages. The complainant had no idea who was sending the messages, and shared her worries about them with the appellant. He tried to reassure her that he and his friends would protect her. When the complainant wanted to involve the police, he said he would lodge a complaint on her behalf. Over a period of four years, the appellant sent her numerous text messages appearing to be sent by different police officers. The messages were designed to encourage her to maintain the relationship with the appellant and to sleep with him.

The appellant was arrested and, when interviewed, eventually admitted that he had been responsible for the creation of the entire fictitious scheme. There had been occasions when sexual intercourse had taken place while the complainant was not truly consenting. Following advice from counsel as to the effect of s.76, the appellant pleaded guilty to inter alia four counts of rape. In his basis of plea, he acknowledged that he had persuaded the complainant to have sexual intercourse with him more frequently than she otherwise would have done and that the persuasion had taken the form of the pressures imposed on her by the complicated scheme he had fabricated.

On appeal against conviction, the appellant argued that the deception did not amount to a deception as to the nature or purpose of the act, and accordingly the conclusive presumptions could not be established. The Court of Appeal agreed, holding that the complainant had been deceived not as to the nature or purpose of the sexual intercourse, but as to the situation in which she had found herself. No conclusive presumption arose merely because a complainant was deceived in some way or other by disingenuous blandishments or common-or-garden lies by the defendant. These may well be deceptive and persuasive, but they will rarely go to the nature or purpose of intercourse. However, the Court dismissed the appeal on the basis that, in the light of the appellant's admissions, the complainant had not exercised a free choice or consent for the purposes of s.74 of the 2003 Act. There was no doubt that, on some occasions at least, the complainant had not consented and that the appellant was perfectly aware of that.

Deception as to the purpose of the act

1.145   Section 76(2)(a) of the 2003 Act is relevant only in the comparatively rare case where the defendant deliberately deceived the complainant about the nature or purpose of one or other form of sexual intercourse. The ambit of s.76 is limited to the "act" to which the deception relates and to deceptions as to the "nature or purpose" of the act, as opposed to the act's quality. Beyond this limited type of case, and assuming that none of the evidential presumptions in s.75 applies, the

---

[34] [2007] 2 Cr. App. R. 34.

issue of consent in rape must be addressed by reference to the definition of consent in s.74 and the provision as to reasonable belief in consent in s.1(2).

Section 76(2)(a) reflects the common law to the extent that, where the complainant was induced to consent on the basis of a fraudulent misrepresentation as to the nature of the act, there was no consent. Section 76(2)(a) also, however, extends to deceptions as to the *purpose* of the act. In *Jheeta*,[35] the Court of Appeal preferred *Green*[36] to *Tabassum*[37] as an example where s.76(2)(a) would operate. In that case, a qualified doctor carried out bogus medical examinations of young men in the course of which they were wired up to monitors while they were masturbated. As the purported object was to assess their potential for impotence, there was a deception as to the "purpose" of the physical act.

Deception as to HIV status

In *R. v B*[38] the Court of Appeal pointed out that the 2003 Act does not expressly 1.153 concern itself with deceptions other than those identified in s.76, let alone implied deceptions.

In that case, the Court held that evidence of the appellant's HIV status should have been excluded where the issue was consent. The appellant's failure to disclose that he was HIV positive did not affect the issue of consent in rape where there was no allegation that the appellant had deceived the complainant, rather that he had forcibly attacked her.

The appellant was convicted of raping the complainant, with whom he had intercourse in the street shortly after meeting her in a nightclub. On arrest, he informed the custody officer that he was HIV positive. He had not disclosed this to the complainant before they had sex. The issue at trial was consent. The judge allowed the prosecution to adduce evidence that the appellant was HIV positive at the time of the offence. He directed the jury that this was relevant to whether the complainant had the freedom or capacity to consent to sexual intercourse in the absence of that knowledge, and that they should consider whether a man diagnosed as HIV positive would be more or less likely to seek consent prior to intercourse. On appeal, the appellant argued that the evidence as to his HIV status was unfairly prejudicial and should have been excluded, and that the effect of the judge's directions had been to withdraw the issue of consent from the jury.

The Court of Appeal allowed the appeal, on the ground that the appellant's failure to disclose his HIV status to the complainant was not relevant to the issue of consent and should have been excluded. The issue for the jury was whether or not the complainant consented to sexual intercourse, not whether she consented to intercourse with a person suffering from a sexually transmitted disease. The fact

---

[35] [2007] EWCA Crim 1699.

[36] [2002] EWCA Crim 1501, identified by Professor David Ormerod in *Smith and Hogan, Criminal Law* (11th edition) as a better example of facts where s.76 might apply.

[37] [2000] 2 Cr. App. R. 328, discussed in the main work. This decision, which pre-dated the SOA 2003, was described by the late Professor Sir John Smith as a "doubtful case".

[38] [2006] EWCA Crim 2945. For the effect of mistake on consent generally, see J. Herring, *Mistaken sex* [2005] Crim. L.R. 511.

that a person had such a disease that was not identified to another person did not vitiate any consent that may have been given concerning any sexual activity.

However, the party who had the disease would have no defence to the harm created by the sexual activity merely by virtue of that consent, as the consent related to the sexual activity and not the disease: *Mohammed Dica*[39] considered. The Court added that the issue of consent in relation to those carrying sexually transmitted diseases requires debate as a matter of public and social policy. This is particularly so as there are questions regarding personal autonomy and whether existing statutory offences should encompass the disclosure of diseases or whether tailor-made offences ought to be created.

Whereas *R. v B* appears to have settled the law for the time being where there is no deception as to the defendant's HIV status, there remains a powerful argument that s.74 of the 2003 Act was intended to and has provided a new definition of consent, which is now a concept significantly wider than simply involving an awareness of the physical nature of the act and agreeing to it.[40]

In any event, in *R. v B* there was no question of any deception. Clearly the position is different where a defendant conceals his HIV status and lies to the complainant about it. In those circumstances, there is a compelling argument that this is relevant to whether the complainant is consenting, i.e. agreeing by choice with the freedom and capacity to make that choice in accordance with s.74 of the 2003 Act. At the very least, a lie about HIV status would be relevant to a complainant's state of mind unless he or she was willing to run the risk of contracting the disease.

The situation is more difficult where there is an established sexual relationship between the parties, the defendant becomes HIV positive and he fails to reveal it to his sexual partner. It could be argued that this amounts to an implied deception in that the continuing consensual sexual relationship depends on openness about such a fundamental matter. In *Konzani*[41] the Court of Appeal considered the position of a defendant charged under s.20 of the Offences against the Person Act 1860 with having recklessly transmitted the HIV virus to his partner through consensual sexual intercourse. The Court acknowledged that, on any view, the concealment of this fact from a partner almost inevitably means she is deceived as to HIV status and so is not in a position to give an informed consent to take the

---

[39] [2004] 2 Cr. App. R. 28.

[40] For strong criticism of the decision in *R. v B*, see Professor L.H. Leigh, *Two cases on consent in rape*, Archbold News, Issue 5, 8 June 2007. Professor Leigh suggests that an answer to the problem can be found in the reasoning in the minority judgment of McLachlin J. (now C.J.C.) in *Cuerrier* [1998] S.C.R. 371; [1999] 2 L.R.C.29 (Canadian S.Ct.). He argues that it would be possible for a English court to conclude that a person cannot be said to have agreed by choice to intercourse where she has been actively misled and is unaware of the fact that her partner suffers from HIV or another STI, on the basis that the deception goes to the very nature of the sexual act. As McLachlin J. stated in *Cuerrier*: " . . . The complainant does not consent to the transmission of diseased fluid into his or her body. This deception in a very real sense goes to the nature of the sexual act, changing it from an act that has certain natural consequences (whether pleasure, pain or pregnancy), to a potential sentence of disease or death."

[41] [2005] 2 Cr. App. R. 14. For discussion see Mathew Wait, *Knowledge, autonomy and consent: R. v Konzani* [2005] Crim. L.R. 763; Samantha Ryan, *Reckless transmission of HIV: Knowledge and culpability* [2006] Crim. L.R. 981.

risk of contracting the disease. This begs the question whether depriving a sexual partner of the opportunity to decide whether to take such a risk is relevant for a jury in a rape case when deciding whether the complainant consented to penetration.

The narrow construction given to the "nature or purpose" of the relevant act in s.76(2)(a) of the 2003 Act means that intentional deception as to HIV status will not trigger the conclusive presumptions about consent under s.76.[42]

In *Barnes*,[43] Lord Woolf C.J. summarised the effect of the decision in *Mohammed* **1.155** *Dica*. An HIV positive defendant who infected a sexual partner with the HIV virus would be guilty of an offence "contrary to s.20 of the 1861 Act if, being aware of his condition, he had sexual intercourse . . . without disclosing his condition." On the other hand, he would have a defence if he had made his partner aware of his condition, and she "with that knowledge consented to sexual intercourse with him because [she was] still prepared to accept the risks involved." In *Konzani* (discussed in para.1.153 above), the Court of Appeal made it clear that for a complainant's consent to the risks of contracting the HIV virus to be a defence, their consent must be an informed consent. Where a defendant deliberately conceals his HIV status, he cannot then assert he had an honest belief in his partner's informed consent to the risk of transmission of the disease, unless there is some evidence that might form the basis for such a belief. Normally, silence in these circumstances is incongruous with such an informed consent.

Absence of reasonable belief in consent

When should the jury be directed on absence of reasonable belief?

In *Taran*[44] the Court of Appeal emphasised that, whilst the absence of reasonable **1.161** belief is now part of the definition of rape, this does not mean that the judge is bound to give a direction on the point in every case. The judge's task is not to read to the jury an abstract lecture on the law but to explain to them in simple terms those parts of the law that arise for application in the case they are trying. A direction on absence of reasonable belief clearly falls to be given when, but only when, there is material upon which a jury might come to a conclusion that (a) the complainant did not in fact consent, but (b) the defendant thought she was consenting. There was no such material in *Taran*, where the complainant's evidence was that she was struggling to get away and making it abundantly clear that she did not consent, and the appellant's case was that, far from giving the impression of hesitant consent, the complainant was throwing herself at him. There was simply no room, on the case of either party, for any misunderstanding by the appellant as to the presence of consent.

---

[42] See *Jheeta* [2007] EWCA Crim 1699. But cf. McLachlin J. in *Cuerrier*, cited above n.41.
[43] [2004] EWCA Crim 3246.
[44] [2006] EWCA 1498.

Mistake as to identity of complainant

1.161A See *Whitta*,[45] discussed in para.2.41 below. Although this was a case of assault by penetration under s.2 of the 2003 Act, the issue could arise equally in a rape case. The Court of Appeal expressed doubts (obiter) as to the correctness of the trial judge's ruling that the defendant could not avail himself of the defence of mistaken identity in seeking to establish that there was or may have been a reasonable belief on his part that the complainant consented. The effect of this ruling is that there would be no defence to rape if a defendant made a mistake as to the identity of the person whom he penetrated, however reasonable the mistake. The Court noted that a possible alternative way of dealing with this very rare set of circumstances would be to hold that the offence is committed if a reasonable (and therefore sober) person would have realised that the person being penetrated or sexually touched was not the person whom the defendant thought he was consensually penetrating. This approach is, with respect, to be preferred to that taken by the judge at trial.

Can self-induced intoxication ever be a defence to rape?

1.183 The 2007 Edition of *Archbold*[46] states that "it is a matter for the jury alone to decide whether a belief is reasonable: and that any rule to the effect that a person who is affected by alcohol or drugs could never make a 'reasonable' mistake would be an unwarranted intrusion into the province of a jury, and calculated to lead to harsh results where there are factors other than the defendant's inebriation that caused him to have the mistaken belief." It would be most surprising if the adoption of the more objective test in the Sexual Offences Act 2003 has led to juries being able to take into account evidence of a self-induced intoxication in considering whether a defendant's belief is reasonable.[47]

We suggest that the following represents the correct approach. When a jury needs to consider whether a defendant may have reasonably believed that the complainant was consenting, there are two distinct questions:

(i) May the defendant have genuinely believed the complainant was consenting? Here the jury are entitled to take into account any evidence of the defendant's intoxication. If the jury are sure that the defendant did not have such a belief, the prosecution have proved the mental element. If the jury conclude that the defendant may have had such a belief, they need to consider question (ii).

(ii) Was the belief reasonable in all the circumstances? Here intoxication is *not* relevant and the jury must consider whether the belief would have been reasonable for a sober man in all the circumstances.

[45] [2006] EWCA Crim 2626.
[46] para.17–116 (p.1778).
[47] Self-induced intoxication was not relevant to mental element under the old law when there was a subjective test. See Woods(W) (1982) 74 Cr. App. R. 312 ; Fotheringham (1989) 88 Cr. App. R. 206.

Intentional penetration

Since the redefined offence of rape in s.1(1) of the 2003 Act requires the   **1.186**
prosecution to prove that the defendant intended to penetrate the vagina, anus or
mouth of another person with his penis, we argued in the main work that, on the
orthodox interpretation of *DPP v Majewski*,[48] this part of the mental element of
rape technically requires a specific intent and can, in principle, be negatived by
evidence of self-induced intoxication. However, at para.2.72, in discussing sexual
assault, we anticipated that the courts would look for a way to avoid this result, to
discourage routine claims that the defendant acted as he did in a self-inflicted state
of drunken or drug-induced confusion. The Court of Appeal achieved this in the
case of *Heard*,[49] by adopting a radical reinterpretation of *Majewski*. The Court
held that, properly understood, the distinction between a specific intent and a
basic intent in the sense used in *Majewski* is that a specific intent (sometimes also
called an "ulterior intent" and described as a "bolted on intent" by the trial judge
in *Heard*) requires proof of a state of mind addressing something beyond the
prohibited act itself, namely its consequences. Applying this "revisionist"[50]
interpretation of *Majewski* to the offence of rape, it would appear to follow that
since the mental element required in rape is nothing more than an intention to do
the prohibited act, voluntary intoxication can provide no defence. Following the
reasoning in *Heard*, it would seem that all the prosecution need establish is that the
defendant deliberately penetrated the complainant's vagina, anus or mouth with
his penis. Whilst the Court in *Heard* stated obiter that an accidental touching
cannot amount to a sexual assault, this principle would seem to have no practical
application to rape.

---

[48] [1977] A.C. 443 (HL).
[49] [2007] Crim. L.R. 654, discussed in para.2.72 below.
[50] So described by Professor David Ormerod in his commentary at [2007] Crim. L.R. 654 at
p.657.

CHAPTER 2

SEXUAL ASSAULTS AND SEXUAL ACTIVITY WITHOUT CONSENT

ASSAULT BY PENETRATION

MODE OF TRIAL AND PUNISHMENT

The offence under s.2 is a specified sexual offence in respect of which a sentence **2.08** of imprisonment for public protection may be imposed under the Criminal Justice Act 2003.[1]

FORM OF INDICTMENT

The use of specimen charges was considered in *Canavan*,[2] where the Court of **2.10** Appeal held that it is a fundamental principle of sentencing that a person should be sentenced only for the offences of which he has been convicted, or which he has admitted, and not for other offences of which those were specimens. The Court clearly appreciated that its decision would require prosecutors to include more counts in their indictments, so that there would be sufficient proof of the offender's criminality to enable the court to pass an appropriate sentence. However, it did not think this "need be unduly burdensome or render the trial unmanageable". This comment was perhaps somewhat optimistic. Although the decision is impeccably principled and logical, it does pose a dilemma for prosecutors and the courts in cases involving multiple offences in which an accurate picture of the defendant's criminality could be given only by overloading the indictment in a way that would require the defendant to plead to too many

---

[1] s.224 and Sch.15, Pt 2.
[2] [1998] 1 Cr. App. R. 70; and see *Clark* [1996] 2 Cr. App. R.(S.) 351; *Tovey and Smith* [2005] EWCA Crim 530.

offences, or the jury to bring in verdicts in respect of too many counts. Problems of this sort are particularly liable to arise in sex cases, especially those involving offences against children, in which the complaint is of multiple offending over a period of perhaps years but the complainant is unable to recall other than in vague terms when the various offences took place. It follows that, in at least some cases, the need to ensure a fair trial and the practicalities of trial management will compel the prosecutor to draw up an indictment that gives something less than the full picture.[3]

This problem may be mitigated, if not wholly resolved, by the recent amendment of the Criminal Procedure Rules to permit more than one incident of the same offence to be charged in one count: see para.15.67C below. The Criminal Procedure Rules Committee has stated that this facility may be used "when, for example, a defendant is alleged to have repeatedly assaulted the same victim in the same way over a period of time".[4] The Committee's intention in creating this new rule was to take account, amongst other things, of the potential under the old rules for a perceived unfairness to a victim of multiple offending where, out of many alleged offences, only a few are prosecuted as examples, giving the impression that the victim's distress has been underestimated or that he or she has not been believed.[5]

Sentencing

2.12   For the definitive guideline published by the Sentencing Guidelines Council on sentencing under the 2003 Act, see para.1.18. The guideline states that the factors to be taken into consideration in sentencing offences of assault by penetration are as follows[6]:

> "1. The sentences for public protection *must* be considered in all cases of assault by penetration. They are designed to ensure that sexual offenders are not released into the community if they present a significant risk of serious harm. Within any indeterminate sentence, the minimum term will generally be half the appropriate determinate sentence. The starting points will be relevant, therefore, to the process of fixing any minimum term that may be necessary.
> 2. This offence involves penetration of the vagina or anus only, with objects or body parts. It may include penile penetration where the means of penetration is only established during the trial.
> 3. All the non-consensual offences involve a high level of culpability on the part of the offender, since that person will have acted either deliberately without the victim's consent or without giving due care to whether the victim was able to or did, in fact, consent.
> 4. The planning of an offence indicates a higher level of culpability than an opportunistic or impulsive offence.

---

[3] cf. *Tovey and Smith*, last note, at para.36.
[4] See guidance to the Rules, dated March 27, 2007.
[5] Taken from a note prepared by the Secretariat to the Committee dated March 27, 2007 and published with the guidance, above.
[6] Pt 2A.

5. An offender's culpability may be reduced if the offender and victim engaged in consensual sexual activity on the same occasion and immediately before the offence took place. Factors relevant to culpability in such circumstances include the type of consensual activity that occurred, similarity to what then occurs, and timing. However, the seriousness of the non-consensual act may overwhelm any other consideration.
6. The seriousness of the violation of the victim's sexual autonomy may depend on a number of factors, but the nature of the sexual behaviour will be the primary indicator of the degree of harm caused in the first instance.
7. The presence of any of the general aggravating factors identified in the Council guideline on seriousness[7] or any of the additional factors identified in the guidelines will indicate a sentence above the normal starting point.
8. Brief penetration with fingers, toes or tongue may result in a significantly lower sentence where no physical harm is caused to the victim."

For the impact on sentence of the age of the victim and the offender, see para.3.15.

The starting points, sentencing ranges and aggravating and mitigating factors for the offences of assault by penetration under s.2 (assault by penetration) and s.6 (assault of a child under 13 by penetration) are as follows:

Type/nature of activity	Starting points	Sentencing ranges
Penetration with an object or body part, accompanied by any one of the following: abduction or detention; more than one offender acting together; abuse of trust; offence motivated by prejudice (race, religion, sexual orientation, physical disability); sustained attack	**13 years custody** if the victim is under 13	**11–17 years custody**
	10 years custody if the victim is 13 or over but under 16	**8–13 years custody**
	8 years custody if the victim is 16 or over	**6–11 years custody**
Penetration with an object— in general, the larger or more dangerous the object, the higher the sentence should be	**7 years custody** if the victim is under 13	**5–10 years custody**
	5 years custody if the victim is 13 or over but under 16	**4–8 years custody**
	3 years custody if the victim is 16 or over	**2–5 years custody**

[7] Published December 2004.

Type/nature of activity	Starting points	Sentencing ranges
Penetration with a body part (fingers, toes or tongue) where no physical harm is sustained by the victim	**5 years custody** if the victim is under 13	**4–8 years custody**
	4 years custody if the victim is 13 or over but under 16	**3–7 years custody**
	2 years custody if the victim is 16 or over	**1–4 years custody**

Additional aggravating factors	Additional mitigating factors
1. Background of intimidation or coercion	*Where the victim is aged 16 or over*
2. Use of drugs, alcohol or other substance to facilitate the offence	Victim engaged in consensual sexual activity with the offender on the same occasion and immediately before the offence
3. Threats to prevent victim reporting the incident	
4. Abduction or detention	*Where the victim is under 16*
5. Offender aware that he or she is suffering from a sexually transmitted infection	• Sexual activity between two children (one of whom is the offender) was mutually agreed and experimental [8]
6. Physical harm arising from the penetration	• Reasonable belief (by a young offender) that the victim was aged 16 or over
7. Offender ejaculated or caused the victim to ejaculate	Penetration is minimal or for a short duration

A person convicted[9] of assault by penetration is automatically subject to notification requirements in accordance with the SOA 2003, s.80 and Sch.3.

2.12A   Before the definitive guideline was issued, valuable guidance on sentencing for assault by penetration was given by the Court of Appeal in *Attorney General's*

---

[8] As to whether prosecution is appropriate in such cases, see paras 3.7 *et seq.* and 4.10 *et seq.* of the main work and para.3.9 below.

[9] Or found not guilty by reason of insanity, found to be under a disability and to have done the act charged, or cautioned.

Reference (No. 104 of 2004) (Wayne Garvey).[10] The decision is broadly consistent with the guideline and so remains of interest.[11] The Court of Appeal stated:

"In our judgment the re-definition of the offence of rape in section 1 of the [Sexual Offences] Act [2003] and the introduction of the new offence of assault by penetration in section 2, with a maximum sentence of life imprisonment in relation to both of these offences, must mean that the sentences to be passed by the court in relation to digital penetration are at a higher level than would have been appropriate had they been dealt with as offences of indecent assault, subject to the lesser maximum. We comment, in passing, that digital penetration was always regarded by the courts as a particularly serious feature of indecent assault."

While deploring too rigid or formulaic an approach, the Court gave the following guidance[12]:

"i. The starting point for an adult for rape as now defined by section 1(1) of the Sexual Offences Act 2003 should be five years, whether penetration is of the vagina, anus or mouth, and whether the victim is male of female, and should be varied upwards or downwards in accordance with the aggravating and mitigating features and higher starting points identified in *Milberry*. The court must also take into account a guilty plea (section 152 of the Powers of Criminal Courts (Sentencing) Act 2000).

ii. In the case of an adult victim, whether male or female, bearing in mind the absence of the risk of pregnancy or infection inherent in rape, the starting point for assault by penetration, as defined in section 2 of the Act, should, generally, be somewhat lower than that for rape—that is, in the region of four years. If non-penile penetration is by an object of such size or character that, by reference to the age of the victim or otherwise, there is a significant risk of physical injury, the starting point should be five years. The aggravating and mitigating features and higher starting points identified in *Milberry* should also apply to assault by penetration, and a plea of guilty must also be taken into account.

iii. If, in assault by penetration, the degree of penetration or the time which penetration lasts is minimal, a lower starting point than four or five years is likely to be appropriate.

iv. For young offenders, the sentence for rape and assault by penetration should be significantly shorter than that for an adult (see paragraph 30 of *Milberry*)."

Garvey involved the non-consensual digital penetration of the complainant's vagina. The offender followed the complainant home from a party at which she had consumed a large quantity of alcohol, knowing that she would leave the front door open for her husband. He entered the house and, when she was asleep, climbed into her bed and digitally penetrated her for between five and 10 minutes, before she awoke and ordered him to leave. He was indicted on a single count of assault by penetration, contrary to s.2 of the 2003 Act. He pleaded guilty at the

[10] [2004] EWCA Crim 2672. See also *Minshull* [2004] EWCA Crim 2673 and *Attorney General's Reference (No. 128 of 2004) (Peter Philip Holness)* [2004] EWCA Crim 3066.

[11] But the Court of Appeal has cautioned that sentencing decisions that are neither guideline cases nor expressed to be of general application are unlikely to be a reliable guide to the appropriate sentencing bracket for a particular type of offence, because the facts and circumstances of cases vary infinitely: *Lyon* [2005] EWCA Crim 1365. As a result, the Court is generally reluctant to look at cases which are merely illustrative of the sentence appropriate on particular facts, and will exercise particular caution in relation to judgments given on Attorney-General References, which, unless they expressly contain statements of general application, are unlikely to identify a general sentencing level.

[12] At para.28.

preliminary hearing and was sentenced to 18 months' imprisonment. The Court of Appeal, in the light of the guidance set out above, concluded that the sentence was unduly lenient. Having regard to the aggravating features of intrusion into the victim's home and bed when she was asleep and vulnerable, it would have expected a sentence after trial of six years' imprisonment. In the light of the guilty plea, it would have expected a sentence of four years' imprisonment. Taking into account double jeopardy, i.e. that the offender was being sentenced for a second time, the Court quashed the original sentence and substituted one of three years and three months' imprisonment.

Consent

Consent and public policy

2.28 Footnote 24: The exceptions include physical injury inflicted during contact sports, where the conduct that causes the injury does not go beyond what a player might reasonably be considered to have accepted: *Barnes.*[13]

2.40 See also *Meachen.*[14] The complainant and the appellant met at a club and returned to the complainant's house. She had been drinking and had no recollection of events at the house, save that the appellant was with her at one point on her living room sofa. When she awoke the next morning she was in immense pain and had suffered considerable blood loss from her peri-anal area. The medical evidence was that she had suffered serious anal injuries most likely caused by "fisting" or penetration by a blunt object. The appellant's case was that they had both willingly taken GHB before becoming sexually intimate. The complainant had, he said, enjoyed penetration of her vagina and anus with his fingers. She had ended up astride him with three of his fingers in her anus and his thumb in her vagina, and she had thrust up and down on his fingers for some four or five minutes before giving every sign of reaching a climax. He noticed some blood on his fingers and assumed the complainant was having her period. When he left the house, he did not know that she was injured. The appellant was charged with rape, indecent assault, causing grievous bodily harm with intent (s.18 of the Offences Against the Person Act 1860) and, in the alternative, maliciously inflicting grievous bodily harm (s.20 of the 1860 Act). At the end of the prosecution case, the judge directed an acquittal on the count of rape on the basis that there was insufficient evidence of penile penetration. He also ruled, relying on *Emmett,*[15] that there was no defence in law to the counts charging indecent assault and the offence under s.20 of the 1860 Act. In the light of that ruling, the appellant pleaded guilty to those counts and the trial proceeded on the s.18 count, on which he was convicted.

On appeal, the Court of Appeal upheld the conviction under s.18 but quashed those for indecent assault and under s.20. In relation to those charges, it held,

---

[13] [2004] EWCA Crim 3246; [2005] Crim. L.R. 381.
[14] [2006] EWCA Crim 2414.
[15] [1999] EWCA Crim 1710, discussed at para.2.35 of the main work.

following an extensive citation of authority, that consent cannot provide a defence where the incident to which the charge relates involved the intentional or reckless infliction of harm, but can provide a defence if the harm was unintentionally and accidentally caused. In the present case, at the time the judge had made his ruling there was, on the appellant's account, an issue as to whether he had been reckless as to the risk of causing harm, or whether the serious injury that occurred was the unintentional and accidental result of consensual sexual activity. In those circumstances, the appellant should have been permitted to run a consent defence and the judge's ruling to the contrary was incorrect, so that the convictions had to be quashed. The Court added that it was unnecessary to consider the further question whether it is only in relation to the deliberate infliction of actual bodily harm that consent is ruled out, so that the defence may apply where the defendant was reckless as to causing actual bodily harm and the complainant consented to the risk of that level of harm.[16]

On this point, i.e. whether consent is ruled out in relation to the reckless infliction of harm or only its intentional infliction, see *Mohammed Dica*.[17] That case involved an appeal against conviction on two counts of maliciously inflicting grievous bodily harm (s.20 of the Offences Against the Person Act 1861). The appellant was an HIV-positive man who had infected two women with the virus by having unprotected sex with them. His evidence would have been that both complainants were aware of his condition at the time the sex took place. However, at the close of the prosecution case the judge ruled, following *Brown*,[18] that the women's consent could provide no defence. The appellant therefore gave no evidence and was convicted on both counts. His appeal was allowed on the ground that the judge should not have withdrawn the issue of consent from the jury. The Court of Appeal, having cited *Brown*, *Donovan*,[19] *Boyea*[20] and *Emmett*,[21] drew a distinction for this purpose between the intentional and reckless infliction of harm. It said[22]:

> "These authorities demonstrate that violent conduct involving the deliberate and intentional infliction of bodily harm is . . . unlawful notwithstanding that its purpose is the sexual gratification of one or both participants . . . It does not follow from them, and they do not suggest, that consensual acts of sexual intercourse are unlawful merely because there may be a known risk to the health of one or other participant. These participants are not intent on spreading or becoming infected with disease through sexual intercourse. They are not indulging in serious violence for the purposes of sexual gratification. They are simply prepared, knowingly, to run the risk—not the certainty—of infection, as well as all the other risks inherent in and possible consequences of sexual intercourse, such as, and despite the most careful precautions,

---

[16] In so far as this comment suggest there is a distinction between actual bodily harm and some lesser degree of harm, it is misguided, since actual bodily harm comprises any harm, however transient or trifling, with the result that there can be no lesser degree of harm. See para.2.36 of the main work, n.39.

[17] [2004] EWCA Crim 1103; [2004] Crim. L.R. 944.

[18] [1993] 2 W.L.R. 556, discussed in the main work at para.2.30 *et seq.*

[19] [1934] 2 K.B. 498, discussed in the main work at para.2.27 *et seq.*

[20] [1992] Crim. L.R. 574, discussed in the main work at para.2.38 *et seq.*

[21] [1999] EWCA Crim 1710, discussed in the main work at para.2.35 *et seq.*

[22] At paras 46–52.

an unintended pregnancy. At one extreme there is casual sex between complete strangers, sometimes protected, sometimes not, when the attendant risks are known to be higher, and at the other, there is sexual intercourse between couples in a long-term and loving, and trusting relationship, which may from time to time also carry risks.

The first of these categories is self-explanatory and needs no amplification. By way of illustration we shall provide two examples of cases which would fall within the second.

In the first, one of a couple suffers from HIV. It may be the man: it may be the woman. The circumstances in which HIV was contracted are irrelevant. They could result from a contaminated blood transfusion, or an earlier relationship with a previous sexual partner, who unknown to the sufferer with whom we are concerned, was himself or herself infected with HIV. The parties are Roman Catholics. They are conscientiously unable to use artificial contraception. They both know of the risk that the healthy partner may become infected with HIV. Our second example is that of a young couple, desperate for a family, who are advised that if the wife were to become pregnant and give birth, her long-term health, indeed her life itself, would be at risk. Together the couple decide to run that risk, and she becomes pregnant. She may be advised that the foetus should be aborted, on the grounds of her health, yet, nevertheless, decide to bring her baby to term. If she does, and suffers ill health, is the male partner to be criminally liable for having sexual intercourse with her, notwithstanding that he knew of the risk to her health? If he is liable to be prosecuted, was she not a party to whatever crime was committed? And should the law interfere with the Roman Catholic couple, and require them, at the peril of criminal sanctions, to choose between bringing their sexual relationship to an end or violating their consciences by using contraception?

These, and similar risks, have always been taken by adults consenting to sexual intercourse. Different situations, no less potentially fraught, have to be addressed by them. Modern society has not thought to criminalise those who have willingly accepted the risks, and we know of no cases where one or other of the consenting adults has been prosecuted, let alone convicted, for the consequences of doing so.

The problems of *criminalising* the consensual taking of risks like these include the sheer impracticability of enforcement and the haphazard nature of its impact. The process would undermine the general understanding of the community that sexual relationships are pre-eminently private and essentially personal to the individuals involved in them. And if adults were to be liable to prosecution for the consequences of taking known risks with their health, it would seem odd that this should be confined to risks taken in the context of sexual intercourse, while they are nevertheless permitted to take the risks inherent in so many other aspects of everyday life, including, again for example, the mother or father of a child suffering a serious contagious illness, who holds the child's hand, and comforts or kisses him or her goodnight.

In our judgement, interference of this kind with personal autonomy, and its level and extent, may only be made by Parliament."

The decision has been cited as authority that "the law treats . . . consent as invalid only in respect of intentionally inflicted harms".[23] This may be too wide a reading. The language and examples used by the Court suggest that it was addressing the operation of consent in relation to the reckless infliction of harm in the context of heterosexual intercourse. Its apparent focus was the risk to health, through disease or pregnancy, involved in "ordinary" sex of this sort. It is not clear

---

[23] See Professor Ormerod's commentaries on *Barnes* [2005] Crim. L.R. 381, at p.383, and *Dica*, above, at p.948.

what the Court's attitude would be to the reckless infliction of harm in another sexual context, e.g. a sado-masochistic encounter or activity of the sort the appellant claimed had taken place in *Meachen*. However, the Court's approving citation of *Brown*, *Donovan*, *Boyea* and *Emmett* does suggest that it would incline against allowing consent to operate in such circumstances. If that is right, the decision merely perpetuates the difficulty presented by *Brown*, that the courts apparently remain disposed in the sexual context to limit the operation of consent as a defence to the infliction of harm, whether intentional or reckless, depending upon their assessment of the nature and extent of the risks involved. Despite the ringing terms of the last sentence of the extract cited above, the decision is unlikely to mark a change of direction in favour of absolute personal autonomy in relation to sexual activity carrying the risk of harm.

MENTAL ELEMENT

The effect of mistaken identity on the requirement of absence of reasonable belief   **2.41** in consent was considered, briefly, in the strange case of *Attorney General's Reference (No.79 of 2006) (Whitta)*.[24] The appellant met a girl at a party and an understanding developed that they would have sex later. The girl went to bed. After some time the appellant, as he thought, followed her. He entered the bedroom in which he thought the girl was sleeping, took off his glasses, got into bed and digitally penetrated the vagina of the occupant, who turned out to be the mother of the party host. She protested and the appellant left the room. He pleaded guilty to assault by penetration, following a ruling by the trial judge that the jury was not entitled to consider the mistake of identity as a relevant circumstance in assessing whether the appellant had a reasonable belief in consent. The basis of the learned judge's reasoning was that s.2 is worded to relate to a named complainant ("B") and in this case the appellant could not reasonably have believed that he had the complainant's consent. The position was unaffected by s.2(2), which states that whether a belief is reasonable is to be determined having regard to "all the circumstances", including any steps A has taken to ascertain whether B consents. The judge held that this provision cannot widen the scope of the jury's consideration to bring in the defendant's state of mind in relation to a third party.

The matter came before the Court of Appeal on an appeal against sentence, and the Court was therefore not concerned with the correctness of the judge's ruling. But it noted in passing that an alternative way of dealing with this "very rare set of circumstances" would be to hold that the offence is committed if a reasonable (and therefore sober) person would have realised that the person being penetrated was not the person whom the defendant thought he was penetrating. This amounts to a rejection of the judge's analysis, under which there is no scope for reasonable belief in consent to operate unless the defendant believes that the person he actually penetrated was consenting. But the Court of Appeal was surely

---

[24] [2006] EWCA Crim 2626.

right implicitly to reject that analysis and to allow scope for mistake as to identity to operate in this way. The judge appears to have been misled by the unusual drafting style of the 2003 Act, which throughout refers to the offender as "A" and the victim as "B", into concluding that any belief in consent, however reasonable, must relate to "B", i.e. the named complainant, and not a third person. This seems to read too much into what is ultimately a matter of drafting technique. If Parliament had intended to produce the result achieved in *Whitta*, which may fairly be regarded as harsh, if not draconian, it would surely have said so expressly.

2.44 In the light of the decision in *Heard*,[25] discussed in para.2.72 below, the offence in s.2 appears to be one of basic intent, such that voluntary intoxication through drink or drugs will provide no defence. It will suffice if the defendant's acts were deliberate. Recklessness is insufficient.

SEXUAL ASSAULT

Mode of Trial and Punishment

2.46 As from a day to be appointed the maximum sentence on summary conviction is 12 months' imprisonment: Criminal Justice Act 2003, s.282(2), (3). The increase has no application to offences committed before the substitution takes effect: s.282(4). The offence under s.3 is a specified sexual offence in respect of which a sentence of imprisonment for public protection may be imposed under the Criminal Justice Act 2003.[26]

Sentencing

2.49 For the definitive guideline published by the Sentencing Guidelines Council on sentencing under the 2003 Act, see para.1.18. The guideline states that the factors to be taken into consideration in sentencing offences of sexual assault are as follows[27]:

> "1. The sentences for public protection *must* be considered in all cases of sexual assault. They are designed to ensure that sexual offenders are not released into the community if they present a significant risk of serious harm.
> 2. The offence of 'sexual assault' covers all forms of sexual touching and therefore covers a wide range of offending behaviour. Some offences may justify a lesser sentence where the actions were more offensive than threatening and comprised a single act rather than more persistent behaviour.
> 3. The nature of the sexual activity will be the *primary* factor in assessing the seriousness of an offence and should be used as the starting point from which to begin the process of assessing the overall seriousness of the offending behaviour.

[25] [2007] EWCA Crim 125.
[26] s.224 and Sch.15, Pt 2.
[27] Pt 2B.

4. The presence of aggravating factors can make an offence significantly more serious than the nature of the activity alone might suggest.

5. For the purpose of the guideline, types of sexual touching are broadly grouped in terms of seriousness. An offence may involve activities from more than one group. In all cases, the fact that the offender has ejaculated or has caused the victim to ejaculate will increase the seriousness of the offence.

6. An offender's culpability may be reduced if the offender and victim engaged in consensual sexual activity on the same occasion and immediately before the offence took place. Factors relevant to culpability in such circumstances include the type of consensual activity that occurred, similarity to what then occurs, and timing. However, the seriousness of the non-consensual act may overwhelm any other consideration.

7. Where this offence is being dealt with in a magistrates' court, more detailed guidance is provided in the Magistrates' Court Sentencing Guidelines (MCSG)."

For the impact on sentence of the age of the victim and the offender, see para.3.15.

The starting points, sentencing ranges and aggravating and mitigating factors for the offences of sexual assault (s.3) and sexual assault on a child under 13 (s.7) are as follows:

Type/nature of activity	Starting points	Sentencing ranges
Contact between naked genitalia of offender and naked genitalia, face or mouth of the victim	**5 years custody** if the victim is under 13	**4–8 years custody**
	3 years custody if the victim is aged 13 or over	**2–5 years custody**
Contact between naked genitalia of offender and another part of victim's body Contact with genitalia of victim by offender using part of his or her body other than the genitalia, or an object Contact between either the clothed genitalia of offender and naked genitalia of victim or naked genitalia of offender and clothed genitalia of victim	**2 years custody** if the victim is under 13	**1–4 years custody**
	12 months custody if the victim is aged 13 or over	**26 weeks–2 years custody**

Type/nature of activity	Starting points	Sentencing ranges
Contact between part of offender's body (other than the genitalia) with part of the victim's body (other than the genitalia)	26 weeks custody if the victim is under 13 Community order if the victim is aged 13 or over	4 weeks–18 months custody An appropriate non-custodial sentence*

* "Non-custodial sentence" in this context suggests a community order or a fine. In most instances, an offence will have crossed the threshold for a community order. However, in accordance with normal sentencing practice, a court is not precluded from imposing a financial penalty where that is determined to be the appropriate sentence.

Additional aggravating factors	Additional mitigating factors
1. Offender ejaculated or caused victim to ejaculate 2. Background of intimidation or coercion 3. Use of drugs, alcohol or other substance to facilitate the offence 4. Threats to prevent victim reporting the incident 5. Abduction or detention 6. Offender aware that he or she is suffering from a sexually transmitted infection 7. Physical harm caused 8. Prolonged activity or contact	*Where the victim is aged 16 or over* Victim engaged in consensual sexual activity with the offender on the same occasion and immediately before the offence *Where the victim is under 16* • Sexual activity between two children (one of whom is the offender) was mutually agreed and experimental[28] • Reasonable belief (by a young offender) that the victim was aged 16 or over • Youth and immaturity of the offender • Minimal or fleeting contact

A person convicted[29] under s.3 is automatically subject to notification requirements in accordance with the SOA 2003, s.80 and Sch.3, if (a) where they were under 18 at the time of the offence, they are sentenced to at least 12 months' imprisonment, or (b) in any other case, the victim was under 18 and the offender is, in respect of the offence, sentenced to a term of imprisonment, detained in a hospital or given a community sentence of at least 12 months.

[28] As to whether prosecution is appropriate in such cases, see paras 3.7 *et seq.* and 4.10 *et seq.* of the main work and para.3.9, below.
[29] Or found not guilty by reason of insanity, found to be under a disability and to have done the act charged, or cautioned.

"Touches Another Person"

The decision in *R. v H*[30] clarifies the non-exhaustive nature of the definition of   **2.56**
"touching" in s.79(8) of the 2003 Act. That provision states that touching includes
touching with any part of the body, with anything else and through anything, and
in particular includes touching amounting to penetration. The Court of Appeal in
R. v H held that touching the clothing worn by a person is within the definition,
even though the person is not touched through the clothing. Accordingly, the
appellant's act in pulling the complainant's tracksuit bottoms constituted a
"touching" for the purposes of a charge under s.3.

"Sexual"

In *R. v H*[31] the Court of Appeal considered the correct approach to the application   **2.59**
of s.78(b) of the SOA 2003. It held that the provision contains two requirements:
first, that the touching (or other activity) because of its nature *may* be sexual, and
secondly, that the touching because of its circumstances or the purpose of any
person in relation to it (or both) *is* sexual. The existence of these two requirements
complicates the tasks of the judge and jury. If there is a submission of "no case",
the judge must decide whether there is a case to be left to the jury. He will answer
that question by determining first, whether it would be possible for a reasonable
person to consider that the touching because of its nature may be sexual, and
secondly, whether it would be possible for a reasonable person to conclude,
because of the circumstances of the touching or the purpose of any person in
relation to it (or both), that it is sexual. If the judge comes to the conclusion that
a reasonable person could possibly answer those questions adversely to the
defendant, then the matter must be left to the jury.

When directing the jury, the Court suggested that the judge should identify two
distinct questions: first, would they, as twelve reasonable people, consider that
because of its nature the touching could be sexual? If the answer to that question
was "No", then they would find the defendant not guilty. If "Yes", they would
have to go on and ask themselves (again as twelve reasonable people) whether in
view of the circumstances and/or the purpose of any person in relation to the
touching, the touching was in fact sexual. If they were satisfied that it was, they
would find the defendant guilty. If they were not so satisfied, they would find him
not guilty.

The Court added that in this suggested approach, the reference in the first
question to the nature of the touching is a reference to the actual touching that
took place. In answering that question, the jury will not be concerned with the
circumstances that pertained before or after the touching took place, nor with any
evidence as to the purpose of any person in relation to the touching.

---

[30] [2005] 2 Cr. App. R. 149.
[31] [2005] 2 Cr. App. R. 149.

In *R. v H*, the victim was walking along a path when the appellant approached and asked her the time. She answered him and he then said "Do you fancy a shag?". The victim kept walking and the appellant followed her. He came up beside her and asked if she was shy. He then grabbed her tracksuit bottoms by the fabric in the area of the right pocket and attempted to pull her towards him. At trial, the appellant submitted there was no case to answer as nothing had occurred that a reasonable person could regard as "sexual" within the meaning of the Act. The trial judge took the view that there were clearly circumstances in what had occurred, including the words alleged to have been spoken beforehand, which could result in what had occurred properly being regarded as sexual. The Court of Appeal said that in approaching the matter in this way the judge had not adopted the required two–stage approach to s.78(b) but had rather looked at the matter as a whole. The problem with that approach was that in a borderline case a person's intention or other circumstances may appear to show that what had happened was sexual, although the nature of the touching might not have been sexual. For the reasons already given, that approach is not appropriate, although the Court recognized that in the great majority of cases the answer will be the same whether the two–stage approach is adopted or the position is looked at as a whole. It went on to hold that despite the judge's misdirection, the appellant's conviction was safe.

In the course of its decision the Court referred to the old case of *George*,[32] in which it was held that the act of a shoe fetishist in removing a woman's shoe was not capable of being indecent. Lord Ackner had cited *George* with apparent approval in *Court*,[33] the indecent assault case from which the definition of "sexual" in s.78 derives. However, the Court of Appeal in *R. v H* expressed the view that under the new law, it would be for the jury to decide whether the act that took place in that case could be sexual.[34] This indicates that a broader range of conduct is capable of being caught by the offence of sexual assault than the old offence of indecent assault, and highlights the potentially wide scope of the application of s.78(b). As Professor Ormerod has commented: "Fetishism knows no bounds [and] it will only be the most unusual fetishes where A derives sexual gratification from the most innocuous conduct that will definitely fall outside the scope of the [offence]."[35]

2.65 In relation to the final example given in this paragraph, see the case of *Kumar*.[36] The appellant, a G.P., was convicted on three counts of indecently assaulting female patients. In relation to one count, relating to a purported breast examination, he appealed on the ground that the judge had wrongly left it open to the jury to convict if they thought that the examination might have been

---

[32] [1956] Crim. L.R. 52, referred to in the main work at para.2.60, fn.65.
[33] [1989] A.C. 28.
[34] Presumably on the basis that a reasonable person could find that it might be: see the discussion of the approach to submissions of "no case", above.
[35] [2005] Crim. L.R. 737.
[36] [2006] EWCA Crim 1946.

legitimate, but that the appellant used it as "cover" for a secret intention to gain sexual gratification. Such a secret intention, he argued, could not turn a legitimate examination into an indecent assault. The appeal was rejected on the basis that the Crown's case throughout had been that, whilst a breast examination was required, it was improperly conducted. It had never been suggested that this was a "secret intent" case, and in those circumstances the judge's direction did not render the conviction unsafe. The Court of Appeal did, however, cite dicta from *Court*[37] to the effect that a necessary medical examination properly conducted, but with the secret intention of gaining sexual gratification, does not constitute an indecent assault. The House of Lords in *Court* held that evidence of a secret indecent intention could be adduced to prove indecent assault only where the defendant's act was "ambiguous", in that it was capable of bearing either an innocent or an indecent interpretation.

The position is similar under the new offence of sexual assault—which is perhaps unsurprising given that the definition of "sexual" in the 2003 Act draws heavily on the approach taken to indecency by the House in *Court*. Under the new law, the admissibility of evidence of a secret indecent intention will turn on whether the defendant's conduct because of its nature could be sexual: s.78(b) of the Sexual Offences Act 2003. We suggest that this test could not be satisfied by a necessary medical examination, properly conducted. However, it might be satisfied if the examination, though necessary, were conducted in an inappropriate manner: see, in this respect, the facts of the Canadian case of *Bolduc and Bird*,[38] where a doctor carried out a proper vaginal examination but allowed a friend to be present, masquerading as a medical student, for purposes of sexual gratification.

MENTAL ELEMENT

Intention and intoxication

In *Heard*,[39] the appellant, who had been drinking heavily, undid his trousers, took **2.72** his penis in his hand and rubbed it up and down the thigh of a police officer. He was convicted of sexual assault on a direction by the trial judge that the touching under s.3 has to be deliberate and the offence is one of basic rather than specific intent, such that drunkenness can provide no defence.

The Court of Appeal held that the judge had been right to rule that the touching must be deliberate. Reckless touching will not do. On the evidence, the appellant plainly intended to touch the police officer with his penis. That he was drunk may have meant either that he was disinhibited and did something he would not have done if sober, and/or that he did not remember it afterwards. Neither of those matters would destroy the intentional character of the touching, on the basis that "[i]n the homely language employed daily in directions to juries in cases of

[37] [1989] A.C. 28, HL.
[38] (1967) 63 D.L.R. (2d) 82.
[39] [2007] EWCA Crim 125.

violence and sexual misbehaviour, 'a drunken intent is still an intent'". The judge's direction amounted to telling the jury that they must be sure the appellant's mind (drunken or otherwise) had gone with his physical act of touching. It seemed to the Court that in the great majority of alleged sexual assaults, or comparable sexual crimes, the defendant's mind, albeit in some cases a drunken mind, will have gone with the touching, penetration or other prohibited act.

The Court did, however, say that it was possible to envisage exceptional cases in which the intoxication was such that the defendant's mind did not go with his act. It referred to *Lipman*,[40] in which the appellant had contended that when he killed his victim by stuffing bedclothes down her throat he was under the illusion, induced by hallucinatory drugs voluntarily taken, that he was fighting for his life against snakes. If the equivalent state of mind were to exist in someone who committed an act of sexual touching or penetration, the question whether their act was intentional would be directly in point. Another potential example would be an intoxicated person whose control of his limbs is uncoordinated or impaired, so that in consequence he stumbles or flails about against another person, touching them in a way which, objectively viewed, is sexual—e.g. because he touches a woman on her private parts. Can such a person be heard to say that what happened was not deliberate when, if he had been sober, it would not have happened at all? In such a case, the Court said there is no offence whether the person is sober or intoxicated. This is not because their intoxication impacts on intention, as intention is not in question. What is in question is impairment or control of the limbs. In such cases the judge might well find it useful to add to the direction that "a drunken intent is still an intent", the corollary that "a drunken accident is still an accident". Where a defendant claims accident, it will be for the jury to decide whether he is doing so truthfully or as a means of disguising the reality that he intended to touch.

The remaining question for the Court was whether the judge had been right to direct the jury that drunkenness was not a defence to a charge of sexual assault. It held that he had, citing *DPP v Majewski*,[41] on the basis that sexual assault is an offence of basic intent and not one of specific intent, which the Court defined as requiring proof of a state of mind addressing something beyond the prohibited act itself, namely its consequences. In reaching this conclusion the Court stated that there is a large element of policy in the decision whether voluntary intoxication can or cannot be relied upon in relation to an offence. It noted the decision in *R. v C*[42] that indecent assault was a crime of basic intent, at least unless the act was an equivocal one so that the defendant's purpose had to be examined. The Court was satisfied that Parliament had not intended in passing the 2003 Act to change the law by allowing voluntary intoxication to provide a defence where previously it did not. It concluded that voluntary intoxication, whether through the taking of

---

[40] (1969) 55 Cr. App. R. 600.
[41] [1977] A.C. 443.
[42] [1992] Crim. L.R. 642.

drink, drugs or other mind-altering substances, cannot be relied upon as negating intention on a charge of sexual assault.

Though it is difficult to quarrel with the conclusions reached in *Heard*, the decision is open to criticism for way the Court distinguished between the concepts of specific and basic intent. The generally accepted understanding, worked out through the case law following *Majewski*, was that offences of specific intent are those requiring proof of intention, whilst offences of basic intent, to which voluntary intoxication can provide no defence, are those requiring some lesser form of *mens rea*, including recklessness. As noted in the main work, sexual assault appears on this analysis to be a crime of specific intent in relation to the element of intentional touching. We did, however, anticipate that the courts would look for a way to analyse the offence as one of basic intent, in order to discourage defences based upon intoxication. The Court of Appeal in *Heard* did just that. But its reasoning, and specifically its definition of offences of specific intent as those that require a state of mind addressing not merely the prohibited act but the consequences of that act, threatens to unsettle the law relating to *mens rea* and voluntary intoxication generally. This point goes beyond the scope of this book, and those who wish to pursue it should start with the trenchant and persuasive commentary on *Heard* by Professor Ormerod.[43] The implications for other sexual offences of the Court's approach to the distinction between offences of specific and basic intent are noted as appropriate below.

Professor Ormerod also criticises *Heard* for giving excessive scope to the concept of "accident", by treating it as covering not only acts that are not voluntary or willed, but also those that *are* willed but have unintended though foreseen consequences. In fact, the only relevant example given in the judgment is an intoxicated person whose control of his limbs is uncoordinated or impaired, so that he stumbles or flails about against another person.[44] This looks like a clear case of non-willed or accidental touching, given that there is no suggestion that the person has foreseen the risk of touching someone else (though if, despite his intoxication, he had indeed foreseen that risk, Professor Ormerod's point would apply).

CAUSING A PERSON TO ENGAGE IN SEXUAL ACTIVITY WITHOUT CONSENT

MODE OF TRIAL AND PUNISHMENT

As from a day to be appointed the maximum sentence on summary conviction is   **2.74** 12 months' imprisonment: Criminal Justice Act 2003, s.282(2), (3). The increase has no application to offences committed before the substitution takes effect:

---

[43] [2007] Crim. L.R. 654.
[44] At para.20, *per* Hughes L.J.

s.282(4). The offence under s.4 is a specified sexual offence in respect of which a sentence of imprisonment for public protection may be imposed under the Criminal Justice Act 2003.[45]

Sentencing

2.77   For the definitive guideline published by the Sentencing Guidelines Council on sentencing under the 2003 Act, see para.1.18. The guideline states that the factors to be taken into consideration in sentencing offences under s.4 (causing a person to engage in sexual activity without consent), s.8 (causing or inciting a child under 13 to sexual activity) and s.31 (causing or inciting a person with a mental disorder impeding choice to engage in sexual activity) are as follows[46]:

> "1. The sentences for public protection *must* be considered in all cases of causing sexual activity. They are designed to ensure that sexual offenders are not released into the community if they present a significant risk of serious harm. Within any indeterminate sentence, the minimum term will generally be half the appropriate determinate sentence. The starting points will be relevant, therefore, to the process of fixing any minimum term that may be necessary.
> 2. The same degree of seriousness applies whether an offender causes an act to take place, incites an act that actually takes place, or incites an act that does not take place only because it is prevented by factors beyond the control of the offender.
> 3. The same starting points apply whether the activity was caused or incited and whether or not the incited activity took place, but some reduction will generally be appropriate when the incited activity does not, in fact, take place.
> 4. Where an offender voluntarily desists from any action taken to incite a sexual act or personally, and of their own volition, intervenes to prevent from taking place a sexual act that he or she has incited, this should be treated as a mitigating factor.
> 5. The effect of the incitement is relevant to the length of the sentence to be imposed. A court should take into account the degree to which the intended victim may have suffered as a result of knowing or believing that an offence would take place."

For the impact on sentence of the age of the victim and the offender, see para.3.15.

The starting points, sentencing ranges and aggravating and mitigating factors for the offences under ss.4, 8 and 31 are as follows:

---

[45] s.224 and Sch.15, Pt 2.
[46] Pt 2B.

Type/nature of activity	Starting points	Sentencing ranges
Penetration with any one of the following aggravating factors: abduction or detention; offender aware that he or she is suffering from a sexually transmitted infection; more than one offender acting together; abuse of trust; offence motivated by prejudice (race, religion, sexual orientation, physical disability); sustained attack	**13 years custody** if the victim is a child under 13 or a person with a mental disorder **10 years custody** if the victim is 13 or over but under 16 **8 years custody** if the victim is 16 or over	**11–17 years custody** **8–13 years custody** **6–11 years custody**
Rape accompanied by any one of the following: abduction or detention; offender aware that he is suffering from a sexually transmitted infection; more than one offender acting together; abuse of trust; offence motivated by prejudice (race, religion, sexual orientation, physical disability); sustained attack	**13 years custody** if the victim is under 13 **10 years custody** if the victim is a child aged 13 or over but under 16 **8 years custody** if the victim is 16 or over	**11–17 years custody** **8–13 years custody** **6–11 years custody**
Single offence of penetration of/by single offender with no aggravating or mitigating factors	**7 years custody** if the victim is a child under 13 or a person with a mental disorder **5 years custody** if the victim is 13 or over but under 16 **3 years custody** if the victim is 16 or over	**5–10 years custody** **4–8 years custody** **2–5 years custody**

Type/nature of activity	Starting points	Sentencing ranges
Contact between naked genitalia of offender and naked genitalia of victim, *or* causing two or more victims to engage in such activity with each other, *or* causing victim to masturbate him/herself	**5 years custody** if the victim is a child under 13 or a person with a mental disorder **3 years custody**	4–8 years custody 2–5 years custody
Contact between naked genitalia of offender and another part of victim's body, *or* causing two or more victims to engage in such activity with each other Contact with naked genitalia of victim by offender using part of the body other than the genitalia or an object, *or* causing two or more victims to engage in such activity with each other Contact between either the clothed genitalia of offender and naked genitalia of victim, between naked genitalia of offender and clothed genitalia of victim, *or* causing two or more victims to engage in such activity with each other	**2 years custody** if the victim is a child under 13 or a person with a mental disorder **12 months custody**	1–4 years custody 26 weeks–2 years custody
Contact between part of offender's body (other than the genitalia) with part of victim's body (other than the genitalia)	**26 weeks custody** if the victim is a child under 13 or a person with a mental disorder **Community order**	4 weeks–18 months custody An appropriate non-custodial sentence*

* "Non-custodial sentence" in this context suggests a community order or a fine. In most instances, an offence will have crossed the threshold for a community order. However, in accordance with normal sentencing practice, a court is not precluded from imposing a financial penalty where that is determined to be the appropriate sentence.

Additional aggravating factors	Additional mitigating factors
1. Offender ejaculated or caused victim to ejaculate	
2. History of intimidation or coercion	
3. Use of drugs, alcohol or other substance to facilitate the offence	
4. Threats to prevent victim reporting the incident	
5. Abduction or detention	
6. Offender aware that he or she is suffering from a sexually transmitted infection	

A person convicted[47] under s.4 is automatically subject to notification requirements in accordance with the SOA 2003, s.80 and Sch.3.

MENTAL ELEMENT

In the light of the decision in *Heard*,[48] discussed in para.2.72 above, the offence in   **2.90** s.4 appears to be one of basic intent, such that voluntary intoxication through drink or drugs will provide no defence. It will suffice if the defendant's acts were deliberate. Recklessness is insufficient.

[47] Or found not guilty by reason of insanity, found to be under a disability and to have done the act charged, or cautioned.
[48] [2007] EWCA Crim 125.

CHAPTER 3

OFFENCES AGAINST CHILDREN UNDER 13

INTRODUCTION

Footnote 5: see the discussion below in relation to para.3.23.   **3.4**

The compatibility of s.5 of the 2003 Act with Art.8 of the ECHR was considered   **3.9**
by the Court of Appeal in *R. v G*,[1] which is currently under appeal to the House
of Lords. In that case, the appellant pleaded guilty under s.5 to rape of the
complainant. He had been 15 at the relevant time and she had been 12. The
offence took place in the appellant's bedroom relatively shortly after the two had
met. The complainant maintained that she had not consented. In due course the
appellant pleaded guilty on the following basis:

   (i) The complainant willingly agreed to have sexual intercourse with the
     defendant.

  (ii) At the time the defendant believed the complainant was 15 years old.
     She told him so on an earlier occasion.

 (iii) The defendant nonetheless pleads guilty to the SOA 2003 offence
     having been advised that, by reason of the fact that the complainant was
     under 13 at the relevant time, the offence is committed irrespective
     of:

     (a) consent

     (b) reasonable belief in consent

     (c) a reasonable belief as to age.

The prosecution initially declined to accept this basis of plea, but did so after
the complainant accepted that she had indeed told the appellant that she was 15
and in the light of her reluctance to attend court to give evidence. The judge
imposed a 12 month detention and training order, the effect of which was to make

---

[1] [2006] EWCA Crim 821.

the appellant subject to the notification requirements under Pt 2 of the 2003 Act.

On appeal against conviction, the appellant argued that his prosecution, conviction and sentence, taken individually or together, constituted a disproportionate interference with respect for his private life under Art.8. In particular, he argued that it is inappropriate to prosecute a child under s.5 where consensual sexual intercourse has taken place, since a conviction will result in the child being labelled a rapist and subject him to notification requirements as a sex offender and a maximum sentence of detention for life. It may not be appropriate to prosecute a child at all in such a case, but if it is, the prosecution should be under s.13 (sexual activity with a child under 16 by a person under 18), where a conviction labels the child as one who has had sexual activity with another child, does not subject him to the notification requirements unless he is sentenced to at least 12 months' imprisonment and carries a maximum sentence of five years' imprisonment. In support of this argument, the appellant relied on a statement made by Lord Falconer of Thoroton during the passage of the Bill, to the effect that where the sexual activity takes place between minors by mutual consent, prosecution would not be the inevitable outcome and one would not expect the full weight of the criminal law to be used against them.[2] He also relied on the third sentence of para.3.9 of the main work.

The appellant accepted that, because the complainant alleged that he made her submit to sexual intercourse against her will, it was initially appropriate for him to be charged under s.5. He submitted, however, that that charge ceased to be appropriate once the prosecution had informed the court that they were prepared to accept the appellant's basis of plea. By proceeding with the s.5 charge after that point, the court subjected the appellant to consequences so severe that the interference with his rights under Art.8(1) could not be justified under Art.8(2).

The appeal was dismissed. The Court of Appeal accepted the possibility that prosecution of a child under s.5 rather than under s.13, or indeed prosecution at all, in relation to consensual sexual intercourse may, on the particular facts, produce consequences that amount to an interference with the child's Art.8(1) rights that are not justified under Art.8(2). Where, however, as here, no criticism can be made of an initial charge under s.5, it does not follow that the judge must necessarily substitute an alternative charge under s.13 if it transpires that the sexual activity was, or must be treated as, consensual. The judge's sentencing powers on conviction under s.5 range from absolute discharge to detention for life. If it transpires that the facts of the offence are, or must be treated as, less serious than those that originally justified the s.5 charge, the judge should normally be able, by an appropriate sentence, to ensure that there is no unjustified interference with the defendant's Art.8(1) rights. In the present case, the Court did not

---

[2] *Hansard*, vol.646, cols.1176–7 (April 1, 2003).

consider that the judge had infringed Art.8 by proceeding to sentence the appellant under s.5, and the appeal on this ground was therefore dismissed.

The Court's acknowledgement that the prosecution of a child may, on the particular facts, amount to a breach of Art.8 is significant and welcome. However, as Professor Ashworth has commented, it is hard to see why *R. v G* was not such a case. What twist in the story could one imagine that would take the case over the border into breach of Art.8 territory? We await the decision of the House of Lords with interest. See also on this point *E v DPP*[3], discussed in para.4.14, below.

On a related point, see Michael Bohlander, *The Sexual Offences Act 2003 and the* Tyrrell *Principle—Criminalising the Victims?* [2005] Crim. L.R. 701, in which the Act is criticised for permitting the prosecution as accessories of children and other vulnerable individuals who are properly regarded as "victims" and deserve the protection of the principle in *Tyrrell*.[4]

RAPE OF A CHILD UNDER 13

MODE OF TRIAL AND PUNISHMENT

The offence under s.5 is a specified sexual offence in respect of which a sentence   **3.13** of imprisonment for public protection may be imposed under the Criminal Justice Act 2003.[5]

SENTENCING

For the definitive guideline published by the Sentencing Guidelines Council in   **3.15** relation to sentencing for offences under the 2003 Act, see para.1.18. In relation to the age of the victim, the guideline states[6]:

> "2.7 The extreme youth or old age of a victim should be an aggravating factor.
> 2.8 In addition, in principle, the younger the child and the greater the age gap between the offender and the victim, the higher the sentence should be.
> 2.9 However, the youth and immaturity of the offender must also be taken into account in each case.
> 2.10 The court in *Millberry*[7] adopted the principle that a sexual offence against a child is more serious than the same offence perpetrated against an adult and attracts a higher starting point. No distinction was made between children aged 13 and over but under 16, and those aged under 13.

---

[3] [2005] EWHC 147 (Admin).
[4] [1894] 1 Q.B. 710.
[5] s.224 and Sch.15, Pt 2.
[6] para.2.7 *et seq.*
[7] [2003] 2 Cr. App. R.(S.) 31.

2.11 Special weight has subsequently been accorded to the protection of very young children by the introduction of a range of strict liability offences in the SOA 2003 specifically designed to protect children under 13:
- The offences of 'rape of a child under 13', 'assault by penetration of a child under 13' and 'causing a child under 13 to engage in sexual activity' where the activity included sexual penetration carry the maximum life penalty.
- The maximum penalty for the new offence of 'sexual assault of a child under 13' is 14 years, as opposed to a maximum of 10 years for the generic 'sexual assault' offence.

2.12 In keeping with the principles of protection established in the SOA 2003, the Council has determined that:
- higher starting points in cases involving victims under 13 should normally apply, but there may be exceptions;
- particular care will need to be taken when applying the starting points in certain cases, such as those involving young offenders or offenders whose judgement is impaired by a mental disorder; and
- proximity in age between a young victim and an offender is also a relevant consideration."

On disparity of age the guideline also provides:

"1.15 The age of the offender will . . . be significant in the sentencing exercise in relation to non-consensual offences, where no special sentencing provisions have been provided for in the legislation. Its significance is particularly acute in relation to the strict liability offences such as 'rape of a child under 13', where the maximum penalty is life imprisonment, especially if an offender is very young and the disparity in age between the offender and the victim is very small."

The guideline states that the factors to be taken into consideration in relation to offences of rape, including rape of a child under 13 (s.5), are as follows[8]:

"1. The sentences for public protection *must* be considered in all cases of rape.
   a) As a result, imprisonment for life or an order of imprisonment for public protection will be imposed in some cases. Both sentences are designed to ensure that sexual offenders are not released into the community if they present a significant risk of serious harm.
   b) Life imprisonment is the maximum for the offence. Such a sentence may be imposed either as a result of the offence itself where a number of aggravating factors are present, or because the offender meets the dangerousness criterion.
   c) Within any indeterminate sentence, the minimum term will generally be half the appropriate determinate sentence. The starting points will be relevant, therefore, to the process of fixing any minimum term that may be necessary.
2. Rape includes penile penetration of the mouth.
3. There is no distinction in the starting points for penetration of the vagina, anus or mouth.
4. All the non-consensual offences involve a high level of culpability on the part of the offender, since that person will have acted either deliberately without the victim's consent or without giving due care to whether the victim was able to or did, in fact, consent.

[8] Pt 2A.

48

5. The planning of an offence indicates a higher level of culpability than an opportunistic or impulsive offence.

6. An offender's culpability may be reduced if the offender and victim engaged in consensual sexual activity on the same occasion and immediately before the offence took place. Factors relevant to culpability in such circumstances include the type of consensual activity that occurred, similarity to what then occurs, and timing. However, the seriousness of the non-consensual act may overwhelm any other consideration.

7. The seriousness of the violation of the victim's sexual autonomy may depend on a number of factors, but the nature of the sexual behaviour will be the primary indicator of the degree of harm caused in the first instance.

8. The presence of any of the general aggravating factors identified in the Council guideline on seriousness or any of the additional factors identified in the guidelines will indicate a sentence above the normal starting point."

The starting points, sentencing ranges and aggravating and mitigating factors for the offences of rape and rape of a child under 13 (s.5) are as follows:

Type/nature of activity	Starting points	Sentencing ranges
Repeated rape of same victim over a course of time or rape involving multiple victims	15 years custody	13–19 years custody
Rape accompanied by any one of the following: abduction or detention; offender aware that he is suffering from a sexually transmitted infection; more than one offender acting together; abuse of trust; offence motivated by prejudice (race, religion, sexual orientation, physical disability); sustained attack	13 years custody if the victim is under 13	11–17 years custody
	10 years custody if the victim is a child aged 13 or over but under 16	8–13 years custody
	8 years custody if the victim is 16 or over	6–11 years custody
Single offence of rape by single offender	10 years custody if the victim is under 13	8–13 years custody
	8 years custody if the victim is 13 or over but under 16	6–11 years custody
	5 years custody if the victim is 16 or over	4–8 years custody

Additional aggravating factors	Additional mitigating factors
1. Offender ejaculated or caused victim to ejaculate 2. Background of intimidation or coercion 3. Use of drugs, alcohol or other substance to facilitate the offence 4. Threats to prevent victim reporting the incident 5. Abduction or detention 6. Offender aware that he is suffering from a sexually transmitted infection 7. Pregnancy or infection results	*Where the victim is aged 16 or over* Victim engaged in consensual sexual activity with the offender on the same occasion and immediately before the offence *Where the victim is under 16* ● Sexual activity between two children (one of whom is the offender) was mutually agreed and experimental ● Reasonable belief (by a young offender) that the victim was aged 16 or over

A person convicted[9] of rape of a child under 13 is automatically subject to notification requirements in accordance with the SOA 2003, s.80 and Sch.3.

Mental Element

3.23   It was settled in *R. v G*[10] that the s.5 offence does not require *mens rea* as to age, so that a defendant will be liable to conviction even if he was labouring under a mistaken belief that the girl was 13 or over. The facts of the case are set out in para.3.9 above. The appellant argued on appeal that, if s.5 could not be "read down" through the introduction of such a *mens rea* requirement, it was incompatible with Art.6(2) of the ECHR (right to a fair trial). The Court of Appeal noted that under normal principles the prosecution would have to prove *mens rea*, in the form of an absence of belief on the part of the defendant that the complainant was 13 or over. In *B (a minor) v DPP*,[11] the House of Lords held that such a mental element was a necessary ingredient of the offence of gross indecency with or towards a child under 14, in s.1(1) of the Indecency with Children Act 1960. However, the House also held that the need for a mental element can be negatived by "an implication that is compellingly clear".[12] Counsel for the

---

[9] Or found not guilty by reason of insanity, found to be under a disability and to have done the act charged, or cautioned.
[10] Above n.1.
[11] [2000] 2 A.C. 428.
[12] At 464, *per* Lord Nicholls of Birkenhead.

appellant in *R. v G* accepted that such an implication arises in relation to s.5, because of the contrast between the express references to reasonable belief that a child is 16 or over in, for instance, s.9, and the absence of any such reference in relation to children under 13. Thus, on its natural meaning, s.5 creates an offence even if the defendant reasonably believes the child to be 13 or over.

The Court went on to consider the appellant's argument that, in order to make s.5 compatible with the Convention, it should be "read down" so as to require the prosecution to establish that the defendant did not believe the victim to be 13 or over. The appellant submitted that an absolute offence is capable of infringing Art.6(2) unless it is "within reasonable limits". Section 5 did not fall within reasonable limits because it can have consequences which are wholly unreasonable, in that it makes a 15-year-old who has had sexual intercourse with a consenting 12-year-old, whom he reasonably believes to be 15, liable to conviction for rape of a child, carrying with it the stigma to which such a conviction gives rise, the notification obligation and a potential sentence of life imprisonment. The Court, citing Strasbourg and domestic authorities, held that even on the assumption that those potential consequences of s.5 are inherently objectionable, they did not render s.5 incompatible with Art.6(2). This is because Art.6(2) is concerned with the procedural fairness of a trial, not with the substantive law that falls to be applied at the trial. It follows that a trial will not be rendered unfair merely because the offence in question is an absolute offence.[13]

In the light of the decision in *Heard*,[14] discussed in para.2.72 above, the offence in s.5 appears to be one of basic intent, such that voluntary intoxication through drink or drugs will provide no defence. It will suffice if the defendant's acts were deliberate. Recklessness is insufficient. **3.24**

ASSAULT OF A CHILD UNDER 13 BY PENETRATION

MODE OF TRIAL AND PUNISHMENT

The offence under s.6 is a specified sexual offence in respect of which a sentence of imprisonment for public protection may be imposed under the Criminal Justice Act 2003.[15] **3.28**

---

[13] *R. v G* was followed on this point in *S. v DPP* [2006] EWHC 2231 (Admin). It is noteworthy that the appellant in *S.* was initially charged under s.5 but, following representations from his solicitors, the CPS decided to amend the charge to a charge under s.9 and s.13.

[14] [2007] EWCA Crim 125.

[15] s.224 and Sch.15, Pt 2.

3.31   For the definitive guideline published by the Sentencing Guidelines Council on sentencing under the 2003 Act, see para.1.18. The guideline states that the factors to be taken into consideration in relation to offences of assault by penetration, including assault by penetration of a child under 13 (s.6), are as follows[16]:

> "1. The sentences for public protection *must* be considered in all cases of assault by penetration. They are designed to ensure that sexual offenders are not released into the community if they present a significant risk of serious harm. Within any indeterminate sentence, the minimum term will generally be half the appropriate determinate sentence. The starting points will be relevant, therefore, to the process of fixing any minimum term that may be necessary.
> 2. This offence involves penetration of the vagina or anus only, with objects or body parts. It may include penile penetration where the means of penetration is only established during the trial.
> 3. All the non-consensual offences involve a high level of culpability on the part of the offender, since that person will have acted either deliberately without the victim's consent or without giving due care to whether the victim was able to or did, in fact, consent.
> 4. The planning of an offence indicates a higher level of culpability than an opportunistic or impulsive offence.
> 5. An offender's culpability may be reduced if the offender and victim engaged in consensual sexual activity on the same occasion and immediately before the offence took place. Factors relevant to culpability in such circumstances include the type of consensual activity that occurred, similarity to what then occurs, and timing. However, the seriousness of the non-consensual act may overwhelm any other consideration.
> 6. The seriousness of the violation of the victim's sexual autonomy may depend on a number of factors, but the nature of the sexual behaviour will be the primary indicator of the degree of harm caused in the first instance.
> 7. The presence of any of the general aggravating factors identified in the Council guideline on seriousness or any of the additional factors identified in the guidelines will indicate a sentence above the normal starting point.
> 8. Brief penetration with fingers, toes or tongue may result in a significantly lower sentence where no physical harm is caused to the victim."

For the impact on sentence of the age of the victim and the offender, see para.3.15.

The starting points, sentencing ranges and aggravating and mitigating factors for offences of assault by penetration (s.2 and s.7 of the 2003 Act) are as follows:

---

[16] Pt 2A.

Type/nature of activity	Starting points	Sentencing ranges
Penetration with an object or body part, accompanied by any one of the following: abduction or detention; more than one offender acting together; abuse of trust; offence motivated by prejudice (race, religion, sexual orientation, physical disability); sustained attack	**13 years custody** if the victim is under 13 **10 years custody** if the victim is 13 or over but under 16 **8 years custody** if the victim is 16 or over	**11–17 years custody** **8–13 years custody** **6–11 years custody**
Penetration with an object— in general, the larger or more dangerous the object, the higher the sentence should be	**7 years custody** if the victim is under 13 **5 years custody** if the victim is 13 or over but under 16 **3 years custody** if the victim is 16 or over	**5–10 years custody** **4–8 years custody** **2–5 years custody**
Penetration with a body part (fingers, toes or tongue) where no physical harm is sustained by the victim	**5 years custody** if the victim is under 13 **4 years custody** if the victim is 13 or over but under 16 **2 years custody** if the victim is 16 or over	**4–8 years custody** **3–7 years custody** **1–4 years custody**

Additional aggravating factors	Additional mitigating factors
1. Background of intimidation or coercion 2. Use of drugs, alcohol or other substance to facilitate the offence 3. Threats to prevent victim reporting the incident	

Additional aggravating factors	Additional mitigating factors
4. Abduction or detention	*Where the victim is aged 16 or over*
5. Offender aware that he or she is suffering from a sexually transmitted infection	Victim engaged in consensual sexual activity with the offender on the same occasion and immediately before the offence
6. Physical harm arising from the penetration	*Where the victim is under 16*
7. Offender ejaculated or caused the victim to ejaculate	• Sexual activity between two children (one of whom is the offender) was mutually agreed and experimental
	• Reasonable belief (by a young offender) that the victim was aged 16 or over
	• Penetration is minimal or for a short duration

A person convicted[17] under s.6 is automatically subject to notification requirements in accordance with the SOA 2003, s.80 and Sch.3.

Mental Element

3.38   In the light of the decision in *Heard*,[18] discussed in para.2.72 above, the offence in s.6 appears to be one of basic intent, such that voluntary intoxication through drink or drugs will provide no defence. It will suffice if the defendant's acts were deliberate. Recklessness is insufficient.

SEXUAL ASSAULT OF A CHILD UNDER 13

Mode of Trial and Punishment

3.42   As from a day to be appointed the maximum sentence on summary conviction is 12 months' imprisonment: Criminal Justice Act 2003, s.282(2), (3). The increase has no application to offences committed before the substitution takes effect: s.282(4). The offence under s.7 is a specified sexual offence in respect of which a

---

[17] Or found not guilty by reason of insanity, found to be under a disability and to have done the act charged, or cautioned.
[18] [2007] EWCA Crim 125.

sentence of imprisonment for public protection may be imposed under the CJA 2003.[19]

SENTENCING

For the definitive guideline published by the Sentencing Guidelines Council on sentencing under the 2003 Act, see para.2.12. The guideline states that the factors to be taken into consideration in relation to offences of sexual assault, including sexual assault of a child under 13 (s.7), are as follows[20]: **3.44**

"1. The sentences for public protection *must* be considered in all cases of sexual assault. They are designed to ensure that sexual offenders are not released into the community if they present a significant risk of serious harm.

2. The offence of 'sexual assault' covers all forms of sexual touching and therefore covers a wide range of offending behaviour. Some offences may justify a lesser sentence where the actions were more offensive than threatening and comprised a single act rather than more persistent behaviour.

3. The nature of the sexual activity will be the *primary* factor in assessing the seriousness of an offence and should be used as the starting point from which to begin the process of assessing the overall seriousness of the offending behaviour.

4. The presence of aggravating factors can make an offence significantly more serious than the nature of the activity alone might suggest.

5. For the purpose of the guideline, types of sexual touching are broadly grouped in terms of seriousness. An offence may involve activities from more than one group. In all cases, the fact that the offender has ejaculated or has caused the victim to ejaculate will increase the seriousness of the offence.

6. An offender's culpability may be reduced if the offender and victim engaged in consensual sexual activity on the same occasion and immediately before the offence took place. Factors relevant to culpability in such circumstances include the type of consensual activity that occurred, similarity to what then occurs, and timing. However, the seriousness of the non-consensual act may overwhelm any other consideration.

7. Where this offence is being dealt with in a magistrates' court, more detailed guidance is provided in the Magistrates' Court Sentencing Guidelines (MCSG)."

The starting points, sentencing ranges and aggravating and mitigating factors for the offence under s.7 are as follows (they apply also to the offence of sexual assault under s.3):

[19] s.224 and Sch.15, Pt 2.
[20] Pt 2B.

Type/nature of activity	Starting points	Sentencing ranges
Contact between naked genitalia of offender and naked genitalia, face or mouth of the victim	**5 years custody** if the victim is under 13 **3 years custody** if the victim is aged 13 or over	**4–8 years custody** **2–5 years custody**
Contact between naked genitalia of offender and another part of victim's body Contact with genitalia of victim by offender using part of his or her body other than the genitalia, or an object Contact between either the clothed genitalia of offender and naked genitalia of victim or naked genitalia of offender and clothed genitalia of victim	**2 years custody** if the victim is under 13 **12 months custody** if the victim is aged 13 or over	**1–4 years custody** **26 weeks–2 years custody**
Contact between part of offender's body (other than the genitalia) with part of the victim's body (other than the genitalia)	**26 weeks custody** if the victim is under 13 **Community order** if the victim is aged 13 or over	**4 weeks–18 months custody** **An appropriate non-custodial sentence***

* "Non-custodial sentence" in this context suggests a community order or a fine. In most instances, an offence will have crossed the threshold for a community order. However, in accordance with normal sentencing practice, a court is not precluded from imposing a financial penalty where that is determined to be the appropriate sentence.

Additional aggravating factors	Additional mitigating factors
1. Offender ejaculated or caused victim to ejaculate	*Where the victim is aged 16 or over*
	Victim engaged in consensual sexual activity with the offender on the same occasion and immediately before the offence
2. Background of intimidation or coercion	
3. Use of drugs, alcohol or other substance to facilitate the offence	*Where the victim is under 16*
4. Threats to prevent victim reporting the incident	• Sexual activity between two children (one of whom is the offender) was mutually agreed and experimental
5. Abduction or detention	
6. Offender aware that he or she is suffering from a sexually transmitted infection	• Reasonable belief (by a young offender) that the victim was aged 16 or over
7. Physical harm caused	• Youth and immaturity of the offender
8. Prolonged activity or contact	
	• Minimal or fleeting contact

A person convicted[21] under s.7 is automatically subject to notification requirements in accordance with the SOA 2003, s.80 and Sch.3, if they were 18 or over at the time of the offence or they are sentenced to at least 12 months' imprisonment.

MENTAL ELEMENT

In the light of the decision in *Heard*,[22] discussed in para.2.72 above, the offence in s.7 appears to be one of basic intent, such that voluntary intoxication through drink or drugs will provide no defence. It will suffice if the defendant's acts were deliberate. Recklessness is insufficient.   **3.51**

CAUSING OR INCITING A CHILD UNDER 13 TO ENGAGE IN SEXUAL ACTIVITY

DEFINITION

Section 8(1) creates two offences, one of intentionally causing and one of intentionally inciting a person under 13 to engage in sexual activity: *Walker.*[23]   **3.52**

---

[21] Or found not guilty by reason of insanity, found to be under a disability and to have done the act charged, or cautioned.
[22] [2007] EWCA Crim 125.
[23] [2006] EWCA Crim 1907.

Mode of Trial and Punishment

3.56 As from a day to be appointed the maximum sentence on summary conviction is 12 months' imprisonment: Criminal Justice Act 2003, s.282(2), (3). The increase has no application to offences committed before the substitution takes effect: s.282(4). The offence under s.8 is a specified sexual offence in respect of which a sentence of imprisonment for public protection may be imposed under the Criminal Justice Act 2003.[24]

Sentencing

3.58 For the definitive guideline published by the Sentencing Guidelines Council on sentencing under the 2003 Act, see para.1.18. The guideline states that the factors to be taken into consideration in sentencing offences under s.8 (causing or inciting a child under 13 to engage in sexual activity) are as follows:

> "1. The sentences for public protection *must* be considered in all cases of causing sexual activity. They are designed to ensure that sexual offenders are not released into the community if they present a significant risk of serious harm. Within any indeterminate sentence, the minimum term will generally be half the appropriate determinate sentence. The starting points will be relevant, therefore, to the process of fixing any minimum term that may be necessary.
> 2. The same degree of seriousness applies whether an offender causes an act to take place, incites an act that actually takes place, or incites an act that does not take place only because it is prevented by factors beyond the control of the offender.
> 3. The same starting points apply whether the activity was caused or incited and whether or not the incited activity took place, but some reduction will generally be appropriate when the incited activity does not, in fact, take place.
> 4. Where an offender voluntarily desists from any action taken to incite a sexual act or personally, and of their own volition, intervenes to prevent from taking place a sexual act that he or she has incited, this should be treated as a mitigating factor.
> 5. The effect of the incitement is relevant to the length of the sentence to be imposed. A court should take into account the degree to which the intended victim may have suffered as a result of knowing or believing that an offence would take place."

For the impact on sentence of the age of the victim and the offender, see para.3.15.

The starting points, sentencing ranges and aggravating and mitigating factors for offences under s.8 are as follows:

---

[24] s.224 and Sch.15, Pt 2.

Type/nature of activity	Starting points	Sentencing ranges
Penetration with any one of the following aggravating factors: abduction or detention; offender aware that he or she is suffering from a sexually transmitted infection; more than one offender acting together; abuse of trust; offence motivated by prejudice (race, religion, sexual orientation, physical disability); sustained attack	**13 years custody** if the victim is a child under 13 or a person with a mental disorder	**11–17 years custody**
	10 years custody if the victim is 13 or over but under 16	**8–13 years custody**
	8 years custody if the victim is 16 or over	**6–11 years custody**
Rape accompanied by any one of the following: abduction or detention; offender aware that he is suffering from a sexually transmitted infection; more than one offender acting together; abuse of trust; offence motivated by prejudice (race, religion, sexual orientation, physical disability); sustained attack	**13 years custody** if the victim is under 13	**11–17 years custody**
	10 years custody if the victim is a child aged 13 or over but under 16	**8–13 years custody**
	8 years custody if the victim is 16 or over	**6–11 years custody**
Single offence of penetration of/by single offender with no aggravating or mitigating factors	**7 years custody** if the victim is a child under 13 or a person with a mental disorder	**5–10 years custody**
	5 years custody if the victim is 13 or over but under 16	**4–8 years custody**
	3 years custody if the victim is 16 or over	**2–5 years custody**

Type/nature of activity	Starting points	Sentencing ranges
Contact between naked genitalia of offender and naked genitalia of victim, *or* causing two or more victims to engage in such activity with each other, *or* causing victim to masturbate him/herself	**5 years custody** if the victim is a child under 13 or a person with a mental disorder **3 years custody**	**4–8 years custody** **2–5 years custody**
Contact between naked genitalia of offender and another part of victim's body, *or* causing two or more victims to engage in such activity with each other Contact with naked genitalia of victim by offender using part of the body other than the genitalia or an object, *or* causing two or more victims to engage in such activity with each other Contact between either the clothed genitalia of offender and naked genitalia of victim, between naked genitalia of offender and clothed genitalia of victim, *or* causing two or more victims to engage in such activity with each other	**2 years custody** if the victim is a child under 13 or a person with a mental disorder **12 months custody**	**1–4 years custody** **26 weeks–2 years custody**
Contact between part of offender's body (other than the genitalia) with part of victim's body (other than the genitalia)	**26 weeks custody** if the victim is a child under 13 or a person with a mental disorder **Community order**	**4 weeks–18 months custody** **An appropriate non-custodial sentence***

* "Non–custodial sentence" in this context suggests a community order or a fine. In most instances, an offence will have crossed the threshold for a community order. However, in accordance with normal sentencing practice, a court is not precluded from imposing a financial penalty where that is determined to be the appropriate sentence.

Additional aggravating factors	Additional mitigating factors
1. Offender ejaculated or caused victim to ejaculate	
2. History of intimidation or coercion	
3. Use of drugs, alcohol or other substance to facilitate the offence	
4. Threats to prevent victim reporting the incident	
5. Abduction or detention	
6. Offender aware that he or she is suffering from a sexually transmitted infection	

A person convicted[25] under s.8 is automatically subject to notification requirements in accordance with the SOA 2003, s.80 and Sch.3.

PARTIES TO THE OFFENCE

In *Jones*,[26] the Court of Appeal rejected the argument that the offence of   **3.61** incitement in s.8 requires incitement of an identified or identifiable child. Rather, the offence can be committed by a person who, with the requisite intention, makes a statement which in specific terms directly incites a child under the age of 13 to engage in sexual activity, whether or not the statement is addressed to any specific or identifiable person. The appellant in *Jones* had left graffiti messages on toilet doors in trains and stations seeking girls aged 8 to 13 for sex and giving a mobile telephone number. He was charged under s.62 of the 2003 Act in relation to these messages, but the Court indicated that he could properly have been charged with the incitement offence in s.8. It follows by analogy that the incitement offence will be committed by a person who posts such a message on an internet website or in a blog.

---

[25] Or found not guilty by reason of insanity, found to be under a disability and to have done the act charged, or cautioned.
[26] [2007] EWCA Crim 1118.

"Causes or Incites another Person . . . to Engage in an Activity"

3.63 The appellant in *Jones*[27] left graffiti messages on toilet doors in trains and stations seeking girls aged 8 to 13 for sex and giving a mobile telephone number. A journalist who saw one of the messages sent him a text message, and he replied in terms indicating that he was looking for an opportunity to incite a child to have penetrative sex. The journalist reported the matter to the police, who commenced an undercover operation in which a police officer calling herself "Amy" exchanged text messages with the appellant. By this means a meeting was arranged at which the appellant was arrested. He was charged under s.62 of the 2003 Act in relation to the graffiti messages and, in relation to Amy, with attempting to cause or incite a child under the age of 13 to engage in penetrative sexual activity. The prosecution case in relation to the attempt charge was that, based upon the text messages exchanged, the appellant had intended to meet with Amy and engage in penetrative sex with her. The appellant applied for this count to be stayed as an abuse of process on a number of grounds, including, first, that this was a case of entrapment by the police, and secondly, that he lacked the intention necessary for an attempt because did not intend to incite an actual child to sexual activity, but an adult pretending to be a child. The stay was refused and the appellant was convicted on this count. He appealed, renewing the two arguments that had failed at trial and adding a third, that he should have been charged with an attempt to commit the less serious offence under s.10 of the 2003 Act.

The Court of Appeal dismissed all these arguments. On entrapment, it held, following an extensive citation of authority, including *Looseley*,[28] that by sending the text messages the police had neither incited nor instigated the crime nor lured the appellant into committing it. They had simply provided him with an opportunity to commit an offence which he had already attempted to commit in his text exchanges with the journalist, but in circumstances in which no harm could come to the victim.

The Court also rejected the appellant's argument that he had not intended to incite an actual child under 13 to engage in sexual activity. The Court followed the decision of the House of Lords in *Shivpuri*[29] to the effect that a person may be convicted of an attempt if they do an act more than merely preparatory to the full offence intending to commit that offence, notwithstanding the commission of the full offence is on the true facts impossible. It was clear on the evidence that the appellant had intended to incite a child under 13 to engage in penetrative sexual activity and he had done an act more than merely preparatory to the commission of the offence. It was impossible for him to complete the offence because the person whom he intended to incite, Amy, was in fact not aged under 13 but an adult. This impossibility did not preclude his conviction for attempted incitement.

---

[27] [2007] EWCA Crim 1118.
[28] [2001] UKHL 53.
[29] [1987] A.C. 1.

The appellant's third argument was that he had been charged with a more serious offence than was warranted. It was, he said, only because the police had chosen Amy's age as 12 that he was charged with attempting the offence under s.8. If they had instead chosen to tell him that Amy was 13, he would have been charged with attempting the less serious offence under s.10. There was no evidence that it mattered to him that Amy was 12 rather than 13, nor that he would have behaved any differently had Amy claimed to be 13. The Court said that the question was whether the police had acted improperly by choosing 12 rather than 13 as Amy's age. It did not consider that they had. The appellant's graffiti messages were directed to girls aged 8 to 13. It was the appellant who asked Amy her age and, when she gave it as 12, from that point the appellant believed that he was inciting a child under 13. In those circumstances he was properly charged with attempting the more serious offence under s.8.

MENTAL ELEMENT

In *Walker*[30] the appellant rang a telephone box near to which children were playing   3.68 and, when the complainant answered, asked her to show him her "fanny". He was convicted of the incitement offence under s.8 but appealed on the basis that he had not intended the girl to act on his words. The Court of Appeal dismissed the appeal, holding that the incitement offence may be committed although the defendant did not intend that the incited activity should take place. This is a surprising decision, given that incitement is usually defined as seeking to bring something about through encouragement or persuasion: see para.3.63 of the main work.

In the light of the decision in *Heard*,[31] discussed in para.2.72 above, s.8 appears to create offences of basic intent, such that voluntary intoxication through drink or drugs will provide no defence. It will suffice if the defendant's acts were deliberate. Recklessness is insufficient.

[30] [2006] EWCA Crim 1907.
[31] [2007] EWCA Crim 125.

CHAPTER 4

CHILD SEX OFFENCES

INTRODUCTION

To the cases cited in footnote 2, add *Figg*[1] and *Cronshaw*.[2] However, in *R. v J*,[3] the **4.04** House of Lords held that the long-standing practice of charging indecent assault where the offence of unlawful sexual intercourse was time-barred was impermissible, because it deprived the statutory bar of meaningful effect. The current state of the law in the light of that decision and subsequent authorities is that, where intercourse with a girl under the age of 16 took place before the commencement of the Sexual Offences Act 2003 (May 1, 2004) and a charge of unlawful sexual intercourse is now time-barred, indecent assault cannot be charged instead, either on its own (as in *R. v J*) or as an alternative to a charge of rape (*W.R.*[4] and *Cottrell and Fletcher*[5]). But if in such a case the defendant is charged with rape, the judge may properly leave indecent assault to the jury as an alternative verdict (*Timmins*[6] and *Phillips*[7]). The Court of Appeal in *Cottrell and Fletcher* noted the fortuitous impact of the case law where indecent assault is charged as an alternative to rape (unacceptable) and where it is left to the jury as an alternative verdict (acceptable). The Court in *Timmins* certified the point as one of general public importance, but the House of Lords refused leave to appeal. One may speculate that this was because the number of cases in which the distinction could be significant is small

---

[1] [2003] EWCA Crim 2751; [2004] Crim. L.R. 386.
[2] [2004] EWCA Crim 2057; [2004] Crim. L.R. 1044.
[3] [2004] UKHL 42; [2005] 1 A.C. 562.
[4] [2005] EWCA Crim 1907.
[5] [2007] EWCA Crim 2016.
[6] [2005] EWCA Crim 2909; [2006] 1 Cr. App. R. 18.
[7] [2007] EWCA Crim 485.

and destined to get smaller, being confined to cases predating the 2003 Act. The law is nonetheless in an unsatisfactory state. For trenchant but well-aimed criticism of *R. v J* and its consequences, see Jonathan Rogers, *Fundamentally objectionable* [2007] N.L.J. 1252–3.

4.14 The claimant in *S. v DPP*[8] was charged under s.5 of the 2003 Act (rape of a child under 13) following an incident in which, aged 15, he had sexual intercourse with a girl of 12. However, following representations from his solicitors, the CPS amended the charge to one under ss.9 and 13. The reason for this decision is not given in the judgment, but it appears to have been influenced by a psychologist's report to the effect that the only inappropriate element in the claimant's behaviour was that he had engaged in sexual behaviour with a partner who was not a peer. The Administrative Court nonetheless refused to quash the decision to prosecute under ss.9 and 13 on the ground that, if the prosecution were able to prove their allegation that the claimant had known the complainant's age, the circumstances could be described as exploitative such that a reasonable prosecutor could consider a prosecution to be in the public interest.

For a pre-2003 Act decision in which prosecution in a case of consensual sexual activity between teenagers was held compatible with Art.8 of the ECHR, see *E. v DPP*.[9] Two 15-year-olds had consensual sex and the boy was convicted by the magistrates of unlawful sexual intercourse with a girl under 16 (s.6(1) of the Sexual Offences Act 1956). On appeal, the Divisional Court rejected the argument that the prosecution breached the boy's Art.8 rights. It held that, having regard to the "tender age" of those involved, proscription of consensual sexual intercourse between 15-year-olds does not constitute an interference with private life within the meaning of Art.8(1). Moreover, even if it did, the proscription would be justified under Art.8(2) because of the need to protect girls from the risk of pregnancy. The decision is short and not fully satisfactory. First, it is hard to see how the fact that those affected are of "tender age" prevents the offence from interfering with their Art.8(1) rights. The age of the individuals, and the legislative aim of protecting the young, are surely relevant to the issue of justification under Art.8(2) rather than to the question whether the offence interfered with private life, which it would seem clearly to do. Secondly, the Court took a disappointingly absolutist line by stating that the offence *did not* engage Art.8(1) rights, suggesting that this would be so regardless of the circumstances. By contrast, the Court of Appeal in *R. v G*[10] stated that whether Art.8(1) is engaged in cases of consensual sexual activity between teenagers depends on the facts. This is surely the preferable approach (although *R. v G* is itself less than fully satisfactory: see further para.3.9 above).

---

[8] [2006] EWHC 2231 (Admin).
[9] [2005] EWHC 147 (Admin).
[10] [2006] EWCA Crim. 821.

SEXUAL ACTIVITY WITH A CHILD

Mode of Trial and Punishment

As from a day to be appointed the maximum sentence on summary conviction is **4.20** 12 months' imprisonment: Criminal Justice Act 2003, s.282(2), (3). The increase has no application to offences committed before the substitution takes effect: s.282(4). The offence under s.9 is a specified sexual offence in respect of which a sentence of imprisonment for public protection may be imposed under the Criminal Justice Act 2003.[11]

Sentencing

For the definitive guideline published by the Sentencing Guidelines Council in **4.22** relation to sentencing for offences under the 2003 Act, see para.1.18. In relation to offences under s.9 (sexual activity with a child) and s.10 (causing or inciting a child to engage in sexual activity), the guideline states that the factors to take into consideration are:

"1. The sentences for public protection *must* be considered in all cases. They are designed to ensure that sexual offenders are not released into the community if they present a significant risk of serious harm.

2. The culpability of the offender will be the primary indicator of offence seriousness, and the nature of the sexual activity will provide a guide as to the seriousness of the harm caused to the victim. Other factors will include:
   - the age and degree of vulnerability of the victim—as a general indication, the younger the child, the more vulnerable he or she is likely to be, although older children may also suffer serious and long-term psychological damage as a result of sexual abuse;
   - the age gap between the child and the offender;
   - the youth and immaturity of the offender; and
   - any breach of trust arising from a family relationship between the child and the offender, or from the offender's professional or other responsibility for the child's welfare, will make an offence more serious.

3. The same starting points apply whether the activity was caused or incited. Where an offence was incited but did not take place as a result of the voluntary intervention of the offender, that is likely to reduce the severity of the sentence imposed."[12]

The starting points, sentencing ranges and aggravating and mitigating factors for offences under ss.9 and 10 are as follows:

[11] s.224 and Sch.15, Pt 2.
[12] Pt 3A.

Type/nature of activity	Starting points	Sentencing ranges
Penile penetration of the vagina, anus or mouth *or* penetration of the vagina or anus with another body part or an object	4 years custody	3–7 years custody
Contact between naked genitalia of offender and naked genitalia or another part of victim's body, particularly face or mouth	2 years custody	1–4 years custody
Contact between naked genitalia of offender *or* victim and clothed genitalia of victim or offender or contact with naked genitalia of victim by offender using part of his or her body other than the genitalia or an object	12 months custody	26 weeks–2 years custody
Contact between part of offender's body (other than the genitalia) with part of the victim's body (other than the genitalia)	Community order	An appropriate non-custodial sentence*

* "Non–custodial sentence" in this context suggests a community order or a fine. In most instances, an offence will have crossed the threshold for a community order. However, in accordance with normal sentencing practice, a court is not precluded from imposing a financial penalty where that is determined to be the appropriate sentence.

Additional aggravating factors	Additional mitigating factors
1. Offender ejaculated or caused victim to ejaculate	1. Offender intervenes to prevent incited offence from taking place
2. Threats to prevent victim reporting the incident	2. Small disparity in age between the offender and the victim
3. Offender aware that he or she is suffering from a sexually transmitted infection	

A person convicted[13] under s.9 or s.10 is automatically subject to notification requirements in accordance with the SOA 2003, s.80 and Sch.3.

See *Corran and others*[14] for a pre-guideline decision in which the Court of Appeal gave guidance on sentencing under s.9. The decision remains of value to the extent that it is consistent with the definitive guideline.

MENTAL ELEMENT

In the light of the decision in *Heard*,[15] discussed in para.2.72 above, the offence in **4.34** s.9 appears to be one of basic intent, such that voluntary intoxication through drink or drugs will provide no defence. It will suffice if the defendant's acts were deliberate. Recklessness is insufficient.

CAUSING OR INCITING A CHILD TO ENGAGE IN SEXUAL ACTIVITY

MODE OF TRIAL AND PUNISHMENT

As from a day to be appointed the maximum sentence on summary conviction is **4.38** 12 months' imprisonment: Criminal Justice Act 2003, s.282(2), (3). The increase has no application to offences committed before the substitution takes effect: s.282(4). The offence under s.10 is a specified sexual offence in respect of which a sentence of imprisonment for public protection may be imposed under the Criminal Justice Act 2003.[16]

SENTENCING

For the definitive guideline published by the Sentencing Guidelines Council in **4.40** relation to sentencing for offences under the 2003 Act, see para.1.18. The provisions of the guideline relating to the offence under s.10 (causing or inciting a child to engage in sexual activity) are set out at para.4.22 above.

See *Corran and others*[17] for a pre-guideline decision in which the Court of Appeal gave guidance on sentencing under s.10. The decision remains of value to the extent that it is consistent with the definitive guideline.

---

[13] Or found not guilty by reason of insanity, found to be under a disability and to have done the act charged, or cautioned.

[14] [2005] EWCA Crim 192; [2005] Crim. L.R. 404.

[15] [2007] EWCA Crim 125.

[16] s.224 and Sch.15, Pt 2.

[17] Above n.14.

"Causes or Incites Another Person . . . to Engage in an Activity"

4.45 For the meaning of these terms, see para.3.63 above.

Mental Element

4.51 In the light of the decision in *Heard*,[18] discussed in para.2.72 above, the offence in s.10 appears to be one of basic intent, such that voluntary intoxication through drink or drugs will provide no defence. It will suffice if the defendant's acts were deliberate. Recklessness is insufficient.

ENGAGING IN SEXUAL ACTIVITY IN THE PRESENCE OF A CHILD

Mode of Trial and Punishment

4.53 As from a day to be appointed the maximum sentence on summary conviction is 12 months' imprisonment: Criminal Justice Act 2003, s.282(2), (3). The increase has no application to offences committed before the substitution takes effect: s.282(4). The offence under s.11 is a specified sexual offence in respect of which a sentence of imprisonment for public protection may be imposed under the Criminal Justice Act 2003.[19]

Sentencing

4.54 For the definitive guideline published by the Sentencing Guidelines Council in relation to sentencing for offences under the 2003 Act, see para.1.18. In relation to the offences under s.11 (engaging in sexual activity in the presence of a child) and s.32 (engaging in sexual activity in the presence of a person with a mental disorder impeding choice), the guideline sets out the following factors to take into consideration:

> "1. The sentences for public protection *must* be considered in all cases of engaging in sexual activity in the presence of a child. They are designed to ensure that sexual offenders are not released into the community if they present a significant risk of serious harm.
> 2. This offence involves intentionally, and for the purpose of obtaining sexual gratification, engaging in sexual activity in the presence of a person under 16, knowing or believing that person to be aware of the activity.

---

[18] Above n.15.
[19] s.224 and Sch.15, Pt 2.

3. The guidelines are predicated on the principle that the more serious the nature of the sexual activity a victim is forced to witness, the higher the sentencing starting point should be.
4. This offence will potentially be serious enough to merit a custodial sentence. In an individual case the court will need to consider whether there are particular mitigating factors that move the sentence below the custodial threshold."[20]

The starting points, sentencing ranges and aggravating and mitigating factors for the offences under ss.11 and 32 are as follows:

Type/nature of activity	Starting points	Sentencing ranges
Consensual intercourse or other forms of consensual penetration	2 years custody	1–4 years custody
Masturbation (of oneself or another person)	18 months custody	12 months–2 years 6 months custody
Consensual sexual touching involving naked genitalia	12 months custody	26 weeks–18 months custody
Consensual sexual touching of naked body parts but not involving naked genitalia	26 weeks custody	4 weeks–18 months custody

Additional aggravating factors	Additional mitigating factors
1. Background of intimidation or coercion	
2. Use of drugs, alcohol or other substance to facilitate the offence	
3. Threats to prevent victim reporting the incident	
4. Abduction or detention	

A person convicted[21] under s.11 or s.32 is automatically subject to notification requirements in accordance with the SOA 2003, s.80 and Sch.3.

[20] Pt 2D.
[21] Or found not guilty by reason of insanity, found to be under a disability and to have done the act charged, or cautioned.

See *Corran and others*[22] for a pre-guideline decision in which the Court of Appeal gave guidance on sentencing under s.11. The decision remains of value to the extent that it is consistent with the definitive guideline.

MENTAL ELEMENT

4.64 For the meaning of "for the purpose of obtaining sexual gratification", see *Abdullahi*,[23] discussed in para.4.79 below.

The view expressed in the main work that the purpose of obtaining sexual gratification must relate to the presence or observation of the child, rather than to the sexual activity itself, derives some support from *W v T*.[24] In that case, which involved a sentencing appeal, the appellants had pleaded guilty under s.11 following an incident in which they had engaged in sexual activity whilst being watched (and photographed) by the nine-year-old daughter of one of them. In delivering the judgment of the Court of Appeal, Mitting J. said:

> "The offence contains a number of elements of which one, the purpose of engaging in sexual activity in the presence or observation of a child, must be the obtaining of sexual gratification from that presence or observation."

The point was not, however, the subject of argument.

4.65 In the light of the decision in *Heard*,[25] discussed in para.2.72 above, the requirement that the defendant did the prohibited act for the purpose of obtaining sexual gratification makes the s.11 offence one of specific intent, such that voluntary intoxication through drink or drugs will provide a defence if it may have prevented the defendant forming that purpose.

Corrigendum: The reference in the main work to para.5.87 should be to para.5.67.

CAUSING A CHILD TO WATCH A SEXUAL ACT

MODE OF TRIAL AND PUNISHMENT

4.68 As from a day to be appointed the maximum sentence on summary conviction is 12 months' imprisonment: Criminal Justice Act 2003, s.282(2), (3). The increase has no application to offences committed before the substitution takes effect: s.282(4). The offence under s.12 is a specified sexual offence in respect of which

---

[22] Above n.14.
[23] [2006] EWCA Crim 2060.
[24] [2005] EWCA Crim 2448.
[25] [2007] EWCA Crim 125.

a sentence of imprisonment for public protection may be imposed under the Criminal Justice Act 2003.[26]

SENTENCING

For the definitive guideline published by the Sentencing Guidelines Council in relation to sentencing for offences under the 2003 Act, see para.1.18. In relation to the offences under s.12 (causing a child to watch a sexual act) and s.33 (causing a person with a mental disorder impeding choice to watch a sexual act), the guideline sets out the following factors to take into consideration: **4.69**

> "1. The sentences for public protection *must* be considered in all cases. They are designed to ensure that sexual offenders are not released into the community if they present a significant risk of serious harm.
> 2. This offence includes intentionally causing or inciting, for the purpose of sexual gratification, a person under 16 to watch sexual activity or look at a photograph or pseudo-photograph of sexual activity.
> 3. The guidelines are predicated on the principle that the more serious the nature of the sexual activity a victim is caused to witness, the higher the sentencing starting point should be.
> 4. This offence will potentially be serious enough to merit a custodial sentence. In an individual case the court will need to consider whether there are particular mitigating factors that should move the sentence below the custodial threshold.
> 5. The same starting points apply whether the activity was caused or incited and whether or not the incited activity took place."

The starting points, sentencing ranges and aggravating and mitigating factors for the offences under ss.12 and 33 are as follows:

Type/nature of activity	Starting points	Sentencing ranges
Live sexual activity	18 months custody	12 months–2 years custody
Moving or still images of people engaged in sexual activity involving penetration	32 weeks custody	26 weeks–12 months custody
Moving or still images of people engaged in sexual activity other than penetration	Community order	Community order–26 weeks custody
Consensual sexual touching of naked body parts but not involving naked genitalia	26 weeks custody	4 weeks–18 months custody

[26] s.224 and Sch.15, Pt 2.

Additional aggravating factors	Additional mitigating factors
1. Background of intimidation or coercion	
2. Use of drugs, alcohol or other substance to facilitate the offence	
3. Threats to prevent victim reporting the incident	
4. Abduction or detention	
5. Images of violent activity	

A person convicted[27] under s.12 or s.33 is automatically subject to notification requirements in accordance with the SOA 2003, s.80 and Sch.3.

See *Corran and others*[28] for a pre-guideline decision in which the Court of Appeal gave guidance on sentencing under s.12. The decision remains of value to the extent that it is consistent with the definitive guideline.

"To Watch a Third Person Engaging in an Activity, or to Look at an Image of any Person Engaging in an Activity"

4.74 For an example of the offence being committed where A causes B (a child) to view an image of him (A) engaging in sexual activity, see *N.G.*,[29] in which an adult caused a child of 12 to watch him masturbating via a webcam.

Mental Element

4.79 For the meaning of "for the purpose of obtaining sexual gratification", see *Abdullahi*.[30] The appellant plied the 13-year-old complainant with drink and drugs and caused him to watch pornographic films depicting heterosexual and homosexual activity. Later, he touched the complainant's penis. He was convicted of offences under ss.9 and 12 of the 2003 Act (sexual activity with a child and causing

---

[27] Or found not guilty by reason of insanity, found to be under a disability and to have done the act charged, or cautioned.
[28] Above n.14.
[29] [2006] EWCA Crim 2694.
[30] [2006] EWCA Crim 2060.

a child to watch a sexual act). In relation to the count under s.12, the trial judge directed the jury that they could convict if they were satisfied that the appellant did what he did "for the purpose of obtaining sexual gratification, either by enjoying seeing [the complainant] looking at the images or with a view to getting [the complainant] in the mood to provide sexual gratification to the defendant later". The appellant appealed, arguing that "for the purpose of obtaining sexual gratification" means for the purpose of *immediate* sexual gratification; that the judge had misdirected the jury that future gratification was sufficient; and that cases of future gratification or "putting the child in the mood" should be prosecuted instead under s.14 (arranging or facilitating the commission of a child sex offence). The Court of Appeal rejected this argument, holding that s.12 covers cases where the purpose is immediate gratification, or deferred gratification, or both immediate and deferred gratification. This is, with respect, an eminently sensible interpretation which avoids setting an evidential hurdle that prosecutors could often find impossible to surmount, in the form of a requirement to prove an immediate rather than a future sexual purpose. The decision does, however, have the effect of creating a significant overlap between the offences in ss.12 and 14.[31]

In the light of the decision in *Heard*,[32] discussed in para.2.72 above, the requirement that the defendant did the prohibited act for the purpose of obtaining sexual gratification makes the s.12 offence one of specific intent, such that voluntary intoxication through drink or drugs will provide a defence if it may have prevented the defendant forming that purpose.

CHILD SEX OFFENCES COMMITTED BY CHILDREN OR YOUNG PERSONS

MODE OF TRIAL AND PUNISHMENT

As from a day to be appointed the maximum sentence on summary conviction is **4.85** 12 months' imprisonment: Criminal Justice Act 2003, s.282(2), (3). The increase has no application to offences committed before the substitution takes effect: s.282(4). The offence under s.13 is a specified sexual offence in respect of which a sentence of imprisonment for public protection may be imposed under the Criminal Justice Act 2003.[33]

---

[31] See further the valuable commentary by Professor Ormerod at [2006] Crim. L.R. 185–6, and the articles cited therein.
[32] [2007] EWCA Crim 125.
[33] s.224 and Sch.15, Pt 2.

4.86 For the definitive guideline published by the Sentencing Guidelines Council in relation to sentencing for offences under the 2003 Act, see para.1.18. The guideline provides the following guidance for sentencing offences under ss.9–12 of the 2003 Act committed by a person under the age of 18. The starting points are based upon a first-time offender aged 17 who pleaded not guilty. For younger offenders, sentencers should consider whether a lower starting point is justified in recognition of the offender's age or immaturity.

The starting points, sentencing ranges and aggravating and mitigating factors for the offences under ss.9–12 are as follows. Section 9:

Type/nature of activity	Starting points	Sentencing ranges
Offence involving penetration where one or more aggravating factors exist or where there is a substantial age gap between the parties	**Detention and Training Order 12 months**	**Detention and Training Order 6–24 months**
CUSTODY THRESHOLD		
Any form of sexual activity (non-penetrative or penetrative) not involving any aggravating factors	**Community order**	**An appropriate non-custodial sentence***

Additional aggravating factors	Additional mitigating factors
1. Background of intimidation or coercion	1. Relationship of genuine affection
2. Use of drugs, alcohol or other substance to facilitate the offence	2. Youth and immaturity of offender
3. Threats to prevent victim reporting the incident	
4. Abduction or detention	
5. Offender aware that he or she is suffering from a sexually transmitted infection	

Section 10:

Type/nature of activity	Starting points	Sentencing ranges
Offence involving penetration where one or more aggravating factors exist or where there is a substantial age gap between the parties	**Detention and Training Order 12 months**	**Detention and Training Order 6–24 months**
CUSTODY THRESHOLD		
Any form of sexual activity (non-penetrative or penetrative) not involving any aggravating factors	**Community order**	**An appropriate non-custodial sentence***

Additional aggravating factors	Additional mitigating factors
1. Background of intimidation or coercion 2. Use of drugs, alcohol or other substance to facilitate the offence 3. Threats to prevent victim reporting the incident 4. Abduction or detention 5. Offender aware that he or she is suffering from a sexually transmitted infection	1. Relationship of genuine affection 2. Offender intervenes to prevent incited offence from taking place 3. Youth and immaturity of offender

Section 11:

Type/nature of activity	Starting points	Sentencing ranges
Sexual activity involving penetration where one or more aggravating factors exist	Detention and Training Order 12 months	Detention and Training Order 6–24 months
CUSTODY THRESHOLD		
Any form of sexual activity (non-penetrative or penetrative) not involving any aggravating factors	Community order	An appropriate non-custodial sentence*

Additional aggravating factors	Additional mitigating factors
1. Background of intimidation or coercion 2. Use of drugs, alcohol or other substance to facilitate the offence 3. Threats to prevent victim reporting the incident 4. Abduction or detention	1. Youth and immaturity of offender

Section 12:

Type/nature of activity	Starting points	Sentencing ranges
Live sexual activity	Detention and Training Order 8 months	Detention and Training Order 6–12 months
CUSTODY THRESHOLD		
Moving or still images of people engaged in sexual acts involving penetration	Community order	An appropriate non-custodial sentence*

Type/nature of activity	Starting points	Sentencing ranges
Moving or still images of people engaged in sexual acts other than penetration	Community order	An appropriate non-custodial sentence*

Additional aggravating factors	Additional mitigating factors
1. Background of intimidation or coercion	1. Youth and immaturity of offender
2. Use of drugs, alcohol or other substance to facilitate the offence	
3. Threats to prevent victim reporting the incident	
4. Abduction or detention	
5. Images of violent activity	

* "Non-custodial sentence" in this context suggests a youth community order (as defined in the Criminal Justice Act 2003, s.147(2)) or a fine. In most instances, an offence will have crossed the threshold for a community order. However, in accordance with normal sentencing practice, a court is not precluded from imposing a financial penalty where that is determined to be the appropriate sentence.

A person convicted[34] under s.13 is automatically subject to notification requirements in accordance with the SOA 2003, s.80 and Sch.3, if they are sentenced to at least 12 months' imprisonment.

ARRANGING OR FACILITATING COMMISSION OF A CHILD SEX OFFENCE

MODE OF TRIAL AND PUNISHMENT

As from a day to be appointed the maximum sentence on summary conviction is 4.93 12 months' imprisonment: Criminal Justice Act 2003, s.282(2), (3). The increase has no application to offences committed before the substitution takes effect: s.282(4). The offence under s.14 is a specified sexual offence in respect of which

---

[34] Or found not guilty by reason of insanity, found to be under a disability and to have done the act charged, or cautioned.

a sentence of imprisonment for public protection may be imposed under the Criminal Justice Act 2003.[35]

SENTENCING

4.94 For the definitive guideline published by the Sentencing Guidelines Council in relation to sentencing for offences under the 2003 Act, see para.1.18. In relation to the offence under s.14, the guideline sets out the following factors to take into consideration:

> "1. The sentences for public protection *must* be considered in all cases. They are designed to ensure that sexual offenders are not released into the community if they present a significant risk of serious harm.
> 2. Sentencers should refer to the individual guideline for the substantive offence under ss. 9–13 of the SOA 2003 that was arranged or facilitated.
> 3. In cases where there is no commercial exploitation, the range of behaviour within, and the type of offender charged with, this offence will be wide. In some cases, a starting point below the suggested starting point for the substantive child sex offence may be appropriate."

The starting points, sentencing ranges and aggravating and mitigating factors for the s.14 offence are as follows:

Type/nature of activity	Starting points and sentencing ranges
Where the activity is arranged or facilitated as part of a commercial enterprise, even if the offender is under 18	As this offence is primarily aimed at persons organising the commission of relevant sexual offences for gain, and sometimes across international borders, this is the most likely aggravating factor Starting points and sentencing ranges should be increased above those for the relevant substantive offence under sections 9–13
Basic offence as defined in the SOA 2003 assuming no aggravating or mitigating factors	The starting point and sentencing range should be commensurate with that for the relevant substantive offence under sections 9–13

[35] s.224 and Sch.15, Pt 2.

Additional aggravating factors	Additional mitigating factors
1. Background of intimidation or coercion	1. Youth and immaturity of offender
2. Use of drugs, alcohol or other substance to facilitate the offence	
3. Threats to prevent victim reporting the incident	
4. Abduction or detention	
5. Number of victims involved	

A person convicted[36] under s.14 is automatically subject to notification requirements in accordance with the SOA 2003, s.80 and Sch.3, if they were 18 or over at the time of the offence or they are sentenced to at least 12 months' imprisonment.

EXCEPTION FOR ACTS DONE TO PROTECT THE CHILD

Gillick was followed in *R. (On the Application of Axon) v Secretary of State for Health*,[37] which concerned an unsuccessful challenge to Department of Health guidance to health professionals on giving advice and treatment on sexual matters to children under the age of 16. It was common ground between the parties that a medical professional who gives advice and treatment to a young person relating to contraception and sexual and reproductive health, including abortion, does not incur criminal liability.[38]   **4.101**

MEETING A CHILD FOLLOWING SEXUAL GROOMING ETC.

DEFINITION

See generally on the s.15 offence, Alisdair A. Gillespie, *Tackling Grooming* Pol. J.   **4.109**
2004, 77(3), 239; Alasdair A. Gillespie, *Indecent Images, Grooming and the Law* [2006] Crim. L.R. 412.

---

[36] Or found not guilty by reason of insanity, found to be under a disability and to have done the act charged, or cautioned.
[37] [2006] EWHC 37 (Admin).
[38] At para.26.

MODE OF TRIAL AND PUNISHMENT

4.110 As from a day to be appointed the maximum sentence on summary conviction is 12 months' imprisonment: Criminal Justice Act 2003, s.282(2), (3). The increase has no application to offences committed before the substitution takes effect: s.282(4). The offence under s.15 is a specified sexual offence in respect of which a sentence of imprisonment for public protection may be imposed under the Criminal Justice Act 2003.[39]

SENTENCING

4.112 For the definitive guideline published by the Sentencing Guidelines Council in relation to sentencing for offences under the 2003 Act, see para.1.18. In relation to the offence under s.15 (meeting a child following sexual grooming), the guideline sets out the following factors to take into consideration:

"1. The sentences for public protection *must* be considered in all cases. They are designed to ensure that sexual offenders are not released into the community if they present a significant risk of serious harm.

2. In a case where no substantive sexual offence has in fact been committed, the main dimension of seriousness will be the offender's *intention*—the more serious the offence intended, the higher the offender's culpability.

3. The *harm* to the victim in such cases will invariably be less than that resulting from a completed offence, although the *risk* to which the victim has been put is always a relevant factor.

4. In some cases, where the offender has come quite close to fulfilling his or her intention, the victim may have been put in considerable fear, and physical injury to the victim is a possible feature.

5. In addition to the generic aggravating factors identified in the Council guideline on seriousness, the main factors determining the seriousness of a preparatory offence are:
   • the seriousness of the intended offence (which will affect both the offender's culpability and the degree of risk to which the victim has been exposed);
   • the degree to which the offence was planned;
   • the sophistication of the grooming;
   • the determination of the offender;
   • how close the offender came to success;
   • the reason why the offender did not succeed, i.e. whether it was a change of mind or whether someone or something prevented the offender from continuing; and
   • any physical or psychological injury suffered by the victim.

6. The starting point should be commensurate with that for the preparatory offence actually committed, with an enhancement to reflect the nature and severity of the intended sexual offence."

The starting points, sentencing ranges and aggravating and mitigating factors for the s.15 offence are as follows:

---

[39] s.224 and Sch.15, Pt 2.

Type/nature of activity	Starting points	Sentencing ranges
Where the intent is to commit an assault by penetration or rape	**4 years custody** if the victim is under 13	**3–7 years custody**
	2 years custody if the victim is 13 or over but under 16	**1–4 years custody**
Where the intent is to coerce the child into sexual activity	**2 years custody** if the victim is under 13	**1–4 years custody**
	18 months custody if the victim is 13 or over but under 16	**12 months–2 years 6 months custody**

Additional aggravating factors	Additional mitigating factors
1. Background of intimidation or coercion	
2. Use of drugs, alcohol or other substance to facilitate the offence	
3. Offender aware that he or she is suffering from a sexually transmitted infection	
4. Abduction or detention	

A person convicted[40] under s.14 is automatically subject to notification requirements in accordance with the SOA 2003, s.80 and Sch.3.

MENTAL ELEMENT

In the light of the decision in *Heard*,[41] discussed in para.2.72 above, the **4.125** requirement that the defendant did the prohibited act whilst intending to do something to or in respect of B which would involve the commission of a relevant offence, makes the s.15 offence one of specific intent, such that voluntary intoxication through drink or drugs will provide a defence if it may have prevented the defendant forming that intention.

---

[40] Or found not guilty by reason of insanity, found to be under a disability and to have done the act charged, or cautioned.
[41] [2007] EWCA Crim 125.

ABUSE OF POSITION OF TRUST

ABUSE OF POSITION OF TRUST: SEXUAL ACTIVITY WITH A CHILD

MODE OF TRIAL AND PUNISHMENT

As from a day to be appointed the maximum sentence on summary conviction is **5.09** 12 months' imprisonment: Criminal Justice Act 2003, s.282(2), (3). The increase has no application to offences committed before the substitution takes effect: s.282(4). The offence under s.16 is a specified sexual offence in respect of which a sentence of imprisonment for public protection may be imposed under the Criminal Justice Act 2003.[1]

SENTENCING

For the definitive guideline published by the Sentencing Guidelines Council in **5.11** relation to sentencing for offences under the 2003 Act, see para.1.18. In relation to the offences under s.16 (abuse of position of trust: sexual activity with a child) and s.17 (abuse of position of trust: causing or inciting a child to engage in sexual activity), the guideline states that the factors to take into consideration are as follows:

> "1. The sentences for public protection *must* be considered in all cases. They are designed to ensure that sexual offenders are not released into the community if they present a significant risk of serious harm.

[1] s.224 and Sch.15, Pt 2.

2. The culpability of the offender will be the primary indicator of offence seriousness, and the nature of the sexual activity will provide a guide as to the seriousness of the harm caused to the victim. Other factors will include:
   - the age and degree of vulnerability of the victim—as a general indication, the younger the child, the more vulnerable he or she is likely to be, although older children may also suffer serious and long-term psychological damage as a result of sexual abuse;
   - the age gap between the child and the offender; and
   - the youth and immaturity of the offender.
3. These offences will only be charged where the victim is aged 16 or 17. Therefore, the sentencing starting points in the guidelines are only intended for those cases and are significantly lower than those for a child sex offence involving the same type of sexual activity, which should be applied in all other cases.
4. When sentencing for an abuse of trust offence, evidence of serious coercion, threats or trauma are aggravating factors that should move a sentence well beyond the starting point.
5. Some relationships caught within the scope of these offences, although unlawful, will be wholly consensual. The length of time over which a relationship has been sustained and the proximity in age between the parties could point to a relationship born out of genuine affection. Each case must be considered carefully on its own facts."

The starting points, sentencing ranges and aggravating and mitigating factors for the offences under ss.16 and 17 are as follows. The starting points are intended to be used only in relation to victims aged 16 or 17. Where the victim is a child under 16, one of the child sex offences in ss.9 to 13 should normally be charged. If one of the abuse of trust offences has nevertheless been charged, the starting points should be the same as they would be for the relevant child sex offence.

Type/nature of activity	Starting points	Sentencing ranges
Penile penetration of the vagina, anus or mouth *or* penetration of the vagina or anus with another body part or an object	18 months custody	12 months–2 years 6 months custody
Contact between naked genitalia of offender and naked genitalia or another part of victim's body, particularly face or mouth	2 years custody	1–4 years custody
Other forms of non-penetrative activity	26 weeks custody	4 weeks–18 months custody

Type/nature of activity	Starting points	Sentencing ranges
Contact between part of offender's body (other than the genitalia) with part of the victim's body (other than the genitalia)	Community order	An appropriate non-custodial sentence*

* "Non-custodial sentence" in this context suggests a community order or a fine. In most instances, an offence will have crossed the threshold for a community order. However, in accordance with normal sentencing practice, a court is not precluded from imposing a financial penalty where that is determined to be the appropriate sentence.

Additional aggravating factors	Additional mitigating factors
1. Background of intimidation or coercion	1. Small disparity in age between victim and offender
2. Offender ejaculated or caused the victim to ejaculate	2. Relationship of genuine affection
3. Use of drugs, alcohol or other substance to facilitate the offence	3. No element of corruption
4. Offender aware that he or she is suffering from a sexually transmitted infection	

A person convicted[2] under s.16 or s.17 is automatically subject to notification requirements in accordance with the SOA 2003, s.80 and Sch.3, if, in respect of the offence, they are sentenced to a term of imprisonment, detained in a hospital or given a community sentence of at least 12 months.

"POSITION OF TRUST"

In 2005 the Department for Culture, Media and Sport (DCMS) issued a paper   5.25
entitled *Consultation on the Scope and Implementation of the Sexual Offences Act 2003 in Relation to Sports Coaches*, on whether sports coaches should be brought within the scope of the abuse of trust offences.[3] The consultation period ended on March 21, 2005. The DCMS has since decided against extending the offences to cover sports coaches, on the ground that appropriate protection is now provided by the Safeguarding Vulnerable Groups Act 2006.

---

[2] Or found not guilty by reason of insanity, found to be under a disability and to have done the act charged, or cautioned.
[3] See generally Yvonne Williams, *Playing it safe* [2005] N.L.J. 234–5 (February 18, 2005).

Marriage Exception

Marriage Exception

5.28 The Civil Partnership Act 2004 has extended the exception to civil partners.[3A] Section 23 of the 2003 Act as amended now provides:

> "**Sections 16 to 19: exception for spouses and civil partners**
> **23.**—(1) Conduct by a person (A) which would otherwise be an offence under any of sections 16 to 19 against another person (B) is not an offence under that section if at the time—
>   (a) B is 16 or over, and
>   (b) A and B are lawfully married or civil partners of each other.
> (2) In proceedings for such an offence it is for the defendant to prove that A and B were at the time lawfully married or civil partners of each other."

Mental Element

5.34 In the light of the decision in *Heard*,[4] discussed in para.2.72 above, the offence in s.16 appears to be one of basic intent, such that voluntary intoxication through drink or drugs will provide no defence. It will suffice if the defendant's acts were deliberate. Recklessness is insufficient.

ABUSE OF POSITION OF TRUST: CAUSING OR INCITING A CHILD TO ENGAGE IN SEXUAL ACTIVITY

Mode of Trial and Punishment

5.38 As from a day to be appointed the maximum sentence on summary conviction is 12 months' imprisonment: Criminal Justice Act 2003, s.282(2), (3). The increase has no application to offences committed before the substitution takes effect: s.282(4). The offence under s.17 is a specified sexual offence in respect of which a sentence of imprisonment for public protection may be imposed under the Criminal Justice Act 2003.[5]

Sentencing

5.39 For the definitive guideline published by the Sentencing Guidelines Council in relation to sentencing for offences under the 2003 Act, see para.1.18. The guideline applies to offences under s.17 (abuse of position of trust: causing or inciting a child to engage in sexual activity) as they do for the offence under s.16 (abuse of position of trust: sexual activity with a child): see para.5.11 above. The same starting points apply whether the activity was caused or incited. Where an

---

[3A] s.261(1) and Sch.27, para.173.
[4] [2007] EWCA Crim 125.
[5] s.224 and Sch.15, Pt 2.

offence was incited but did not take place as a result of the voluntary intervention of the offender, that is likely to reduce the severity of the sentence imposed.

MENTAL ELEMENT

In the light of the decision in *Heard*,[6] discussed in para.2.72 above, the offence in 5.50 s.17 appears to be one of basic intent, such that voluntary intoxication through drink or drugs will provide no defence. It will suffice if the defendant's acts were deliberate. Recklessness is insufficient.

ABUSE OF POSITION OF TRUST: ENGAGING IN SEXUAL ACTIVITY IN THE PRESENCE OF A CHILD

MODE OF TRIAL AND PUNISHMENT

As from a day to be appointed the maximum sentence on summary conviction is 5.54 12 months' imprisonment: Criminal Justice Act 2003, s.282(2), (3). The increase has no application to offences committed before the substitution takes effect: s.282(4). The offence under s.18 is a specified sexual offence in respect of which a sentence of imprisonment for public protection may be imposed under the Criminal Justice Act 2003.[7]

SENTENCING

For the definitive guideline published by the Sentencing Guidelines Council in 5.55 relation to sentencing for offences under the 2003 Act, see para.1.18. In relation to the offence under s.18 (abuse of position of trust: engaging in sexual activity in the presence of a child), the guideline states that the factors to take into consideration are as follows:

"1. The sentences for public protection *must* be considered in all cases. They are designed to ensure that sexual offenders are not released into the community if they present a significant risk of serious harm.
2. The guidelines are predicated on the principle that the more serious the nature of the sexual activity a victim is forced to witness, the higher the sentencing starting point should be.
3. These offences will only be charged where the victim is aged 16 or 17. Therefore, the sentencing starting points in the guidelines are only intended for those cases and are significantly lower than those for a child sex offence involving the same type of sexual activity, which should be applied in all other cases.
4. These offences will potentially be serious enough to merit a custodial sentence. In an individual case, the court will need to consider whether there are particular mitigating factors that should move the sentence below the custodial threshold."

[6] [2007] EWCA Crim 125.
[7] s.224 and Sch.15, Pt 2.

The starting points, sentencing ranges and aggravating and mitigating factors for the s.18 offence are as follows.

Type/nature of activity	Starting points	Sentencing ranges
Consensual intercourse or other forms of consensual penetration	2 years custody	1–4 years custody
Masturbation (of oneself or another person)	18 months custody	12 months–2 years 6 months custody
Consensual sexual touching involving naked genitalia	12 months custody	26 weeks–2 years custody
Consensual sexual touching of naked body parts but not involving naked genitalia	26 weeks custody	4 weeks–18 months custody

Additional aggravating factors	Additional mitigating factors
1. Background of intimidation or coercion	
2. Use of drugs, alcohol or other substance to facilitate the offence	
3. Threats to prevent victim reporting the incident	
4. Abduction or detention	

A person convicted[8] under s.18 is automatically subject to notification requirements in accordance with the SOA 2003, s.80 and Sch.3, if, in respect of the offence, they are sentenced to a term of imprisonment, detained in a hospital or given a community sentence of at least 12 months.

Mental Element

5.67   In the light of the decision in *Heard*,[9] discussed in para.2.72 above, the requirement that the defendant did the prohibited act for the purpose of obtaining

---

[8] Or found not guilty by reason of insanity, found to be under a disability and to have done the act charged, or cautioned.
[9] [2007] EWCA Crim 125.

sexual gratification makes the s.18 offence one of specific intent, such that voluntary intoxication through drink or drugs will provide a defence if it may have prevented the defendant forming that purpose.

ABUSE OF POSITION OF TRUST: CAUSING A CHILD TO WATCH A SEXUAL ACT

MODE OF TRIAL AND PUNISHMENT

As from a day to be appointed the maximum sentence on summary conviction is **5.72** 12 months' imprisonment: Criminal Justice Act 2003, s.282(2), (3). The increase has no application to offences committed before the substitution takes effect: s.282(4). The offence under s.19 is a specified sexual offence in respect of which a sentence of imprisonment for public protection may be imposed under the Criminal Justice Act 2003.[10]

SENTENCING

For the definitive guideline published by the Sentencing Guidelines Council in **5.73** relation to sentencing for offences under the 2003 Act, see para.1.18. In relation to the offence under s.19 (abuse of position of trust: causing a child to watch a sexual act), the guideline states that the factors to take into consideration are as follows:

> "1. The sentences for public protection *must* be considered in all cases. They are designed to ensure that sexual offenders are not released into the community if they present a significant risk of serious harm.
> 2. The culpability of the offender will be the primary indicator of offence seriousness, and the nature of the sexual activity will provide a guide as to the seriousness of the harm caused to the victim. Other factors will include:
>   - the age and degree of vulnerability of the victim—as a general indication, the younger the child, the more vulnerable he or she is likely to be, although older children may also suffer serious and long-term psychological damage as a result of sexual abuse;
>   - the age gap between the child and the offender; and
>   - the youth and immaturity of the offender.
> 3. Serious coercion, threats, corruption or trauma are aggravating factors that should move a sentence well beyond the starting point.
> 4. Some relationships caught within the scope of these offences, although unlawful, will be wholly consensual. The length of time over which a relationship has been sustained and the proximity in age between the parties could point to a relationship born out of genuine affection. Each case must be considered carefully on its own facts.
> 5. These offences will only be charged where the victim is aged 16 or 17. Therefore, the sentencing starting points in the guidelines are only intended for those cases

---

[10] s.224 and Sch.15, Pt 2.

and are significantly lower than those for a child sex offence involving the same type of sexual activity, which should be applied in all other cases.

6. The guideline is predicated on the principle that the more serious the nature of the sexual activity a victim is forced to witness, the higher the sentencing starting point should be.

7. The offence will potentially be serious enough to merit a custodial sentence. In an individual case, the court will need to consider whether there are particular mitigating factors that should move the sentence below the custodial threshold.''

The starting points, sentencing ranges and aggravating and mitigating factors for the s.19 offence are as follows:

Type/nature of activity	Starting points	Sentencing ranges
Live sexual activity	18 months custody	12 months–2 years custody
Moving or still images of people engaged in sexual activity involving penetration	32 weeks custody	26 weeks–12 months custody
Moving or still images of people engaged in sexual activity other than penetration	Community order	Community order–26 weeks custody

Additional aggravating factors	Additional mitigating factors
1. Background of intimidation or coercion	1. Small disparity in age between victim and offender
2. Use of drugs, alcohol or other substance to facilitate the offence	
3. Threats to prevent victim reporting the incident	
4. Abduction or detention	
5. Images of violent activity	

A person convicted[11] under s.19 is automatically subject to notification requirements in accordance with the SOA 2003, s.80 and Sch.3, if, in respect of

---

[11] Or found not guilty by reason of insanity, found to be under a disability and to have done the act charged, or cautioned.

the offence, they are sentenced to a term of imprisonment, detained in a hospital or given a community sentence of at least 12 months.

MENTAL ELEMENT

In the light of the decision in *Heard*,[12] discussed in para.2.72 above, the requirement that the defendant did the prohibited act for the purpose of obtaining sexual gratification makes the s.19 offence one of specific intent, such that voluntary intoxication through drink or drugs will provide a defence if it may have prevented the defendant forming that purpose. 5.85

[12] [2007] EWCA Crim 125.

CHAPTER 6

FAMILIAL SEX OFFENCES

SEXUAL ACTIVITY WITH A CHILD FAMILY MEMBER

MODE OF TRIAL AND PUNISHMENT

As from a day to be appointed the maximum sentence on summary conviction is **6.12** 12 months' imprisonment: Criminal Justice Act 2003, s.282(2), (3). The increase has no application to offences committed before the substitution takes effect: s.282(4). The offence under s.26 is a specified sexual offence in respect of which a sentence of imprisonment for public protection may be imposed under the Criminal Justice Act 2003.[1]

SENTENCING

For the definitive guideline published by the Sentencing Guidelines Council on **6.14** sentencing under the 2003 Act, see para.1.18 above. The guideline states that the factors to be taken into consideration in relation to offences under s.25 (sexual activity with a child family member) and s.26 (inciting a child family member to engage in sexual activity) are as follows[2]:

"1. The new sentences for public protection must be considered in all cases. They are designed to ensure that sexual offenders are not released into the community if they present a significant risk of serious harm.
2. The culpability of the offender will be the primary indicator of offence seriousness, and the nature of the sexual activity will provide a guide as to the seriousness of the harm caused to the victim. Other factors will include:

---

[1] s.224 and Sch.15, Pt 2.
[2] Pt 3A.

95

- the age and degree of vulnerability of the victim—as a general indication, the younger the child, the more vulnerable he or she is likely to be, although older children may also suffer serious and long-term psychological damage as a result of sexual abuse;
- the age gap between the child and the offender; and
- the youth and immaturity of the offender.

3. The starting points for sentencing for the familial child sex offences should be between 25% and 50% higher than those for the generic child sex offences in all cases where the victim is aged 13 or over but under 16; the closer the familial relationship, using the statutory definitions as a guide, the higher the increase that should be applied.

4. Where a victim is over the age of consent, the starting points assume that the offender is a close relative.

5. Where the victim of a familial child sex offence is aged 16 or 17 when the sexual activity is commenced and the sexual relationship is unlawful only because it takes place within a familial setting, the starting points for sentencing should be in line with those for the generic abuse of trust offences.

6. Evidence that a victim has been 'groomed' by the offender to agree to take part in sexual activity will aggravate the seriousness of the offence."

The starting points, sentencing ranges and aggravating and mitigating factors for the offences under ss.25 and 26 are different according to whether the offender is an adult or under 18:

Adult offenders

In relation to adults, i.e. those aged 18 or over, the starting points (etc.) are split in two. The first set apply where: (a) the victim is 13 or over but under 16, regardless of the familial relationship with the offender; (b) the victim is 16 or 17 but the sexual relationship commenced when the victim was under 16; or (c) the victim is aged 16 or 17 and the offender is a blood relative. They are as follows:

Type/nature of activity	Starting points	Sentencing ranges
Penile penetration of the vagina, anus or mouth or penetration of the vagina or anus with another body part or an object	5 years custody	4–8 years custody
Contact between naked genitalia of offender and naked genitalia of victim	4 years custody	3–7 years custody

Type/nature of activity	Starting points	Sentencing ranges
Contact between naked genitalia of offender or victim and clothed genitalia of the victim or offender Contact between naked genitalia of victim by another part of the offender's body or an object, or between the naked genitalia of offender and another part of victim's body	18 months custody	12 months–2 years 6 months custody
Contact between part of offender's body (other than the genitalia) with part of the victim's body (other than the genitalia)	Community order	An appropriate non-custodial sentence*

In cases where the victim was aged 16 or 17 when the sexual relationship commenced and the relationship is only unlawful because of the abuse of trust implicit in the offence, the guidelines are as follows[3]:

Type/nature of activity	Starting points	Sentencing ranges
Penile penetration of the vagina, anus or mouth or penetration of the vagina or anus with another body part or an object	2 years custody	1-4 years custody
Any other form of non-penetrative sexual activity involving the naked contact between the offender and victim	12 months custody	26 weeks–2 years custody

[3] For a pre-guidelines example of sentencing for an offence under s.25 committed in these circumstances, see *Thomas* [2006] Crim. L.R. 71.

Type/nature of activity	Starting points	Sentencing ranges
Contact between clothed part of offender's body (other than the genitalia) with clothed part of victim's body (other than the genitalia)	**Community order**	**An appropriate non-custodial sentence***

* "Non-custodial sentence" in this context suggests a community order or a fine. In most instances, an offence will have crossed the threshold for a community order. However, in accordance with normal sentencing practice, a court is not precluded from imposing a financial penalty where that is determined to be the appropriate sentence.

Additional aggravating factors	Additional mitigating factors
1. Background of intimidation or coercion	1. Small disparity in age between victim and offender
2. Use of drugs, alcohol or other substance	
3. Threats deterring the victim from reporting the incident	
4. Offender aware that he or she is suffering from a sexually transmitted infection	
5. Closeness of familial relationship	

A person convicted[4] under s.25 or s.26 who was aged 18 or over at the time of the offence is automatically subject to notification requirements in accordance with the SOA 2003, s.80 and Sch.3.

Offenders under 18

Where the offender is under 18, the starting points (etc.) are as follows. They are based upon a first-time offender aged 17 who pleaded not guilty. For younger offenders, sentencers should consider whether a lower starting point is justified in recognition of the offender's age or immaturity:

[4] Or found not guilty by reason of insanity, found to be under a disability and to have done the act charged, or cautioned.

Type/nature of activity	Starting points	Sentencing ranges
Offence involving penetration where one or more aggravating factors exist or where there is a substantial age gap between the parties	Detention and Training Order 18 months	Detention and Training Order 6–24 months
CUSTODY THRESHOLD		
Any form of sexual activity that does not involve any aggravating factors	Community order	An appropriate non-custodial sentence*

* "Non-custodial sentence" in this context suggests a youth community order (as defined in the Criminal Justice Act 2003, s.147(2)) or a fine. In most instances, an offence will have crossed the threshold for a community order. However, in accordance with normal sentencing practice, a court is not precluded from imposing a financial penalty where that is determined to be the appropriate sentence.

Additional aggravating factors	Additional mitigating factors
1. Background of intimidation or coercion	1. Small disparity in age between victim and offender
2. Use of drugs, alcohol or other substance	2. Relationship of genuine affection
3. Threats deterring the victim from reporting the incident	3. Youth and immaturity of offender
4. Offender aware that he or she is suffering from a sexually transmitted infection	

A person convicted[5] under s.25 or s.26 who was under 18 at the time of the offence is automatically subject to notification requirements in accordance with the SOA 2003, s.80 and Sch.3, if they are sentenced to at least 12 months' imprisonment.

[5] Or found not guilty by reason of insanity, found to be under a disability and to have done the act charged, or cautioned.

Mental Element

6.33A In the light of the decision in *Heard*,[6] discussed in para.2.72 above, the offence in s.25 appears to be one of basic intent, such that voluntary intoxication through drink or drugs will provide no defence. It will suffice if the defendant's acts were deliberate. Recklessness is insufficient.

Marriage Exception

6.34 The Civil Partnership Act 2004 has extended the exception to civil partners.[6A] Section 28 of the 2003 Act as amended now provides:

> "**Sections 25 and 26: exception for spouses and civil partners**
> **28.**—(1) Conduct by a person (A) which would otherwise be an offence under section 25 or 26 against another person (B) is not an offence under that section if at the time—
> (a) B is 16 or over, and
> (b) A and B are lawfully married or civil partners of each other.
> (2) In proceedings for such an offence it is for the defendant to prove that A and B were at the time lawfully married or civil partners of each other."

INCITING A CHILD FAMILY MEMBER TO ENGAGE IN SEXUAL ACTIVITY

Mode of Trial and Punishment

6.41 As from a day to be appointed the maximum sentence on summary conviction is 12 months' imprisonment: Criminal Justice Act 2003, s.282(2), (3). The increase has no application to offences committed before the substitution takes effect: s.282(4). The offence under s.26 is a specified sexual offence in respect of which a sentence of imprisonment for public protection may be imposed under the Criminal Justice Act 2003.[7]

Sentencing

6.42 For the definitive guideline published by the Sentencing Guidelines Council in relation to sentencing for offences under the 2003 Act, see para.1.18 above. The provisions of the guideline applicable to offences under s.26 are set out at para.6.14, above.

---

[6] [2007] EWCA Crim 125.
[6A] s.261(1) and Sch.27, para.174.
[7] s.224 and Sch.15, Pt 2.

MENTAL ELEMENT

In the light of the decision in *Heard*,[8] discussed in para.2.72 above, the offence in **6.46** s.26 appears to be one of basic intent, such that voluntary intoxication through drink or drugs will provide no defence. It will suffice if the defendant's acts were deliberate. Recklessness is insufficient.

SEX WITH AN ADULT RELATIVE: PENETRATION

MODE OF TRIAL AND PUNISHMENT

As from a day to be appointed the maximum sentence on summary conviction is **6.51** 12 months' imprisonment: Criminal Justice Act 2003, s.282(2), (3). The increase has no application to offences committed before the substitution takes effect: s.282(4). The offence under s.64 is a specified sexual offence in respect of which a sentence of imprisonment for public protection may be imposed under the Criminal Justice Act 2003.[9]

SENTENCING

For the definitive guideline published by the Sentencing Guidelines Council on **6.53** sentencing under the 2003 Act, see para.1.18 above. The guideline states that the factors to be taken into consideration in relation to offences under ss.64 and 65 (of sex with an adult relative) are as follows[10]:

"1. The sentences for public protection must be considered in all cases. They are designed to ensure that sexual offenders are not released into the community if they present a significant risk of serious harm.
2. The two offences within this category are triable either way and carry a maximum penalty of 2 years' imprisonment on conviction on indictment. The relatively low maximum penalty for these offences reflects the fact that they involve sexual relationships between consenting adults.
3. For these offences, unlike those against child family members, the relationship between offender and victim is narrowly defined in terms of close blood relationships only: 'a parent, grandparent, child, grandchild, brother, sister, half-brother, half-sister, uncle, aunt, nephew or niece'.
4. It is a defence to both offences that the offender was unaware of the blood relationship, unless it is proved that he or she could reasonably have been expected to be aware of it.

---

[8] [2007] EWCA Crim 125.
[9] s.224 and Sch.15, Pt 2.
[10] Pt 3A.

5. These offences could be charged in a wide range of circumstances and the most important issue for the sentencer to consider is the particular circumstances in which an offence has taken place and the harm that has been caused or risked:
   - Where an offence involves no harm to a victim (other than the offensiveness of the conduct to society at large), the starting point for sentencing should normally be a community order.
   - Where there is evidence of the exploitation of a victim or significant aggravation, the normal starting point should be a custodial sentence.
   - The presence of certain aggravating factors should merit a higher custodial starting point.
6. Examples of aggravating factors especially relevant to these offences include:
   - high level of coercion or humiliation of the victim;
   - imbalance of power;
   - evidence of grooming;
   - age gap between the parties;
   - history of sexual offending;
   - sexual intercourse with the express intention of conceiving a child or resulting in the conception of a child; and
   no attempt taken to prevent the transmission of a sexual infection."

The starting points, sentencing ranges and aggravating and mitigating factors for the offences under ss.64 and 65 are as follows:

Type/nature of activity	Starting points	Sentencing ranges
Where there is evidence of long-term grooming that took place at a time when the person being groomed was under 18	**12 months custody if offender is 18 or over**	**26 weeks–2 years custody**
Where there is evidence of grooming of one party by the other at a time when both parties were over the age of 18	**Community order**	**An appropriate non-custodial sentence***
Sexual penetration with no aggravating factors	**Community order**	**An appropriate non-custodial sentence***

* "Non-custodial sentence" in this context suggests a community order or a fine. In most instances, an offence will have crossed the threshold for a community order. However, in accordance with normal sentencing practice, a court is not precluded from imposing a financial penalty where that is determined to be the appropriate sentence.

Additional aggravating factors	Additional mitigating factors
1. Background of intimidation or coercion	1. Small disparity in age between victim and offender
2. Use of drugs, alcohol or other substance to facilitate the offence	2. Relationship of genuine affection
3. Threats to prevent the victim reporting an offence	
4. Evidence of long-term grooming	
5. Offender aware that he or she is suffering from a sexually transmitted infection	
6. Where there is evidence that no effort was made to avoid pregnancy or the sexual transmission of infection	

A person convicted[11] under s.64 or s.65 is automatically subject to notification requirements in accordance with the SOA 2003, s.80 and Sch.3, if (a) where they were under 18 at the time of the offence, they are sentenced to a term of at least 12 months' imprisonment, or (b) in any other case, they are, in respect of the offence, sentenced to a term of imprisonment or detained in a hospital.

MENTAL ELEMENT

In the light of the decision in *Heard*,[12] discussed in para.2.72 above, the offence in   **6.64** s.64 appears to be one of basic intent, such that voluntary intoxication through drink or drugs will provide no defence. It will suffice if the defendant's acts were deliberate. Recklessness is insufficient.

SEX WITH AN ADULT RELATIVE: CONSENTING TO PENETRATION

MODE OF TRIAL AND PUNISHMENT

As from a day to be appointed the maximum sentence on summary conviction is   **6.69** 12 months' imprisonment: Criminal Justice Act 2003, s.282(2), (3). The increase

---

[11] Or found not guilty by reason of insanity, found to be under a disability and to have done the act charged, or cautioned.
[12] [2007] EWCA Crim 125.

has no application to offences committed before the substitution takes effect: s.282(4). The offence under s.65 is a specified sexual offence in respect of which a sentence of imprisonment for public protection may be imposed under the Criminal Justice Act 2003.[13]

SENTENCING

6.71 For the definitive guideline published by the Sentencing Guidelines Council in relation to sentencing for offences under the 2003 Act, see para.1.18 above. The provisions of the guideline applicable to offences under s.65 are set out at para.6.53 above.

MENTAL ELEMENT

6.74 In the light of the decision in *Heard*,[14] discussed in para.2.72 above, the offence in s.65 appears to be one of basic intent, such that voluntary intoxication through drink or drugs will provide no defence. It will suffice if the defendant's acts were deliberate. Recklessness is insufficient.

---

[13] s.224 and Sch.15, Pt 2.
[14] [2007] EWCA Crim 125.

CHAPTER 7

SEXUAL OFFENCES AGAINST THOSE WITH A MENTAL DISORDER

INTRODUCTION

Competence of witnesses suffering from mental disorder

Section 116 of the Criminal Justice Act 2003, which came into force on April 4, **7.19**
2005, may be used in the interests of justice to admit the statement or video-
recorded interview of a witness who, by the time of trial, is unable to testify
through fear or physical or mental illness.[A]

[A] *DPP v R* [2007] EWHC 1842 (Admin) s.116(2)(b) is not concerned only with the ability of the
prospective witness to get to court.

105

There may also be circumstances in which a witness's previous statement is admissible under s.120 of the Criminal Justice Act 2003. A mandatory requirement of s.120 is that, during the course of the witness's evidence, he indicates that to the best of his belief he made the statement, and that to the best of his belief it states the truth.[1] In those circumstances, provided that any of the following conditions is met, the statement is admissible.[2] The first condition is that the statement identifies or describes a person, object or place. The second is that the statement was made by the witness when the matters stated were fresh in his memory, but he does not remember them, and cannot reasonably be expected to remember them, well enough to give oral evidence of them in the proceedings. The third condition is that:

(a) the witness claims to be a person against whom an offence has been committed,

(b) the offence is one to which the proceedings relate,

(c) the statement consists of a complaint made by the witness (whether to a person in authority or not) about conduct which would, if proved, constitute the offence or part of the offence,

(d) the complaint was made as soon as could reasonably be expected after the alleged conduct,

(e) the complaint was not made as a result of a threat or a promise, and

(f) before the statement is adduced the witness gives oral evidence in connection with its subject matter.

While s.116 would have to be relied upon in cases such as *Sed (Ali Dahir)*,[3] where the complaint was suffering from the advanced stages of Alzheimer's disease, s.120 may be of use when a witness's recollection is severely limited but nonetheless they are able to recall making what they believe to be a true statement.

OFFENCES AGAINST A PERSON WITH MENTAL DISORDER IMPEDING CHOICE

SEXUAL ACTIVITY WITH A PERSON WITH A MENTAL DISORDER IMPEDING CHOICE

Mode of Trial and Punishment

7.23   As from a day to be appointed the maximum sentence on summary conviction is 12 months' imprisonment: Criminal Justice Act 2003, s.282(2), (3). The increase has no application to offences committed before the substitution takes effect: s.282(4). The offence under s.30 is a specified sexual offence in respect of which a sentence of imprisonment for public protection may be imposed under the Criminal Justice Act 2003.[4]

---

[1] s.120(4)(b).
[2] s.120(4)(a), (5)–(7).
[3] [2004] EWCA Crim 1294; [2005] 1 Cr. App. R. 4, cited in the main work, para.7.19, n.40.
[4] s.224 and Sch.15, Pt 2.

SENTENCING

For the definitive guideline published by the Sentencing Guidelines Council on **7.25** sentencing under the 2003 Act, see para.1.18. The guideline states that the factors to be taken into consideration in relation to the offences under ss.30, 34 and 35 of the Act are as follows[5]:

> "1. The sentences for public protection *must* be considered in all cases. They are designed to ensure that sexual offenders are not released into the community if they present a significant risk of serious harm. Within any indeterminate sentence, the minimum term will generally be half the appropriate determinate sentence. The starting points will be relevant, therefore, to the process of fixing any minimum term that may be necessary.
> 2. The starting points for sentencing for a sexual offence should be the same whether the victim has a mental disorder impeding choice, or has a mental disorder that makes him or her vulnerable to inducement, threat or deception.
> 3. The same starting points apply whether the activity was caused or incited. Where an offence was incited but did not take place as a result of the voluntary intervention of the offender, that is likely to reduce the severity of the sentence imposed."

The starting points, sentencing ranges and aggravating and mitigating factors for the offences under ss.30, 34 and 35 are as follows:

Type/nature of activity	Starting points	Sentencing ranges
Penetration with any of the aggravating factors: abduction or detention; offender aware that he or she is suffering from a sexually transmitted infection; more than one offender acting together; offence motivated by prejudice (race, religion, sexual orientation, physical disability); sustained or repeated activity	**13 years custody**	**11–17 years custody**
Single offence of penetration of/by single offender with no aggravating or mitigating factors	**10 years custody**	**8–13 years custody**

[5] Pt 3B.

Type/nature of activity	Starting points	Sentencing ranges
Contact between naked genitalia of offender and naked genitalia of victim	5 years custody	4–8 years custody
Contact between naked genitalia of offender and another part of victim's body *or* naked genitalia of victim by offender using part of his or her body other than the genitalia Contact between clothed genitalia of offender and naked genitalia of victim *or* naked genitalia of offender and clothed genitalia of victim	15 months custody	36 weeks–3 years custody
Contact between part of offender's body (other than the genitalia) with parts of victim's body (other than the genitalia)	26 weeks custody	4 weeks–18 months custody

Additional aggravating factors	Additional mitigating factors
1. Background of intimidation or coercion 2. Offender ejaculated or caused the victim to ejaculate 3. Use of drugs, alcohol or other substance to facilitate the offence 4. Threats to prevent the victim reporting the incident 5. Abduction or detention 6. Offender is aware that he or she is suffering from a sexually transmitted infection	1. Relationship of genuine affection 2. Offender had a mental disorder at the time of the offence that significantly affected his or her culpability

A person convicted[6] under s.30 is automatically subject to notification requirements in accordance with the SOA 2003, s.80 and Sch.3.

"Unable to Refuse"

In *Hulme v DPP*,[7] the appellant, aged 73, was convicted under s.30(1) for touching **7.32**
the private parts of the complainant, aged 27. She suffered from cerebral palsy and
had a mental age well below her chronological age. On appeal, the appellant
submitted that there was no evidence on which the justices could have concluded
that the complainant was "unable to refuse" within the meaning of s.30(2) of the
2003 Act. She was capable of both choosing and communicating her choice and,
on the evidence, she did indeed make a choice: she chose not to consent to the
appellant's activity, she communicated her choice and he overrode it. Effectively,
the submission was that the appellant had been charged with an inappropriate
offence and should have been charged instead with sexual assault under s.3 of the
2003 Act.

The Divisional Court, having analysed the justices' findings, held that they had
been entitled to conclude that the complainant was unable to refuse because of or
for a reason related to a mental disorder. The Court interpreted the justices as
essentially saying that, although the complainant did not want the appellant to act
in the way that he did, she was unable effectively to communicate her choice to the
appellant. There was evidence capable of supporting this finding, in that the
complainant had said that, when the appellant touched her private parts and
pressed hard, she did not know what to do or say, although it made her feel sad,
hurt and upset. If the justices accepted that she did not want him to continue but
did not know what to say or do, that could only sensibly be because of her mental
condition.

"Because of or for a Reason Related to a Mental Disorder"

Section 1 of the Mental Health Act 2007, which is not yet in force, simplifies and **7.33**
extends the definition of "mental disorder" by substituting the following
definition in s.1(2) of the 1983 Act:

> "'mental disorder' means any disorder or disability of the mind; and 'mentally
> disordered' shall be construed accordingly;"

The 2007 Act also removes from s.1(2) the concepts of mental illness, mental
impairment, severe mental impairment and psychopathic disorder. The effect is to
widen the application of the provisions in question to all mental disorders, not just
those which fall within one of the abolished categories. Practical examples of
disorders which will be covered by the new definition of "mental disorder" are
forms of personality disorder which would not be considered legally to be "mental

---

[6] Or found not guilty by reason of insanity, found to be under a disability and to have done the act
charged, or cautioned.
[7] [2006] EWHC 1347 (Admin).

illness" and which do not fall within the current definition of psychopathic disorder because they do not result in abnormally aggressive or seriously irresponsible conduct on the part of the person concerned. Other examples almost certainly include certain types of psychological dysfunction arising from brain injury or damage in adulthood. Examples of clinically recognised mental disorders include mental illnesses such as schizophrenia, bipolar disorder, anxiety or depression, as well as personality disorders, eating disorders, autistic spectrum disorders and learning disabilities. Under the new definition, disorders or disabilities of the brain are not mental disorders unless (and only to the extent that) they give rise to a disability or disorder of the mind as well.

Section 2 of the 2007 Act provides that for the purpose of certain provisions of the 1983 Act, a person may not be considered to be suffering from a mental disorder simply as a result of having a learning disability, unless that disability is associated with abnormally aggressive or seriously irresponsible conduct on the part of the person concerned. The provisions in question include the criteria for detention and for the use of guardianship and guardianship orders. It seems to follow from s.2 that in other contexts, including Pt 1 of the Sexual Offences Act 2003, a person with a learning disability *may* be considered to be suffering from a "mental disorder". There is certainly nothing in the 2007 Act to preclude this result.

MENTAL ELEMENT

7.43   In the light of the decision in *Heard*,[8] discussed in para.2.72 above, the offence in s.30 appears to be one of basic intent, such that voluntary intoxication through drink or drugs will provide no defence. It will suffice if the defendant's acts were deliberate. Recklessness is insufficient.

CAUSING OR INCITING A PERSON, WITH A MENTAL DISORDER IMPEDING CHOICE, TO ENGAGE IN SEXUAL ACTIVITY

MODE OF TRIAL AND PUNISHMENT

7.48   As from a day to be appointed the maximum sentence on summary conviction is 12 months' imprisonment: Criminal Justice Act 2003, s.282(2), (3). The increase has no application to offences committed before the substitution takes effect: s.282(4). The offence under s.31 is a specified sexual offence in respect of which a sentence of imprisonment for public protection may be imposed under the Criminal Justice Act 2003.[9]

---

[8] [2007] EWCA Crim 125.
[9] s.224 and Sch.15, Pt 2.

For the definitive guideline published by the Sentencing Guidelines Council on sentencing under the 2003 Act, see para.1.18. The provisions of the guideline relating to the offence under s.31 of the Act are set out at para.2.77 above.

A person convicted[10] under s.31 is automatically subject to notification requirements in accordance with the SOA 2003, s.80 and Sch.3.

MENTAL ELEMENT

In the light of the decision in *Heard*,[11] discussed in para.2.72 above, the offence in   7.55
s.31 appears to be one of basic intent, such that voluntary intoxication through drink or drugs will provide no defence. It will suffice if the defendant's acts were deliberate. Recklessness is insufficient.

ENGAGING IN SEXUAL ACTIVITY IN THE PRESENCE OF A PERSON WITH A MENTAL DISORDER IMPEDING CHOICE

MODE OF TRIAL AND PUNISHMENT

As from a day to be appointed the maximum sentence on summary conviction is   7.58
12 months' imprisonment: Criminal Justice Act 2003, s.282(2), (3). The increase has no application to offences committed before the substitution takes effect: s.282(4). The offence under s.32 is a specified sexual offence in respect of which a sentence of imprisonment for public protection may be imposed under the Criminal Justice Act 2003.[12]

For the definitive guideline published by the Sentencing Guidelines Council on sentencing under the 2003 Act, see para.1.18. The provisions of the guideline relating to the offence under s.32 of the Act are set out at para.4.54 above.

A person convicted[13] under s.32 is automatically subject to notification requirements in accordance with the SOA 2003, s.80 and Sch.3.

MENTAL ELEMENT

In the light of the decision in *Heard*,[14] discussed in para.2.72 above, the   7.65
requirement that the defendant did the prohibited act for the purpose of obtaining sexual gratification makes the s.32 offence one of specific intent, such that voluntary intoxication through drink or drugs will provide a defence if it may have prevented the defendant forming that purpose.

[10] Or found not guilty by reason of insanity, found to be under a disability and to have done the act charged, or cautioned.
[11] [2007] EWCA Crim 125.
[12] s.224 and Sch.15, Pt 2.
[13] Or found not guilty by reason of insanity, found to be under a disability and to have done the act charged, or cautioned.
[14] [2007] EWCA Crim 125.

CAUSING A PERSON, WITH A MENTAL DISORDER IMPEDING CHOICE, TO WATCH A SEXUAL ACT

Mode of Trial and Punishment

7.68 As from a day to be appointed the maximum sentence on summary conviction is 12 months' imprisonment: Criminal Justice Act 2003, s.282(2), (3). The increase has no application to offences committed before the substitution takes effect: s.282(4). The offence under s.33 is a specified sexual offence in respect of which a sentence of imprisonment for public protection may be imposed under the Criminal Justice Act 2003.[15]

For the definitive guideline published by the Sentencing Guidelines Council on sentencing under the 2003 Act, see para.1.18. The provisions of the guideline relating to the offence under s.33 of the Act are set out at para.4.69 above.

A person convicted[16] under s.33 is automatically subject to notification requirements in accordance with the SOA 2003, s.80 and Sch.3.

Mental Element

7.75 In the light of the decision in *Heard*,[17] discussed in para.2.72 above, the requirement that the defendant did the prohibited act for the purpose of obtaining sexual gratification makes the s.33 offence one of specific intent, such that voluntary intoxication through drink or drugs will provide a defence if it may have prevented the defendant forming that purpose.

INDUCEMENTS ETC. TO PERSONS WITH A MENTAL DISORDER

INDUCEMENT, THREAT OR DECEPTION TO PROCURE SEXUAL ACTIVITY WITH A PERSON WITH A MENTAL DISORDER

Mode of Trial and Punishment

7.79 As from a day to be appointed the maximum sentence on summary conviction is 12 months' imprisonment: Criminal Justice Act 2003, s.282(2), (3). The increase has no application to offences committed before the substitution takes effect: s.282(4). The offence under s.34 is a specified sexual offence in respect of which

---

[15] s.224 and Sch.15, Pt 2.
[16] Or found not guilty by reason of insanity, found to be under a disability and to have done the act charged, or cautioned.
[17] [2007] EWCA Crim 125.

a sentence of imprisonment for public protection may be imposed under the Criminal Justice Act 2003.[18]

For the definitive guideline published by the Sentencing Guidelines Council on sentencing under the 2003 Act, see para.1.18. The provisions of the guideline relating to the offence under s.34 of the Act are set out at para.7.25 above.

A person convicted[19] under s.34 is automatically subject to notification requirements in accordance with the SOA 2003, s.80 and Sch.3.

MENTAL ELEMENT

In the light of the decision in *Heard*,[20] discussed in para.2.72 above, the offence in   7.85 s.34 appears to be one of basic intent, such that voluntary intoxication through drink or drugs will provide no defence. It will suffice if the defendant's acts were deliberate. Recklessness is insufficient.

CAUSING A PERSON WITH A MENTAL DISORDER TO ENGAGE IN OR AGREE TO ENGAGE IN SEXUAL ACTIVITY BY INDUCEMENT, THREAT OR DECEPTION

MODE OF TRIAL AND PUNISHMENT

As from a day to be appointed the maximum sentence on summary conviction is   7.88 12 months' imprisonment: Criminal Justice Act 2003, s.282(2), (3). The increase has no application to offences committed before the substitution takes effect: s.282(4). The offence under s.35 is a specified sexual offence in respect of which a sentence of imprisonment for public protection may be imposed under the Criminal Justice Act 2003.[21]

For the definitive guideline published by the Sentencing Guidelines Council on sentencing under the 2003 Act, see para.1.18. The provisions of the guideline relating to the offence under s.35 of the Act are set out at para.7.25 above.

A person convicted[22] under s.35 is automatically subject to notification requirements in accordance with the SOA 2003, s.80 and Sch.3.

---

[18] s.224 and Sch.15, Pt 2.

[19] Or found not guilty by reason of insanity, found to be under a disability and to have done the act charged, or cautioned.

[20] [2007] EWCA Crim 125.

[21] s.224 and Sch.15, Pt 2.

[22] Or found not guilty by reason of insanity, found to be under a disability and to have done the act charged, or cautioned.

Mental Element

7.94   In the light of the decision in *Heard*,[23] discussed in para.2.72 above, the offence in s.35 appears to be one of basic intent, such that voluntary intoxication through drink or drugs will provide no defence. It will suffice if the defendant's acts were deliberate. Recklessness is insufficient.

ENGAGING IN SEXUAL ACTIVITY IN THE PRESENCE, PROCURED BY INDUCEMENT, THREAT OR DECEPTION, OF A PERSON WITH A MENTAL DISORDER

Mode of Trial and Punishment

7.96   As from a day to be appointed the maximum sentence on summary conviction is 12 months' imprisonment: Criminal Justice Act 2003, s.282(2), (3). The increase has no application to offences committed before the substitution takes effect: s.282(4). The offence under s.36 is a specified sexual offence in respect of which a sentence of imprisonment for public protection may be imposed under the Criminal Justice Act 2003.[24]

For the definitive guideline published by the Sentencing Guidelines Council on sentencing under the 2003 Act, see para.1.18. The guideline states that the factors to be taken into consideration in relation to the offences under ss.36 and 40 (care workers) of the Act are as follows[25]:

> "1. The sentences for public protection *must* be considered in all cases. They are designed to ensure that sexual offenders are not released into the community if they present a significant risk of serious harm.
> 2. The starting points for sentencing for a sexual offence should be the same whether the victim has a mental disorder impeding choice, or has a mental disorder that makes him or her vulnerable to inducement, threat or deception.
> 3. The guidelines are predicated on the principle that the more serious the nature of the sexual activity a victim is forced to witness, the higher the sentencing starting point should be.
> 4. These offences will potentially be serious enough to merit a custodial sentence. In an individual case, the court will need to consider whether there are particular mitigating factors that should move the sentence below the custodial threshold."

The starting points, sentencing ranges and aggravating and mitigating factors for the offences under ss.36 and 40 are as follows:

[23] [2007] EWCA Crim 125.
[24] s.224 and Sch.15, Pt 2.
[25] Pt 3B.

Type/nature of activity	Starting points	Sentencing ranges
Consensual intercourse or other forms of consensual penetration	2 years custody	1–4 years custody
Masturbation (of oneself or another person)	18 months custody	12 months–2 years 6 months custody
Consensual sexual touching involving naked genitalia	12 months custody	26 weeks–2 years custody
Consensual sexual touching of naked body parts but not involving naked genitalia	26 weeks custody	4 weeks–18 months custody

Additional aggravating factors	Additional mitigating factors
1. Background of intimidation or coercion	
2. Use of drugs, alcohol or other substance to facilitate the offence	
3. Threats to prevent victim reporting the incident	
4. Abduction or detention	

A person convicted[26] under s.36 is automatically subject to notification requirements in accordance with the SOA 2003, s.80 and Sch.3.

MENTAL ELEMENT

In the light of the decision in *Heard*,[27] discussed in para.2.72 above, the **7.101** requirement that the defendant did the prohibited act for the purpose of obtaining sexual gratification makes the s.36 offence one of specific intent, such that

---

[26] Or found not guilty by reason of insanity, found to be under a disability and to have done the act charged, or cautioned.

[27] [2007] EWCA Crim 125.

voluntary intoxication through drink or drugs will provide a defence if it may have prevented the defendant forming that purpose.

CAUSING A PERSON WITH A MENTAL DISORDER TO WATCH A SEXUAL ACT BY INDUCEMENT, THREAT OR DECEPTION

Mᴏᴅᴇ ᴏꜰ Tʀɪᴀʟ ᴀɴᴅ Pᴜɴɪꜱʜᴍᴇɴᴛ

7.104 As from a day to be appointed the maximum sentence on summary conviction is 12 months' imprisonment: Criminal Justice Act 2003, s.282(2), (3). The increase has no application to offences committed before the substitution takes effect: s.282(4). The offence under s.37 is a specified sexual offence in respect of which a sentence of imprisonment for public protection may be imposed under the CJA 2003.[28]

For the definitive guideline published by the Sentencing Guidelines Council on sentencing under the 2003 Act, see para.1.18. The guideline states that the factors to be taken into consideration in relation to the offences under ss.37 and 41 (care workers) of the Act are as follows[29]:

"1. The sentences for public protection *must* be considered in all cases. They are designed to ensure that sexual offenders are not released into the community if they present a significant risk of serious harm.
2. The starting points for sentencing for a sexual offence should be the same whether the victim has a mental disorder impeding choice, or has a mental disorder that makes him or her vulnerable to inducement, threat or deception.
3. The guidelines are predicated on the principle that the more serious the nature of the sexual activity a victim is forced to witness, the higher the sentencing starting point should be.
4. These offences will potentially be serious enough to merit a custodial sentence. In an individual case, the court will need to consider whether there are particular mitigating factors that move the sentence below the custodial threshold.
5. The same starting points apply whether the activity was caused or incited. Where an offence was incited but did not take place as a result of the voluntary intervention of the offender, that is likely to reduce the severity of the sentence imposed."

The starting points, sentencing ranges and aggravating and mitigating factors for the offences under ss.37 and 41 are as follows:

---

[28] s.224 and Sch.15, Pt 2.
[29] Pt 3B.

Type/nature of activity	Starting points	Sentencing ranges
Live sexual activity	18 months custody	12 months–2 years custody
Moving or still images of people engaged in sexual activity involving penetration	32 weeks custody	26 weeks–12 months custody
Moving or still images of people engaging in sexual activity other than penetration	Community order	Community order-26 weeks custody

Additional aggravating factors	Additional mitigating factors
1. Background of intimidation or coercion	
2. Use of drugs, alcohol or other substance to facilitate the offence	
3. Threats to prevent victim reporting the incident	
4. Abduction or detention	
5. Images of violent activity	

A person convicted[30] under s.37 is automatically subject to notification requirements in accordance with the SOA 2003, s.80 and Sch.3.

Mental Element

In the light of the decision in *Heard*,[31] discussed in para.2.72 above, the 7.111 requirement that the defendant did the prohibited act for the purpose of obtaining sexual gratification makes the s.37 offence one of specific intent, such that voluntary intoxication through drink or drugs will provide a defence if it may have prevented the defendant forming that purpose.

---

[30] Or found not guilty by reason of insanity, found to be under a disability and to have done the act charged, or cautioned.
[31] [2007] EWCA Crim 125.

OFFENCES RELATING TO CARE WORKERS

CARE WORKERS: SEXUAL ACTIVITY WITH A PERSON WITH A MENTAL DISORDER

Mode of Trial and Punishment

7.117   As from a day to be appointed the maximum sentence on summary conviction is 12 months' imprisonment: Criminal Justice Act 2003, s.282(2), (3). The increase has no application to offences committed before the substitution takes effect: s.282(4). The offence under s.38 is a specified sexual offence in respect of which a sentence of imprisonment for public protection may be imposed under the Criminal Justice Act 2003.[32]

Sentencing

7.118   For the definitive guideline published by the Sentencing Guidelines Council on sentencing under the 2003 Act, see para.1.18. The guideline states that the factors to be taken into consideration in relation to the offences under ss.38 and 39 of the Act are as follows[33]:

> "1. The sentences for public protection *must* be considered in all cases. They are designed to ensure that sexual offenders are not released into the community if they present a significant risk of serious harm.
> 2. The starting points for sentencing are predicated on the fact that these offences are designed to be charged where victims have the capacity to choose and where there is no clear evidence of inducement, threat or deception."

The starting points, sentencing ranges and aggravating and mitigating factors for the offences under ss.38 and 39 are as follows:

Type/nature of activity	Starting points	Sentencing ranges
Basic offence of sexual activity involving penetration, assuming no aggravating or mitigating factors	3 years custody	2–5 years custody

---

[32] s.224 and Sch.15, Pt 2.
[33] Pt 3B.

Type/nature of activity	Starting points	Sentencing ranges
Other forms of non-penetrative activity	12 months custody	26 weeks–2 years custody
Naked contact between part of the offender's body with part of the victim's body	Community order	An appropriate non-custodial sentence*

* "Non-custodial sentence" in this context suggests a community order or a fine. In most instances, an offence will have crossed the threshold for a community order. However, in accordance with normal sentencing practice, a court is not precluded from imposing a financial penalty where that is determined to be the appropriate sentence.

Additional aggravating factors	Additional mitigating factors
1. History of intimidation	
2. Use of drugs, alcohol or other substance to facilitate the offence	
3. Threats to prevent victim reporting the incident	
4. Abduction or detention	
5. Offender aware that he or she is suffering from a sexually transmitted infection	

A person convicted[34] under s.38 is automatically subject to notification requirements in accordance with the SOA 2003, s.80 and Sch.3, if (a) where the offender was under 18 at the time of the offence, they are sentenced to at least 12 months' imprisonment, or (b) in any other case, the offender is, in respect of the offence, sentenced to a term of imprisonment, detained in a hospital or given a community sentence of at least 12 months.

An instructive decision on sentencing under s.38, which pre-dates the definitive guideline but is consistent with it, is *Bradford*.[35] The complainant was a woman in her 30s who suffered from post-natal depression following the birth of her daughter in 2004. She was diagnosed as suffering from medium to severe depression, a mental disorder within the meaning of s.1 of the Mental Health Act 2003. The appellant was her social worker. The complainant became flattered by

7.118A

---

[34] Or found not guilty by reason of insanity, found to be under a disability and to have done the act charged, or cautioned.
[35] [2006] EWCA Crim 2629.

his attentions and began to be obsessed with him. Her vulnerability was demonstrated by the fact that she had panic attacks and would harm herself when she did not have contact with him. The appellant suggested to her that a particular residential care home would suit her. He visited her there and they had sexual intercourse in her room. On the third such occasion, the appellant said that he could not stay for long, which culminated in the complainant becoming distressed and disclosing to staff what had happened between them. When arrested, the appellant denied that anything improper had taken place. However, he later pleaded guilty to an offence under s.38. In sentencing, the judge said that the offence was extremely serious and had devastated the complainant. He found that the fact that the complainant had been "willing" was irrelevant, and sentenced the appellant to 17 months' imprisonment.

The Court of Appeal noted that s.38 had created a new offence, the aim of which was to protect people who, because of their mental disorder, were vulnerable to sexual advances from those who cared for them and who were in a position of trust in relation to them. The rationale of the offence was that, because the victim suffered from a mental disorder, they would not be able to make an informed choice about sexual activity. The issue of consent was not relevant to whether the offence had been committed.

Whilst the Court felt unable to give guidance as to the general level of sentence, as that was a matter for the Sentencing Guidelines Council, it did give some consideration to the recommendation in the Council's consultation document that an appropriate starting point on conviction for an offence under s.38 was three years' imprisonment. The appellant's sentence was within the suggested bracket. In all the circumstances, including the appellant's previous good character, guilty plea and personal mitigation, the sentence was perfectly proper. The appellant had taken advantage of an extremely vulnerable person and had led her into a sexual relationship, which had devastating effects upon her. Further, there had been an element of planning.

Parties to the Offence

7.119 *Corrigendum*: For offences outside the UK, see para.7.26 of the main work.

Mental Element

7.127 In the light of the decision in *Heard*,[36] discussed in para.2.72 above, the offence in s.38 appears to be one of basic intent, such that voluntary intoxication through drink or drugs will provide no defence. It will suffice if the defendant's acts were deliberate. Recklessness is insufficient.

[36] [2007] EWCA Crim 125.

MARRIAGE EXCEPTION

The Civil Partnership Act 2004[37] has extended the exception to civil partners.　7.130
Section 43 of the 2003 Act as amended now provides:

> "**Sections 25 and 26: exception for spouses and civil partners**
> **43.**—(1) Conduct by a person (A) which would otherwise be an offence under any of
> sections 38 to 41 against another person (B) is not an offence under that section if at
> the time—
> 　　(a) B is 16 or over, and
> 　　(b) A and B are lawfully married or civil partners of each other.
> (2) In proceedings for such an offence it is for the defendant to prove that A and B
> were at the time lawfully married or civil partners of each other."

CARE WORKERS: CAUSING OR INCITING SEXUAL ACTIVITY

MODE OF TRIAL AND PUNISHMENT

As from a day to be appointed the maximum sentence on summary conviction is　7.133
12 months' imprisonment: Criminal Justice Act 2003, s.282(2), (3). The increase
has no application to offences committed before the substitution takes effect:
s.282(4). The offence under s.39 is a specified sexual offence in respect of which
a sentence of imprisonment for public protection may be imposed under the
Criminal Justice Act 2003.[38]

For the definitive guideline published by the Sentencing Guidelines Council on
sentencing under the 2003 Act, see para.1.18. The provisions of the guideline
relating to the offence under s.39 of the Act are set out at para.7.118 above.

A person convicted[39] under s.39 is automatically subject to notification
requirements in accordance with the SOA 2003, s.80 and Sch.3, if (a) where the
offender was under 18 at the time of the offence, they are sentenced to at least 12
months' imprisonment, or (b) in any other case, the offender is, in respect of the
offence, sentenced to a term of imprisonment, detained in a hospital or given a
community sentence of at least 12 months.

MENTAL ELEMENT

In the light of the decision in *Heard*,[40] discussed in para.2.72 above, the offence in　7.138
s.39 appears to be one of basic intent, such that voluntary intoxication through
drink or drugs will provide no defence. It will suffice if the defendant's acts were
deliberate. Recklessness is insufficient.

---

[37] s.261(1) and Sch.27, para.175.
[38] s.224 and Sch.15, Pt 2.
[39] Or found not guilty by reason of insanity, found to be under a disability and to have done the act
charged, or cautioned.
[40] [2007] EWCA Crim 125.

CARE WORKERS: SEXUAL ACTIVITY IN THE PRESENCE OF A PERSON WITH A MENTAL DISORDER

Mode of Trial and Punishment

7.142   As from a day to be appointed the maximum sentence on summary conviction is 12 months' imprisonment: Criminal Justice Act 2003, s.282(2), (3). The increase has no application to offences committed before the substitution takes effect: s.282(4). The offence under s.40 is a specified sexual offence in respect of which a sentence of imprisonment for public protection may be imposed under the Criminal Justice Act 2003.[41]

For the definitive guideline published by the Sentencing Guidelines Council on sentencing under the 2003 Act, see para.1.18. The provisions of the guideline relating to the offence under s.40 of the Act are set out at para.7.96 above.

A person convicted[42] under s.40 is automatically subject to notification requirements in accordance with the SOA 2003, s.80 and Sch.3, if (a) where the offender was under 18 at the time of the offence, they are sentenced to at least 12 months' imprisonment, or (b) in any other case, the offender is, in respect of the offence, sentenced to a term of imprisonment, detained in a hospital or given a community sentence of at least 12 months.

Mental Element

7.148   In the light of the decision in *Heard*,[43] discussed in para.2.72 above, the requirement that the defendant did the prohibited act for the purpose of obtaining sexual gratification makes the s.40 offence one of specific intent, such that voluntary intoxication through drink or drugs will provide a defence if it may have prevented the defendant forming that purpose.

CARE WORKERS: CAUSING A PERSON WITH A MENTAL DISORDER TO WATCH A SEXUAL ACT

Mode of Trial and Punishment

7.152   As from a day to be appointed the maximum sentence on summary conviction is 12 months' imprisonment: Criminal Justice Act 2003, s.282(2), (3). The increase has no application to offences committed before the substitution takes effect: s.282(4). The offence under s.41 is a specified sexual offence in respect of which

---

[41] s.224 and Sch.15, Pt 2.

[42] Or found not guilty by reason of insanity, found to be under a disability and to have done the act charged, or cautioned.

[43] [2007] EWCA Crim 125.

a sentence of imprisonment for public protection may be imposed under the Criminal Justice Act 2003.[44]

For the definitive guideline published by the Sentencing Guidelines Council on sentencing under the 2003 Act, see para.1.18. The provisions of the guideline relating to the offence under s.41 of the Act are set out at para.7.104 above.

A person convicted[45] under s.41 is automatically subject to notification requirements in accordance with the SOA 2003, s.80 and Sch.3, if (a) where the offender was under 18 at the time of the offence, they are sentenced to at least 12 months' imprisonment, or (b) in any other case, the offender is, in respect of the offence, sentenced to a term of imprisonment, detained in a hospital or given a community sentence of at least 12 months.

Parties to the Offence

Corrigendum: For offences outside the UK, see para.7.26 of the main work.   7.153

Mental Element

In the light of the decision in *Heard*,[46] discussed in para.2.72 above, the   7.158 requirement that the defendant did the prohibited act for the purpose of obtaining sexual gratification makes the s.41 offence one of specific intent, such that voluntary intoxication through drink or drugs will provide a defence if it may have prevented the defendant forming that purpose.

---

[44] s.224 and Sch.15, Pt 2.
[45] Or found not guilty by reason of insanity, found to be under a disability and to have done the act charged, or cautioned.
[46] [2007] EWCA Crim 125.

INDECENT PHOTOGRAPHS OF CHILDREN

TAKING (ETC.) AN INDECENT PHOTOGRAPH OR PSEUDO-PHOTOGRAPH OF A CHILD

MODE OF TRIAL AND PUNISHMENT

As from a day to be appointed the maximum sentence on summary conviction is **8.04** 12 months' imprisonment: Criminal Justice Act 2003, s.282(2), (3). The increase has no application to offences committed before the substitution takes effect: s.282(4). An offence under s.1 is a specified sexual offence in respect of which a sentence of imprisonment for public protection may be imposed under the Criminal Justice Act 2003.[1]

Restriction on prosecution

It is not necessary for the DPP personally to consent to the institution of **8.05** proceedings, as any consent given by a Crown Prosecutor is to be treated as having been given by the DPP: Prosecution of Offences Act 1985, s.1(7).

In the light of *Ashton*[2], which was followed in *R. v D*,[3] it appears that absence of **8.05A** consent is no longer fatal to a prosecution, provided that allowing it to continue causes no injustice.

The appellant in *Ashton* pleaded guilty to one charge under s.1(1)(a) of the Protection of Children Act 1978 and one charge under s.160(1) of the Criminal

---

[1] s.224 and Sch.15, Pt 2.
[2] [2006] EWCA Crim 794.
[3] [2007] Crim. L.R. 240.

Justice Act 1988. He was committed to the Crown Court for sentence. At the sentencing hearing, the prosecution erroneously told the court that consent to prosecute had not been obtained and invited the judge to sit as a District Judge (Magistrates' Courts) under the power contained in s.66 of the Courts Act 2003. The aim appears to have been to put right the previous irregularity, on the basis that the necessary consent was by then available. The judge acceded to the invitation and went on to determine the mode of trial, whereupon the appellant pleaded guilty. The judge then committed him to the Crown Court for sentence and proceeded to sentence him. The Court of Appeal dismissed an appeal against conviction, holding that as the proceedings were originally instituted by or with the consent of the DPP, the initial committal for sentence was valid and legally effective. The Court went on to review *obiter* the legality of the steps taken by the judge and concluded that, although they were legally unnecessary, they contravened no statutory prohibition. But it stressed that in most cases where there has been a procedural failure of the sort that was thought to have occurred in *Ashton*, it will be unnecessary for the Circuit Judge, using s.66, to carry out a process of rectification by exercising the powers of a District Judge. Instead, the court should approach the matter in accordance with the principles derived from the decisions in *Soneji*[4] and *Sekhon and others*,[5] by first asking itself whether the intention of Parliament was that any act following the failure to obtain consent should be invalid. If the answer to that question is no, then the court should go on to consider the interests of justice generally, and most particularly whether there is a real possibility that either the prosecution or the defence may suffer prejudice on account of the failure. If there is such a risk, the court must decide whether it is just to allow the proceedings to continue. Although the Court of Appeal expressed no view on the first of these questions, i.e. whether Parliament intended the failure to obtain consent for a prosecution under the 1978 or 1988 Act to invalidate all that follows, it is tolerably clear, not least from its decision that rectification by way of s.66 was unnecessary, that it thought Parliament did *not* so intend. The key questions in practice will therefore be whether the failure creates a real possibility of prejudice, and if so, whether it is just for the proceedings to continue.

The approach set out by the Court of Appeal in *Ashton* was applied by H.H. Judge Brown sitting in Lewes Crown Court in *R. v D*.[6] The defendant was charged with 20 offences of possession contrary to s.160(1) of the 1988 Act in relation to images downloaded from the internet. Consent to prosecute was not obtained. The defendant was committed for trial and at the PCMH, an indictment was preferred that charged him with 16 counts of "making" indecent images under s.1(1)(a) of the 1978 Act. The judge gave leave for the indictment to be signed out of time and the defendant gave notice of his intention to apply to quash it on the ground that proceedings had been instituted without the consent of the DPP. Prior to the hearing of the application, the purported consent of the DPP was given by a senior Crown Prosecutor. The defendant argued that this consent was given too late and

[4] [2005] UKHL 49.
[5] [2002] EWCA Crim 2954.
[6] [2007] Crim. L.R. 240.

could not retrospectively authorize the institution of the proceedings, relying on *Angel*[7] and *Pearce*.[8] He contended that these authorities had not been overruled by *Ashton* and were binding on the Crown Court. H.H. Judge Brown rejected the application, holding that *Angel* and *Pearce* were distinguishable since in those cases there had never been a consent to the charges on which the defendants had been convicted. He went on to apply *Ashton*, holding that the failure to give prior consent was properly to be described as a procedural failure and one which did not take away the court's jurisdiction. Accordingly, he was required to consider the interests of justice generally and, in particular, whether there was a real possibility of prejudice to either the prosecution or the defence. Although the maximum penalty for the "making" offences (10 years' imprisonment) was greater than for the "possession" offences, the "factual matrix" was the same for both, and the defendant was not taken by surprise by any change in the nature of the evidence against him. It was essential from the point of view of both the defendant and the public that the appropriate charges were brought and, if contested, decided on the evidence presented by both sides. The learned judge accordingly concluded that the interests of justice required that the Crown be allowed to proceed on the charges under the 1978 Act.

This reasoning is, with respect, convincing and the result unsurprising in the light of *Ashton* and the later case of *Clark*,[9] in which the absence of the required signature of "the proper officer of the court" from a voluntary bill of indictment was held not to invalidate the subsequent trial or convictions. Indeed, Professor Ormerod has commented that the learned judge in *R. v D.* "was perhaps more hesitant than he needed to be by seeking to distinguish the cases of *Angel* and *Pearce . . .* , where unlike the present case no consent from the DPP was ever obtained. If *Ashton* is as revolutionary as it seems to be, even apparently non-distinguishable binding authorities might be cast aside."[10] It should however be noted that, at the time of writing, the decision in *Clarke* is on its way to the House of Lords. There may therefore be a further twist in the story before the correct approach to procedural error is definitively settled.

SENTENCING

The guideline case of *Oliver, Hartrey and Baldwin*[11] has been superseded by the   **8.07** definitive guideline published by the Sentencing Guidelines Council in relation to sentencing for offences under the 2003 Act, which also covers the offences relating to indecent photographs of children under the Protection of Children Act 1978 and s.160 of the Criminal Justice Act 1988.[12] For the background to the guideline, see para.1.18 above.

---

[7] [1968] 1 W.L.R. 669, see main work at para.8.05.
[8] [1981] Crim. L.R. 639.
[9] [2006] Crim. L.R. 1011.
[10] [2007] Crim. L.R. 242.
[11] [2003] 1 Cr. App. R. 28.
[12] Pt 6A.

Oliver identified five different levels of offence of increasing seriousness for sentencing purposes, and also aggravating and mitigating factors. The aggravating and mitigating factors remain relevant and are included in the guideline. However, the Sentencing Guidelines Council reviewed *Oliver* in terms of the nature of the images falling into each level of offence, on the basis that:

- Images depicting non-penetrative activity are less serious than images depicting penetrative activity.
- Images of non-penetrative activity between children are generally less serious than images depicting non-penetrative activity between adults and children.[13]
- All acts falling within the definitions of rape and assault by penetration, which carry the maximum life penalty, should be classified as level 4.

The guideline retains five levels of offence, but with two key changes from the *Oliver* scheme.[14] First, images depicting penetrative sexual activity between children were, under *Oliver*, placed at level 2. They were accordingly treated as less serious than images depicting non-penetrative sexual activity between adults and children (level 3), which seemed counter-intuitive. Secondly, *Oliver* had been to some extent overtaken by the 2003 Act's treatment of oral penetration as equivalent in seriousness to vaginal or anal penetration (see e.g. the extension of rape to cover oral penetration of the complainant's mouth by the defendant's penis). This development indicated that images depicting oral penetration between adults and children should be moved from level 3 to level 4, i.e. from non-penetrative to penetrative sexual activity between adults and children. The definitive guideline addresses both these points. It states that the factors to take into consideration in sentencing for offences relating to indecent photographs of children under the 1978 and 1988 Acts are as follows:

"1. The levels of seriousness (in ascending order) for sentencing for offences involving pornographic images are:

Level 1   Images depicting erotic posing with no sexual activity
Level 2   Non-penetrative sexual activity between children, or solo masturbation by a child
Level 3   Non-penetrative sexual activity between adults and children
Level 4   Penetrative sexual activity involving a child or children, or both children and adults
Level 5   Sadism or penetration of, or by, an animal

2. Offences involving any form of sexual penetration of the vagina or anus, or penile penetration of the mouth (except where they involve sadism or intercourse with an animal, which fall within level 5), should be classified as activity at level 4.

3. Pseudo-photographs generally should be treated less seriously than real photographs.

---

[13] H.H. Judge Beatrice Bolton queried the correctness of this point in her lecture on sentencing powers at the JSB Serious Sexual Offences Seminar in July 2007, on the basis that choreographed videos and posed pictures may be equally if not more exploitative of the children concerned, who are often being forced to do unspeakable things to each other.

[14] The adjustments meet criticisms made of *Oliver*: see e.g. Alisdair A. Gillespie, *Sentencing crimes; updating Oliver* [2005] N.L.J. 1517.

4. Sentences should be lower than those involving photographs of children under 16 where:
   - an offender possesses only a few indecent photographs, none of which includes sadism or penetration of, or by, an animal; and
   - the images are of children aged 16 or 17; and
   - the photographs are retained solely for the use of the offender.
5. The fact that the subject of the indecent photograph(s) is aged 16 or 17 has *no* impact on sentencing starting points where the activity depicted is at level 5.
6. Starting points for sentencing for possession of indecent photographs should be higher where the subject of the indecent photograph(s) is a child under 13.
7. Registration requirements attach to a conviction for this offence dependent upon the age of the subject portrayed in the indecent photograph(s) and the sentence imposed.
8. Courts should consider making an order disqualifying an offender (adult or juvenile) from working with children regardless of the sentence imposed.
9. Courts should consider making an order for the forfeiture of any possessions (for example, computers or cameras) used in connection with the commission of the offence."

The guideline notes that the court cannot make inferences about the status of unknown material, because of the fundamental principle that a person may only be convicted and sentenced according to the facts that have been proved. However, if an offender has used devices to destroy or hide material then it falls within the general aggravating factor "An attempt to conceal or dispose of evidence".[15]

Although it may be distressing, judges should view a good sample of the material before them, so that they can form their own impression of its seriousness and of the offender's proclivities.[16]

The starting points, sentencing ranges and aggravating and mitigating factors for the indecent photograph offences set out in the guideline are as follows:

Type/nature of activity	Starting points	Sentencing ranges
Offender commissioned or encouraged the production of level 4 or 5 images Offender involved in the production of level 4 or 5 images	6 years custody	4–9 years custody
Level 4 or 5 images shown or distributed	3 years custody	2–5 years custody

[15] Pt 6A.10.
[16] This was the "strong advice" given by H.H. Judge Bolton in her lecture on sentencing powers to the JSB Serious Sexual Offences Seminar in July 2007.

Type/nature of activity	Starting points	Sentencing ranges
Offender involved in the production of, or has traded in, material at levels 1–3	2 years custody	1–4 years custody
Possession of a large quantity of level 4 or 5 material for personal use only Large number of level 3 images shown or distributed	12 months custody	26 weeks–2 years custody
Possession of a large quantity of level 3 material for personal use Possession of a small number of images at level 4 or 5 Large number of level 2 images shown or distributed Small number of level 3 images shown or distributed	26 weeks custody	4 weeks–18 months custody
Offender in possession of a large amount of material at level 2 or a small amount at level 3 Offender has shown or distributed material at level 1 or 2 on a limited scale Offender has exchanged images at level 1 or 2 with other collectors, but with no element of financial gain	12 weeks custody	4 weeks–26 weeks custody

Type/nature of activity	Starting points	Sentencing ranges
Possession of a large amount of level 1 material and/or no more than a small amount of level 2, and the material is for personal use and has not been distributed or shown to others	Community order	An appropriate non-custodial sentence*

* "Non-custodial sentence" in this context suggests a community order or a fine. In most instances, an offence will have crossed the threshold for a community order. However, in accordance with normal sentencing practice, a court is not precluded from imposing a financial penalty where that is determined to be the appropriate sentence.

Additional aggravating factors	Additional mitigating factors
1. Images shown or distributed to others, especially children	1. A few images held solely for personal use
2. Collection is systematically stored or organised, indicating a sophisticated approach to trading or a high level of personal interest	2. Images viewed but not stored
3. Images stored, made available or distributed in such a way that they can be inadvertently accessed by others[17]	3. A few images held solely for personal use and it is established both that the subject is aged 16 or 17 and that he or she was consenting.
4. Use of drugs, alcohol or other substance to facilitate the offence of making or taking	
5. Background of intimidation or coercion	
6. Threats to prevent victim reporting the activity	
7. Threats to disclose victim's activity to friends or relatives	
8. Financial or other gain	

[17] H.H. Judge Beatrice Bolton has suggested that, where photographs are held on a computer which has a file-sharing facility, the existence of that facility should be treated as an aggravating factor in that it enables the offender to "swap or trade" in photographs, even if there is no evidence that he has in fact done so: lecture on sentencing powers at the JSB Serious Sexual Offences Seminar in July 2007.

A person convicted[18] of an offence under s.1 of the 1978 Act is automatically subject to notification requirements in accordance with the SOA 2003, s.80 and Sch.3, if the images showed persons under 16 and the offender was 18 or over at the time of the offence or is sentenced to at least 12 months' imprisonment.

While the "making" offence under s.1(1)(a) of the 1978 Act carries a maximum sentence of 10 years' imprisonment and "possession" under s.160 of the 1988 Act a maximum sentence of five years' imprisonment, neither *Oliver* nor the definitive guideline makes any distinction between the "making" and "possession" of indecent photographs if the images were accessed for the personal use of the defendant and not further disseminated. Instead, a distinction is drawn between the deliberate saving of an image and mere viewing of it. In *Oliver*, the Court said that "merely locating an image on the internet will generally be less serious than downloading it".[19] This approach is echoed as a mitigating factor in the definitive guideline. However, internet browsing of indecent photographs which are not deliberately saved by the user nevertheless results in those images being saved in the internet browser cache as an automated function of the browser software. Where such images are recovered, the offender will commonly be charged with making the image rather than possession of it. This is because the file data that is saved along with the offending image by the browser software will provide evidence of when the image was created, i.e. made. Ironically, given the disparity in maximum sentences between the making and possession offences, an offender would stand to receive a lesser sentence for making an image recovered in this way from his browser than if he possessed the same image in a stored format.

"INDECENT"

8.23   In *Nicklass*,[20] the Court of Appeal upheld the appellant's conviction on three counts of possession of an indecent photograph of a child (s.160(1) of the Criminal Justice Act 1988), where the judge had given a lengthy direction to the jury in the course of which he invited them to consider whether the photographs were indecent by reference to "contemporary standards of modesty and privacy". The Court held that, while that reference was "out of place", at the end of the direction the jury could have been left with no other impression than that the question they had to decide was whether the photographs were indecent, i.e. the statutory test, and the conviction was therefore safe.

8.23A   In *Murray*,[21] a video seized from the appellant contained, in the first part, a TV programme in which a doctor examined the genitalia of a naked boy who suffered from a genital defect. The programme had a commentary explaining what the doctor was doing. The second part of the video consisted of some of the earlier

---

[18] Or found not guilty by reason of insanity, found to be under a disability and to have done the act charged, or cautioned.
[19] At para.12.
[20] [2006] EWCA Crim 2613.
[21] [2004] EWCA Crim 2211.

images, but without the commentary, slowed down and clearly focusing on the boy's penis and its manipulation. The appellant was charged with possessing an indecent photograph of a child (s.160(1) of the Criminal Justice Act 1988). At trial, the defence argued that, because the prosecution had accepted that the programme with commentary in the first part of the video was not indecent, the images in the second part which had been abstracted from the programme could not be indecent either, because they were merely the original programme slowed down. The judge held that the alterations made to the original programme by removing the commentary, slowing it down and focusing on the part in which the penis was manipulated, could make an image which the jury could find to be indecent. He directed the jury accordingly and they convicted. An appeal against conviction was unsuccessful, the Court of Appeal holding that the jury were asked to look at a quite separate set of images from the images constituting the original programme and were entitled to look at those images independently of the programme and to determine whether, objectively speaking, they were indecent, applying recognized standards of propriety. Accordingly, the judge had accurately directed the jury both that there were separate images which they were entitled to consider and as to their approach to the question of whether those images were indecent.

"PHOTOGRAPH"

8.28 Clause 68 of the Criminal Justice and Immigration Bill, which is currently before Parliament,[22] will extend the definition of a photograph in the 1978 Act to include a tracing or other image derived from a photograph. The clause inserts in the Act a new s.7(4A) as follows:

"(4A) References to a photograph also include—
(a) a tracing or other image, whether made by electronic or other means (of whatever nature)—
(i) which is not itself a photograph or pseudo-photograph, but
(ii) which is derived from the whole or part of a photograph or pseudo-photograph (or a combination of either or both); and
(b) data stored on a computer disc or by other electronic means which is capable of conversion into an image within paragraph (a);
and subsection (8)[23] applies in relation to such an image as it applies in relation to a pseudo-photograph."

"PSEUDO-PHOTOGRAPH"

8.30 Clause 68 of the Criminal Justice and Immigration Bill, which is currently before Parliament,[24] will correct a drafting error in s.7(9)(b) of the 1978 Act, by replacing "a pseudo-photograph" with "an indecent pseudo-photograph".

---

[22] First Reading was on June 26, 2007.
[23] For s.7(8) of the 1978 Act, see para.8.30 of the main work.
[24] See n.22, above.

SECTION 1(1)(A)—"TO MAKE"

8.35   Footnote 41: "to make" has been given the same meaning in Scotland: *Smart v H.M Advocate*.[25]

SECTION 1(1)(B)—"DISTRIBUTE OR SHOW"

8.36   For a Scottish decision to the same effect as *Fellows and Arnold*, see *Peebles v H.M Advocate*.[26]

8.37   In *R. v C.*,[27] the Court of Appeal approved (*obiter*) *DPP v Armstrong* in holding that a defendant may be convicted of incitement without proof that the person incited intended to commit the offence. It is sufficient that the defendant intended or believed that, if person acted as incited, they would do so with the fault required for the offence.

8.37A   The extra-jurisdictional reach of the offence of incitement to distribute indecent photographs of children was considered in *Tompkins*.[28] The respondent had accessed a website operated and controlled by a US company, which ran a number of sites offering access to commercial child pornography. Following a raid on the company's premises by US law enforcement authorities, the respondent's details together with those of other UK visitors to the company's sites were passed to the police in the UK. The respondent was arrested during the ensuing investigation ("Operation Ore") and was charged with incitement to distribute indecent photographs of children. The case had a tortured procedural history culminating in a Crown Court ruling that the respondent's conduct had not amounted to incitement, since it was not an offence to incite the commission of a crime abroad unless the crime was one in respect of which an indictment would lie in this jurisdiction. The proceedings were stayed pending the outcome of a prosecution appeal to the Court of Appeal under s.58 of the Criminal Justice Act 2003 (prosecution appeals against terminating rulings). On the appeal, the respondent conceded that the courts of England and Wales "possess jurisdiction over an allegation of incitement to distribute indecent photographs of children contrary to the common law even where the incitee is abroad provided that the distribution occurs at least in part in England and Wales". However, he argued that the procedure adopted earlier in the case meant that there had been no valid committal to the Crown Court that could give rise to a prosecution right of appeal.

The Court of Appeal rejected this argument and went on to allow the appeal. On the jurisdictional point, the Court stated that the concession made by the respondent was correctly made. Without hearing detailed argument, it held to be well-founded the Crown's submission that, if a person carries out an act of

[25] 2007 J.C. 119.
[26] [2007] HCJAC 6.
[27] [2005] EWCA Crim 2827.
[28] [2006] EWCA Crim 2132.

incitement in this country to a person outside the jurisdiction, which amounts to an encouragement to that other person to commit an offence in this jurisdiction, then the courts of England and Wales have jurisdiction to try that offence on ordinary principles as the offence incited would be an attack on the Queen's peace. Since sending indecent photographs from a website abroad to a computer in this country constitutes an offence in this country contrary to s.1(1)(b) of the Protection of Children Act 1978 (citing *Goldman*[29] and *Waddon*, unreported), it followed that the Crown Court had had jurisdiction to entertain the charge brought against the respondent.

Professor Ormerod has noted[30] that the respondent's liability turned on the Court of Appeal's assumption that the US company's dissemination of the images to him in England would constitute a "distribution" here for the purposes of the offence under s.1(1)(b) of the 1978 Act, as well as in the US. However, neither of the two cases cited in support of this point, is decisive. *Waddon* is not precisely on point since the offence alleged was one under the Obscene Publications Act 1959, and the question was whether "publication" had occurred in this jurisdiction. Publication is given an extended meaning under s.1(3) of the 1959 Act. Moreover, the jurisdictional point was conceded. As for *Goldman*, that is also perhaps distinguishable in that the material in question was a video tape which would have arrived in physical form in the UK. Nevertheless, Professor Ormerod concludes, by reference to the definition in s.1(2) of the 1978 Act, that the Court was right to reach the conclusion that there was a "distribution" by the US company sending images to the respondent. Section 1(2) provides that a person is to be regarded as distributing an image "if he parts with possession of it to, or exposes or offers it for acquisition by, another person". In this case, the images on the internet would be exposed for acquisition by the respondent in the UK and the offence the respondent had incited would therefore have been committed in the UK if it had been completed.

R. (on the application of O.) v Coventry Magistrates' Court is reported at [2004]   **8.38**
Crim. L.R. 948.

SECTION 1(1)(C)—"HAVE IN HIS POSSESSION . . . WITH A VIEW TO THEIR BEING DISTRIBUTED OR SHOWN"

The concept of "possession" in relation to material emptied from a computer   **8.39**
recycle bin was considered in *Porter*,[31] which repays some attention. The police raided the appellant's house and seized two computers which were linked to the internet almost permanently. They recovered 3575 still images and 40 movie files of child pornography from the hard disk drives. The appellant was charged with 15 offences of making an indecent photograph of a child (s.1(1)(a) of the 1978 Act) and two offences of possession of indecent photographs of children (s.160(1) of the

---

[29] [2001] EWCA Crim 1684.
[30] [2007] Crim. L.R. 235.
[31] [2006] EWCA Crim 560.

Criminal Justice Act 1988), relating respectively to the still images and the movie files. Of the 3575 still images, 875 had been deleted in the sense that they had been placed in the recycle bin of the relevant computer, which had then been emptied. The remaining 2700 still images had been saved in the database of a programme called ACDSee, which was designed for viewing graphic images and was used by photographers. When opened in "gallery view", the programme created thumbnail images of the pictures viewed. There would originally have been larger images associated with each thumbnail, and if one had clicked on the thumbnail, the larger image could have been viewed. However, all the larger images had been deleted, with the effect that the thumbnail could no longer be viewed in gallery view. But a trace of each thumbnail (the "metadata") remained in the programme's database.

Of the 40 movie files, 7 had been placed in the recycle bin which had then been emptied. The remaining 33 files had not been saved, but were recovered from the browser cache (temporary internet files).

The Crown conceded that the appellant did not have the software to retrieve or view the deleted still or movie files and that the thumbnail images were only retrievable with the use of specialist forensic techniques and equipment provided by the US Government which would not have been available to the public. It was common ground that the appellant could have acquired software to enable him to retrieve the items which had been emptied from the recycle bin, including by downloading it from the internet. There was no evidence that he had attempted to do this.

At the close of the prosecution case, the appellant submitted that there was no case to answer in relation to the charges of possessing the 3575 still images and the seven movie files, as he had done all he could to divest himself of possession of these by deleting them. The judge rejected this submission, holding that a computer file remains on the hard drive, and so is capable of being possessed, even if it has been deleted. In summing up, he directed the jury that possession means knowingly having something under one's custody or control, and that the fact that an image is on a deleted file does not mean that the user is not in possession of it, if the file remains on a hard disk in his possession.

On appeal, the appellant submitted that a person does not have possession of indecent photographs on the hard disk drive of his computer unless the images are "readily accessible to the accused for viewing at the time when they are said to be possessed, or capable of being made so accessible without the need to obtain additional specialist software". He further submitted that a person who has at some time in the past been in possession of such images, but who has taken all reasonable steps to destroy them or make them irretrievable by him (such as by placing them in the recycle bin of his computer and emptying the bin) is no longer in possession of them.

The Crown submitted in response that, so long as images remain on the hard disk drive and are recoverable and capable of being viewed, they are in the possession of a person who has control of the hard disk drive. Applying that approach to this case, the Crown conceded that the appellant was not in possession of the 2700 still images which had been saved using the ACDSee programme. But it submitted that he was in possession of the 7 movie files and 875 still images which had been emptied from the recycle bin.

The Court of Appeal said it was superficially attractive to say that all that is required to prove a breach of s.160(1) is that, to the knowledge of the defendant, the images were on the hard disk drive of the computer which was in his custody and control at the material time. It can be argued that possession is an ordinary English word which should be given its normal meaning. Parliament has mitigated the harshness that would result from this by expressly providing three defences in s.160(2) and impliedly providing that knowledge is an essential element of the offence. On this interpretation (which was adopted by the judge in the present case), the fact that the images may be difficult or even impossible to retrieve is irrelevant.

But the possible consequences of this approach were so unreasonable that the Court was unwilling to accept it unless compelled to do so by the express words of the statute or by necessary implication. The unreasonableness was illustrated by the present case. The only way in which the appellant could have retrieved the 2700 still images which had been saved by the ACDSee programme would have been by the use of specialist techniques and equipment supplied only with the authority of the US Government and unavailable to the general public. It was accepted by the Crown that in reality the appellant could not have retrieved these images. In the Court's judgment, it offended common sense to say that they were in the appellant's possession, and the Crown's concession meant that it did not so contend.

It was not, however, necessary to postulate such an extreme example to demonstrate that the judge's view would lead to unreasonable results. Suppose that a person receives unsolicited images of child pornography as an attachment to an email. He is shocked by what he sees and immediately deletes the attachment and deletes it from the recycle bin. Suppose further that he knows that the images are retrievable from the hard disk drive, but he believes that they can only be retrieved and removed by specialists who have software and equipment which he does not have. It does not occur to him to seek to acquire the software or engage a specialist for this purpose. So far as he is concerned, he has no intention of ever seeking to retrieve the images and he has done all that is reasonably necessary to make them irretrievable. The Court thought it would be surprising if Parliament had intended that such a person should be guilty of an offence under s.160(1).

Moreover, an interpretation which rendered such a person guilty of an offence would sit uneasily with s.160(2)(c), under which a person who inadvertently comes into possession of images and gets rid of them within a reasonable time is not guilty of the offence. On the judge's interpretation, the s.160(2)(c) defence would not be available to a person who had saved the images in ACDSee or a similar programme. It is true that the appellant in the present case could not invoke s.160(2)(c) because the images had been sent to him at his request. But the point remained that, on the judge's interpretation, the defence may be available to a defendant who has received hard copy photographs and has adopted the simple remedy of getting rid of them within a reasonable time, whereas it would not be available to a defendant who had received such images on his computer, even if they were saved in ACDSee or a similar programme, because the images were still on the computer's hard disk drive.

In the Court's judgment, such an interpretation was not compelled either by the express words of the statute or by necessary implication. So what was the correct interpretation? The Court cited authorities to the effect that "possession" in the law of drugs involves custody or control, and went on[32]:

> " . . . in seeking to elucidate the meaning of 'possession' in section 160(1) in the present context, we see no reason not to import the concept of having custody or control of the images. In the special case of deleted computer images, if a person cannot retrieve or gain access to an image, in our view he no longer has custody or control of it. He has put it beyond his reach just as does a person who destroys or otherwise gets rid of a hard copy photograph. For this reason, it is not appropriate to say that a person who cannot retrieve an image from the hard disk drive is in possession of the image because he is in possession of the hard disk drive and the computer.
>
>   . . . [T]he first question for the jury is whether the defendant in a case of this kind has possession of the image at the relevant time, in the sense of custody or control of the image at that time. If at the alleged time of possession the image is beyond his control, then for the reasons given earlier he will not possess it. If, however, at that time the image is within his control, for example, because he has the ability to produce it on his screen, to make a hard copy of it, or to send it to someone else, then he will possess it. It will be a matter for the jury to decide whether images are beyond the control of the defendant having regard to all the factors in the case, including his knowledge and particular circumstances. Thus, images which have been emptied from the recycle bin may be considered to be within the control of a defendant who is skilled in the use of computers and in fact owns the software necessary to retrieve such images; whereas such images may be considered not to be within the control of a defendant who does not possess these skills and does not own such software.
>
> We acknowledge that this introduces a subjective element into the concept of physical possession. But we note that the defences provided by section 160(2) import a consideration of the knowledge and behaviour of the particular defendant. Moreover, on any view, an important element of subjectivity is introduced by the requirement of knowledge. It follows that this is not an area where Parliament has enacted an absolute offence. In these circumstances, we see no objection to interpreting the word 'possession' in the particular context of the possession of images in a computer as referring to images that are within the defendant's control.
>
> It will, therefore, be a matter for the jury to decide whether images on a hard disk drive are within the control of the defendant, and to do so having regard to all the circumstances of the case. Such is the speed at which computer technology is developing that what a jury may consider not to be within a defendant's control today may be considered by a jury to be within a defendant's control in the near future. Further, in the course of time more and more people will become skilled in the use of computers. This too will be a relevant factor for the jury to take into account."

It followed that the judge had been right to reject the submission of "no case" in relation to the counts of possession. But his summing up was flawed, in that he directed the jury that the only issue for them to decide was whether the appellant

---

[32] At paras 20–28.

knew that the images were indecent or likely to be indecent. He did not direct them about the factual state of affairs necessary to constitute possession, so removing from them that vital issue. Nor did he direct them about the mental element required for possession, which in principle would require proof that the appellant did not believe that the image in question was beyond his control—though as the Court had not heard argument on that point, it expressed no concluded view on it. For the reasons given, the convictions on the counts of possession were quashed.

Professor Ormerod has questioned whether the Court's approach to "possession" might have the undesirable effect of rendering arbitrary the application of the s.160(1) offence in deletion cases, by making liability turn on the defendant's ability to retrieve the deleted images.[33] Why, he asks, should the "defence" of deletion be available to the computer illiterate but not to the knowledgeable? One might respond that liability should fall only where it is merited, and the Court of Appeal makes a convincing case that in relation to deleted images, it should fall on the person who has the software and computing skills to call up the images, but not on the one who does not. In other words, the computer illiterate ought to be able to defeat a charge of possession because, whilst it may remain possible in theory for them to call up the images, in practice they lack the necessary computing skills and software. If there is a problem with the Court's approach, it is rather the evidential complexity that it will generate in deletion cases. The prosecution may well find it difficult to establish that the defendant has the computing skills necessary for liability (note that the appellant in *Porter* himself worked in IT), and expert evidence is likely to be necessary to establish just how retrievable the images were.

Finally, the Court noted that the problem it was required to address would not have arisen if the appellant had been charged with possession during the period from the time when he viewed the images until he deleted them. There is, however, a practical difficulty with this approach, in that when an image is emptied from the recycle bin, as in *Porter*, the computer operating system places it in the unallocated disc space of the computer hard disc drive, where the image will remain unless and until it is overwritten by the saving of further data to the disc drive or the wiping of the data using file erasion software. However, although an image that has not been overwritten remains retrievable by specialist software, the file data in the form of the dates of file creation, last modification and last access are not retained. Accordingly, in the absence of other evidence, it will not be possible for the prosecution to say when an image was created and when it was deleted. One might add that another way in which the problem might have been avoided was if the appellant had been charged with the more serious offence of making the indecent photographs by downloading them from the internet (see para.8.32 of the main work). Professor Ormerod points out that, by allowing deletion to operate as a "defence" to the s.160 charge, the Court of Appeal has increased the likelihood that individuals will be charged with the more serious

---

[33] [2006] Crim. L.R. 748.

"making" offence, to which there is no defence either of quick disposal (as in s.160(2)(c) of the 1988 Act) or of deletion. See para.8.07 above on the equivalence in seriousness between of the "making" and "possession" offences where images are for the sole use of the offender.

"CHILD"

8.42   The altering of the definition of a "child" by s.45 of the Sexual Offences Act 2003 to include those aged 16 and 17 has resulted in cases in which guilty pleas are tendered to offences involving indecent photographs of children on the basis that the subjects of the photographs are under 18 but not under 16. Where a defendant pleads on this basis, it will be for the judge to decide whether the images are of persons under 16. The Sentencing Guidelines Council's definitive guideline provides that offences relating to images of 16 and 17-years-olds are less serious than offences relating to images of those under 16, unless they are level 5 images. In addition, offences involving images of 16 and 17-year-olds do not trigger the notification requirements under Part 2 of the 2003 Act.

EXCEPTIONS FOR CONSENT WITHIN MARRIAGE OR OTHER RELATIONSHIP

8.45   On the nature of the reverse burden imposed on the defendant by s.1A, see Alisdair A. Gillespie, *Child pornography: balancing substantive and evidential law to safeguard children effectively from abuse*, E. & P. 2005, 9(1), 29–49.

EXCEPTION FOR CRIMINAL PROCEEDINGS AND INVESTIGATION

8.48   Clause 68 of the Criminal Justice and Immigation Bill, which is currently before Parliament,[34] will extend to members of the Secret Intelligence Service (MI6) the exception in s.1B applicable to members of GCHQ and MI5.

8.49   A Memorandum of Understanding concerning s.46 of the SOA 2003, which introduced the new defences in s.1B of the 1978 Act, was agreed in October 2004 between the Crown Prosecution Service and the Association of Chief Police Officers. The MoU is set out at Appendix B to this Supplement.

DEFENCES TO CHARGES UNDER SECTION 1(1)(B),(C)

8.52   Section 1(4) imposes a legal rather than a mere evidential burden on the defendant: *Collier*.[35] See further Alisdair A. Gillespie, *Child pornography: balancing substantive and evidential law to safeguard children effectively from abuse*, E. & P. 2005, 9(1), 29–49.

8.55   *Collier* is reported at [2005] 1 W.L.R. 843. It is a decision on the scope of the defence in s.160(2)(b) of the Criminal Justice Act 1988, which applies on a charge

[34] First Reading was on June 26, 2007.
[35] [2005] 1 W.L.R. 843, at para.18.

of simple possession where the defendant had not seen the photograph and "did not know, nor had any cause to suspect, it to be indecent". *Collier* establishes that the defence applies where the defendant knew the photograph to be indecent, but did not know and had no reason to suspect it to be of a child. The decision extends by analogy to the parallel defence in s.1(4) of the 1978 Act. Its effect is that, on a charge in relation to which the statutory defence is available, the prosecution has to prove merely that the defendant knew the photograph to be indecent and not that it was of a child, since if that had to be proved, the defence would never come into play. This is in contrast with the position where the statutory defence is unavailable. In *Smith and Jayson*[36] (referred to para.8.56 of the main work), it was held in relation to the offence of making or taking an indecent photograph of a child (s.1(1)(a) of the 1978 Act), to which the s.1(4) defence is not available, that the prosecution must prove that the defendant knew the image was, or was likely to be, of a child. The Court of Appeal in *Collier* pointed out that it follows "very ironically" that the prosecution has a heavier burden in the absence of the statutory defence, since then it must prove that the defendant knew not only that the photograph was indecent but also that it was of a child.

The Court in *Collier* distinguished *Land*[37] (para.8.60 of the main work), where it was held in relation to the offence of possession of indecent photographs of a child with a view to their being distributed or shown (s.1(1)(c) of the 1978 Act) that, where the statutory defence was unavailable *because the defendant had seen the photographs*, it was sufficient for the prosecution to prove that he knew he was in possession of indecent photographs. It was *not* required to prove that he knew the photographs to be of children. In other words, *Land* establishes that in cases where the defendant has seen the photographs, there is strict liability as to age and he takes the risk that the subjects are children. We question whether this is just. Should liability as to age be strict, in the light of the approach taken by the House of Lords to the same issue in *B. v DPP*?[38] If the defendant honestly believes that the photographs he possesses are of adults, should that not preclude his conviction?

The position established by these cases is less than wholly satisfactory and intervention by Parliament is desirable in order to establish greater coherence in the application of the criminal law in this area.

MENTAL ELEMENT

Section 1(1)(a)—taking or making an indecent photograph or pseudo-photograph

Smith and Jayson is reported at [2003] 1 Cr. App. R. 212. It was followed in *Smart*   8.56
v H.M Advocate.[39]

---

[36] [2003] 1 Cr. App. R. 212.
[37] [1998] 1 Cr. App. R. 301.
[38] [2000] 1 All E.R. 833.
[39] 2007 J.C. 119.

Section 1(1)(c)—possession of indecent photographs or pseudo-photographs with a view to their being distributed or shown

8.61   On the mental element of "possession", see *Porter*,[40] discussed above para.8.39.

8.62   For US authorities to the same effect as *Atkins v DPP; Goodland v DPP*, see *US v Kuchinski (John Charles)* (November 27, 2006) (9th Cir. (US)) and *US v Diodoro (Anthony)* (November 2, 2006) (Pennsylvania), discussed in C.T.L.R. 2007, 13(3), pp. 63–4.

8.64   The meaning of the words "with a view to" in s.1(1)(c) was considered by the Court of Appeal in *Dooley*.[41] The appellant had been a member of Kazaa, an internet file-sharing network that enables users to share any type of computer file. Users become part of the network by downloading the necessary software from the internet. All members have a "My Shared Folder", the files in which, when the computer is connected to the internet, can be accessed by any Kazaa member and downloaded to their own "My Shared Folder". A police search of the appellant's home found on his computer several thousand indecent images of children, which had been obtained using Kazaa. Six images (to which the indictment related) were found in the appellant's "My Shared Folder", where they had been for 10 days. His case was that whenever he had downloaded images from the system, he had transferred them from his "My Shared Folder" to another part of his computer, where they would not be accessible by others; and that had been his intention in relation to the six images that had remained in his "My Shared Folder", but he simply had not removed them by the time of the police search.

   In a pre-trial ruling, the judge held that there was a difference between the meaning of the words "with a view to" and "with the intention of", and that while the appellant's case would be capable of providing him with a defence if he had been charged with possessing the six images with intent to distribute or show them, it provided him only with mitigation in relation to the offence under s.1(1)(c). That was because it was necessary for the prosecution to prove only that, when the appellant had downloaded a particular photograph, he had done so in the knowledge that it was likely to be seen by other members of the file-sharing system. In the light of this ruling, the appellant pleaded guilty and then appealed.

   He was successful, the Court of Appeal holding that there is a distinction between doing something "with the intention of . . . " and doing something "with a view to . . . ", and that a person does X "with a view to" doing Y if one of his reasons for doing X is to do Y. Therefore, in a case such as the present case, although it may be very important to examine the defendant's knowledge in the way in which the judge had done, the question which the jury should resolve is whether at least one of the reasons why he had left the images in his "My Shared

---

[40] [2006] EWCA Crim 560.
[41] [2005] EWCA Crim 3093.

Folder" was so that others could have access to them. If so, he would be in possession of those images with a view to their being distributed or shown by himself.

In *Dooley*, the appellant knew that the files in his "My Shared Folder" were accessible by other members of the Kazaa network, that being the way he had himself built up his own collection of images. This knowledge was powerful evidence from which the jury might properly infer that one of his reasons for keeping material in the folder was to distribute it to or share it with others. In this respect, see also *Peebles v H.M Advocate*,[42] in which *Dooley* was cited with approval. The appellant in that case was convicted of the Scottish equivalent of the s.1(1)(c) offence, contained in s.52(1)(c) of the Civic Government (Scotland) Act 1982. He had also downloaded the Kazaa software from the internet and stored indecent images in his "My Shared Folder". There was evidence before the court that when installing the software, he had enabled the file-sharing function. One ground of appeal was that there was no evidence of *mens rea*, but the appellant abandoned this ground during argument before the High Court of Justiciary. The Court observed that the evidence that the appellant had enabled the file-sharing function entitled the jury to infer that one of his reasons for so doing was to allow others to have access to the files in his "My Shared Folder". On that basis they could properly conclude that he held the files with a view to their being distributed or shown by himself.

The words "with a view to" comprise a mental element going beyond the **8.64A** prohibited act to the consequences of that act, and on the reasoning in *Heard*[43] (discussed para.2.72 above) this serves to confirm that the s.1(1)(c) offence is one of specific intent. Accordingly, self-induced intoxication will provide a defence if it prevented D acting "with a view to" the distribution or sharing of the images. As indicated in the main work, where intoxication may be an issue, a charge of simple possession under s.160(1) of the Criminal Justice Act 1988 should be brought instead.

Section 1(1)(d)—publishing or causing to be published an advertisement

FORENSIC EVIDENCE

In *Skinner*,[44] the Court of Appeal was required to consider whether information **8.66** copied from one website to another and adduced in the form of a printed screen image amounted to real evidence admissible under s.27 of the Criminal Justice Act 1988 (since replaced by s.133 of the Criminal Justice Act 2003). The appellant was convicted of possessing indecent images of children (s.160(1) of the Criminal

---

[42] [2007] HCJAC 6.
[43] [2007] EWCA Crim 125.
[44] [2005] EWCA Crim 1439.

Justice Act 1988), the images having been found on CD-ROM discs found at his home. His defence had been that he had found the discs but had been unable to open them and had not known or had cause to suspect that they contained indecent images of children. To rebut this defence, the Crown sought to adduce exhibit "SR1", which comprised printouts of screen images from the Kaaza website (see further para 8.64 above). These showed that a user identifying himself as "Poloman@Kaaza" had offered for access by others on the website certain files with names indicative of child pornographic content. Superimposed on one of the screen images was a smaller window containing material in DOS format, which revealed the internet protocol address of "Poloman@Kaaza". Inquiries of BT had identified the appellant as the offeror, and this prompted the search of his home.

The issue was whether exhibit SR1 was admissible in evidence. On a voir dire, the police officer who printed out the screen images gave evidence that he had accessed them by entering a secure website, but he refused to identify the website, saying that there was a "source" involved; he did not know whether the source was an individual or a facility; he could not tell how the information was posted onto the secure website or whether one or a number of persons were involved; the information had been copied from a Word document, so he could not tell whether it had been altered; and he could not say whether the information had been received by another source and posted by a second or third person onto the website from which he had obtained it.

The judge permitted SR1 to be adduced on the ground that it was real evidence and not hearsay. He considered s.27 of the Criminal Justice Act 1988, which provided that, where a statement contained in a document was admissible in evidence, it might be proved by production of the document or a copy thereof (or the material part of it) authenticated in such manner as the court may approve, it being irrelevant how many removes there were between the copy and the original. The judge ruled that the original for these purposes was what appeared on the Kaaza site screen. It had been copied to a site that the prosecution declined to identify and then to a police computer and printed out. He held that this was entirely within the process contemplated by s.27.

On appeal, the appellant argued that SR1 should not have been admitted, first because copying the screen images electronically to another computer or website rendered them hearsay, and secondly because there had been no evidence to explain the process by which the original screen image had come to be on the police computer, and no public interest immunity ruling to the effect that such an explanation need not be given.

The Court of Appeal said that the screen images had probably (and it emphasized the word "probably") been real evidence rather than hearsay. This was so despite their being copied from the original website, because their content neither required nor acquired any human input other than that of a person responsible for the content of the website in the first place. As for s.27 of the 1988 Act, the case did not involve the straightforward use of a computer and the police officer did not give and was unable to give any proper explanation of the electronic process involved. That being the case, there had been no material upon which the judge could properly have concluded either that the images were real evidence or that they were authentic in a manner which he might approve. The Court nonetheless went on to hold the appellant's conviction safe on the basis that the screen images could have had only a limited influence on the outcome of the trial, given the other evidence before the court.

The admissibility of copy documents is now regulated by s.133 of the Criminal Justice Act 2003, which replaces s.27 of the 1988 Act and provides as follows:

> "Where a statement in a document is admissible as evidence in criminal proceedings, the statement may be proved by producing either
> (a) the document, or
> (b) (whether or not the document exists) a copy of the document or of the material part of it
> authenticated in whatever way the court may approve."

Section 133 is intended to cover all forms of copying, including the use of imaging technology: para.436 of the Explanatory Notes. Of course, even if the requirements of s.133 are met in relation to a document copied in this way, the defendant may argue that the evidence establishes a link with the relevant computer, but not with him, if others may have had access to the machine.

Finally, where a party to criminal proceedings seeks to adduce in evidence a representation of fact made otherwise than by a person, they must now satisfy the accuracy safeguard introduced by s.129 of the Criminal Justice Act 2003:

> "(1) Where a representation of any fact—
> (a) is made otherwise than by a person, but
> (b) depends for its accuracy on information supplied (directly or indirectly) by a person,
> the representation is not admissible in criminal proceedings as evidence of the fact unless it is proved that the information was accurate."

This safeguard will apply in relation to computer-generated evidence where the accuracy of the evidence depends on information inputted by a person, such as the date and time a file was created or sent. In such cases, compliance with the safeguard in s.129 may be very difficult.

R. (on the application of O.) v Coventry Magistrate' Court is reported at [2004] **8.67**
Crim. L.R. 948.

POSSESSION OF AN INDECENT PHOTOGRAPH OR PSEUDO-PHOTOGRAPH OF A CHILD

MODE OF TRIAL AND PUNISHMENT

As from a day to be appointed the maximum sentence on summary conviction is **8.69**
12 months' imprisonment: Criminal Justice Act 2003, s.282(2), (3). The increase

has no application to offences committed before the substitution takes effect: s.282(4). An offence under s.160 is a specified sexual offence in respect of which a sentence of imprisonment for public protection may be imposed under the Criminal Justice Act 2003.[45]

Restriction on prosecution

8.70   See the discussion in para.8.05 above.

SENTENCING

8.72   See the discussion in para.8.07 above. A person convicted[46] of an offence under s.160(1) of the 1988 Act is automatically subject to notification requirements in accordance with the SOA 2003, s.80 and Sch.3, if the images showed persons under 16 and the offender was 18 or over at the time of the offence or is sentenced to at least 12 months' imprisonment.

"INDECENT PHOTOGRAPH OR PSEUDO-PHOTOGRAPH"

8.75   See the discussion in para.8.23 above.

"POSSESSION"

8.78   For the meaning of "possession", see para.8.39 above.

DEFENCES

8.80   For the application of the defence in s.160(2)(b), see the discussion in paras 8.52 and 8.55 above. See also Dr. Yaman Akdeniz, *Possession and dispossession: a critical assessment of defences in cases of possession of indecent photographs of children* [2007] Crim. L.R. 274.

MENTAL ELEMENT

8.81   For the mental element required for "possession", see para.8.61 above.

---

[45] s.224 and Sch.15, Pt 2.
[46] Or found not guilty by reason of insanity, found to be under a disability and to have done the act charged, or cautioned.

CHAPTER 9

CHILD ABDUCTION

DEFINITION

Section 2(1)(a) and (b) creates two separate offences, and neither is an alternative **9.06** verdict for the other: *Foster v DPP*.[1] It follows from the wording of the section that an offence may be committed either by taking a child so as to (a) remove her from, or (b) keep her out of the lawful control of any person, or by detaining a child so as to (a) remove her from, or (b) keep her out of the lawful control of any person. The Divisional Court in *Foster* accordingly held that "there will be circumstances when a child may be removed from lawful control by detention rather than taking. The most obvious example is an occasion when the child is in the company of another with the agreement of his parent or guardian, but ceases to be so when knowingly detained beyond the period agreed. In [this] example, when consent knowingly expired, removal occurred." The Court went on to hold that if the child was already out of lawful control, then any subsequent taking or detention could only have the effect of keeping the child out of the lawful control of someone entitled to it: see para.9.15 below.

MODE OF TRIAL AND PUNISHMENT

As from a day to be appointed the maximum sentence on summary conviction is **9.07** 12 months' imprisonment: Criminal Justice Act 2003, s.282(2), (3). The increase has no application to offences committed before the substitution takes effect: s.282(4). An offence under s.2(1) is not a specified violent or sexual offence in respect of which a sentence of imprisonment for public protection may be imposed

---

[1] [2004] EWHC 2955 (Admin); [2005] 1 W.L.R. 1402, at para.7.

under the Criminal Justice Act 2003.[2] Nor is it an offence for which a court may make an order under s.28 of the Criminal Justice and Court Services Act 2000 disqualifying the offender from working with children: *Prime (Roy Vincent)*.[3]

ALTERNATIVE VERDICT

9.08 See *Foster v DPP*, para.9.06 above.

SENTENCING

9.09 In *Bailey (William)*,[4] the appellant was convicted of attempted child abduction. He had approached an eight-year-old boy and asked if he would like an ice-cream. The boy went to ask his father, who called the police. The appellant had a long criminal record which included a conviction for indecent assault on a boy under the age of 14 and another for abduction of a child. A pre-sentence report indicated a very high risk that he would re-offend and a potential risk of serious harm to the public, in particular to young males. The judge imposed a longer than com-mensurate sentence under s.80(2)(b) of the Powers of Criminal Courts (Sentenc-ing) Act 2000 (since repealed: see Ch.22 of the main work), stating that a commensurate sentence would have been five years' imprisonment. The Court of Appeal held, on an appeal against sentence, that the judge had no power to impose a longer than commensurate sentence since the offence under s.2(1) was not a "sexual offence" for the purposes of s.80(2)(b) (citing *Wrench*[5]) and there was no finding that the appellant had had physical contact with the boy such as to make his offence "violent" (distinguishing *Newsome*[6]). However, although the statutory maximum for the substantive offence is seven years' imprisonment, the Court held that a sentence of five years' imprisonment for an attempt was not excessive given the judge's finding that the appellant clearly intended indecency towards the victim; the appellant's appalling record, which included convictions for offences of the same kind; and his failure to plead guilty or show remorse.

"WITHOUT LAWFUL AUTHORITY OR REASONABLE EXCUSE"

9.13 The Divisional Court in *Foster v DPP*[7] cited *Re Owens*[8] as a case in which a reasonable excuse "plainly" existed. The applicant in *Re Owens* was committed for extradition to the USA, where she had been indicted on kidnapping charges the equivalent of s.2(1) of the 1984 Act. She applied successfully for a writ of *habeas corpus* on the ground that there was no prima facie case against her. The agreed facts included that, to the applicant's knowledge, the two children who were the

---

[2] s.224 and Sch.15.
[3] [2004] EWCA Crim 2009, [2005] 1 Cr. App. R.(S.) 45.
[4] [2004] EWCA Crim 3058, [2005] 2 Cr. App. R.(S.) 16.
[5] [1996] 1 Cr. App. R.(S.) 145.
[6] [1997] 2 Cr. App. R.(S.) 69.
[7] Above n.1.
[8] [2000] 1 Cr. App. R. 195.

subject of the alleged offence, for whom she was caring and whose nanny she had been, had no parent with lawful control over them. Their father had been killed, their mother had never sought to exercise control over them and the applicant believed that the mother had abandoned them. The applicant took the children to their father's funeral in the USA from Germany, where, until his death, the father had been serving as a soldier in the US military. She was unaware when she flew back that their grandmother had that day been granted an *ex parte* order for temporary custody. Although the argument in *Re Owens* turned on the *mens rea* for the s.2(1) offence (for which see below para.9.22), the court in *Foster* said that, had a prosecution proceeded, it was difficult to see how the prosecutor could have established that the applicant did not have a reasonable excuse. She plainly did: she was in actual control of the children and had been since their father's death; she had taken them to the USA to attend his funeral; and although she knew that their grandmother intended to apply for custody, she was unaware that the application had been lodged when she took the children back to Germany, having taken legal advice that it was permissible for her to do so.

"TAKES OR DETAINS"

In *Foster v DPP*,[9] the Divisional Court held that the offence of abduction of a child   **9.15** so as to remove her from a person having lawful control of her could not be proved, where the child was no longer in the lawful control of her foster parents when the appellants detained her. At the relevant time the complainant, S, was aged 15 and living with foster parents, in whose control she lawfully was for the purposes of s.2 of the 1984 Act. On the afternoon of March 1, 2003, she met the second appellant, R, who took her to his home. He believed at this point that she was aged 16 or over. When S failed to return home that evening, her foster father reported her missing to the police. The police telephoned R's home at 1.30am the following day and told him that they were looking for S, who was under age and had been reported as missing. R passed on that information to the first appellant, F. At about 2am the police arrived at R's home. The appellants told them that S had been there, but had since left. That was a lie, as they knew S was hiding in the attic to avoid being found by the police. At 7am the police revisited R, found S in the living room and took her home. The appellants were charged with an offence contrary to ss.2(1)(a) and 4 of the Child Abduction Act 1984, the particulars of offence stating that "On 2nd March 2003 . . . without lawful authority or reasonable excuse [they] detained S, a child under the age of 16, so as to remove her from the lawful control of . . . a person having lawful control of the child . . . ". Before the deputy district judge in the magistrates' court, the appellants submitted that S's foster parents had lost control of her on March 1 so that, if any offence was committed on March 2, it could only have been abduction contrary to s.2(1)(b) of the Act, namely keeping S out of the lawful control of any person entitled to lawful control of her, with which they were not charged and

---

[9] Above n.1.

which was not an alternative to the charges laid. The deputy district judge found at the close of the prosecution case that an act of removal took place on March 2 when, knowing S's true age, the appellants took no steps to return her. The appellants appealed successfully by way of case stated. The Divisional Court held that R's action in taking S to his home had the effect of removing her from the control of her foster parents and F's complicit action in detaining S at the house had the effect of removing or keeping her from the control of her foster parents. However, neither man was guilty of the offence of abduction on March 1, since at that point both believed S to be aged 16 or over. Had it not been for their belief, they would have been guilty of abduction on that day. The factual situation had however changed dramatically by 1.30am on March 2. The appellants had been told that S was 15, was missing from home and being sought by the police. Assuming, for the purposes of the appeal, that S did not wish to be restored to her foster parents and took advantage of the appellants' willingness to allow her to hide from the police and stay the night, then they detained her within the meaning of s.2(1), since that willingness constituted an inducement to stay with them, as contemplated by s.3(c) of the Act. However, those acts of the appellants did not have the effect of removing S from the lawful control of her foster parents, since by the time they were committed she had already left that control. It is clear from the wording of s.2 that Parliament intended a material distinction to be drawn between the two forms of the s.2 offence, which, when applied to facts such as those of the present case, is critical to guilt or innocence. Paragraph (a) uses the word "having" as the verb which qualifies or explains lawful control of the child, while paragraph (b) uses the words "entitled to lawful control of the child". From that two conclusions follow. The first is that the distinction between removal from a person having control, and keeping from a person entitled to control, is intended to reflect two materially different states of affairs. One requires the child to be in the lawful control of someone when taken or detained. The other requires only that the child is kept out of the lawful control of someone entitled to it when they are taken or detained. Paragraph (b) would cover a situation in which the child has run away from lawful control and is, whilst out of lawful control, detained unlawfully by the defendant. The second conclusion to be drawn from the distinction between removal from a person having lawful control and keeping from a person entitled to control is that, when laid in a charge, each is a material averment which alleges one of two separate forms of the s.2 offence. In the present case, by the time the appellants knew that their inducements to S were unlawful, she was no longer in the lawful custody of her foster parents. Accordingly, the offence charged under s.2(1)(a) was not proved.

"Lawful Control"

9.20   *Leather*[10] was approved in *Foster v DPP*,[11] where the Court said "the word 'remove' is intended to convey a substitution of the authority by an accused for

---

[10] (1994) 98 Cr. App. R. 179.
[11] Above n.1.

that of the person lawfully having it, and not the physical removal of the child from any particular place".[12]

MENTAL ELEMENT

The apparent conflict between the objective construction of s.2 adopted in *Mousir*[13] and the subjective approach taken in *Re Owens*[14] was considered in *Foster v DPP*.[15] Pitchford J., giving the judgment of the Divisional Court, examined the authorities at some length and concluded that *Mousir* is to be preferred. He noted that in that case, the Court of Appeal gave "emphatic" approval to the defence concession that the objective approach applies, and also that a direction to the jury in objective terms was subsequently approved in *Leather*[16] (albeit *Mousir* was not cited). Pitchford J. observed, with great respect to the Divisional Court in *Re Owens*, that the argument for a subjective construction could not survive the judgment of the Court of Appeal in *Mousir* and *Leather*. He concluded that the *mens rea* of the abduction offence is "an intentional or reckless taking or detention of a child under the age of 16, the effect or objective consequence of which is to remove or to keep that child within the meaning of section 2(1)(a) or (b)." **9.22**

The main work considers the question "What if the defendant believes the child is 16 or over at the outset but later learns that she is younger?", and suggests that the answer must turn on the defendant's state of mind when the "taking" or "detaining" occurs. See further on this issue *Foster v DPP*,[17] discussed above para.9.15. **9.23**

[12] At para.18.
[13] [1987] Crim. L.R. 562.
[14] Above n.8.
[15] Above n.1.
[16] Above n.10.
[17] Above n.1.

CHAPTER 10

PROSTITUTION: EXPLOITATION AND TRAFFICKING

A. ABUSE OF CHILDREN THROUGH PROSTITUTION AND PORNOGRAPHY

PAYING FOR SEXUAL SERVICES OF A CHILD

MODE OF TRIAL AND PUNISHMENT

As from a day to be appointed the maximum sentence on summary conviction is **10.21** 12 months' imprisonment: Criminal Justice Act 2003, s.282(2), (3). The increase has no application to offences committed before the substitution takes effect: s.282(4). The offence under s.47 is a specified sexual offence in respect of which a sentence of imprisonment for public protection may be imposed under the Criminal Justice Act 2003.[1]

---

[1] s.224 and Sch.15, Pt 2.

10.22 For the definitive guideline published by the Sentencing Guidelines Council on sentencing under the 2003 Act, see para.1.18. The guideline states that the factors to be taken into consideration in sentencing offences under s.47 (paying for sexual services of a child) are as follows[2]:

> "1. The sentences for public protection must be considered in all cases. They are designed to ensure that sexual offenders are not released into the community if they present a significant risk of serious harm. Within any indeterminate sentence, the minimum term will generally be half the appropriate determinate sentence. The starting points will be relevant, therefore, to the process of fixing any minimum term that may be necessary.
>
> 2. The offence of 'paying for sexual services of a child' is the only offence in this group that involves actual physical sexual activity between an offender and a victim.
>
> 3. It carries staged maximum penalties according to the age of the victim (in this case under 16, or over 16 but under 18) and also, specifically in relation to victims under 13, whether the sexual services provided or offered involved penetrative activity.
>
> 4. The starting points for sentencing for the offence of 'paying for sexual services of a child', where the victim is aged 13 or over but under 16, are higher than those for the offence of 'sexual activity with a child', to reflect the fact that the victim has been commercially exploited.
>
> 5. Starting points for victims aged 16 or 17 are lower than the equivalent starting points for victims aged 13 to 15, in line with the difference in the maximum penalty, to reflect the fact that the victim is above the legal age of consent.
>
> 6. The starting points where the victim is aged 13 or over but under 16 are higher than those for the offence of 'sexual activity with a child', to reflect the fact that the victim has been commercially exploited.
>
> 7. The starting points for sentencing for the offence of 'paying for sexual services of a child' where the victim is under 13 are higher than those for the specific 'under 13' offences covering the same type of sexual activity, to reflect the fact that the victim has been commercially exploited.
>
> 8. The offence of 'paying for sexual services of a child' includes higher maximum penalties to cater for those (albeit rare) cases where the age of the victim is only established during the course of a trial. The same principle has been applied to the starting points for sentencing."

The starting points, sentencing ranges and aggravating and mitigating factors for the offences under s.47 of the 2003 Act are as follows:

[2] Pt 6B.

Type/nature of activity	Starting points	Sentencing ranges
History of paying for penetrative sex with children under 18	If the victim is under 13, the offence of "rape of a child under 13" or "assault of a child under 13 by penetration" would normally be charged. Any commercial element to the offence and any history of repeat offending would be aggravating factors. However, if this offence is charged—**15 years custody**	**13–19 years custody**
	7 years custody if the victim is 13 or over but under 16	**5–10 years custody**
	3 years custody if the victim is aged 16 or 17	**2–5 years custody**
Penile penetration of the vagina, anus or mouth or penetration of the vagina or anus with another body part or an object	If the victim is under 13, the offence of "rape of a child under 13" or "assault of a child under 13 by penetration" would normally be charged. Any commercial element to the offence would be an aggravating factor. However, if this offence is charged—**12 years custody**	**10–16 years custody**
	5 years custody if the victim is 13 or over but under 16	**4–8 years custody**
	2 years custody if the victim is aged 16 or 17	**1–4 years custody**

Type/nature of activity	Starting points	Sentencing ranges
Sexual touching falling short of penetration	If the victim is under 13, the offence of "sexual assault of a child under 13" would normally be charged. Any commercial element to the offence would be an aggravating factor. However, if this offence is charged—**5 years custody**	**4–8 years custody**
	4 years custody if the victim is 13 or over but under 16	**3–7 years custody**
	12 months custody if the victim is aged 16 or 17	**26 weeks–2 years custody**

Additional aggravating factors	Additional mitigating factors
1. Use of drugs, alcohol or other substance to secure the victim's compliance	
2. Abduction or detention	
3. Threats to prevent victim reporting the activity	
4. Threats to disclose victim's activity to friends or relatives	
5. Offender aware that he or she is suffering from a sexually transmitted infection	

A person convicted[3] under s.47 is automatically subject to notification requirements in accordance with the SOA 2003, s.80 and Sch.3, if the victim (or other

---

[3] Or found not guilty by reason of insanity, found to be under a disability and to have done the act charged, or cautioned.

party) was under 16 and the offender was 18 or over or is sentenced to at least 12 months' imprisonment.

CAUSING OR INCITING CHILD PROSTITUTION OR PORNOGRAPHY

MODE OF TRIAL AND PUNISHMENT

As from a day to be appointed the maximum sentence on summary conviction is **10.31** 12 months' imprisonment: Criminal Justice Act 2003, s.282(2), (3). The increase has no application to offences committed before the substitution takes effect: s.282(4). The offence under s.48 is a specified sexual offence in respect of which a sentence of imprisonment for public protection may be imposed under the Criminal Justice Act 2003.[4]

SENTENCING

For the definitive guideline published by the Sentencing Guidelines Council on **10.32** sentencing under the 2003 Act, see para.1.18. The guideline states that the factors to be taken into consideration in sentencing offences under ss.48–50 are as follows[5]:

> "1. The sentences for public protection must be considered in all cases. They are designed to ensure that sexual offenders are not released into the community if they present a significant risk of serious harm.
> 2. Three offences fall within this group:
>   - Causing or inciting child prostitution or child pornography
>   - Controlling a child prostitute or a child involved in pornography
>   - Arranging or facilitating child prostitution or pornography
> 3. The level of involvement of the offender is a fundamental element of the 'abuse of children through prostitution and pornography' offences.
> 4. Financial reward may not always be a factor in someone's involvement in these offences. Thus the offences cover anyone who takes part in any way, for whatever reason, in a child's involvement in prostitution or pornography. However, most offenders will stand to gain in some way from their involvement, and sentencing starting points need to be relatively high, in line with established principles about the serious nature of commercial exploitation.
> 5. The courts should consider making an order confiscating any profits stemming from the offender's criminal lifestyle or forfeiting any possessions (for example cameras, computers, property) used in connection with the commission of the offence.
> 6. Evidence of an offender's involvement in, or management of, a well-planned or large-scale commercial operation resulting in sexual exploitation should be treated

[4] s.224 and Sch.15, Pt 2.
[5] Pt 6B.

as an aggravating factor for sentencing: the greater the offender's degree of involvement, the more serious the offence.

7. The starting point for the child prostitution and pornography offences will always be a custodial sentence.

8. The same starting points apply whether the activity was caused or incited. Where an offence was incited but did not take place as a result of the voluntary intervention of the offender, that is likely to reduce the severity of the sentence imposed.

9. The presence of any of the general aggravating factors identified in the Council guideline on seriousness[6] or any of the additional factors identified in the guidelines will indicate a sentence above the normal starting point.

10. In cases where a number of children are involved, consecutive sentences may be appropriate, leading to cumulative sentences significantly higher than the suggested starting points for individual offences.

11. In cases where the offender is, to a degree, another victim, a court may wish to take a more lenient stance. A court might consider whether the circumstances of the offender should mitigate sentence. This will depend on the merits of each case."

The starting points, sentencing ranges and aggravating and mitigating factors applicable to the offences under ss.48–50 are as follows:

Type/nature of activity	Starting points	Sentencing ranges
Penetrative activity Organised commercial exploitation	If the victim is under 13, the offence of "causing or inciting a child under 13 to engage in sexual activity" would normally be charged. The commercial element of the offence would be an aggravating factor. However, if this offence is charged—**10 years custody**	**8–13 years custody**
	8 years custody if the victim is 13 or over but under 16	**6–11 years custody**
	4 years custody if the victim is aged 16 or 17	**3–7 years custody**

[6] Issued December 2004.

Type/nature of activity	Starting points	Sentencing ranges
Penetrative activity Offender's involvement is minimal and not perpetrated for gain	If the victim is under 13, the offence of "causing or inciting a child under 13 to engage in sexual activity" would normally be charged. The commercial element of the offence would be an aggravating factor. However, if this offence is charged—**8 years custody**	6–11 years custody
	5 years custody if the victim is 13 or over but under 16	4–8 years custody
	2 years custody if the victim is aged 16 or 17	1–4 years custody
Non-penetrative activity Organised commercial exploitation	If the victim is under 13, the offence of "causing or inciting a child under 13 to engage in sexual activity" would normally be charged. The commercial element of the offence would be an aggravating factor. However, if this offence is charged—**8 years custody**	6–11 years custody
	6 years custody if the victim is 13 or over but under 16	4–9 years custody
	3 years custody if the victim is aged 16 or 17	2–5 years custody

Type/nature of activity	Starting points	Sentencing ranges
Non-penetrative activity Offender's involvement is minimal and not perpetrated for gain	If the victim is under 13, the offence of "causing or inciting a child under 13 to engage in sexual activity" would normally be charged. The commercial element of the offence would be an aggravating factor. However, if this offence is charged—**6 years custody**	**4–9 years custody**
	3 years custody if the victim is aged 13 or over but under 16	**2–5 years custody**
	12 months custody if the victim is aged 16 or 17	**26 weeks–2 years custody**

Additional aggravating factors	Additional mitigating factors
1. Background of threats or intimidation	1. Offender also being controlled in prostitution or pornography and subject to threats or intimidation
2. Large-scale commercial operation	
3. Use of drugs, alcohol or other substance to secure the victim's compliance	
4. Induced dependency on drugs	
5. Forcing a victim to violate another person	
6. Victim has been manipulated into physical and emotional dependence on the offender	
7. Abduction or detention	

Additional aggravating factors	Additional mitigating factors
8. Threats to prevent victim reporting the activity	
9. Threats to disclose victim's activity to friends or relatives	
10. Storing, making available or distributing images in such a way that they can be inadvertently accessed by others	
11. Images distributed to other children or persons known to the victim	
12. Financial or other gain	

A person convicted[7] under s.48 is automatically subject to notification requirements in accordance with the SOA 2003, s.80 and Sch.3,[8] if he was 18 or over at the time of the offence or is sentenced to at least 12 months' imprisonment.

CONTROLLING A CHILD PROSTITUTE OR A CHILD INVOLVED IN PORNOGRAPHY

MODE OF TRIAL AND PUNISHMENT

As from a day to be appointed the maximum sentence on summary conviction is **10.44** 12 months' imprisonment: Criminal Justice Act 2003, s.282(2), (3). The increase has no application to offences committed before the substitution takes effect: s.282(4). The offence under s.49 is a specified sexual offence in respect of which a sentence of imprisonment for public protection may be imposed under the Criminal Justice Act 2003.[9]

SENTENCING

For the definitive guideline published by the Sentencing Guidelines Council on **10.46** sentencing under the 2003 Act, see para.1.18. The provisions of the guideline relating to offences under s.49 are set out at para.10.32 above.

---

[7] Or found not guilty by reason of insanity, found to be under a disability and to have done the act charged, or cautioned.
[8] As amended by SI 2007/296.
[9] s.224 and Sch.15, Pt 2.

A person convicted[10] under s.49 is automatically subject to notification requirements in accordance with the SOA 2003, s.80 and Sch.3,[11] if he was 18 or over at the time of the offence or is sentenced to at least 12 months' imprisonment.

ARRANGING OR FACILITATING CHILD PROSTITUTION OR PORNOGRAPHY

Mode of Trial and Punishment

10.58   As from a day to be appointed the maximum sentence on summary conviction is 12 months' imprisonment: Criminal Justice Act 2003, s.282(2), (3). The increase has no application to offences committed before the substitution takes effect: s.282(4). The offence under s.50 is a specified sexual offence in respect of which a sentence of imprisonment for public protection may be imposed under the Criminal Justice Act 2003.[12]

Sentencing

10.59   For the definitive guideline published by the Sentencing Guidelines Council on sentencing under the 2003 Act, see para.1.18. The provisions of the guideline relating to offences under s.50 are set out at para.10.32 above.

A person convicted[13] under s.50 is automatically subject to notification requirements in accordance with the SOA 2003, s.80 and Sch.3,[14] if he was 18 or over at the time of the offence or is sentenced to at least 12 months' imprisonment.

B. EXPLOITATION OF PROSTITUTION

CAUSING OR INCITING PROSTITUTION FOR GAIN

Mode of Trial and Punishment

10.71   As from a day to be appointed the maximum sentence on summary conviction is 12 months' imprisonment: Criminal Justice Act 2003, s.282(2), (3). The increase has no application to offences committed before the substitution takes effect: s.282(4). The offence under s.52 is a specified sexual offence in respect of which

---

[10] Or found not guilty by reason of insanity, found to be under a disability and to have done the act charged, or cautioned.

[11] As amended by SI 2007/296.

[12] s.224 and Sch.15, Pt 2.

[13] Or found not guilty by reason of insanity, found to be under a disability and to have done the act charged, or cautioned.

[14] As amended by SI 2007/296.

a sentence of imprisonment for public protection may be imposed under the Criminal Justice Act 2003.[15]

SENTENCING

For the definitive guideline published by the Sentencing Guidelines Council on   **10.72**
sentencing under the 2003 Act, see para.1.18. The guideline states that the factors to be taken into consideration in sentencing offences under s.52 (causing or inciting prostitution for gain) and s.53 (controlling prostitution for gain) are as follows[16]:

> "1. The sentences for public protection must be considered in all cases. They are designed to ensure that sexual offenders are not released into the community if they present a significant risk of serious harm.
> 2. The degree of coercion, both in terms of recruitment and subsequent control of a prostitute's activities, is highly relevant to sentencing.
> 3. The degree to which a victim is exploited or controlled, the harm suffered as a result, the level of involvement of the offender, the scale of the operation and the timescale over which it has been run will all be relevant in terms of assessing the seriousness of the offence.
> 4. Where an offender has profited from his or her involvement in the prostitution of others, the courts should always consider making a confiscation order approximately equivalent to the profits enjoyed.
> 5. The presence of any of the general aggravating factors identified in the Council guideline on seriousness[17] or any of the additional factors identified in the guidelines will indicate a sentence above the normal starting point.
> 6. Where there is evidence that an offender convicted of an exploitation of prostitution offence is not actively involved in the coercion or control of the victim(s), that he or she acted through fear or intimidation and that he or she is trying to exit prostitution, the courts may wish to consider whether, in the particular circumstances of the case, this should mitigate sentence.
> 7. The starting points are the same whether prostitution was caused or incited and whether or not the incited activity took place. Where the offence was incited, the sentencer should begin from the starting point that the offence was incited, taking account of the nature of the harm that would have been caused had the offence taken place and calculating the final sentence to reflect that no actual harm was occasioned to the victim, but being mindful that the intended victim may have suffered as a result of knowing or believing the offence would take place.
> 8. The starting point for the exploitation of prostitution offences where an offender's involvement was minimal, and he or she has not actively engaged in the coercion or control of those engaged in prostitution, is a non-custodial sentence.
> 9. A fine may be more appropriate for very minimal involvement.
> 10. Where an offender has profited from his or her involvement in the prostitution of others, the court should consider making a confiscation order[18] approximately equivalent to the profits enjoyed.
> 11. Where this offence is being dealt with in a magistrates' court, more detailed guidance is provided in the Magistrates' Court Sentencing Guidelines (MCSG)."

[15] s.224 and Sch.15, Pt 2.
[16] Pt 6C.
[17] Issued December 2004.
[18] Under the Criminal Justice Act 1988 as amended by the Proceeds of Crime Act 2002.

The starting points, sentencing ranges and aggravating and mitigating factors for offences under ss.52 and 53 are as follows:

Type/nature of activity	Starting points	Sentencing ranges
Evidence of physical and/or mental coercion	3 years custody	2–5 years custody
No coercion or corruption, but the offender is closely involved in the victim's prostitution	12 months custody	26 weeks–2 years custody
No evidence that the victim was physically coerced or corrupted, and the involvement of the offender was minimal	Community order	An appropriate non-custodial sentence*

* "Non-custodial sentence" in this context suggests a community order or a fine. In most instances, an offence will have crossed the threshold for a community order. However, in accordance with normal sentencing practice, a court is not precluded from imposing a financial penalty where that is determined to be the appropriate sentence.

Additional aggravating factors	Additional mitigating factors
1. Background of threats, intimidation or coercion	1. Offender also being controlled in prostitution and subject to threats or intimidation
2. Large-scale commercial operation	
3. Substantial gain (in the region of £5,000 and upwards)	
4. Use of drugs, alcohol or other substance to secure the victim's compliance	
5. Induced dependency on drugs	
6. Abduction or detention	
7. Threats to prevent victim reporting the activity	
8. Threats to disclose victim's activity to friends or relatives	

CONTROLLING PROSTITUTION FOR GAIN

MODE OF TRIAL AND PUNISHMENT

As from a day to be appointed the maximum sentence on summary conviction is   **10.84**
12 months' imprisonment: Criminal Justice Act 2003, s.282(2), (3). The increase
has no application to offences committed before the substitution takes effect:
s.282(4). The offence under s.53 is a specified sexual offence in respect of which
a sentence of imprisonment for public protection may be imposed under the
Criminal Justice Act 2003.[19]

SENTENCING

For the definitive guideline published by the Sentencing Guidelines Council on   **10.86**
sentencing under the 2003 Act, see para.1.18. The provisions of the guideline
relating to offences under s.53 are set out at para.10.72 above.

"CONTROLS ANY OF THE ACTIVITIES OF ANOTHER PERSON RELATING TO THAT
PERSON'S PROSTITUTION"

In *Massey*,[19A] the complainant, then 19, met the appellant, then 35, when she was   **10.96**
already working as a prostitute. She told him of her troubled background, i.e. she
had been taken into care when she was two years old, had committed various
offences and had developed an addiction to drugs. Their relationship developed
and the complainant went to live with the appellant. The relationship was
turbulent. During it, the complainant continued to work as a prostitute. After 10
years she left the appellant and complained to the police that he had forced her to
work as a prostitute and had lived on her earnings. The appellant denied the
allegations. He was charged under s.53 with controlling prostitution for gain and
with living on the earnings of prostitution (s.30(1) of the SOA 1956). At trial, the
complainant said that the appellant took all her money, set up a website for her to
advertise her services and kept a log of the work she did. The appellant was
domineering and violent, and she did what he wanted because she felt intimidated.
The appellant said that he had taken her in through pity, had not liked her working
as a prostitute and had tried to convince her to stop. The judge directed the jury
to the effect that "control" required the complainant to have acted under
compulsion, but did not require proof that the appellant had forced her into
prostitution. The Court of Appeal dismissed an appeal, holding that "control"

---

[19] s.224 and Sch.15, Pt 2.
[19A] [2007] All ER (D) 295 (Oct).

includes, but is not limited to, forcing another to carry out the relevant activity. It can be exercised in a variety of ways, including physical violence and emotional blackmail. But the word does not need to include compulsion, force or coercion. It is enough if the defendant instructed or directed the complainant to carry out the activity of prostitution or to do it in a certain way. The judge had put the matter too high in directing the jury to the effect that the prosecution had to prove an absence of free will. However, the direction as a whole could not have misled the jury on the meaning of "control" and in all the circumstances the appellant's conviction was safe.

10.96A   In *Drew and others*,[20] H.H.J. Rivlin sitting at Southwark Crown Court ruled that "control" in s.53 of the 2003 Act is a "simple everyday word" the meaning of which may embrace compulsion, as one of its more extreme manifestations, but also any one of a number of situations involving the power to exert influence over another person's behaviour in connection with a particular activity. Thus, "control" could well include a person "ordering", "directing", "instructing" or "requiring" a prostitute either to do or not to do something in connection with any of her activities in that capacity, in circumstances in which she is expected, and feels obliged, to comply. The learned judge rejected the suggestion by one defendant that he had not controlled the prostitutes but merely "managed" them, stating that in dictionary after dictionary one of the definitions of the word "manage" includes the word "control". He went on to hold[21] that s.53 may cover, for example, controlling the prostitute's days and hours of employment, where she should work, the price to be charged by her and the commission to be paid to the agency, the services which she shall or shall not render, or the clothing she should or should not wear in the course of her work. The fact that a prostitute may be willing to work on these terms, and be subject to one kind of control or another, may possibly amount to a mitigating circumstance, but cannot affect the issue of criminal responsibility. The judge went on to hold that in the case before him there was sufficient evidence of control to go before the jury: although there was no evidence of compulsion or coercion, there was evidence, including documentary evidence, that the prostitutes were subject to "quite rigorous control", including as to their working times, the services they should offer, the items they were to have with them whilst working, their charges and the arrangements for payment.

10.103   In *Drew and others*,[22] H.H.J. Rivlin sitting at Southwark Crown Court rejected the proposition advanced on behalf of some of the defendants that a charge under s.53 requires proof that the prostitute concerned was exploited by the defendant, as opposed to an equal partner in the business. He said that the section requires only

---

[20] Unreported, December 2006. The case resulted in acquittals and so there will be no appeal.
[21] Citing with approval pp.309–311 of the main work.
[22] *Op. cit.* n.20.

that the defendant acted in the expectation of gain, and the absence of exploitation, whilst it may go to mitigation, cannot extinguish criminal liability.

C. TRAFFICKING

TRAFFICKING INTO THE UK FOR SEXUAL EXPLOITATION

MODE OF TRIAL AND PUNISHMENT

As from a day to be appointed the maximum sentence on summary conviction is **10.108** 12 months' imprisonment: Criminal Justice Act 2003, s.282(2), (3). The increase has no application to offences committed before the substitution takes effect: s.282(4). The offence under s.57 is a specified sexual offence in respect of which a sentence of imprisonment for public protection may be imposed under the Criminal Justice Act 2003.[23]

SENTENCING

For the definitive guideline published by the Sentencing Guidelines Council on **10.109** sentencing under the 2003 Act, see para.1.18. The guideline states that the factors to be taken into consideration in sentencing offences under ss.57–59 (trafficking into, within or out of the UK) are as follows[24]:

"1. The sentences for public protection must be considered in all cases. They are designed to ensure that sexual offenders are not released into the community if they present a significant risk of serious harm.
2. The type of activity covered by the various trafficking offences in the SOA 2003 is broadly the same, the only difference being the geographical area within which the trafficked persons are moved. The harm being addressed is sexual exploitation, but here either children or adults may be involved as victims.
3. The offences are designed to cover anyone involved in any stage of the trafficking operation, whether or not there is evidence of gain. This is serious offending behaviour, which society as a whole finds repugnant, and a financial or community penalty would rarely be an appropriate disposal.
4. The degree of coercion used and the level of control over the trafficked person's liberty will be relevant to assessing the seriousness of the offender's behaviour. The nature of the sexual exploitation to which the victim is exposed will also be relevant, as will the victim's age and vulnerability.
5. In general terms the greater the level of involvement, the more serious the crime. Those at the top of an organised trafficking chain may have very little personal involvement with day-to-day operations and may have no knowledge at all of

---

[23] s.224 and Sch.15, Pt 2.
[24] Pt 6D.

individual victims. However, being in control of a money-making operation that is based on the degradation, exploitation and abuse of vulnerable people may be equally, if not more, serious than the actions of an individual who is personally involved at an operational level.

6. The presence of any of the general aggravating factors identified in the Council guideline on seriousness[25] or any of the additional factors identified in the guidelines will indicate a sentence above the normal starting point.

7. Circumstances such as the fact that the offender is also a victim of trafficking and that their actions were governed by fear could be a mitigating factor if not accepted as a defence.

8. The starting point for sentencing for offences of trafficking for sexual exploitation should be a custodial sentence. Aggravating factors such as participation in a large-scale commercial enterprise involving a high degree of planning, organisation or sophistication, financial or other gain, and the coercion and vulnerability of victims should move sentences towards the maximum 14 years.

9. In cases where a number of children are involved, consecutive sentences may be appropriate, leading to cumulative sentences significantly higher than the suggested starting points for individual offences.

10. Where an offender has profited from his or her involvement in the prostitution of others, the court should consider making a confiscation order[26] approximately equivalent to the profits enjoyed.

11. The court may order the forfeiture of a vehicle used, or intended to be used, in connection with the offence.[27]"

The starting points, sentencing ranges and aggravating and mitigating factors for offences under ss.57–59 are as follows:

Type/nature of activity	Starting points	Sentencing ranges
Involvement at any level in any stage of the trafficking operation where the victim was coerced	6 years custody	4–9 years custody
Involvement at any level in any stage of the trafficking operation where there was no coercion of the victim	2 years custody	1–4 years custody

Note: If the victim is under 13, one of the specific under 13 offences would normally be charged. Any commercial exploitation element would be an aggravating factor.

[25] Issued December 2004.

[26] Under the Criminal Justice Act 1988 as amended by the Proceeds of Crime Act 2002.

[27] Sexual Offences Act 2003, s.60A, as inserted by the Violent Crime Reduction Act 2006, s.54 and Sch.4.

Additional aggravating factors	Additional mitigating factors
1. Large-scale commercial operation	1. Coercion of the offender by a third party
2. High degree of planning or sophistication	2. No evidence of personal gain
3. Large number of people trafficked	3. Limited involvement
4. Substantial financial (in the region of £5,000 and upwards) or other gain	
5. Fraud	
6. Financial extortion of the victim	
7. Deception	
8. Use of force, threats of force or other forms of coercion	
9. Threats against victim or members of victim's family	
10. Abduction or detention	
11. Restriction of victim's liberty	
12. Inhumane treatment	
13. Confiscation of victim's passport	

Two recent sentencing decisions are instructive. In *Attorney General's Reference* **10.109A**
(Nos 129 and 132 of 2006),[28] the Court of Appeal took into account the Sentencing
Guidelines Council's draft guideline which, in relation to the s.57 offence, was
almost identical to the definitive guideline. There were two cases before the Court.
The first involved an enterprise which enabled women from a variety of overseas
countries to enter the UK in order to work as prostitutes. The defendants
controlled the work the prostitutes undertook and received 60 per cent of their
earnings. The defendant Z received some £240,000 during the period of police
surveillance. He admitted his involvement from the outset and pleaded guilty on
arraignment to conspiracy to commit the s.57 offence, conspiracy to control
prostitution for gain (s.53 of the 2003 Act) and an immigration offence. He was
sentenced to seven years' imprisonment for the trafficking offence, four years
concurrent for the prostitution offence and seven years concurrent for the
immigration offence. His female co-defendant, D–F, was convicted following a
trial and sentenced to five years' imprisonment for the trafficking offence, three
years concurrent for the prostitution offence and five years concurrent for the

[28] [2007] EWCA Crim 762.

immigration offence. In the Court of Appeal, Lord Phillips of Worth Matravers C.J., presiding, said[29]:

> "In this case the nature of the immigration assistance was first of all to inform the prostitutes that the easiest way of entering the country was via Ireland, and then to instruct them to fill in their immigration forms with the false information that the purpose for which they were entering the country was tourism. They were then provided with visas to enter the country on that basis. Most of them left before those visas expired. However, instead of spending their time in this country in innocent tourism, they spent their time working as prostitutes. They then returned home, so that there was no long-term increase of illegal immigrants in this country, and indeed never more than four or five at a time as a result of the applicants' activities. It seems to us that the immigration offence was part and parcel of the trafficking offence and, of course, it aggravated that offence.
>
> The remaining elements of the trafficking offence lacked most of the aggravating factors identified by the Sentencing Guidelines Council. There was no deception or coercion. There was assistance for prostitutes who wanted to come to this country —assistance with their entering the country illegally and organisation of their business while they were here on a substantial scale and for a substantial profit."

In the circumstances, the Court considered the sentence imposed on Z to be manifestly excessive. It reduced the sentences for the trafficking and immigration offences to five years' imprisonment concurrent, making a total sentence of five years. As for D-F, the judge had been entitled to treat her more leniently, despite the fact that she did not plead guilty, as she was very much under the control of Z and only received a modest share of the profits of the enterprise. The Court considered her sentence also to be manifestly excessive. It reduced the sentences for the trafficking and immigration offences to four years' imprisonment concurrent, making a total sentence in her case of four years.

10.109B   In the other case before the Court in *Attorney General's Reference (Nos. 129 and 132 of 2006)*, the defendant T was involved in the trafficking of Malaysian women into the UK for the purpose of prostitution at brothels in London and Birmingham. Documents seized by the police showed that T had received very substantial income from the brothels, in the management of which he was involved. Aggravating features were the scale of offending (with receipts in the order of £2 million) and, in one case, the existence of coercion. T was sentenced on guilty pleas to five years' imprisonment for conspiracy to commit the s.57 offence, with a concurrent sentence of $2\frac{1}{2}$ years' imprisonment for an offence under s.53 of controlling prostitution for gain. The Court of Appeal compared his case with that of *Roci and another*,[30] in which there were very late guilty pleas. The offenders in that case were concerned in the importation into the UK and control of prostitutes from Lithuania. The women came to this country willingly, but were coerced to work in unpleasant circumstances and in ways contrary to their wishes and to pay over most of their earnings. The Court considered a sentence of nine

---

[29] At paras 45–6.
[30] [2005] EWCA Crim 3404; [2006] 2 Cr. App. R.(S.) 15. For further pre-guideline sentencing decisions, see *Maka* [2005] EWCA Crim 3365; *Ramaj and Atesogullari* [2006] EWCA Crim 448; *Kizlaite and Axhami* [2006] EWCA Crim 1492.

years' imprisonment to be appropriate in that case. In relation to T, the Court stated:

> "We have compared the facts of this case with those in *Roci*. Although here there was the single case of coercion, the picture in *Roci* is of a much more rigid regime of exploitation, albeit lacking the gravity of the single aggravating feature that we have to deal with. Overall we consider that the two cases are comparable and that the appropriate starting point in this case should have been ten years. From that starting point there fell to be a full reduction for the guilty plea, and then there was the further reduction made by the judge to reflect personal mitigation. Initially we were sceptical as to its justification. However, we are told that the applicant's wife, whose life expectancy is very limited, has returned to Malaysia where she is likely to die in circumstance where the applicant will not see her again.
>
> In these circumstances, have regard to that item of mitigation and to the principle of double jeopardy, we have reached the conclusion that while this was a lenient sentence, it did not amount to a sentence that was unduly lenient so that it should be increased. For that reason we propose to leave the sentence as it stands."

The second instructive decision is *Makai*,[31] in which sentence was passed before **10.109C** publication of the definitive guideline, but the matter came before the Court of Appeal on an appeal against sentence after that date. M, aged 22 and of previous good character, pleaded guilty on arraignment to conspiracy to commit the s.57 offence. He was sentenced to 40 months' imprisonment. M and his co-defendant were involved in recruiting and arranging for Hungarian women to come to the UK to work as prostitutes in brothels here. The women responded to adverts placed by the co-accused on Hungarian websites and bought their own air tickets to the UK. M met them on arrival and passed them on to other men who were more closely involved in the trade. He was paid a fee of about £3,000 a time. The conspiracy to which he pleaded guilty related to two women. They were not prostitutes before they came to the UK, but the prosecution accepted that they would have known for what work they were being recruited. One worked as a prostitute in Glasgow. The other claimed to have been raped by the men to whom she was handed over, before being taken to a brothel. She was then taken to a club in Birmingham and was kept under the control of those in charge of the brothel there, her personal effects and documents of identity being taken from her. The prosecution did not suggest that M or his co-defendant knew what happened to the women once they had been handed over, but the judge approached the case on the basis that they lacked concern as to what the women were being led into.

The Court of Appeal held that the scale of offending in this case was much smaller than in *Attorney General's Reference (Nos 129 and 132 of 2006)* or *Roci*. In particular, M handed over the women to others and was not himself concerned in brothel management. Moreover, the additional aggravating factors listed in the guideline did not apply in M's case save, to a limited extent, "substantial financial (in the region of £5,000 and upwards) or other gain". However, the Court noted the guideline's acknowledgement of the seriousness of the trafficking chain, even in the absence of knowledge of what happens to individual victims.

---

[31] [2007] EWCA Crim 1652.

The Court agreed with the judge on the importance of the risks to women handed on for a fee in the way the complainants in this case were. It noted that M was in his early twenties, without previous convictions, and was entitled to a 20 per cent discount for his late plea. It concluded, not without hesitation, that the sentence of 40 months' imprisonment was manifestly excessive given the comparatively limited scale of the operation and the absence of aggravating factors. The judge did not have the benefit of the definitive guideline and took as his starting point a figure in the appropriate sentencing range, but at the top of it, i.e. four years. A sentence of 30 months' imprisonment would have been appropriate, after a discount for the guilty plea.

TRAFFICKING WITHIN THE UK FOR SEXUAL EXPLOITATION

MODE OF TRIAL AND PUNISHMENT

10.117   As from a day to be appointed the maximum sentence on summary conviction is 12 months' imprisonment: Criminal Justice Act 2003, s.282(2), (3). The increase has no application to offences committed before the substitution takes effect: s.282(4). The offence under s.58 is a specified sexual offence in respect of which a sentence of imprisonment for public protection may be imposed under the Criminal Justice Act 2003.[32]

SENTENCING

10.118   For the definitive guideline published by the Sentencing Guidelines Council on sentencing under the 2003 Act, see para.1.18. The provisions of the guideline relating to offences under s.58 are set out at para.10.109 above.

TRAFFICKING OUT OF THE UK FOR SEXUAL EXPLOITATION

MODE OF TRIAL AND PUNISHMENT

10.126   As from a day to be appointed the maximum sentence on summary conviction is 12 months' imprisonment: Criminal Justice Act 2003, s.282(2), (3). The increase has no application to offences committed before the substitution takes effect: s.282(4). The offence under s.59 is a specified sexual offence in respect of which a sentence of imprisonment for public protection may be imposed under the Criminal Justice Act 2003.[33]

---

[32] s.224 and Sch.15, Pt 2.
[33] s.224 and Sch.15, Pt 2.

SENTENCING

For the definitive guideline published by the Sentencing Guidelines Council on   **10.126**
sentencing under the 2003 Act, see para.1.18. The provisions of the guideline
relating to offences under s.59 are set out at para.10.109 above.

CHAPTER 11

OFF-STREET PROSTITUTION AND RELATED OFFENCES

INTRODUCTION

In July 2004, the Home Office published *Paying the Price: a Consultation Paper on Prostitution*, which was intended to be "the starting point for the development of a realistic and coherent strategy to deal with prostitution".[1] The Paper set out the Government's intentions with regard to prostitution, which were to address the issues of prevention, protection and support, and justice. Following the close of the consultation period, in January 2006 the Home Office published *A Coordinated Prostitution Strategy*. The focus of the strategy is on street prostitution and it is therefore considered in para.12.10 below. In relation to off-street prostitution, the strategy concentrates almost exclusively on the targeting of commercial sexual exploitation, in particular of young or trafficked victims.[2] The implication is that the Government sees off-street prostitution as a significant problem only if it is

11.08

---

[1] Home Secretary's Foreword, p.5. For discussion, see Belinda Brooks-Gordon, *Clients and Commercial Sex: Reflections on Paying the Price: a Consultation Paper on Prostitution* [2005] Crim. L.R. 425.

[2] See generally s.5.

exploitative or causes community concern. This is borne out by the key objectives of the strategy, which are to:

> "● challenge the view that street prostitution is inevitable and here to stay,
> ● achieve an overall reduction in street prostitution,
> ● improve the safety and quality of life of communities affected by prostitution, including those directly involved in street sex markets, and
> ● reduce all forms of commercial sexual exploitation."[3]

There is a distinct sense here of an issue being ducked, not least as it was in relation to off-street prostitution that the responses to *Paying the Price* were most divided. The essential question posed in the consultation paper was: should the off-street market be managed or policed? Some respondents argued for decriminalisation and others for regimes of licensing or registration, but the majority were sceptical of the ability of such regimes to reduce violence and exploitation. There were real concerns based on evidence from overseas that those unwilling or unable to comply with such a regime would be driven into an illegal sector or onto the streets, where it would be harder to address the issues represented by their activities. There were also fears that both the legal and illegal sectors would grow as a result of an increasing acceptance of prostitution. Against that background, the Government decided broadly to maintain the status quo, i.e. to retain the criminalisation of off-street prostitution, but with one significant change. This addresses a concern that the current definition of a "brothel", as premises where two or more women work together, gives an incentive to off-street prostitutes to work in isolation, which in turn inhibits their ability to protect themselves from violence. The Government noted significant support from respondents for a change in the law to allow two or three women to work together without the premises becoming a "brothel" and it undertook to bring forward legislation to effect this change.

One can understand the reasoning behind this proposal, given the vulnerability of women working alone to offences of violence, including robbery. However, the proposal is at least potentially in tension with one of the key objectives of the strategy, which is to improve the quality of life of communities. Quality of life will be affected by nuisance behaviour, and such behaviour is more likely to be associated with premises where two or three prostitutes work together than with premises where one works alone. Fiona Mactaggart, the junior Minister at the Home Office who announced the strategy, was quoted as saying that there would have to be more consultation over how to prevent adverse effects on neighbourhoods: "I'm not trying, by having a clear strategy in the street sex market, to move it from the streets to a series of pairs of women working out of flats and causing a nuisance to their neighbours. But I do think that very small-scale operations can operate in a way which is not disruptive to neighbours."[4] At the time of writing, legislation to amend the definition of a "brothel" has yet to be introduced, despite the opportunity offered by the Criminal Justice and Immigration Bill currently

---

[3] Executive Summary.
[4] *Times*, January 18, 2006.

before Parliament. The Government's hesitation may be connected with the recent reported surge in off-street prostitution, associated in large part with the impact of immigration from Eastern Europe.[5]

KEEPING A BROTHEL

As from a day to be appointed the maximum sentence on summary conviction is   **11.10** 12 months' imprisonment: Criminal Justice Act 2003, s.282(2), (3). The increase has no application to offences committed before the substitution takes effect: s.282(4). The offence under s.33 is a specified sexual offence in respect of which a sentence of imprisonment for public protection may be imposed under the Criminal Justice Act 2003.[6]

KEEPING A BROTHEL USED FOR PROSTITUTION

As from a day to be appointed the maximum sentence on summary conviction is   **11.30** 12 months' imprisonment: Criminal Justice Act 2003, s.282(2), (3). The increase has no application to offences committed before the substitution takes effect: s.282(4). The offence under s.33A is not a specified sexual offence in respect of which a sentence of imprisonment for public protection may be imposed under the Criminal Justice Act 2003.[7]

For the definitive guideline published by the Sentencing Guidelines Council on   **11.32** sentencing under the 2003 Act, see para.1.18. The guideline states that the factors to be taken into consideration in sentencing offences under s.33A (keeping a brothel used for prostitution) are as follows[8]:

> "1. The sentences for public protection must be considered in all cases. They are designed to ensure that sexual offenders are not released into the community if they present a significant risk of serious harm.
>   2. The offence covers anyone who keeps, manages or acts or assists in the management of a brothel. The degree of coercion, both in terms of recruitment and subsequent control of a prostitute's activities, is highly relevant to sentencing.

---

[5] See e.g. *Times*, September 28, 2007, pp.6–7.
[6] s.224 and Sch.15, Pt 2. *Cp.* The offence under s.33A, below.
[7] s.224 and Sch.15, Pt 2. *Cp.* The offence under s.33, above.
[8] Pt 6D.

3. The degree to which a victim is exploited or controlled, the harm suffered as a result, the level of involvement of the offender, the scale of the operation and the timescale over which it has been run will all be relevant in terms of assessing the seriousness of the offence.
4. The presence of any of the general aggravating factors identified in the Council guideline on seriousness[9] or any of the additional factors identified in the guidelines will indicate a sentence above the normal starting point.
5. Where there is evidence that an offender convicted of an exploitation of prostitution offence is not actively involved in the coercion or control of the victim(s), that he or she acted through fear or intimidation and that he or she is trying to exit prostitution, the courts may wish to consider whether, in the particular circumstances of the case, this should mitigate sentence.
6. The starting points are the same whether prostitution was caused or incited and whether or not the incited activity took place. Where the offence was incited, the sentencer should begin from the starting point that the offence was incited, taking account of the nature of the harm that would have been caused had the offence taken place and calculating the final sentence to reflect that no actual harm was occasioned to the victim, but being mindful that the intended victim may have suffered as a result of knowing or believing the offence would take place.
7. A non-custodial sentence may be appropriate for very minimal involvement.
8. Where an offender has profited from his or her involvement in the prostitution of others, the courts should always consider making a confiscation order approximately equivalent to the profits enjoyed.
9. Where this offence is being dealt with in a magistrates' court, more detailed guidance is provided in the Magistrates' Court Sentencing Guidelines (MCSG)."

The starting points, sentencing ranges and aggravating and mitigating factors for the offence under s.33A are as follows:

Type/nature of activity	Starting points	Sentencing ranges
Offender is the keeper of a brothel and has made substantial profits in the region of £5,000 and upwards	2 years custody	1–4 years custody
Offender is the keeper of the brothel and is personally involved in its management	12 months custody	26 weeks–2 years custody
Involvement of the offender was minimal	Community order	An appropriate non-custodial sentence*

* "Non-custodial sentence" in this context suggests a community order or a fine. In most instances, an offence will have crossed the threshold for a community order. However, in accordance with normal sentencing practice, a court is not precluded from imposing a financial penalty where that is determined to be the appropriate sentence.

[9] Issued December 2004.

Additional aggravating factors	Additional mitigating factors
1. Background of threats, intimidation or coercion	1. Using employment as a route out of prostitution and not actively involved in exploitation
2. Large-scale commercial operation	2. Coercion by third party
3. Personal involvement in the prostitution of others	
4. Abduction or detention	
5. Financial or other gain	

The guideline also reminds sentencers that a number of financial orders can be made in addition to the sentence imposed for this offence (viz. confiscation, deprivation and compensation orders).

KEEPING A DISORDERLY HOUSE

MODE OF TRIAL AND PUNISHMENT

As from a day to be appointed the maximum sentence on summary conviction is **11.66** 12 months' imprisonment: Criminal Justice Act 2003, s.282(1). The increase has no application to offences committed before the substitution takes effect: s.282(4). The offence of keeping a disorderly house is not a specified sexual offence in respect of which a sentence of imprisonment for public protection may be imposed under the Criminal Justice Act 2003.[10]

---

[10] s.224 and Sch.15, Pt 2.

STREET-BASED PROSTITUTION

INTRODUCTION

In July 2004, the Home Office published *Paying the Price: a Consultation Paper on* **12.10**
Prostitution, which was intended to be "the starting point for the development of
a realistic and coherent strategy to deal with prostitution"[1]. The Paper set out the
Government's intentions with regard to prostitution, which were to address the
issues of prevention, protection and support, and justice. Following the close of
the consultation period, in January 2006 the Home Office published *A Coordinated
Prostitution Strategy.*[2] The four key objectives of the strategy are to:

"● challenge the view that street prostitution is inevitable and here to stay,
● achieve an overall reduction in street prostitution,
● improve the safety and quality of life of communities affected by
  prostitution, including those directly involved in street sex markets, and
● reduce all forms of commercial sexual exploitation."[3]

Changes to the law and its implementation form a relatively limited part of the **12.10A**
package, with greater emphasis being placed on methods of preventing individuals
becoming involved with prostitution, developing routes out for those already
involved and tackling demand by deterring would-be clients. In the latter context,
the Government considered but rejected the Swedish model of decriminalising
prostitution and instead criminalising clients by making it an offence to purchase
sexual services. Many respondents to *Paying the Price* supported the principles
underpinning the Swedish model and the shift of enforcement away from

[1] Home Secretary's Foreword, p.5.
[2] Home Office, January 2006.
[3] Executive Summary.

prostitutes onto those who create a demand for their services.[4] The Government was unpersuaded, citing the differences between the size and nature of the problem in the two countries (1,500 prostitutes in Sweden when the law was changed, an estimated 80,000 in the UK, many of whom, unlike in Sweden, suffer from severe addiction problems). But it did accept that the activities of kerb crawlers are a particular nuisance to communities, and that enforcement of the law against them does have a deterrent effect. So the Government proposes to put kerb crawlers at the heart of local enforcement strategies, in a staged approach: first, using CCTV to identify cars that regularly cruise red light areas and sending the owners a letter warning that they risk prosecution if they return; if that does not work then, for first offenders, offering a place on a re-education programme as an alternative to prosecution or as a condition of a caution; and if all else fails, prosecuting, with encouragement to the courts to use the full range of penalties, including disqualification from driving, and encouragement to the media to name and shame those who are convicted. The strategy separately notes evidence submitted by some respondents that increased enforcement against kerb crawlers will place prostitutes in greater danger, by reducing their opportunities to satisfy themselves that potential clients are "safe". This evidence does not appear to have influenced the strategy.

12.10B   Some respondents to the consultation paper favoured repealing the offence of loitering or soliciting in the street by a common prostitute (s.1 of the Street Offences Act 1959), to reduce the stigmatisation of women and the inhibition they may feel in seeking help and support. The Government accepted that enforcement alone has no long-term effect on street prostitution and tends simply to displace it to other areas or to other forms of criminal activity. But it also said that decriminalisation would send out the wrong message about the acceptability of street prostitution, and make it harder to control the nuisance associated with the street sex trade. So it proposed that the loitering and soliciting offence should be retained, but that the available penalties should be better tailored to meet the needs of prostitutes and to address the factors that keep them on the streets. The Government noted that the offence is a low-level one and at present the courts will usually only consider a fine, which leads to a "revolving door" syndrome as prostitutes go back onto the streets in order to fund their fines. It therefore proposed to introduce a more rehabilitative approach, allowing the courts to order an "appropriate package of interventions" to address the causes of persistent offending behaviour. Part of the reform would involve removing the outdated and offensive concept of "common prostitute", as first recommended by the Criminal Law Revision Committee as long ago as 1984.[5]

---

[4] For argument in favour of criminalizing the use of prostitutes, see M. Madden Dempsey, *Rethinking Wolfenden: Prostitute-use, Criminal law and remote harm* [2005] Crim. L.R. 444.
[5] Sixteenth Report, Prostitution in the Street, Cmnd. 9329 (1984), para.17.

These changes will be implemented by the Criminal Justice and Immigration Bill, which is currently before Parliament.[6] Clause 71 of the Bill removes the concept of "common prostitute" from the loitering and soliciting offence and introduces in its place a requirement of persistence, which aims to capture the essence of the epithet "common" without the offensive overtones. In parallel, the clause removes the little-used provisions whereby a person who was unjustly cautioned for the offence could apply to a magistrates' court for an order that the caution should not be recorded or that the record of it should be expunged. Clause 72 makes provision for the courts to deal with persons convicted of the offence by way of a new form of order to promote rehabilitation instead of by way of criminal punishment. Such orders will require the offender to attend three meetings with a suitably qualified person ("the supervisor"), with the aim of assisting them to address the causes of their offending behaviour and find ways to stop engaging in it.

12.10C The Government also declared an intention to use ASBOs to address the nuisance caused by the behaviour of prostitutes. It admitted that many respondents to *Paying the Price* criticised the effectiveness of ASBOs, some saying that they tend to displace prostitution to other geographical areas and so drive the women away from local support services, others that they fail to address the underlying reasons for the women's involvement in prostitution. The English Collective of Prostitutes stated that ASBOs have operated essentially to re-introduce prison sentences for the offence of loitering and soliciting, some 20 years after they were abolished by s.71 of the Criminal Justice Act 1982. In short, there appears to be little support for the use of ASBOs in this context. Despite this, the Government concluded that they have a role to play in addressing the nuisance to communities associated with street prostitution, as part of a package of measures designed to encourage prostitutes to engage with support services. It said it would be issuing guidance on the subject, which would include advice on how ASBOs, and Acceptable Behaviour Contracts, can be used effectively as part of an overall strategy designed to help those involved in prostitution to get out of it, and advice on drafting prohibitions that do not prevent women accessing support services.

12.10D As regards young people involved in prostitution, there was a wide consensus amongst respondents to the consultation paper in favour of decriminalising loitering and soliciting by those under 18, on the basis that criminalisation tends to undermine the message that they are victims of child abuse. The Government noted that its *Guidance on Safeguarding Children Involved in Prostitution* (published in 2000) requires young people to be treated primarily as victims of abuse, and that since its issue the numbers of cautions and prosecutions of those under 18 have dropped dramatically, to three convictions in 2004. Against that background, the Government's favoured approach is not decriminalisation for under 18s but, as with adults, encouraging the law to operate in a way that provides opportunities

---

[6] The Bill's First Reading was on June 26, 2007.

for diversion into contact with support services that will help young people to get out of prostitution. To this end, it intends to relaunch the existing (2000) guidance to re-emphasise that the criminal law is not to be used against children save in the most exceptional circumstances and as a last resort. It is worth adding in this context that the Government has also been instrumental in setting up the Child Exploitation and Online Protection Centre (CEOP), which is part of the Serious Organised Crime Agency but with its own "brand" and operational freedom. The aim of CEOP, which began work in April 2006, is to bring an holistic approach to bear on the problem of child sexual abuse in the UK and overseas, by combining intelligence-led investigations, law enforcement, victim protection and support, and risk reduction through the education of children particularly about the dangers lurking on the internet.

12.10E Finally, the Government proposed to address the commercial sexual exploitation of individuals involved in prostitution through proactive policing and use of the "robust legal framework" created by the SOA 2003. So there would be no change in the law in this area, but instead the Government would issue guidance on effective investigation and witness support and encourage the reporting of offences (with CEOP as one vehicle for this). In terms of witness support, the Government acknowledged that some respondents had called for adult as well as child victims of prostitution to be treated as vulnerable witnesses for the purposes of the special measures provisions of the Youth Justice and Criminal Evidence Act 1999. It did not reject these calls, but neither did it take them up, simply stating that adult complainants of sexual offences are automatically eligible for special measures, but that to engage the measures, it must be shown that the quality of their evidence is likely to be improved or maximised as far as practicable.

12.10F The responses to the strategy were mixed. It was welcomed by ACPO and by organisations working with children, including the Children's Society and Barnardo's. The Conservative Party criticised it, their spokesman saying "policy cannot simply focus on demand . . . We need to focus on the underlying social problems which force men, women and children into prostitution, such as family breakdown, drug misuse, child abuse, domestic violence and debt." This criticism is perhaps unfair, given that the need to address underlying issues is the theme running through the strategy. The Lib Dems took a more regretful tone, calling the strategy a "missed opportunity" and saying that it would do "very little to reduce the number of prostitutes on the street, to improve the appalling conditions they work in, or to tackle health problems". They favoured the piloting of "managed zones" in designated city areas, a possibility which is in fact considered but rejected in the strategy. The English Collective of Prostitutes, on the other hand, was outraged, calling the proposals "a brutality" and stating that "clamping down on clients does not make women safer, it makes the lives of women more dangerous". In terms of its overall approach, the Collective appears to line up with the Conservative Party, sharing their view that the strategy does not deal with the fundamental issue that "poverty and debt and drug misuse are sending women into the sex industry".

MEANING OF "COMMON PROSTITUTE"

The concept of "common prostitute" will be removed from the loitering and soliciting offence in s.1(1) of the Street Offences Act 1959 by clause 71 of the Criminal Justice and Immigration Bill, which is currently before Parliament: see para.12.10B above.   **12.11**

LOITERING OR SOLICITING BY A COMMON PROSTITUTE

DEFINITION

Clause 71 of the Criminal Justice and Immigration Bill, which is currently before Parliament, will amend s.1(1) of the 1959 Act by substituting "person" for "common prostitute" and inserting "persistently" after "female)". If the Bill is passed, the offence as so amended will read: **12.17**

> "It shall be an offence for a person (whether male or female) persistently to loiter or solicit in a street or public place for the purpose of prostitution."

Clause 71 will also amend s.1(4) of the 1959 Act by inserting the following definition of "persistent":

> "(a) conduct is persistent if it takes place on two or more occasions in any period of three months;
> (b) any reference to a person loitering or soliciting for the purposes of prostitution is a reference to a person loitering or soliciting for the purposes of offering services as a prostitute."

MODE OF TRIAL AND PUNISHMENT

The Criminal Justice and Immigration Bill, currently before Parliament, will insert into the 1959 Act new provisions empowering the courts to make orders to promote the rehabilitation of persons convicted of the offence instead of imposing any form of punishment: see para.12.10B above. Clause 72 of the Bill will insert new subss.(2A)–(2D) into s.1 of the Act and a new s.1A, as follows: **12.18**

> "(2A) The court may deal with a person convicted of an offence under this section by making an order under this subsection requiring the offender to attend three meetings with the person for the time being specified in the order ("the supervisor") or with such other person as the supervisor may direct.
> (2B) The purpose of an order under subsection (2A) is to promote the offender's rehabilitation by assisting the offender, through attendance at those meetings, to—
> (a) address the causes of the conduct constituting the offence; and
> (b) find ways to cease engaging in such conduct in the future.

(2C) Where the court is dealing with an offender who is already subject to an order under subsection (2A) ('the original order'), the court may not make a further order under that subsection unless it first revokes the original order.

(2D) If the court makes an order under subsection (2A) it may not impose any other penalty in respect of the offence.

1A. Orders under section 1(2A): supplementary

(1) This section applies where a court proposes to make an order under subsection (2A) of section 1 in relation to a person convicted of an offence under that section ('the offender').

(2) The order may not be made unless a suitable person has agreed to act as supervisor in relation to the offender.

(3) In subsection (2) 'suitable person' means a person appearing to the court to have appropriate qualifications or experience for helping the offender to make the best use of the meetings for the purpose mentioned in section 1(2B).

(4) The order must specify—

    (a) a date (not more than six months after the date of the order) by which the meetings required by the order must take place;

    (b) the local justice area in which the offender resides or will reside while the order is in force.

(5) The meetings required by the order shall take place at such times and places as the supervisor may determine and shall be of such duration as he may determine.

(6) It is the duty of the supervisor—

    (a) to make any arrangements that are necessary to enable the meetings required by the order to take place; and

    (b) once the order has been complied with, to notify the court which made the order of that fact.

(7) The court making the order must forthwith provide copies of it to the offender and the supervisor.

(8) Subsection (9) applies where—

    (a) the order is made by the Crown Court, or

    (b) the order is made by a magistrates' court but specifies a local justice area for which the court making the order does not act.

(9) The court must provide to a magistrates' court acting for the local justice area specified in the order—

    (a) a copy of the order, and

    (b) any documents and information relating to the case that it considers likely to be of assistance to that court in the exercise of any functions in relation to the order.

(10) An order under section 1(2A) (other than an order that is revoked under section 1(2C) or under the Schedule to this Act) ceases to be in force—

    (a) at the end of the day on which the supervisor notifies the court that the order has been complied with, or

    (b) at the end of the day specified in the order under subsection (4)(a), whichever first occurs."

The Bill will also insert into the 1959 Act a Schedule containing detailed provisions relating to breaches of rehabilitation orders and the amendment of orders.[7] Finally, it will amend the Rehabilitation of Offenders Act 1974 so that the rehabilitation period applicable to a rehabilitation order under s.1(2A) of the 1959 Act will be six months from the date of conviction for the offence in respect of

[7] See Sch.14 to the Bill.

which the order is made. If, after the end of the rehabilitation period, the offender is dealt with again for the offence for which the order was made, and the rehabilitation period applicable to the conviction (taking into account any sentence imposed when so dealing with the offender) ends later than the rehabilitation period previously applicable, the offender shall be treated as not having become a rehabilitated person in respect of that conviction, and that conviction shall for those purposes be treated as not having become spent, in relation to any period falling before the end of the new rehabilitation period.

"COMMON PROSTITUTE"

See para.12.11 above. 12.21

THE CAUTIONING SYSTEM

The non-statutory cautioning system will presumably be abolished once the 12.33 amendments made by the Criminal Justice and Immigration Bill are in force: see paras 12.10B, 12.18 above.

APPLICATION TO COURT BY PERSON CAUTIONED FOR LOITERING OR SOLICITING

Section 2 of the 1959 Act will be repealed by clause 71 of the Criminal Justice and 12.34 Immigration Bill, currently before Parliament: see para.12.10B above.

POWER OF ARREST

Section 1(3) of the 1959 Act was repealed by the Serious Organised Crime and 12.36 Police Act 2005,[8] with effect from January 1, 2006. The general police powers of arrest are set out in s.24 of the Police and Criminal Evidence Act 1984, as substituted by s.110 of the 2005 Act. They empower a constable to arrest a person if he has reasonable grounds for believing that the arrest is necessary inter alia to prevent the person committing an offence against public decency, but only where members of the public going about their normal business cannot reasonably be expected to avoid the person.[9]

ADVERTISING BY OR ON BEHALF OF PROSTITUTES

Footnote 88: Section 24 of the Police and Criminal Evidence Act 1984 was 12.41 substituted by the Serious and Organised Crime and Police Act 2005, s.110: see para.12.36 above.

[8] s.111 and Sch.7, Pt I, para.14.
[9] s.24(4), (5)(c)(iv) and (6).

KERB CRAWLING

DEFINITION

12.43 Footnote 92: Section 24 of the Police and Criminal Evidence Act 1984 was substituted by the Serious and Organised Crime and Police Act 2005, s.110: see para.12.36 above.

ANTI-SOCIAL BEHAVIOUR ORDERS

12.70 For guidance on the making of ASBOs under s.1C of the 1998 Act following conviction of a criminal offence, see *W (A juvenile) v Acton Youth Court*,[10] *Boness and Bebbington*[11] and *W (A juvenile) and another v R*.[12] In the last of these cases, the Court of Appeal set out the following principles:

"(1) Proceedings under section 1C of the 1998 Act are civil in nature, so that hearsay evidence is admissible. But a court must be satisfied to a criminal standard that the defendant has acted in the anti-social manner alleged: see *R. (McCann) v. Crown Court at Manchester* [2003] 1 A.C. 787, para 37.

(2) The test of 'necessity' set out in section 1C(2)(b) of the 1998 Act requires the exercise of judgment or evaluation; it does not require proof beyond reasonable doubt that the order is 'necessary': *McCann*'s case, para 37.

(3) The findings of fact giving rise to the making of the order must be recorded by the court: see the Criminal Procedure Rules 2005, rule 50.4, the form set out in Practice Direction (Criminal Proceedings: Consolidation) [2002] 1 W.L.R. 2870 and *R. v. P. (Shane)* [2004] 2 Cr.App.R.(S.) 343, para 34. We regard this as particularly important.

(4) The terms of the order made must be precise and capable of being understood by the offender: *R. v. P.*, para 34.

(5) The conditions in the order must be enforceable in the sense that the conditions should allow a breach to be readily identified and capable of being proved. Therefore the conditions should not impose generic prohibitions, but should identify and prohibit the particular type of anti-social behaviour that gives rise to the necessity of an anti-social behaviour order: *R. v. Boness* [2006] 1 Cr.App.R.(S.) 690, para 22.

(6) There is power under section 1C(5) of the 1998 Act to suspend the starting point of an anti-social behaviour order until an offender has been released from a custodial sentence. However, where custodial sentences in excess of a few months are passed and the offender is liable to be released on licence and is thus subject to recall, the circumstances in which there would be a demonstrable necessity to make a suspended anti-social behaviour order, to take effect on release, will be limited. But there might be cases where geographical restraints could supplement licence conditions: *R. v. Boness*, para 25.

---

[10] [2005] EWHC 954 (Admin).
[11] [2005] EWCA Crim 2395; [2006] Crim. L.R. 160.
[12] [2006] EWCA Crim 686; [2007] 1 W.L.R. 339.

(7) Because the test for making an anti-social behaviour order and prohibiting an offender from doing something is one of necessity, each separate order prohibiting a person from doing a specified thing must be necessary to protect persons from anti-social behaviour by the offender. Therefore each order must be specifically fashioned to deal with the offender concerned. The court has to ask, 'is this order necessary to protect persons in any place in England and Wales from further anti-social acts by him?': *R. v. Boness*, para 29.

(8) Not all conditions set out in an anti-social behaviour order have to run for the full term of the anti-social behaviour order itself. The test must always be is what is necessary to deal with the particular anti-social behaviour of the offender and what is proportionate in the circumstances: *R. v. Boness*, paras 27, 29 and 37.

(9) The order is there to protect others from anti-social behaviour by the offender. Therefore the court should not impose an order which prohibits an offender from committing specified criminal offences if the sentence which could be passed following conviction (or a guilty plea) for the offence should be a sufficient deterrent: *R. v. Boness*, para 31.

(10) It is unlawful to make an anti-social behaviour order as if it were a further sentence or punishment. An anti-social behaviour order must therefore not be used merely to increase the sentence of imprisonment that the offender is to receive: *R. v. Boness*, para 33."

Although the Act requires the offender to have acted anti-socially after the commencement date, the court is entitled to consider the totality of the offender's behaviour when determining the necessity for an ASBO, including behaviour occurring before that date: *McGrath*.[13]

---

[13] [2005] EWCA Crim 353; [2005] 2 Cr. App. R.(S.) 85.

CHAPTER 13

PREPARATORY OFFENCES

ADMINISTERING A SUBSTANCE WITH INTENT

MODE OF TRIAL AND PUNISHMENT

As from a day to be appointed the maximum sentence on summary conviction is **13.09**
12 months' imprisonment: Criminal Justice Act 2003, s.282(2), (3). The increase
has no application to offences committed before the substitution takes effect:
s.282(4). The offence under s.61 is a specified sexual offence in respect of which
a sentence of imprisonment for public protection may be imposed under the
Criminal Justice Act 2003.[1]

SENTENCING

For the definitive guideline published by the Sentencing Guidelines Council in **13.11**
relation to sentencing for offences under the 2003 Act, see para.1.18. In relation
to the offence under s.61, the guideline states that the factors to take into
consideration are as follows:

> "1. The sentences for public protection must be considered in all cases. They are
>   designed to ensure that sexual offenders are not released into the community if
>   they present a significant risk of serious harm.
> 2. In a case where no substantive sexual offence has in fact been committed, the main
>   dimension of seriousness will be the offender's intention—the more serious the
>   offence intended, the higher the offender's culpability. This is equally so where
>   the offence is committed by an offender for the benefit of another.
> 3. The harm to the victim in such cases will invariably be less than that resulting
>   from a completed offence, although the risk to which the victim has been put is
>   always a relevant factor.

---

[1] s.224 and Sch.15, Pt 2.

4. In some cases, where the offender has come quite close to fulfilling his or her intention, the victim may have been put in considerable fear, and physical injury to the victim is a possible feature, in particular for this offence.
5. In addition to the generic aggravating factors identified in the Council guideline on seriousness,[2] the main factors determining the seriousness of a preparatory offence are:
   - the seriousness of the intended offence (which will affect both the offender's culpability and the degree of risk to which the victim has been exposed);
   - the degree to which the offence was planned;
   - the determination of the offender;
   - how close the offender came to success;
   - the reason why the offender did not succeed, i.e. whether it was a change of mind or whether someone or something prevented the offender from continuing; and any physical or psychological injury suffered by the victim.
6. The starting point should be commensurate with that for the preparatory offence actually committed, with an enhancement to reflect the nature and severity of the intended sexual offence."

The starting points, sentencing ranges and aggravating and mitigating factors for the s.61 offence are as follows:

Type/nature of activity	Starting points	Sentencing ranges
If intended offence is rape or assault by penetration	**8 years custody** if the victim is under 18 **6 years custody** otherwise	**6–9 years custody** **4–9 years custody**
If intended offence is any sexual offence other than rape or assault by penetration	**6 years custody** if the victim is under 13 **4 years custody** otherwise	**4–9 years custody** **3–7 years custody**

Additional aggravating factors	Additional mitigating factors
1. Threats to prevent the victim reporting an offence 2. Abduction or detention 3. Offender aware that he or she, or the person planning to commit the sexual offence, is suffering from a sexually transmitted infection 4. Targeting of the victim	1. Offender intervenes to prevent the intended sexual offence from taking place

[2] Issued December 2004.

A person convicted[3] under s.61 is automatically subject to notification requirements in accordance with the SOA 2003, s.80 and Sch.3.

MENTAL ELEMENT

In the light of the decision in *Heard*,[4] discussed in para.2.72 above, the   **13.20**
requirement that the defendant did the prohibited act with the intention of
stupefying or overpowering B, so as to enable any person to engage in a sexual
activity that involves B, makes the s.61 offence one of specific intent, such that
voluntary intoxication through drink or drugs will provide a defence if it may have
prevented the defendant forming that intention.

COMMITTING AN OFFENCE WITH INTENT TO COMMIT A
SEXUAL OFFENCE

MODE OF TRIAL AND PUNISHMENT

As from a day to be appointed the maximum sentence on summary conviction is   **13.24**
12 months' imprisonment: Criminal Justice Act 2003, s.282(2), (3). The increase
has no application to offences committed before the substitution takes effect:
s.282(4). The offence under s.62 is a specified sexual offence in respect of which
a sentence of imprisonment for public protection may be imposed under the
Criminal Justice Act 2003.[5]

SENTENCING

For the definitive guideline published by the Sentencing Guidelines Council in   **13.27**
relation to sentencing for offences under the 2003 Act, see para.1.18. In relation
to the offence under s.62, the guideline assumes that the intended offence was not
committed. It states that the factors to take into consideration are as follows:

> "1. The sentences for public protection must be considered in all cases. They are
> designed to ensure that sexual offenders are not released into the community if
> they present a significant risk of serious harm. Within any indeterminate sentence,
> the minimum term will generally be half the appropriate determinate sentence.
> The starting points will be relevant, therefore, to the process of fixing any
> minimum term that may be necessary.

---

[3] Or found not guilty by reason of insanity, found to be under a disability and to have done the act
charged, or cautioned.
[4] [2007] EWCA Crim 125.
[5] s.224 and Sch.15, Pt 2.

2. In a case where no substantive sexual offence has in fact been committed, the main dimension of seriousness will be the offender's intention—the more serious the offence intended, the higher the offender's culpability.

3. The harm to the victim in such cases will invariably be less than that resulting from a completed offence, although the risk to which the victim has been put is always a relevant factor.

4. In some cases, where the offender has come quite close to fulfilling his or her intention, the victim may have been put in considerable fear, and physical injury to the victim is a possible feature.

5. In addition to the generic aggravating factors identified in the Council guideline on seriousness,[6] the main factors determining the seriousness of a preparatory offence are:
   - the seriousness of the intended offence (which will affect both the offender's culpability and the degree of risk to which the victim has been exposed);
   - the degree to which the offence was planned;
   - the determination of the offender;
   - how close the offender came to success;
   - the reason why the offender did not succeed, i.e. whether it was a change of mind or whether someone or something prevented the offender from continuing; and
   - any physical or psychological injury suffered by the victim.

6. The starting point should be commensurate with that for the preparatory offence actually committed, with an enhancement to reflect the nature and severity of the intended sexual offence."

The starting points, sentencing ranges and aggravating and mitigating factors for the s.62 offence are as follows:

Type/nature of activity	Starting points and sentencing ranges
Any offence committed with intent to commit a sexual offence, e.g. assault (see item 4 of "Factors to take into consideration" above)	The starting point and sentencing range should be commensurate with that for the preliminary offence actually committed, but with an enhancement to reflect the intention to commit a sexual offence The enhancement will need to be varied depending on the nature and seriousness of the intended sexual offence, but 2 years is suggested as a suitable enhancement where the intent was to commit rape or an assault by penetration

[6] Issued December 2004.

Additional aggravating factors	Additional mitigating factors
1. Use of drugs, alcohol or other substance to facilitate the offence

2. Offender aware that he or she is suffering from a sexually transmitted infection (where the intended offence would have involved penile penetration) | 1. Offender decides, of his or her own volition, not to proceed with the intended sexual offence

2. Incident of brief duration |

A person convicted[7] under s.62 is automatically subject to notification requirements in accordance with the SOA 2003, s.80 and Sch.3, if (a) where he was under 18 at the time of the offence, he is sentenced to at least 12 months' imprisonment or (b) in any other case, the intended victim was under 18 and the offender is, in respect of the offence, sentenced to a term of imprisonment, detained in a hospital or given a community sentence of at least 12 months.

An example of sentencing that pre-dates the guideline but remains instructive is **13.27A** *Wisniewski*.[8] The appellant pleaded guilty to two offences of battery with intent to commit a sexual offence and received consecutive sentences of two and five years' imprisonment. On appeal against sentence, the Court of Appeal said that in cases of battery with intent, the factors of particular relevance to sentence include the method and degree of force used; the nature and extent of the indecency perpetrated and intended; the degree of vulnerability of and harm to the victim; the duration and general circumstances of the attack, including the time, day and place where it occurred; and the level of risk posed by the offender to the public. In the present case, both attacks took place in the middle of the night when the victim was alone and there was no one else about. No weapon was used, no blows were struck, and the indecency that actually occurred was of a limited nature. In the first attack, the violence was limited and the victim sustained only slight physical injuries, though she was obviously upset. In the second, the violence was greater, more prolonged and accompanied by more persistence in pursuit of sexual activity, which, it was common ground, the appellant intended should be rape. The victim was deeply upset and, in view of the appellant's denials, had to undergo the ordeal of attending an identification parade. The fact that the two offences took place within the space of a week was a seriously aggravating feature. Although the appellant was entitled to a discount for his guilty plea, it would have been higher had he made admissions in interview, before the identification parade took place. Taking all those circumstances into account, the Court quashed the two

---

[7] Or found not guilty by reason of insanity, found to be under a disability and to have done the act charged, or cautioned.
[8] [2004] EWCA Crim 3361.

sentences and substituted sentences of 18 months' and three-and-a-half years' imprisonment respectively, making a total sentence of five years.

"Any Offence"

13.30   The width of the s.62 offence is demonstrated by *Jones*,[9] where the appellant was convicted of criminal damage with intent to commit a sexual offence after he left graffiti messages on toilet doors in trains and stations seeking girls aged 8–13 for sex and giving a mobile telephone number.

Mental Element

13.32   In the light of the decision in *Heard*,[10] discussed in para.2.72 above, the requirement that the defendant did the prohibited act with the intention of committing a sexual offence makes the s.62 offence one of specific intent, such that voluntary intoxication through drink or drugs will provide a defence if it may have prevented the defendant forming that intention.

TRESPASS WITH INTENT TO COMMIT A SEXUAL OFFENCE

Mode of Trial and Punishment

13.36   As from a day to be appointed the maximum sentence on summary conviction is 12 months' imprisonment: Criminal Justice Act 2003, s.282(2), (3). The increase has no application to offences committed before the substitution takes effect: s.282(4). The offence under s.63 is a specified sexual offence in respect of which a sentence of imprisonment for public protection may be imposed under the Criminal Justice Act 2003.[11]

Sentencing

13.38   For the definitive guideline published by the Sentencing Guidelines Council in relation to sentencing for offences under the 2003 Act, see para.1.18. In relation to the offence under s.63, the guideline states that the factors to take into consideration are as follows:

> "1. The sentences for public protection must be considered in all cases. They are designed to ensure that sexual offenders are not released into the community if they present a significant risk of serious harm.

[9] [2007] EWCA Crim 1118, discussed in para.3.63, above.
[10] [2007] EWCA Crim 125.
[11] s.224 and Sch.15, Pt 2.

196

2. In a case where no substantive sexual offence has in fact been committed, the main dimension of seriousness will be the offender's intention—the more serious the offence intended, the higher the offender's culpability.

3. The harm to the victim in such cases will invariably be less than that resulting from a completed offence, although the risk to which the victim has been put is always a relevant factor.

4. In some cases, where the offender has come quite close to fulfilling his or her intention, the victim may have been put in considerable fear, and physical injury to the victim is a possible feature.

5. In addition to the generic aggravating factors identified in the Council guideline on seriousness,[12] the main factors determining the seriousness of a preparatory offence are:
   - the seriousness of the intended offence (which will affect both the offender's culpability and the degree of risk to which the victim has been exposed);
   - the degree to which the offence was planned;
   - the determination of the offender;
   - how close the offender came to success;
   - the reason why the offender did not succeed, i.e. whether it was a change of mind or whether someone or something prevented the offender from continuing; and any physical or psychological injury suffered by the victim.

6. The starting point should be commensurate with that for the preparatory offence actually committed, with an enhancement to reflect the nature and severity of the intended sexual offence."

The starting points, sentencing ranges and aggravating and mitigating factors for the s.63 offence are as follows:

Type/nature of activity	Starting points	Sentencing ranges
The intention is to commit rape or an assault by penetration	4 years custody	3–7 years custody
The intended sexual offence is other than rape or assault by penetration	2 years custody	1–4 years custody
Consensual sexual touching involving naked genitalia	12 months custody	26 weeks–2 years custody
Consensual sexual touching of naked body parts but not involving naked genitalia	26 weeks custody	4 weeks–18 months custody

[12] Issued December 2004.

Additional aggravating factors	Additional mitigating factors
1. Offender aware that he or she is suffering from a sexually transmitted infection (where intended offence would have involved penile penetration)	1. Offender decides, of his or her own volition, not to commit the intended sexual offence
2. Targeting of a vulnerable victim	
3. Significant impact on persons present in the premises	

A person convicted[13] under s.63 is automatically subject to notification requirements in accordance with the SOA 2003, s.80 and Sch.3, if (a) where he was under 18 at the time of the offence, he is sentenced to at least 12 months' imprisonment or (b) in any other case, the intended victim was under 18 and the offender is, in respect of the offence, sentenced to a term of imprisonment, detained in a hospital or given a community sentence of at least 12 months.

MENTAL ELEMENT

13.46   In the light of the decision in *Heard*,[14] discussed in para.2.72 above, the requirement that the defendant did the prohibited act (i.e. trespassed) with the intention of committing a sexual offence makes the s.63 offence one of specific intent, such that voluntary intoxication through drink or drugs will provide a defence if it may have prevented the defendant forming that intention.

---

[13] Or found not guilty by reason of insanity, found to be under a disability and to have done the act charged, or cautioned.
[14] [2007] EWCA Crim 125.

CHAPTER 14

OFFENCES AGAINST PUBLIC DECENCY

INTRODUCTION

In *Rimmington; Goldstein,*[1] the House of Lords held, in relation to the common law   **14.03**
offence of public nuisance, that where conduct formerly covered by the offence has
been made the subject of express statutory provision, good practice and respect for
the primacy of statute requires that the matter should be prosecuted under the
relevant statute unless there is good reason for doing otherwise. Further, securing
a higher maximum penalty cannot ordinarily amount to such a reason. The
decision no doubt applies also to the common law offence of outraging public
decency, though the breadth of that offence is such that it may be difficult to
determine in any particular case whether conduct formerly covered by it is now
covered by an express statutory provision. Take, for example, the facts of *Cosco,*[2]
where the appellant was convicted, just before the commencement of the Sexual
Offences Act 2003, on three counts of outraging public decency on evidence that
he had exposed his private parts on a crowded beach, on one occasion whilst trying
to talk to some children. Exposure of the genitals is now an offence under s.66 of
the 2003 Act, but the offence is committed only where the defendant intends that
someone will see his genitals and be caused alarm or distress. There was evidence
in *Cosco* that the appellant had been trying to hide what he was doing with a rolled-
up newspaper, which indicates that he did not intend anyone to see him, let alone
be alarmed or distressed. This suggests that, if the facts were to recur, a
prosecution under s.66 would not be feasible. Yet the appellant's conduct seems

[1] [2005] UKHL 63.
[2] [2005] EWCA Crim 207.

199

clearly deserving of criminal punishment. That being said, we suggest that a prosecution for the common law offence would still be in order, despite the enactment of s.66, and that the need to discourage such behaviour supplies the "good reason" required by *Rimmington; Goldstein.*

OUTRAGING PUBLIC DECENCY

Definition

14.25   On the relationship between the common law offence and the new statutory offences in ss.66, 67 and 70 of the Sexual Offences Act 2003, see the discussion in para.14.03 above.

Mode of Trial and Punishment

14.26   As from a day to be appointed the maximum sentence on summary conviction is 12 months' imprisonment: Criminal Justice Act 2003, s.282(1). The increase has no application to offences committed before the substitution takes effect: s.282(4).

"A Lewd, Obscene or Disgusting Act"

14.30   In *Kirk,*[3] the Court of Appeal held that the words "indecent" and "obscene" in s.85(4) of the Postal Services Act 2000 (offence of sending by post a postal packet on which there are words, marks or designs of an indecent or obscene character) are ordinary words of the English language that would be readily understood by members of a jury. It is unnecessary and postentially misleading for the jury to be given any interpretation of the words, using other words which might narrow or enlarge their meaning. A simple direction using the words "indecent" and "obscene" will be sufficient, and it will be for the jury to set the standard. The Court did not refer to the statement of Lord Parker, C.J., in *Stanley.* Accordingly, after *Kirk,* the safer course for a judge directing a jury on s.85(4) of the 2000 Act is to avoid elaborating in any way the meaning of "indecent" and "obscene". We nonetheless suggest that the statement in *Stanley* remains valid and potentially of assistance in directing a jury in relation to the meaning of the term "lewd, obscne or disgusting act" for the purposes of the offence of outraging public decency.

"Outrage to Public Decency"

14.33   On the meaning of "indecent", see *Kirk,*[4] above para.14.30.

---

[3] [2006] EWCA Crim 725; Crim. L.R. 850.
[4] [2006] EWCA Crim 725; Crim. L.R. 850.

THE "TWO PERSON" RULE

In *Hamilton*,[5] the Court of Appeal held that the "two person" rule does not   **14.40** require anyone actually to witness the defendant's act; it is sufficient that at least two people are present and capable of seeing the act should they happen to look. The appellant admitted "up-skirting" in supermarkets, i.e. taking video footage up the skirts of women shoppers using a camera positioned in a rucksack. Neither the women he filmed nor anyone else had ever noticed what he was doing. He was caught only when police raided his house and found the footage. It was accepted that there must have been a direct line of sight between the camera lens and the object which was being filmed. On that basis the prosecution contended that the lens must have been visible, so that what the appellant was doing could have been seen at the supermarkets. He disputed this, arguing that there was no evidence that his conduct was seen by anyone and therefore it lacked the public element required for the offence to be committed. The trial judge rejected the appellant's argument and directed the jury that it was sufficient if there was a real possibility, when the appellant carried out the filming, that at least two people would have been able to see it if they had looked. The arguments were rehearsed before the Court of Appeal, which exhaustively analysed the case law and concluded as follows[6]:

> "In our view it is necessary to have regard to the purpose of the two person rule; it goes solely to the necessity that there be a public element in the sense of more than one being present and capable of being affected by it. There is in our view no reason to confine the requirement more restrictively and require actual sight or sound of the nature of the act. The public element in the offence is satisfied if the act is done where persons are present and the nature of what is being done is capable of being seen; the principle is that the public are to be protected from acts of a lewd, obscene or disgusting act which are of a nature that outrages public decency and which are capable of being seen in public. As was pointed out in *Bunyan and Morgan*, a person committing such an act may wish as much privacy as possible, if there is a possibility of them being discovered in public, it would nonetheless be an offence. Looking therefore at the purpose of the two person rule, it can, in our view, be satisfied if there are two or more persons present who are capable of seeing the nature of the act, even if they did not actually see it . . .".
>
> Thus in the present case, although no one saw the appellant filming, there was evidence from the videos that there were others present. But was what the appellant was in fact doing capable of being seen, even though no one actually did? It cannot be said . . . that this type of filming is incapable of being seen. Whether on the facts of this case the way in which the appellant filmed up the skirts of the women was capable of being seen was a question for the jury. As is clear from the passage in the summing up which we have set out at paragraph 13, this was an issue expressly left to the jury by the judge. By their verdict of guilty the jury must have concluded that the way the appellant filmed was capable of being seen by those in the supermarket."

It is tempting to regard the Court's assertion that there must be "two or more persons present who are capable of seeing the nature of the act" as settling the issue left unresolved for nearly 150 years since *Elliot and White*,[7] of whether there

[5] [2007] EWCA Crim 2062.
[6] At paras 39–40.
[7] (1861) Le. & Ca. 103.

must be two people actually present and able to see the act if they happen to look, or whether it is sufficient that two persons might reasonably have been expected to be present. However, this particular point did not arise for decision in *Hamilton*, and anything said by the Court which appears to bear upon it must therefore be treated with caution. The assertion quoted above was made in the context of a decision that the "two person" rule does not require that at least two people actually witness the act: it is sufficient if at least two people are present and able to see it. It is possible that, on appropriate facts, the courts would go a step further and, given the purpose of the rule, find it sufficient that, although the defendant is alone when he commits the act, there is a real possibility that at least two people could happen upon him and see what he is doing. For example, D films himself masturbating in broad daylight in a corner of a public park, which happens to be empty at the time, but is generally well-used so that there is a real chance that he could be caught in flagrante by members of the public. We suggest that in those circumstances, the fact that nobody (other than D) is actually present when the act is committed ought not to preclude a conviction, and that there is nothing in *Hamilton* which would have this effect. In short, the point in *Elliot and White* remains open.[8]

14.40A   In *Rose v DPP*[9] the appellant was recorded by a CCTV camera having an act of oral sex performed upon him by a female, in the foyer of a bank containing ATM machines to which the public had access. The next morning, the manageress of the bank, as part of her normal duties, viewed the CCTV recording on which the act was captured. The time on the CCTV was 00:54. The manageress reported the matter to the police and the appellant was charged with outraging public decency. At trial, the appellant did not dispute the factual basis of the allegation, but contended that his act could not have outraged public decency as it was not witnessed at the time it was committed, there having been no passers-by at that time in the morning who might have witnessed it. The District Judge ruled that the witnessing of the event by the manageress satisfied the requirements of the offence.

On appeal, the Divisional Court (Stanley Burton J.) held that the offence of outraging public decency is not committed where the act is seen by only one person other than the participants in it: there must be at least two witnesses for the required public element to be established. In this case, the only evidence of anyone else seeing the act was from the manageress, and on the authorities that was insufficient. The conviction was therefore quashed. The Court added *obiter* that there was considerable force in the appellant's alternative submission that the private viewing of a private recording of an act which had not previously been seen by anyone is insufficient to constitute the offence. That is because "the offence is committed when it is committed", and it would be curious if the offence was completed by a private viewing of a recording, and if it could make a difference,

---

[8] For a similar point arising in the very different context of s.4 of the Public Order Act 1986, see *Holloway v DPP* [2004] EWHC 2621 (Admin), discussed below para.14.116.
[9] [2006] EWHC 852 (Admin), [2006] Crim. L.R. 993.

for example, whether the manageress was in the company of somebody else or not when she saw the video, or whether she showed it to someone else afterwards or not.

The decision in *Rose* represents an orthodox application of the "two person" rule. The novelty of the case lies in the *dicta*. No court has previously considered whether the relevant act must be witnessed by a person's own unaided senses, or whether it is sufficient that it is witnessed through some visual or other medium. We respectfully suggest that the Court was right to doubt that the offence may be committed by the replaying of a CCTV recording. However, viewing of the product of a camera ought to be sufficient where the viewing takes place in real-time, i.e. where the product is broadcast over the internet or on live-feed CCTV.

The second part of this para (beginning "Some scepticism . . . ") was cited with approval by the Court of Appeal in *Hamilton*.[10]   **14.42**

Requirement of "Publicity"

On the requirement of publicity, see generally *Hamilton*.[11]   **14.43**

Mental Element

In the light of the decision in *Heard*,[12] discussed in para.2.72 above, the offence of outraging public decency appears to be one of basic intent, such that voluntary intoxication through drink or drugs will provide no defence. It will suffice if the defendant's acts were deliberate. Recklessness is insufficient.   **14.47**

EXPOSURE

Mode of Trial and Punishment

As from a day to be appointed the maximum sentence on summary conviction is 12 months' imprisonment: Criminal Justice Act 2003, s.282(2), (3). The increase has no application to offences committed before the substitution takes effect: s.282(4). An offence under s.66 is a specified sexual offence in respect of which a   **14.50**

---

[10] [2007] EWCA Crim 2062, at paras 33–34.
[11] [2007] EWCA Crim 2062, at paras 33–34.
[12] [2007] EWCA Crim 125.

sentence of imprisonment for public protection may be imposed under the Criminal Justice Act 2003.[13]

Sentencing

14.52   For the definitive guideline published by the Sentencing Guidelines Council on sentencing under the 2003 Act, see para.1.18. The guideline states that the factors to be taken into consideration in relation to offences under s.66 are as follows[14]:

> "1. The sentences for public protection *must* be considered in all cases. They are designed to ensure that sexual offenders are not released into the community if they present a significant risk of serious harm.
> 2. The offence replaces section 4 of the Vagrancy Act 1824 and section 28 of the Town Police Clauses Act 1847. It is gender neutral (covering exposure of male or female genitalia to a male or female witness) and carries a maximum penalty of 2 years' imprisonment.
> 3. These offences are sometimes more serious than they may, at first, appear. Although there is no physical contact with the victim, the offence may cause serious alarm or distress, especially when the offender behaves aggressively or uses obscenities.
> 4. A pre-sentence report, which can identify sexually deviant tendencies, will be extremely helpful in determining the most appropriate disposal. It will also help determine whether an offender would benefit from participation in a programme designed to help them address those tendencies.
> 5. A person convicted of this offence is subject to notification requirements.
> 6. Where this offence is being dealt with in a magistrates' court, more detailed guidance is provided in the Magistrates' Court Sentencing Guidelines (MCSG)."

The starting points, sentencing ranges and aggravating and mitigating factors for offences under s.66 are as follows:

Type/nature of activity	Starting points	Sentencing ranges
Repeat offender	12 weeks custody	4 weeks–26 weeks custody
Basic offence as defined in the SOA 2003, assuming no aggravating or mitigating factors, or some offences with aggravating factors	Community order	An appropriate non-custodial sentence*

* "Non-custodial sentence" in this context suggests a community order or a fine. In most instances, an offence will have crossed the threshold for a community order. However, in accordance with normal sentencing practice, a court is not precluded from imposing a financial penalty where that is determined to be the appropriate sentence.

[13] s.224 and Sch.15, Pt 2.
[14] Pt 5.

Additional aggravating factors	Additional mitigating factors
1. Threats to prevent the victim reporting an offence	
2. Intimidating behaviour/threats of violence	
3. Victim is a child	

A person convicted[15] of the s.66 offence is automatically subject to notification requirements under the SOA 2003, s.80 and Sch.3, where (a) he was under 18 at the time of the offence and is sentenced to at least 12 months' imprisonment or (b) in any other case, the victim was under 18 or the offender is, in respect of the offence, sentenced to a term of imprisonment, detained in a hospital or given a community sentence of at least 12 months.

In *Mailer*,[16] a pre-guideline case which appears consistent with the guideline, the   **14.52A**
Court of Appeal upheld sentences of six months' imprisonment concurrent in relation to two offences under s.66. In both incidents the appellant, aged 26, had sat next to the same young woman on a city centre bus, despite there being empty seats nearby, and had exposed his penis and masturbated. On both occasions the young woman was shocked, scared and upset. The appellant pleaded guilty. He was a repeat offender, having previously been sentenced for a total of eight offences of indecent exposure to a community rehabilitation order which was still in place. The pre-sentence report opined that a custodial sentence would be counter-productive in the appellant's rehabilitation and recommended participation in a sex offender treatment programme. The Court of Appeal held that, given all that had gone before, a sentence of imprisonment was necessary, as was the length of the term, which the Court noted would result in the appellant's release before the expiry of the community rehabilitation order, so that there would still be time for him to benefit from the sex offender treatment programme.

MENTAL ELEMENT

In the light of the decision in *Heard*,[17] discussed in para.2.72 above, the   **14.57**
requirement that the defendant did the prohibited act with the intention that someone would see his genitals and be caused alarm or distress makes the s.66 offence one of specific intent, such that voluntary intoxication through drink or drugs will provide a defence if it may have prevented the defendant forming that intention.

---

[15] Or found not guilty by reason of insanity, found to be under a disability and to have done the act charged, or cautioned.
[16] [2006] EWCA Crim 665; [2006] 2 Cr. App. R.(S.) 84.
[17] [2007] EWCA Crim 125.

VOYEURISM

Mode of Trial and Punishment

14.60   As from a day to be appointed the maximum sentence on summary conviction is 12 months' imprisonment: Criminal Justice Act 2003, s.282(2), (3). The increase has no application to offences committed before the substitution takes effect: s.282(4). An offence under s.67 is a specified sexual offence in respect of which a sentence of imprisonment for public protection may be imposed under the Criminal Justice Act 2003.[18]

Sentencing

14.62   For the definitive guideline published by the Sentencing Guidelines Council on sentencing under the 2003 Act, see para 1.18. The guideline states that the factors to be taken into consideration in relation to offences under s.67 are as follows[19]:

> "1. The sentences for public protection *must* be considered in all cases. They are designed to ensure that sexual offenders are not released into the community if they present a significant risk of serious harm.
>
> 2. The offence of voyeurism covers cases where someone who has a reasonable expectation of privacy is secretly observed. The offence may be committed in a number of ways:
> - by direct observation on the part of the offender;
> - by operating equipment with the intention of enabling someone else to observe the victim;
> - by recording someone doing a private act, with the intention that the recorded image will be viewed by the offender or another person; or
> - by installing equipment or constructing or adapting a structure with the intention of enabling the offender or another person to observe a private act.
>
> 3. In all cases the observation, or intended observation, must be for the purpose of obtaining sexual gratification and must take place, or be intended to take place, without the consent of the person observed.
>
> 4. The SOA 2003 defines a 'private act', in the context of this offence, as an act carried out in a place which, in the circumstances, would reasonably be expected to provide privacy, and where the victim's genitals, buttocks or breasts are exposed or covered only in underwear; *or* the victim is using a lavatory; *or* the person is 'doing a sexual act that is not of a kind ordinarily done in public'.
>
> 5. The harm inherent in this offence is intrusion of the victim's privacy. Whilst less serious than non-consensual touching, it may nevertheless cause severe distress, embarrassment or humiliation to the victim, especially in cases where a private act is not simply observed by one person, but where an image of it is disseminated for wider viewing. A higher sentencing starting point is recommended for cases where the offender records and shares images with others.
>
> 6. For offences involving the lowest level of offending behaviour, i.e. spying on someone for private pleasure, a non-custodial sentence is recommended as the starting point.

[18] s.224 and Sch.15, Pt 2.
[19] Pt 5.

7. A pre-sentence report, which can identify sexually deviant tendencies, will be extremely helpful in determining the most appropriate disposal. It will also help determine whether an offender would benefit from participation in a programme designed to help them address those tendencies.
8. Where this offence is being dealt with in a magistrates' court, more detailed guidance is provided in the Magistrates' Court Sentencing Guidelines (MCSG)."

The starting points, sentencing ranges and aggravating and mitigating factors for offences under s.67 are as follows:

Type/nature of activity	Starting points	Sentencing ranges
Offence with serious aggravating factors such as recording sexual activity and placing it on a website or circulating it for commercial gain	12 months custody	26 weeks–2 years custody
Offence with aggravating factors such as recording sexual activity and showing it to others	26 weeks custody	4 weeks–18 months custody
Basic offence as defined in the SOA 2003, assuming no aggravating or mitigating factors, e.g. the offender spies through a hole he or she has made in a changing room wall	Community order	An appropriate non-custodial sentence*

* "Non-custodial sentence" in this context suggests a community order or a fine. In most instances, an offence will have crossed the threshold for a community order. However, in accordance with normal sentencing practice, a court is not precluded from imposing a financial penalty where that is determined to be the appropriate sentence.

Additional aggravating factors	Additional mitigating factors
1. Threats to prevent the victim reporting an offence 2. Recording activity and circulating pictures/videos	

Additional aggravating factors	Additional mitigating factors
3. Circulating pictures or videos for commercial gain—particularly if victim is vulnerable, e.g. a child or person with a mental or physical disorder	
4. Distress to victim, e.g. where the pictures/videos are circulated to people known to the victim	

A person convicted[20] of the s.67 offence is automatically subject to notification requirements under the SOA 2003, s.80 and Sch.3, where (a) he was under 18 at the time of the offence and is sentenced to at least 12 months' imprisonment or (b) in any other case, the victim was under 18 or the offender is, in respect of the offence, sentenced to a term of imprisonment, detained in a hospital or given a community sentence of at least 12 months.

14.62A In *I.P.*,[21] a pre-guideline case which appears consistent with the guideline, the Court of Appeal quashed concurrent sentences of eight months' imprisonment in relation to two offences under s.67 and substituted a community rehabilitation order with a condition that the appellant participate in a sex offender treatment programme. The appellant, who was of previous good character, installed a video camera in the loft above the bathroom of his home so that he could watch his step-daughter, aged 24, in the shower. The step-daughter became suspicious and, while the appellant was out of the house, searched it, in company with her mother and sister. They found the camera, which was connected to a screen in the appellant's bedroom. The shower could be seen on the screen. The appellant admitted installing the camera with a view to watching the step-daughter in the shower, and also a cable so that he could view the images on the screen in his bedroom, which he had done three or four times. He pleaded guilty to charges under s.67(1) and (4). On appeal against sentence, the Court of Appeal said that the fact that the appellant had made recordings of the step-daughter having a shower made the case somewhat worse than if he had simply spied on her. However, there was no feature of showing the recordings to other people, circulating copies, posting pictures on the internet or selling the recordings for gain. Given the appellant's previous good character, early admissions and plea of guilty, and taking into account the fact that he had moved out of the family home, a custodial sentence was not justified.

14.62B In *Turner*,[22] the Court of Appeal quashed a sentence of 14 months' imprisonment and substituted one of nine months in relation to one offence under s.67, with two

---

[20] Or found not guilty by reason of insanity, found to be under a disability and to have done the act charged, or cautioned.
[21] [2004] EWCA Crim 2646; [2005] 1 Cr. App. R.(S.) 102.
[22] [2006] EWCA Crim 63; [2006] 2 Cr. App. R.(S.) 51.

more taken into consideration. The appellant, aged 30 and with no previous convictions, was employed as the manager at a sports centre. A woman using the gym noticed that a ceiling tile above the shower had been dislodged and that there was a camera lens in the gap. The matter was reported to the police, who found a video camera in one of the lockers. A number of video cassettes were recovered from the appellant's office and home address. He admitted filming women at the sports centre when they were either in the shower or using the sunbeds. In their victim impact statements, one woman said the incident had left her feeling sick and unable to sleep, and another that she felt violated. The appellant pleaded guilty to all three offences. He accepted that he had exploited his position of trust for sexual gratification and expressed remorse. A pre-sentence report indicated that he was motivated to address his offending behaviour. The sentencing court had a number of character references before it. It was referred to *I.P.*, above. The Court of Appeal considered the case more serious than *I.P.*, as there were four victims and the appellant had abused his position as manager. The latter factor took the case over the custody threshold, but did not justify a sentence as long as 14 months. The Court added that it did not wish to be taken to indicate that in a case where there is an abuse of a person's position, there should necessarily be a custodial sentence, if treatment in the community is in the particular circumstances an appropriate course.

In *Turner*, the Court treated as aggravating factors the number of victims and the appellant's abuse of trust. Neither of those matters is specified as an aggravating factor in the definitive guideline, but the factors that are specified are not exhaustive.[23] We suggest that the decision is a reliable guide to post-guideline sentencing.

MENTAL ELEMENT

In the light of the decision in *Heard*,[24] discussed in para.2.72 above, the **14.69** requirement that the defendant did the prohibited act for the purpose of obtaining sexual gratification means that the offences under s.67 are offences of specific intent, such that voluntary intoxication through drink or drugs will provide a defence if it may have prevented the defendant forming that purpose.

INTERCOURSE WITH AN ANIMAL

DEFINITION

Clause 64 of the Criminal Justice and Immigration Bill, currently before **14.70** Parliament, creates an offence of possession of extreme pornographic images. An

---

[23] Definitive Guideline, p.15(ii).
[24] [2007] EWCA Crim 125.

"extreme pornographic image" is defined as an image which is both pornographic and an extreme image. An image is "pornographic" if it appears to have been produced solely or principally for the purpose of sexual arousal. An "extreme image" is defined to include an image of a person performing or appearing to perform an act of intercourse or oral sex with an animal, where any such act, person or animal depicted in the image is or appears to be real. By clause 67, the offence will be triable either way with a maximum punishment on indictment of two years' imprisonment where the image is of an act of this sort.

Mode of Trial and Punishment

14.71   As from a day to be appointed the maximum sentence on summary conviction under s.69 is 12 months' imprisonment: Criminal Justice Act 2003, s.282(2), (3). The increase has no application to offences committed before the substitution takes effect: s.282(4). An offence under s.69 is a specified sexual offence in respect of which a sentence of imprisonment for public protection may be imposed under the Criminal Justice Act 2003.[25]

Sentencing

14.73   For the definitive guideline published by the Sentencing Guidelines Council on sentencing under the 2003 Act, see para.1.18. The guideline states that the factors to be taken into consideration in relation to offences under s.69 are as follows[26]:

> "1. The sentences for public protection *must* be considered in all cases. They are designed to ensure that sexual offenders are not released into the community if they present a significant risk of serious harm.
> 2. This replaces the previous offence of 'buggery' with an animal, for which the maximum penalty was life imprisonment. The maximum penalty of 2 years' imprisonment attached to this offence is sufficient to recognize an offender's predisposition towards unnatural sexual activity.
> 3. A custodial sentence for an adult for this offence will result in an obligation to comply with notification requirements and this seems to be the most appropriate course of action for a repeat offender. The offence can be charged in addition to existing offences relating to cruelty to animals.
> 4. A pre-sentence report, which can identify sexually deviant tendencies, will be extremely helpful in determining the most appropriate disposal. It will also help determine whether an offender would benefit from participation in a programme designed to help them address those tendencies."

The starting points, sentencing ranges and aggravating and mitigating factors for offences under s.69 are as follows:

---

[25] s.224 and Sch.15, Pt 2.
[26] Pt 5.

Type/nature of activity	Starting points	Sentencing ranges
Basic offence as defined in the SOA 2003, assuming no aggravating or mitigating factors	Community order	An appropriate non-custodial sentence*

* "Non-custodial sentence" in this context suggests a community order or a fine. In most instances, an offence will have crossed the threshold for a community order. However, in accordance with normal sentencing practice, a court is not precluded from imposing a financial penalty where that is determined to be the appropriate sentence.

Additional aggravating factors	Additional mitigating factors
1. Recording activity and/or circulating pictures or videos	1. Symptom of isolation rather than depravity

A person convicted[27] of the s.69 offence is automatically subject to notification requirements under the SOA 2003, s.80 and Sch.3, where (a) he was under 18 at the time of the offence and is sentenced to at least 12 months' imprisonment or (b) in any other case, he is, in respect of the offence, sentenced to a term of imprisonment or detained in a hospital.

MENTAL ELEMENT

In the light of the decision in *Heard*,[28] discussed in para.2.72 above, the offence in 14.86 s.69 appears to be one of basic intent, such that voluntary intoxication through drink or drugs will provide no defence. It will suffice if the defendant's acts were deliberate. Recklessness is insufficient.

SEXUAL PENETRATION OF A CORPSE

DEFINITION

Clause 64 of the Criminal Justice and Immigration Bill, currently before 14.87 Parliament, creates an offence of possession of extreme pornographic images. An "extreme pornographic image" is defined as an image which is both pornographic and an extreme image. An image is "pornographic" if it appears to have been produced solely or principally for the purpose of sexual arousal. An "extreme image" is defined to include an image of an act which involves or appears to involve sexual interference with a human corpse, where any such act depicted in

---

[27] Or found not guilty by reason of insanity, found to be under a disability and to have done the act charged, or cautioned.
[28] [2007] EWCA Crim 125.

the image is or appears to be real. By clause 67, the offence will be triable either way with a maximum punishment on indictment of two years' imprisonment where the image is of an act of this sort.

Mode of Trial and Punishment

14.88   As from a day to be appointed the maximum sentence on summary conviction under s.70 is 12 months' imprisonment: Criminal Justice Act 2003, s.282(2), (3). The increase has no application to offences committed before the substitution takes effect: s.282(4). An offence under s.70 is a specified sexual offence in respect of which a sentence of imprisonment for public protection may be imposed under the Criminal Justice Act 2003.[29]

Sentencing

14.90   For the definitive guideline published by the Sentencing Guidelines Council on sentencing under the 2003 Act, see para.1.18. The guideline states that the factors to be taken into consideration in relation to offences under s.70 are as follows[30]:

> "1. The sentences for public protection *must* be considered in all cases. They are designed to ensure that sexual offenders are not released into the community if they present a significant risk of serious harm.
> 2. Necrophilia is associated with 'other very deviant behaviour', and killers who use the bodies of their victims for sexual gratification cannot, under the existing law, be formally recognized as, or treated as, sexual offenders.
> 3. A pre-sentence report (and in some cases a psychiatric report), which can identify sexually deviant tendencies, will be extremely helpful in determining the most appropriate disposal. It will also help determine whether an offender would benefit from participation in a programme designed to help them address those tendencies."

The starting points, sentencing ranges and aggravating and mitigating factors for offences under s.70 are as follows:

Type/nature of activity	Starting points	Sentencing ranges
Repeat offending and/or aggravating factors	26 weeks custody	4 weeks–18 months custody
Basic offence as defined in the SOA 2003, assuming no aggravating or mitigating factors	Community order	An appropriate non-custodial sentence*

* "Non-custodial sentence" in this context suggests a community order or a fine. In most instances, an offence will have crossed the threshold for a community order. However, in accordance with normal sentencing practice, a court is not precluded from imposing a financial penalty where that is determined to be the appropriate sentence.

[29] s.224 and Sch.15, Pt 2.
[30] Pt 5.

Additional aggravating factors	Additional mitigating factors
1. Distress caused to relatives or friends of the deceased	
2. Physical damage caused to body of the deceased	
3. The corpse was that of a child	
4. The offence was committed in a funeral home or mortuary	

A person convicted[31] of the s.70 offence is automatically subject to notification requirements under the SOA 2003, s.80 and Sch.3, where (a) he was under 18 at the time of the offence and is sentenced to at least 12 months' imprisonment or (b) in any other case, he is, in respect of the offence, sentenced to a term of imprisonment or detained in a hospital.

MENTAL ELEMENT

In the light of the decision in *Heard*,[32] discussed in para.2.72 above, the offence in **14.93** s.70 appears to be one of basic intent, such that voluntary intoxication through drink or drugs will provide no defence. It will suffice if the defendant's acts were deliberate. Recklessness is insufficient.

SEXUAL ACTIVITY IN A PUBLIC LAVATORY

SENTENCING

For the definitive guideline published by the Sentencing Guidelines Council on **14.97** sentencing under the 2003 Act, see para.1.18. The guideline states that the factors to be taken into consideration in relation to offences under s.71 are as follows[33]:

"1. This offence has been introduced to give adults and children the freedom to use public lavatories for the purpose for which they are designed, without the fear of being an unwilling witness to overtly sexual behaviour of a kind that most people would not expect to be conducted in public.
2. This offence, being a public order offence rather than a sexual offence, carries the lowest maximum penalty in the SOA 2003—6 months' imprisonment—and the starting point for sentencing reflects this.

---

[31] Or found not guilty by reason of insanity, found to be under a disability and to have done the act charged, or cautioned.
[32] [2007] EWCA Crim 125.
[33] Pt 5.

3. More detailed guidance is provided in the Magistrates' Court Sentencing Guidelines (MCSG)."

The starting points, sentencing ranges and aggravating and mitigating factors for offences under s.71 are as follows:

Type/nature of activity	Starting points	Sentencing ranges
Repeat offending and/or aggravating factors	Community order	An appropriate non-custodial sentence*
Basic offence as defined in the SOA 2003, assuming no aggravating or mitigating factors	Fine	An appropriate non-custodial sentence*

* "Non-custodial sentence" in this context suggests a community order or a fine. In most instances, an offence will have crossed the threshold for a community order. However, in accordance with normal sentencing practice, a court is not precluded from imposing a financial penalty where that is determined to be the appropriate sentence.

Additional aggravating factors	Additional mitigating factors
1. Intimidating behaviour/threats of violence to member(s) of the public	

Mental Element

14.101   In the light of the decision in *Heard*,[34] discussed in para.2.72 above, the offence in s.71 appears to be one of basic intent, such that voluntary intoxication through drink or drugs will provide no defence. It will suffice if the defendant's acts were deliberate. Recklessness is insufficient.

INSULTING BEHAVIOUR UNDER SECTION 4 OF THE PUBLIC ORDER ACT 1986

Mode of Trial and Punishment

14.103   As from a day to be appointed the maximum sentence on summary conviction is 12 months' imprisonment: Criminal Justice Act 2003, s.282(2), (3). The increase has no application to offences committed before the substitution takes effect: s.282(4).

[34] [2007] EWCA Crim 125.

"Insulting Behaviour"

Footnote 43: See also *Hammond v DPP*.[35]   **14.105**

INSULTING OR DISORDERLY BEHAVIOUR UNDER SECTION 5 OF THE PUBLIC ORDER ACT 1986

"Within the Sight of a Person likely to be Caused"

In *Norwood v DPP*,[36] cited in the main work, the Divisional Court held that it is   **14.116** not necessary that the behaviour is actually seen by someone who is likely to be caused harassment, alarm or distress; it is sufficient that the behaviour is plainly capable of causing harassment, etc., to persons passing by who might see it. The case concerned a poster offensive to Muslims which the appellant placed in the window of his home, and the thrust of the decision is that he could be convicted without proof that the poster had actually been seen by someone of that faith. A similar issue arose in *Holloway v DPP*,[37] in which *Norwood* was not cited. In that case, the appellant had filmed himself naked in a rural location, with school-children playing on a sports field in the background. There was an express finding that no one actually saw the appellant's behaviour. His appeal against conviction was allowed. Silber J. said that for the offence to be committed "some person must have actually seen the abusive or insulting words or behaviour. It is not enought that somebody merely might have seen or could possibly have seen that behaviour".[38] Collins J. expressed himself slightly differently, saying "it is not sufficient that someone might have come on the scene and therefore might have seen what the individual who is charged was doing . . . What, in my view, is required is that there is at least evidence that there was someone who could see, or could hear, at the material time, what the individual was doing."[39] He added: "It may be that what I am saying goes to the evidence which has to be called in order to establish this offence because I do not believe it to be necessary that the prosecution call a person or persons who can say that they did see what was happening. The evidence must be sufficient, so that the court can draw the inference, having regard to the criminal standard, that what he was doing was visible or audible to people who were in the vicinity at the relevant time."[40] In *Taylor v DPP*,[41] a third Divisional Court held that any difference between the approaches taken by the two members of the Court in *Holloway* came down to a question of what evidence is required to prove the offence. It seemed to the Court

---

[35] [2004] EWHC 69 (Admin).
[36] [2003] EWHC 1564 (Admin); [2003] Crim. L.R. 888.
[37] [2004] EWHC 2621 (Admin)
[38] para.17.
[39] paras 28–29.
[40] para.32.
[41] [2006] EWHC 1202 (Admin).

that Collins J. was right in saying that there must be evidence that there was someone able to see or hear the defendant's conduct, and that the prosecution does not have to call evidence that that person did actually see or hear it. But it is not enough to establish that someone might have come on the scene and observed what was going on. This is, with respect, a persuasive analysis that also ensures there is no air gap between *Norwood* and *Holloway*. In the former, it was plain on the evidence that the poster was freely visible to passers-by, whereas in the latter, the most that could be said was that there was a possibility that someone could have stumbled on the scene.

Footnote 64: see also *Taylor v DPP*, above.

EVIDENCE: GENERAL

HEARSAY EVIDENCE

Evidence outside the definition of hearsay in s.115 Criminal Justice Act 2003

Personal diaries often feature in evidence in cases where it is alleged that children **15.03** have been sexually abused. If it is established that a child wrote a diary not intending it to be read by anyone, then relevant entries are direct or real evidence and not hearsay within the definition in s.115 of the Act.[1]

First hand hearsay and competence

Under s.116 Criminal Justice Act 2003, first hand hearsay evidence, whether oral **15.03A** or documentary, is admissible without leave provided certain criteria are met. However, in all cases under s.116, it is necessary to establish that the relevant person was competent at the time of making the relevant statement. Section 123(1) of the 2003 Act provides:

> "Nothing in section 116, 119 or 120 makes a statement admissible as evidence if it was made by a person who did not have the required capability at the time when he made the statement."

Section 123 bases the test of capability on (a) understanding questions put to him about matters stated, and (b) giving answers to such questions which can be understood. A *voir dire* may be held and expert evidence called if necessary. This requirement, somewhat surprisingly, appears to narrow the law at a time when

---

[1] *R. v N(K)* [2006] EWCA Crim 3309.

Parliament was adopting a far more inclusionist approach to the admissibility of evidence. Under the pre-2003 Act provisions, the Court of Appeal in *Ali Sed*[2] held that the video interview of an Alzheimer's sufferer (who was a complainant in case of attempted rape) was rightly admitted under s.23 of the Criminal Justice Act 1987, even though the complainant was not available to give evidence. *Ali Sed* followed *R. v D.,*[3] where it was held in an attempted rape case that the video interview of another Alzheimer's victim was rightly admitted under s.23, and, in particular, there was no requirement for admission under s.23 that the witness be competent.

General guidance as to the admission of hearsay statements where it is the sole, or decisive, evidence against a defendant

When deciding whether to admit the evidence of a statement where the defendant has not had an opportunity to examine the witness, there is only one governing criterion: is the admission of the evidence compatible with a fair trial? In *Konrad Cole and Rocky Keet,*[4] the Lord Chief Justice stated:

> "There are many reasons why it may be impossible to call a witness. Where the defendant is himself responsible for that fact, he is in no position to complain that he has been denied a fair trial if a statement from that witness has been admitted. Where the witness is dead, or cannot be called for some other reason, the question of whether the admission of a statement from that witness will impair the fairness of the trial will depend on the facts of the particular case. Factors that will be likely to be of concern to the court are identified in s.114(2) of the Act."

He went on to point out that that the s.114 list of factors relevant to the interests of justice does not state expressly which way each individual factor is intended to cut. The Court considered that the inference is that the more important and the more reliable the statement appears to be, the stronger the case for its admission. When the factors in s.114 are considered in respect of several statements, the correct approach is not to consider each statement on its own, but to consider each in context. Each statement may be part of a wider picture that is coherent and compelling.

The Court also endorsed the trial judge's remarks that s.116 and its predecessors provide an important weapon in the prosecution armoury in respect of offences alleged to have been aimed at the elderly and vulnerable.

Inconsistent statements: s.119 of the Criminal Justice Act 2003

15.03B   Section 119(1) of the Criminal Justice Act 2003 makes a person's previous inconsistent statement, once admitted, "evidence of any matter stated of which oral evidence by him would be admissible." This provision has potentially a

---

[2] [2004] Crim. L.R. 1036. For present position see *DPP v R* [2007] EWHC 1842 (Admin).
[3] [2002] 2 Cr. App. R. 601. In both *Ali Sed* and *R. v D* there was supporting evidence.
[4] [2007] EWCA Crim 1924.

significant impact in respect of the evidence of complainants of a sexual offence.[5] A good example is *Leach*,[6] where the Court of Appeal upheld a conviction of sexual assault where the first complaint of a 14-year-old to her mother was that the appellant had kissed her. In subsequent interviews, she alleged that he had touched her beneath her underwear. This inconsistent statement became evidence of the truth as well as material which, if the jury thought the inconsistency was significant, could be used to cast doubt upon the truth of what the complainant said. Arguably, judges should be astute to remind juries of any important inconsistencies in a complainant's previous statement, as the jury would be entitled to act upon a previous inconsistent statement as evidence of the truth.[7] It remains to be seen if prosecutors will seek to rely more on the previous statements of complainants who have retracted their statements, particularly where there is other evidence in the case supporting the previous statement.[8] Problems may arise where a complainant has given fundamentally different accounts.[9–11]

EVIDENCE OF RECENT COMPLAINT

THE CRIMINAL JUSTICE ACT 2003

The common law on recent complaint has been superseded by s.120 of the **15.09** Criminal Justice Act 2003, implementing the recommendations of the Law Commission, which came into force on April 4, 2005.[12]

It is important to remember that, as with inconsistent statements under s.119, the Criminal Justice Act 2003 admits previous consistent statements (including those where the recent complaint criteria are established under s.120(4) and (7)) as evidence of the truth of their contents, i.e. a previous statement by the witness is admissible as evidence of any matter stated of which oral evidence by him would be admissible. Judges should, however, continue to remind juries that a complainant's previous complaint does not come from an independent source.[13]

---

[5] For a strong example of s.119 in operation, see *Joyce and Joyce* [2005] EWCA Crim 1785, where two eye-witnesses in respect of a firearms offences became hostile at trial.

[6] [2005] EWCA Crim 58.

[7] *R. v Keith D* [2005] EWCA Crim 3043 (obiter).

[8] *Crown Prosecution Service v CE* [2006] EWCA Crim 1410, the Court of Appeal upheld the trial judge's ruling not to admit a complainant's video evidence in a rape case even though two of the criteria under s.116 were satisfied. The hearsay evidence was the sole or decisive evidence against the accused. The complainant was "potentially a completely flawed witness" and the defendant would be deprived of the opportunity of cross-examining her on a large numbers of issues relating to consent. Cf. two cases under s.23 of the Criminal Justice Act 1988, where the Court of Appeal held that the complainant's video was properly admitted: *Ali Sed* [2004] Crim. L.R.1036; *R. v D* [2002] 2 Cr. App. R. 601.

[9–11] See *Coates* [2007] Crim. L.R. 887.

[12] SI 2005/950.

[13] *R. v A* [2007] All E.R. (D) 143.

The Court of Appeal considered the use of s.120 in *Xhabri*.[14] The complainant, a 17-year-old Latvian, alleged that she had been kidnapped, raped and forced to work as a prostitute. She made telephone calls to her parents and others alleging that she was being detained against her will. At trial the complainant gave evidence of those calls without any objection. The Court of Appeal held that the trial judge had been correct to allow the recipients' evidence to be received as evidence of recent complaint under s.120(7) of the Act.

15.11 Whilst the words "as soon as could reasonably be expected" in s.120(7)(d) appear to replicate those from *Lillyman*,[15] a leading authority under the common law of recent complaint, the Court of Appeal has made it very clear that s.120 is unfettered by the common law requirement that the complaint must have been made at the first reasonable opportunity. In *Openshaw*[16] the complainant made the complaints when she was 17, after she had been abused at home from the age of 9. It follows that, in part, her complaints related to abuse several years before. The Court of Appeal approved the trial judge's approach:

> "There was much debate in the written arguments before us as to whether technically the old rules as to recent complaint had been abolished by the 2003 Act. That seems to us, in spite of the erudition of those arguments, to be largely an arid discussion. The application to admit the evidence was made under the new Act. The learned judge, in our view, correctly concentrated on deciding whether the test of admissibility provided by that Act had been satisfied."

However, the Law Commission had recommended that the requirement of a prompt complaint be retained and there is no change to the previous requirement that the complaint be made as soon as could reasonably be expected. Professor Ormerod has argued that, since Parliament did not take opportunity expressly to relax the requirement of promptness, and the words of the statute replicate those of a leading authority on the common law, the test should be interpreted restrictively. This approach would not allow for years of delay in a historic abuse case, explicable on the basis of a child maturing.[17] The decision in *Openshaw* suggests that the courts will now take a more liberal approach in cases where a complainant may have not made a complaint for a significant period.

This particular debate may be overtaken by events, as a recent Home Office consultation document[18] suggested that s.120(7)(d) should be repealed and that *all* complaints in sexual cases should be admissible, regardless of when they are made. There is a strong argument that evidence of first complaint is illuminating whenever it is made. Delay can often be explained by the maturing of a young complainant or the impact of a close relationship. However, problems will arise where a complainant has made a series of fundamentally different complaints.[18A]

---

[14] [2006] 1 Cr. App. R. 26.
[15] [1896] 2 Q.B. 167 at 171.
[16] [2006] EWCA Crim 556.
[17] See *Birks* [2003] 2 Cr. App. R. 7.
[18] *Convicting Rapists and Protecting Victims—Justice for Victims of Rape.*
[18A] See *Coates* [2007] Crim. L.R. 887.

The Court of Appeal in *Openshaw* also acknowledged that there is no rule that restricts the prosecution to calling just one recipient to give evidence of recent complaint.

Permissible judicial comment in respect of late disclosure by children in respect of allegations of child sex abuse

A judge is entitled to make measured comments in a summing up as to the reasons   **15.11A**
why it might take time for young complainants to make allegations of abuse, in a case where late disclosure is relied on as supporting a defence of fabrication. In *M.M.*[19] the appellant was the step-father of the two complainants. He had moved in with the family. The prosecution case was that he had repeatedly raped one step-daughter over a three year period when she was aged between eight and 10, and indecently assaulted an older step-daughter when she was aged between 11 and 13. The girls did not report what happened until some years afterwards, and significantly after the appellant had left the family home. One of the grounds of appeal was that the summing up was unfair and slanted towards the prosecution and against the defence in that the judge took it on himself to give evidence to the jury about the reasons why the girls might not report incidents that had happened.

After giving the appropriate direction to the jury as to how they should be alive to the possible prejudice to a defendant because of delay, the trial judge giving the following direction:

"You are entitled to consider why these matters did not come to light sooner. The defence say it is because they are not true. The allegations are fabricated. Had they been true, they say, you would have expected a complaint to be made earlier and certainly when the defendant was out of the way. The prosecution say that it is not as simple as that. When children are abused, whether these two girls were abused is what you have to decide, they are often confused about what is happening to them and why it is happening. They are children. That is something you should have in the forefront of your mind when considering this. They might have some inkling that what is going on is wrong. Sometimes children even blame themselves when there is obviously no need for them to do so. A child can be inhibited for a variety of reasons from speaking out. They might be fearful that they may not be believed, a child's word against a mature adult, or they might be scared of the consequences, or fearful of the effect upon relationships which they have come to know. The difficulties, you may think, are compounded in the family situation where they involve a family member for whom the feelings of the child may be ambivalent. The child might not like the abuse but there may be aspects of the abuser that causes the child to view them with some degree of affection. The fallout from disclosures can be unpredictable and sometimes calamitous. So, if a child or children are abused, they are often subject to very mixed emotions, and that can be the case particularly where there is an imposing adult in the household of whom they are perhaps afraid and who has overborne them and has power over them and warned them if they tell.

Whether any of that applies here is a matter for you. Equally, there are sometimes in lives, sometimes earlier, sometime later, when there is a trigger or the need arises to

---

[19] [2007] EWCA Crim 1558.

disclose, speak out. No easy thing to do, you may think, and it takes some courage to do so.

Ladies and gentleman, I make clear to you that I offer these matters to you not by way of direction in law but as things which in common sense and with knowledge of the world you might like to consider in assessing whether you find that there is a reason for the delay here and of course it also affects the honesty and truthfulness of the two girls.

You have heard explanations and it is entirely a matter for you but you may think that some of the things they said on the video and to you, K 'He told me I would get the blame. It's our secret', R, 'I didn't know whether they would believe me or him', both of them scared to an extent. 'I was worried about what would happen. I was worried about his reaction, what people might say.' It is a matter for you but you may think some of those reactions, if they are true, mirror some of the matters I have just been speaking about."

The Court of Appeal stated that this passage, slightly elaborate as it was, did not go beyond the bounds of permissible comment on the part of a judge. The defence was fabrication, the jury were aware of it and in the Court's judgment did need some assistance as to the reasons why it might take time for girls to make allegations of this nature. The judge was entitled to give the measured comment he did. The Court also said that it took the view that this was a fair and not biased summing up.

EVIDENCE OF CHARACTER OF DEFENDANT

The Criminal Justice Act 2003

15.40   The Criminal Justice Act 2003 introduced a statutory scheme regulating the admissibility of evidence of the bad character of defendants and non-defendant witnesses. The provisions came into force in December 2004 and apply in trials that began after 15 December 2004, irrespective of when the prosecution was instituted.[20] The Court of Appeal has handed down a number of important decisions on the operation of the provisions. These decisions have helped to ensure that convictions remain based on evidence, and not prejudice. This chapter will be confined, in the main, to those appeals involving sexual offences.

Notice requirements

15.40A   It is important that there is compliance with the notice requirements in the Criminal Procedure Rules 2005, although it does not follow that non-compliance by the prosecution will lead to the application to introduce bad character evidence being refused.[21] Whilst the courts have been taking the position that a culture of

---

[20] *Bradley* [2005] 1 Cr. App. R. 24.

[21] *Delay (Timothy)* [2006] EWCA Crim 1110, where the Court of Appeal held that the Recorder's decision that the defendant had not suffered any prejudice was not unreasonable even though the application was made at the end of the prosecution case.

non-compliance should not be allowed to take root, the higher courts will not interfere with a conviction unless the appellant can demonstrate prejudice. The main considerations will be (a) the reason for the failure to comply with the rules and (b) whether the other party was prejudiced by the failure. The trial judge's discretion to allow late applications is not limited by the principle that it is only to be exercised in exceptional circumstances.[22]

A late application may mean that the defence do not have sufficient time to investigate important matters. A good example of a case where a late application led to clear prejudice is *R. v M.*,[23] where the Court of Appeal quashed the conviction of a 17 year old for rape. At trial, just before the end of its case, the prosecution applied to admit evidence of two previous allegations of sexual assault against the appellant, dating back to when he was 14, as evidence capable of showing a propensity to commit offences of the kind with which he was charged. The Court of Appeal held that, on the facts of the case, the late application had put undue pressure on the appellant and the judge. The judge had originally rejected the application, but later changed his mind, limiting the evidence that could be called in respect of the two previous allegations to the complainants (apart from the appellant, if he chose to do so). The judge ruled that no other live evidence could be called as to the earlier allegations, even though the appellant denied them. It followed that the appellant had been unable to examine a witness to the first incident to confirm that his acts of oral sex with the complainant had been consensual. Nor could he call the first complainant's doctor to give evidence about the scratches on her breast, which were alleged to have occurred at that time.

The Court of Appeal stated that the time limits in the 2003 Act should be observed. If not, there was a risk of unfairness. A defendant might be reluctant to apply for an adjournment if he and the complainant had already given evidence, and judges might be reluctant to grant an adjournment in such circumstances. The appellant in the instant case had had no opportunity to make any investigations into important matters such as the medical evidence with regard to the scratches, or letters from the complainant describing consensual conduct. There can be real practical problems when the defence need to investigate the facts of previous convictions, and these are likely to be compounded when an application is made late in the day. However where the prosecution has properly carried out its duties of disclosure, and the defence are in a position to make their own enquiries, a speculative application for further particulars is unlikely to succeed.[24]

In *R. (O) v Central Criminal Court*[25] the Divisional Court gave the warning that prosecuting authorities need to be aware of the consequences of late applications, in that they may lead to additional complexity and delay which may have

---

[22] *R. (Robinson) v Sutton Coldfield Magistrates' Court* [2006] 2 Cr. App. R. 13.
[23] [2006] EWCA Crim 1509.
[24] *Alobayadi* [2007] EWCA Crim 2984. See also *R. v K* [2007] EWCA Crim 911.
[25] [2006] EWHC 3542 (Admin).

repercussions on custody time limits and the issue as to whether the prosecution has proceeded with due expedition.

Proving the details of the previous sexual offences

15.40B   The hearsay provisions of the 2003 Act[26] can be used to prove the fact of a previous conviction, but not the circumstances of the offence.[27] The prosecution must decide whether they need any more evidence to achieve the purpose for which they want the evidence to be admitted, i.e. more than the evidence of conviction and the matters that can be formally established. They must ensure that they have available the necessary evidence to support what they require. Often the details of the modus operandi of the previous sexual offending can only be established by the evidence of the complainant.[28] In *Ainscough*[29] the Court of Appeal stressed that it is important for courts to avoid the proliferation of satellite issues, particularly where there is a short trial on a simple issue. It may be possible, in appropriate cases, to prove previous facts by relying on s.116 of the 2003 Act if any of the conditions in s.116(2) are met, or on s.114(1)(d)[30] where the court has had regard to the factors set out in s.114(2). Clearly "bad character" includes foreign convictions, which may be admissible under s.101(d) and (g) in precisely the same way as a domestic conviction. Propensity is unlikely to be affected by the jurisdiction where the offences are committed. The fact of a foreign conviction may be proved under s.7 of the Evidence Act 1851.[31]

The definition of "bad character"

15.40C   "Bad character" is defined by s.98 of the Criminal Justice Act 2003, which provides:

> "References in this Chapter to evidence of 'bad character' are to evidence of, or of a disposition towards, misconduct on his part, other than evidence which—
> (a) has to do with the alleged facts of the offence with which the defendant is charged, or
> (b) is evidence of misconduct in connection with the investigation or prosecution of that offence."

The result is to exclude from the "bad character" regime the central facts of the case. It should be remembered that it does not follow that merely because evidence fails to come within the s.101 gateways, it will be inadmissible. Where the

---

[26] s.117 of the Criminal Justice Act 2003.

[27] *Humphris* [2005] EWCA Crim 2030.

[28] See also *Hogart* [2007] where a civil judgment was held to be admissible under s.117 CJA 2003.

[29] [2006] EWCA Crim 694.

[30] *R. v S* [2007] EWCA Crim 35.

[31] *Kordasinski* [2007] 1 Cr. App. R. 17 (evidence of the appellant's convictions in Poland for rape and kidnapping were admissible for the purpose of proving that he did in fact commit the rape and false imprisonment alleged within this jurisdiction).

exclusions in s.98 are applicable, the evidence will be admissible without further ado.[32]

This may lead to an overlap between the central facts of the case and evidence admissible under the gateway for "important explanatory evidence" in s.101(1)(c). In *McKintosh*,[33] evidence that the appellant had shown the complainant a firearm some months before the alleged rape was held to be part of the alleged facts of the case, in that it explained why she had not complained earlier.[34] Professor Ormerod has argued that in such circumstances, s.101(1)(c) would be a safer route to admissibility.[35]

The term "misconduct" is defined in s.112(1), which provides:

> "'Misconduct' means the commission of an offence or other reprehensible behaviour."

What constitutes "reprehensible behaviour" in a sexual context can provoke lively debate.[36] In *Renda*[37] the Court of Appeal accepted that the word "reprehensible" carries with it some element of culpability or blameworthiness. A definition using such a subjective term means that much will depend on the facts of the particular case. Presumably, homosexual behaviour between consenting adults cannot properly be described in 2007 as "reprehensible behaviour". What about conduct involving a sexual relationship with someone significantly younger than the defendant? In *Manister*[38] the Court of Appeal accepted that the trial judge was wrong to conclude that an earlier sexual relationship between the appellant (aged 36) and a girl of 16 was reprehensible behaviour. However, evidence of the relationship was admissible at common law, in the particular circumstances of the case, because it was relevant to the issue of whether the appellant had a sexual interest in the complainant, in that it was capable of demonstrating that he had a sexual interest in early or mid-teenage girls much younger than himself. It is important to remember that if evidence is admissible at common law, the notice provisions of the 2003 Act do not bite.

It is not unknown for juries to convict a defendant of an offence of violence that occurred at the same time as an alleged sexual offence, such as rape, on which the jury then fail to agree. On a retrial of the rape, the earlier conviction for violence may well be within s.98(a) in that it "had to do with" the sexual allegation because it occurred during the same incident. It will then fall outside the definition of "bad

---

[32] *Edwards and Rowlands and others* [2006] EWCA Crim 3244; [2006] 2 Cr. App. R. 4.

[33] [2006] EWCA Crim 193.

[34] See also *Tirnaveanu* [2007] 2 Cr. App. R. 23 where the Court of Appeal did not accept Professor Ormerod's argument. It also suggested that "to do with" involves a nexus in time with the alleged offence; *Brummitt* [2006] EWCA Crim 1629.

[35] In a lecture to the JSB Serious Sexual Offences Seminar, July 2007.

[36] Roderick Munday, *What constitutes "other reprehensible behaviour" under the bad character provisions of the Criminal Justice Act 2003?* [2005] Crim. L.R. 24. Dr. Munday believes that the definition is dangerously vague and "will prove a nightmare of interpretation".

[37] [2006] 1 Cr. App. R. 24; and see *Osbourne* [2007] EWCA Crim 481, where it was held that "reprehensible behaviour" did not include shouting and being aggressive towards a partner over the care of an infant.

[38] [2005] EWCA Crim 2866; [2006] 1 Cr. App. R. 19 (a consolidated appeal with *Weir*).

character", but be admissible at common law as going to the issue whether the defendant had been violent to the complainant in the context of the rape allegation.[39]

Where there has been an acquittal, or proceedings have been stayed as an abuse of process, the prosecution can still produce evidence to show that the defendant was in fact guilty.[40] In *Smith*[41] the Court of Appeal held that the trial judge had properly admitted allegations of sexual offences which had been stayed as an abuse of process because the defendant had had a legitimate expectation of non-prosecution.

The Gateways

Section 101(1)(c)—"important explanatory evidence"

15.40D   To be admissible the evidence must be both important and explanatory.[42] Nevertheless, the Court of Appeal has given a very wide interpretation to gateway (c). In *Pronick*[43] the Court held that evidence of a previous rape of the complainant by the appellant was properly admissible as explanatory evidence under this gateway. However, it should be remembered that the gateway does not apply if the evidence is readily understandable without the evidence of bad character.[44] In *Smith*,[45] where the appellant had been charged with sexual offences against children, the Court of Appeal approved the approach of the trial judge, who had rejected the submission that evidence of other sexual assaults upon children by the appellant was admissible through gateway (c), but had concluded that it was evidence of propensity under gateway (d).

Evidence of "bad character" that amounts to an explanation for an apparently late disclosure by the complainant may be admissible as "important explanatory evidence". In *R. v S.*[46] the Court of Appeal held that a caution for indecent assault in 2003 was properly admitted as "important explanatory evidence" as to why the appellant's two sisters had then for the first time made allegations that he had raped them 20 years ago.

---

[39] See *R. v W* [2006] EWCA Crim 2308, where the Court of Appeal concluded that a conviction of assault occasioning actual bodily harm was admissible on a retrial of the rape on the basis of common law relevance rather than under gateway s.101(1)(d).

[40] *R. v Z* [2000] 2 A.C. 483.

[41] [2005] EWCA Crim 3244.

[42] The scope of s.101(1)(c) is explained in s.102.

[43] [2006] EWCA Crim 2517.

[44] *Beverley* [2006] EWCA Crim 1287. The Court noted that gateway (c) does not apply where the evidences require "no footnote or lexicon" to be readily understandable. For a classic example of where evidence was properly admitted under this gateway, see *Chohan*, an appeal consolidated with *Edwards* [2006] 1 Cr. App. R. 3.

[45] [2005] EWCA Crim 3244 (an appeal consolidated with *Edwards and Rowlands*).

[46] [2006] EWCA Crim 756.

Section 101(1)(d)—evidence "relevant to an important matter in issue between the defendant and the prosecution"

Under s.101(1)(d), all that is required is that the bad character is relevant to an **15.40E**
"important matter in issue between the prosecution and the defence". The
threshold for admissibility is not an enhanced one, as it was under the old similar
fact rule even in its more liberal later form in *DPP v P*.[47] In *Somanthan*[48] the Court
of Appeal held that if the evidence of a defendant's bad character is relevant to an
important issue between the prosecution and the defence, then, unless there is an
application to exclude the evidence, it is admissible. Leave is not required. The
previous one-stage test, which balanced probative value against prejudicial effect,
is obsolete.

The scope of gateway (d) is expanded by s.101(3)(1)(a), which provides:

"For the purposes of section 101(1)(d) the matters in issue between the defendant and
the prosecution include—
(a) the question whether the defendant has a propensity to commit offences of the
kind with which he is charged, except where his having such as propensity
makes it no more likely that he is guilty of the offence."

In the leading case of *Hanson*,[49] the Court of Appeal stated that where
propensity to commit an offence is relied upon, there are essentially three
questions to be considered:

1. Does the history of conviction(s) establish a propensity to commit
   offences of the kind charged?
2. Does that propensity make it more likely that the defendant committed
   the offence charged?
3. Is it unjust to rely on the conviction(s) of the same description or
   category; and, in any event, will the proceedings be unfair if they are
   admitted?

The Court said that in referring to offences of the same description or category,
s.103(2) is not exhaustive of the types of conviction which might be relied upon
to show evidence of propensity to commit offences of the kind charged. Nor is it
necessarily sufficient, in order to show such propensity, that a conviction should be
of the same description or category as that charged.[50] Furthermore, the Court of
Appeal pointed out that a single previous conviction of an offence of the same
description will often not show propensity. Whilst circumstances demonstrating
probative force are not confined to those sharing striking similarity, if the modus
operandi has significant features shared by the offence it may be more likely to
show propensity, and so evidence of the detail of the offence may be necessary.

It does not follow that there is a minimum number of events necessary to
demonstrate propensity. Whilst, generally speaking, the fewer the number of

---

[47] [1991] 2 A.C. 447; 93 Cr. App. R. 267.
[48] [2005] EWCA Crim 2866 (a conjoined appeal with *Weir*).
[49] [2005] EWCA Crim 824; 2 Cr. App. R. 21.
[50] [2005] EWCA Crim 824; 2 Cr. App. R. 21.

convictions, the weaker the evidence of propensity is likely to be, certain sexual behaviour may, in appropriate circumstances, provide an exception to this general proposition. In *Hanson*, the Court of Appeal observed that a single previous conviction may show propensity where, for example, it shows a tendency to unusual behaviour or where its circumstances demonstrate probative force in relation to the crime charged. The court suggested child sexual abuse or fire-setting as comparatively clear examples, but declined to provide an exhaustive list.

In *P*, one of the appeals conjoined with *Hanson*, the prosecution sought to have the applicant's 1993 conviction for indecent assault on an 11 year old girl put in evidence under gateway (d), as showing a propensity and so making it more likely that he committed offences of rape and indecent assault on his step-daughter (born in May 1996), who made the revelations to her foster mother in March 2004. The earlier offence had taken place over 10 years before. The trial judge concluded that the earlier offence was of the same description and the same category, within the Criminal Justice Act 2003 (Categories of Offences) Order 2004,[51] as the offences charged. He expressly took into account the length of time since the previous offence[52] and observed that "a defendant's sexual mores and motivations are not necessarily affected by the passage of time". He concluded that the passage of time was not here sufficient to make the admission of the evidence unjust. The evidence had significant probative value, and its admission would not adversely affect the fairness of the proceedings.[53] The Court of Appeal described the judge's conclusion as "unassailable". In contrast, in *Leaver*,[54] on a charge of rape, it was held that an old conviction for indecent exposure was not evidence of propensity, nor did it go to the appellant's credibility.

Propensity can be proved by relying on incidents which have occurred since the incident which is the subject matter of the trial.[55] This issue is likely to arise from time to time in the trial of sexual offences. Take the case of a schoolmaster who is alleged to have sexually assaulted some of the boys at the school where he teaches. After his arrest for those offences, he is re-arrested because child pornography has been found on his computer, and it is clear that it had been downloaded after the

---

[51] SI 2004/3346.

[52] On an application to exclude under s.101(3) on the basis that the admission would have such an adverse effect on the fairness of the proceedings that the court ought not to admit it, the court must have regard to the length of time between the matters to which the evidence relates and the matters which form the subject of the offence charged: s.101(4) of the Criminal Justice Act 2003. Note the words of Lord Hope in the Privy Council Scottish case of *DS v Her Majesty's Advocate (Privy Council Appeal No. 12 of 2006)* [2007] UKPC D1: when looking at an "interests of justice test" in the context of the admissibility of a defendant's previous convictions for sexual offences in a trial of a sex case, "the test needs to be exacting in proceedings on indictment, in view of the risk that the jury may attach a significance to the conviction which, due to its age or other factors, it cannot properly bear." (para.49).

[53] The judge also admitted this evidence under gateway (g) on the basis that what the defendant had said in interview was a false allegation giving rise to an attack on the complainant's character within s.106(1)(c)(i).

[54] [2006] EWCA Crim 2988.

[55] *Adenusi* [2006] All E.R. (D.) 231.

alleged earlier offences. His subsequent possession of the child pornography is likely to be admissible in respect of the earlier sexual assaults.[56]

The Court of Appeal has resolved a number of issues which may have a significant impact on the trial of sexual offences. Evidence of propensity may be admissible irrespective of whether the defendant's case in relation to an allegation of sexual assault is one of complete denial or one of innocent explanation.[57] Evidence of propensity can support identification evidence.[58] There is no rule that that because the previous offences are unpleasant, the detail of them should not be admitted.[59] The prosecution may cross-examine a defendant about evidence of his bad character as adduced under gateway (d). The prosecution may well wish to hammer home similarities. When deciding whether the admission of the evidence would have such an adverse effect upon the fairness of the proceedings that the court ought not to admit it, the strength of the rest of the prosecution case is highly relevant.[60]

Where evidence of bad character is introduced, the jury should be given assistance as to its relevance in simple language that is tailored to the facts of the individual case. Once the evidence has been admitted through a gateway, it is open to the jury to attach significance to it in any respect in which it is relevant.[61] However, it is undesirable for the judge to identify to the jury the gateway or gateways through which the evidence has been admitted.[62]

In *Campbell*,[63] the Lord Chief Justice stated that the distinction between propensity to offend and credibility is usually unrealistic. The question of whether a defendant has a propensity for being untruthful will not normally be described as an *important* matter in issue between the defendant and the prosecution. A propensity for untruthfulness will not, of itself, go very far to establishing the committal of a criminal offence. The only circumstance in which there is likely to be an *important* issue as to whether a defendant has a propensity to tell lies is where telling lies is an element of the offence charged, and in such a case, the jury should be directed as to the relevance of the evidence with reference to the particular facts which make the matter important.

The Court of Appeal will only interfere if the trial judge's decision-making has been *Wednesbury* unreasonable.[64] However, a jury warning, along the lines

---

[56] In *Weir* [2006] 1 Cr. App. R. 19, a conviction for sexually assaulting a 13 year old girl was upheld where the trial judge had admitted under gateway (d) a previous caution for taking an indecent photograph of a child. Presumably the same principles can be applied if the chronology were reversed.

[57] *Wilkinson* [2006] EWCA Crim 1332.

[58] *Heath Randall* [2006] EWCA Crim 1413; *Blake* [2006] All E.R. (D.) 361; *Eastlake and Eastlake* [2007] EWCA Crim 603.

[59] *Smith* [2006] All E.R. (D.) 280.

[60] *Brima* [2006] All E.R. (D.) 108.

[61] *Highton* [2005] 1W.L.R. 3472; 1 Cr. App. R. 7.

[62] *Campbell* [2007] 2 Cr. App. R. 28.

[63] Last note. See also *R. v RR* [2007] EWCA Crim 437, where the Court of Appeal accepted that in a trial for various offences relating to child abuse, the appellant's conviction of indecently assaulting his 12 year old granddaughter two years earlier had nothing to do with a propensity to tell lies, as he had pleaded guilty.

[64] *Cushing* [2006] All E.R. (D.) 22; *Chand* [2007] EWHC 90 (Admin).

suggested in *Hanson* as modified by *Campbell*,[65] is crucial. In particular, the jury should be warned against attaching too much weight to bad character evidence, let alone concluding that the defendant is guilty simply because of his bad character.

Section 101(1)(e)—evidence of "substantial probative value in relation to an important matter in issue"

15.40F   Section 101(1)(e) provides that evidence of the defendant's bad character is admissible if:

> "it has substantial probative value in relation to an important matter in issue between the defendant and co-defendant."

This is more restrictive than s.101(1)(d), as the evidence has to have substantial probative value in relation to an important issue, as opposed to relevance to an important matter. If evidence of bad character is only marginally probative or only probative in relation to a minor matter, it should not be admitted.[66] In *Edwards and Rowlands*,[67] the Court of Appeal made it clear that simply because an application is made by a co-defendant, the judge is not bound to admit the evidence. The gateway in s.101(1)(e) must be gone through, and marginally relevant matters should not be admitted through it. In determining an application under s.101(1)(e), analysis with a fine-tooth comb is unlikely to be helpful; it is the context of the case as a whole that matters.

However, although gateway (e) is more restrictive, a defendant whose defence has been undermined by a co-defendant may use it to adduce evidence of that co-defendant's bad character, if it has substantial probative value. It cannot be excluded under s.78 of the Police and Criminal Evidence Act 1984 or s.101(3) of the Criminal Justice Act 2003.[68] The jury is entitled to consider evidence of a co-defendant's bad character when considering the case against that co-defendant, even though the evidence is adduced by another defendant and not the prosecution. However, the prosecution should not refer to such "windfall" evidence in their closing speech unless it is, in any event, admissible at the prosecution's behest.[69] *Lawson*[70] is a recent example of a case in which the Court of Appeal held that a co-defendant's previous conviction had been properly admitted under gateway (e) even though its relevance was confined to the

---

[65] [2007] 2 Cr. App. R. 28, where the Lord Chief Justice questioned the desirability of the judge identifying the gateway or gateways through which the bad character evidence has been admitted by reference to the wording of the Act.

[66] *Edwards and Rowlands* [2006] 2 Cr. App. R. 4.

[67] *Edwards and Rowlands* [2006] 2 Cr. App. R. 4.

[68] But see the surprising but practical decision in *Musone* [2007] 2 Cr. App. R. 29, where it was held that there are limited circumstances where relevant evidence can be excluded after non-compliance with the Criminal Procedure Rules. The failure to give notice within the prescribed period was not due to oversight but because of a deliberate intention to ambush a co-defendant. However, the more credible the evidence, the less likely it is that the judge will exclude it on grounds of a breach of procedural requirement.

[69] *Robinson* [2005] EWCA Crim 3233; [2006] 1 Cr. App. R. 32.

[70] [2006] EWCA Crim 2572.

co-defendant's truthfulness/credibility. The appellant was convicted of manslaughter. The principal defendant pushed the victim into a lake and the victim did not surface. The principal defendant pleaded guilty. The prosecution case was that appellant and a third defendant encouraged him. These two defendants ran cut-throat defences, although it did not follow that one or the other was guilty. Co-defending counsel put the appellant's conviction for wounding to the appellant in cross-examination. This was done without notice, which was reprehensible because it went against established rules and principles of advocacy and the unannounced cross-examination put the judge in a very difficult position. However, the judge was entitled to admit such evidence under gateway (e) in that it was of substantial probative value to an important matter in issue between the accused. The conduct of the appellant's defence had undermined the co-defendant's defence. The issue of who was telling the truth was of substantial importance to the case as a whole. The conviction was properly before the jury on the issue of truthfulness/credibility. The Court of Appeal did, however, observe that not every conviction or episode of bad character on the part of a witness whose truthfulness or credibility is in issue will be capable of having probative value on that question.

Section 101(1)(f)—evidence to correct a false impression given by the defendant

This gateway is further explained in s.105(6), which provides that evidence of bad character is admissible under s.101(1)(f) only if it goes no further than to correct a false impression.[71]   **15.40G**

A graphic example of the gateway in operation is *Somonathan*.[72] The appellant was charged with twice raping a woman who attended a Hindu Temple where he was a priest. The trial judge acceded to a prosecution application under s.101(1)(f) to call a witness who was involved in the running of a Hindu Temple where the appellant had previously worked. The appellant had told the police that he had left his employment at that Temple of his own accord. The witness gave evidence that the appellant had been dismissed from his post because he had lied and because his behaviour towards women had given cause for concern. The Court of Appeal held that the gateway having been opened, the prosecution was entitled to adduce from their witness a full account of what, according to the witness, brought the contract to an end. Part of the false impression given by the appellant in interview and, as it turned out later, by calling seven character witnesses, was that he was a priest who had never behaved inappropriately towards female worshippers at his Temple.

---

[71] This effectively abolishes the rule under the old common law that character is indivisible: see Winfield (1939) 27 Cr. App. R. 139.

[72] [2006] 1 Cr. App. R. 19.

Section 101(1)(g)—the defendant has made an attack on another person's character[73]

15.40H   In contrast to the previous law,[74] this gateway is opened even if the defendant does not give evidence. In *Ball*,[75] the Court of Appeal accepted that the defendant's use in interview of the epithet "slag" to describe the complainant was sufficient to trigger s.101(1)(g) in a case where two violent rapes were alleged and the defence was consensual intercourse after heavy alcohol consumption. In interview, the appellant had told the police that most of the men in the local public house had had sexual intercourse with the complainant. He criticised her sexual promiscuity in very disparaging terms, stating "She's a bag really, you know what I mean, a slag". The judge took the view that this amounted to an attack on the complainant's character for the purposes of s.101(1)(g), as explained and expanded in s.106. The Court of Appeal held that the answers given by the appellant in interview purported to be exculpatory in nature (there was no rape: it was consent) but were said by the Crown, with every justification, to provide evidence which indicated an attitude to the complainant which carried with it the implication that the appellant believed that she would have agreed to sexual intercourse with him, and any other man, at any time and in any circumstances, and that if and when she purported to be unwilling to have sexual intercourse, any such refusal should be disregarded as quite meaningless. In reality, answers which might have been treated as exculpatory, and possibly not admissible on that basis, properly formed part of the prosecution case and were "evidence given of an imputation" under the terms of s.106(1)(c).

Significantly, the trial judge refused to admit the evidence of bad character on the basis that the appellant had made a direct attack upon the credibility of the complainant based on the appellant's instructions that the allegations of rape were fabricated. The Court of Appeal stated that the judge's approach to this part of the case was impeccable.

However, notwithstanding this observation, whatever the law was under the 1898 Act,[75A] defences suggesting consent may well involve an attack on the complainant's character.

NON-DEFENDANT'S BAD CHARACTER

15.40I   Section 100 of the Criminal Justice Act 2003 regulates the admissibility of evidence of bad character against non-defendants in criminal trials, whether they be witnesses or strangers to the proceedings. The provision is designed to protect the feelings and reputations of witnesses, as well as to prevent fact-finders in trials from being distracted by satellite issues.

---

[73] s.106 of the Act elaborates on the application of this gateway.
[74] *Butterwasser* [1948] 1 K.B. 4.
[75] [2005] EWCA Crim 2826 (an appeal consolidated with *Renda*).
[75A] cf. *Turner* [1944] K.B. 463; *Stirland v D.P.P.* [1944] A.C. 315. See also *Selvey v D.P.P.* [1970] A.C. 304 at 339 *Cook* [1959] 2 Q.B. 340 at 347, *per* Devlin J.

Unless all parties to the proceedings agree to the evidence being admitted, such evidence is only admissible if (a) it is important explanatory evidence or (b) it has substantial probative value in relation to a matter which (i) is a matter in issue in the proceedings, and (ii) is of substantial importance in the context of the case as a whole. Evidence may be admitted under s.100 if it is directly relevant to an issue in the proceedings or if it bears upon the credibility of a witness who gives evidence about such an issue.[76]

Furthermore, a previous conviction may be relevant to credibility even though it does not necessarily show a propensity to be untruthful. *R. v S. (Andrew)*[77] is a good illustration of this principle. The complainant was a prostitute. She had previous convictions for theft. She complained that the appellant had raped her. The appellant claimed that she had agreed to the sexual act in return for £10. When afterwards he refused her demand for more money, she threatened to accuse him of rape and tried to grab hold of the gold chain he was wearing. At trial, the judge refused the appellant's application for leave to cross-examine the complainant pursuant to s.100 in relation to convictions for theft, handling and burglary. The Court of Appeal stated that the convictions did not demonstrate a propensity to untruthfulness, as asserted by the appellant, but they did demonstrate the complainant's propensity to act in the way asserted, in short to act dishonestly. Section 100 does not spell this out by providing gateways, as s.101 does in the case of a defendant's bad character, but clearly the convictions for dishonesty were relevant to an important matter in issue between the appellant and the prosecution.

In *Hanson*,[78] the Court of Appeal made the observation that dishonesty is not the same as untruthfulness. In *Stephenson*,[79] Hughes L.J. stated that it did not follow from this that previous convictions that do not involve either the making of false statements or the giving of false evidence are incapable of having substantial probative value in relation to the credibility of a non-defendant under s.100. If the evidence has substantial probative value in relation to a matter in issue in the proceedings and is of substantial importance in the context of the case as a whole, the judge has no discretion and must allow the s.100 application. This principle was demonstrated in *Riley*,[80] where the appellant was charged with wounding contrary to s.18 of the Offences Against the Person Act 1860. His defence was self-defence. The complainant was due to stand trial in respect of an allegation of actual bodily harm on the appellant himself. The appellant applied to cross-examine the complainant about this, on the basis that it was important explanatory evidence which went to the issue of appellant's propensity to violence. The trial judge refused leave on the basis that the application raised an unhelpful satellite

---

[76] *Yaxley-Lennon* [2006] 1 Cr. App. R. 19. See also the Explanatory Notes to the Criminal Justice Act 2003.

[77] [2006] EWCA Crim 1303; [2006] 2 Cr. App. R. 31. See also *Hester and McKray* [2007] EWCA Crim 2127.

[78] Above n.49.

[79] [2006] EWCA Crim 2325.

[80] [2006] EWCA Crim 2030.

issue. The Court of Appeal held that this decision had been wrong.[81] The evidence was capable of showing that the complainant was the aggressor and was therefore important explanatory evidence.

The restriction in s.100 operates cumulatively together with the prohibition imposed by s.41 of the Youth Justice and Criminal Evidence Act 1999. This means that when a defendant wishes to cross-examine a complainant in a sex case, they face a double hurdle, which may be very difficult to surmount.[82] For the purposes of s.41, the term "complainant" is limited to the complainant of the offence that is the subject of the trial. This means that a complainant in a matter of which evidence is admitted under the bad character provisions does not enjoy the protection of s.41.[83] However, such a complainant might be protected by s.100, and even if not so protected, will be protected by the general rules as to common law relevance as informed by the principles underpinning s.41. These principles are designed to outlaw irrelevant and illegitimate lines of reasoning based on the Canadian "twin myths": see further Ch.18 of the main work.

JOINDER AND SEVERANCE

Cross-admissibility

15.67 Although cross-admissibility is not a pre-condition for charges to be properly joined in one indictment,[84] it is likely to arise frequently in sex cases, and when it does, an application for severance is most unlikely to succeed. Traditionally, the facility to rely on similar fact evidence has been a factor in favour of joinder and against severance. The removal of similar fact evidence by s.99(1) of the Criminal Justice Act 2003 means that the old test in *DPP v P.* has gone, and now the gateways in the new bad character provisions must be considered when determining cross-admissibility. The likelihood is that it will be easier to establish propensity than similar fact, and so evidence on one count will be admissible on another more often than in the past, and thus it will more frequently be appropriate for counts to be tried jointly.[85]

---

[81] Nevertheless the Court of Appeal has expressed concerns as to the proliferation of satellite issues: *R. v AJC* [2006] EWCA Crim 284. However, once the Court is of the view that evidence of bad character is of substantial probative value in relation to the credibility of a material witness, it would seem that it has no discretion but to allow the s.100 application.

[82] *R. v V* [2006] EWCA Crim 1901, where the Court observed that in many cases the s.41 hurdle will be the more formidable obstacle to overcome.

[83] *R. v M* [2006] EWCA Crim 1509.

[84] *Christou* [1996] 2 Cr. App. R. 360, where Lord Taylor C.J. set out the factors to be considered. *Thomas* [2006] EWCA Crim 2442 is a recent example of the Court of Appeal approving a judge's decision not to sever counts in a case where the evidence in respect of each count was not cross-admissible (see Commentary in Criminal Law Week 2006, Issue 35).

[85] H.H. Judge Mott in a lecture to the JSB Serious Sexual Offences Seminar, July 2007.

As to the application of the bad character provisions, s.112(2) of the Criminal Justice Act 2003 provides that where a defendant is charged with two or more offences in the same criminal proceedings, the bad character provisions have effect as if each offence were charged in separate proceedings; and references to the offence with which the defendant is charged are to be read accordingly.

The issue of cross-admissibility arose in *Chopra*.[86] The appellant was a dentist who was tried on an indictment alleging indecent touching of three teenage patients over a period spanning 10 years. The trial judge held that the evidence of the several complainants was cross-admissible providing that collusion or contamination between them could be excluded. On appeal, it was submitted that the jury should not have been permitted to treat the evidence of one complainant as supportive of the evidence of another. In each of the cases, the complainant alleged that the appellant had deliberately placed his hand on her breast and squeezed it. In each case, the appellant denied that he had done any such thing and said that nothing resembling in any way a deliberate squeezing of the breast had occurred. The Court of Appeal was satisfied that the evidence in respect of each allegation was, as the trial judge ruled, available to the jury, if it accepted it and if collusion and contamination was excluded, on a basis of cross-admissibility each to support the other. The common law rules as to admissibility of bad character evidence had been abolished by s.99 of the Criminal Justice Act 2003. Accordingly, the evidence in relation to one count can be admissible evidence in relation to another count if, but only if, it passes through one of the gateways in s.101. In this case, the relevant gateway was s.101(1)(d). The evidence of the several complainants was cross-admissible if, but only if, it was relevant to an important matter in issue between the defendant and the prosecution. The present case was one in which, quite clearly, if the evidence did establish a propensity in the appellant occasionally to molest young female patients in the course of dental examination, that did make it more likely that he committed the several offences charged. It followed that the jury could treat the evidence of one complainant as being supportive of another if they were sure that the evidence of the first complainant was true.

The decision in *Chopra* begs the question of how juries should approach an indictment containing similar but separate sexual allegations. Can it be that the new bad character provisions, by abolishing the old common law similar fact rules, prevent the prosecution from submitting that the jury can, if they exclude the possibility of contamination and/or collusion, take the view that it would be an affront to common sense to conclude that several complainants had independently made similar false allegations? The point derives its strength from the fact of several independent complaints, rather than from the fact that a particular allegation, once proved, can support another. We suggest that, in appropriate cases, this remains a logical and legitimate line of reasoning which the jury should consider before passing on to the residual consideration as to whether one

[86] [2006] EWCA Crim 2133.

allegation, once proved, can show propensity, which can then be take into account when considering other allegations.[87]

Cross-admissibility and the danger of unconscious influence

15.67A   Where the bad character provisions in s.101 of the Criminal Justice Act 2003 permit the evidence on one count to be cross-admissible on another, it is important for the judge to direct the jury carefully about the dangers of innocent contamination[88] (or what the standard JSB direction describes as conscious or unconscious influence) as well as the dangers of guilty collusion, if that is or may be a possibility. In *Lamb*,[89] the appellant, a teacher, had been convicted of engaging in sexual activity in breach of trust with two 17 year old girl pupils whom he taught at school. The Court of Appeal took the view that there was a clear possibility that the two complainants had been consciously or unconsciously influenced in their complaints, or their evidence about them, by hearing of, and discussing with one another, the circumstances of their respective incidents. The trial judge had directed the jury on dishonest collusion, but had failed to warn the jury that they must take into account the possibility of conscious or unconscious influence when assessing the weight of the complainants' evidence. Furthermore, the appellant's counsel argued that the judge had over-emphasised the similarities between the incidents, making no allowance for the dissimilarities. The Court of Appeal acknowledged that it is necessary for the judge to give a balanced and accurate account of similarities, as the level of similarity is relevant to the issue of likelihood or unlikelihood of innocent coincidence.

Indictments that straddle the implementation date of the Sexual Offences Act 2003—severance ever justified?

15.67B   The Sexual Offences Act 2003 came into force on May 1, 2004. Section 141 of the Act empowered the Secretary of State to make transitional provisions, but no such provisions were made. It follows that, if there was doubt as to whether an offence occurred before or after the coming into force of the Act, the proceedings would fail because the prosecution would not have proved whether a statutory offence was committed under the old or the new law.[90] This lacuna in the law was filled by s.55 of the Violent Crime Reduction Act 2006, a deeming provision which came

---

[87] See article by James Richardson supporting this line of argument in Criminal Law Week, Issue 2, January 2007. See also *Wallace* [2007] 2 Cr. App. R. 30, where there was a technical reliance on bad character by the prosecution using inferences to be drawn from circumstantial evidence to show that the defendant was involved in a series of robberies. The Court of Appeal took the view that a proper direction as to circumstantial evidence was sufficient, and it was neither here nor there that it may have been bad character evidence requiring admittance through a s.101 gateway. There was clear evidence that the robberies were linked.

[88] See *Lee* [2007] EWCA Crim 764 for a case where the Court of Appeal felt no direction on unconscious influence was necessary. See also *Ryder* (1994) 98 Cr. App. R. 242.

[89] [2007] EWCA Crim 1766.

[90] *A. (Prosecutor's Appeal)* [2006] 1 Cr. App. R. 433 sometimes referred to as *R v C* [2005] EWCA Crim 3533; *Newbon* [2005] Crim. L.R. 738.

into force on February 12, 2007. It covers the situation where a defendant is charged in respect of the same conduct both with an offence under the 2003 Act and with an offence under the old law, and the only thing preventing him being found guilty of either offence is the fact that it has not been proved beyond a reasonable doubt that the time when the conduct took place was either after the coming into force of the 2003 Act offence or before the repeal of the old law, as the case may be. In such circumstances, for the purposes of determining guilt, it shall be conclusively presumed that the time when the conduct took place was when the old law applied, if the old offence attracted a lesser maximum penalty; otherwise, it will be presumed the conduct took place after the implementation of the new law. If the penalties are the same, then it will be conclusively presumed that the conduct took place after the commencement of the 2003 Act.

The question nonetheless arises whether severance will ever be justified where the allegations in an indictment relate to a course of conduct extending both before and after the commencement date of the 2003 Act, i.e. May 1, 2004? In some cases, factually similar conduct occurring before and after commencement will constitute different offences. For example, the 2003 Act redefines rape to include penile penetration of another person's mouth without their consent, which was formerly indecent assault. It follows that such conduct committed before and after commencement will be constitute different offences.

There have also been fundamental changes in the law relating to the meaning of "consent" and the mechanisms for proving its absence. Further, in relation to non-consensual offences, the subjective *Morgan* test in relation to the mental element has been replaced by a more objective test. These changes may complicate trials for non-consensual offences straddling the implementation date, as the jury will need to be directed differently on the consent issues arising in respect of the earlier and later offences.

It is doubtful whether these considerations will ever provide good grounds for an application by the defence to sever the indictment. Severance may be ordered where the court is of the opinion that trying the counts together may prejudice the defence. It is unlikely that prejudice will ever be made out simply on the basis that the jury have to be directed to consider different counts by reference to different legal and/or evidential tests. Even in a very complicated case, any difficulty the jury might have in following and applying different directions on the "old" and "new" counts should be capable of being resolved by the use of written directions.

Multiple offending: count charging more than one incident—Rule 14.2(2) of the Criminal Procedure Rules 2005

Revision of the rule against duplicity

For any case sent, transferred or committed to the Crown Court on or after April   **15.67C** 2, 2007, the rules relating to the form and content of indictments are to be found in the Criminal Procedure Rules 2005, as amended by the Criminal Procedure

(Amendment) Rules 2007.[91] For cases sent (etc.) prior to April 2, 2007, the Indictment Rules 1971 still apply. The 2007 Rules revoke the Indictment Rules 1971 and consolidate them with the procedural rules about indictments, which were already included in Pt 14 of the 2005 Rules. The new Pt 14 is intended to revise and simplify the rules about the service, form and content of indictments.

The new Rules have made an important change to the rule against particularising a series of like offences within a single count, with the result that it is no longer essential for a count to relate to a single act. In due course, this will have significant impact on the indictment of cases involving allegations of repeated sexual abuse. The new Pt 14 permits more than one incident of the same offence to be charged in one count. This will mean a change in the way indictments are drafted in order to reflect a continuing course of conduct. It is now proper to charge one count covering a period over which a number of offences have occurred, instead of charging a number of specimen counts divided up by reference to time and type of assault.

Good practice will develop in respect of the drafting of such counts. It may not be appropriate for a count to cover a period of a number of years. It may still be necessary to include separate counts where significantly different forms of sexual activity are alleged, to enable the sentencer properly to evaluate the gravity of the offender's conduct.

The Criminal Procedure Rules Committee has stated that the facility to charge more than one incident of the commission of an offence in a single count may be used: "when, for example, a defendant is alleged to have repeatedly assaulted the same victim in the same way over a period of time".[92] The Committee's intention in creating this new rule was to take account, amongst other things, of the potential under the old rules for a perceived unfairness to a victim of multiple offending where, out of many alleged offences, only a few are prosecuted as examples, giving the impression that the victim's distress has been underestimated or that he or she has not been believed.[93]

The Consolidated Criminal Practice Direction—Amendment No. 15

15.67D   The new Rules are supplemented by amendments to the Criminal Practice Direction giving guidance on when a "multiple incidents" count under Rule 14.2(2) may be appropriate. The following is the relevant extract:

> "**More than one incident**
> (IV.34.8) Rule 14.(2)(2) of the Criminal Procedure Rules allows a single count to allege more than one incident of the commission of an offence in certain circumstances. Each incident must be of the same offence. The circumstances in which such a count may be appropriate include, but are not limited to, the following:
>   (a) the victim on each occasion was the same . . . ;

---

[91] SI 2007/699.
[92] See guidance to the Rules, dated March 27, 2007.
[93] Taken from a note prepared by the Secretariat to the Committee dated March 27, 2007 and published with the guidance, above.

(b) the alleged incidents involved a marked degree of repetition in the method employed or in their location, or both;

(c) the alleged incidents took place over a clearly defined period, typically (but not necessarily) no more than about a year;

(d) in any event, the defence is such as to apply to every alleged incident without differentiation. Where what is in issue differs between different incidents, a single 'multiple incidents' count will not be appropriate, though it may be appropriate to use two or more such counts according to the circumstances and to the issues raised by the defence.

(IV.34.10) For some offences, particularly sexual offences, the penalty for the offence may have changed during the period over which the alleged incidents took place. In such a case, additional 'multiple incidents' counts should be used so that each count only alleges incidents to which the same maximum penalty applies.

. . .

(IV.34.12) In other cases, such as sexual or physical abuse, a complainant may be in a position only to give evidence of a series of similar incidents without being able to specify when or the precise circumstances in which they occurred. In these cases, a 'multiple incidents' count may be desirable. If on the other hand, the complainant is able to identify particular incidents of the offence by reference to a date or other specific event, but alleges that in addition there were other incidents which the complainant is unable to specify, then it may be desirable to include separate counts for the identified incidents and a 'multiple incidents' count or counts alleging that incidents of the same offence occurred 'many' times. Using a 'multiple incidents' count may be an appropriate alternative to using 'specimen' counts in some cases where repeated sexual or physical abuse is alleged. The choice of count will depend on the particular circumstances of the case and should be determined bearing in mind the implications for sentencing set out in *R v Canavan; R v Kidd; R v Shaw* [1998] 1 Cr App R 79."

Summing up where there are multiple counts

In relation to each count, it is necessary to summarise the evidence which goes to **15.67E** that count and any significant disputes that arise upon that evidence, so that such discrepancies as arise from each witness whose evidence goes to that count are disclosed. It will only confuse a jury if the judge outlines the evidence of one witness in relation to several events and then, possibly a day later, turns to another witness's evidence in relation to the same events. Only by a summary focused upon a particular count can assistance be given to a jury faced with numbers of counts relating to different events.[94]

---

[94] H.H. Judge Tim Mort, lecture to JSB Serious Sexual Offences Seminar, July 2007. See also *Robson and others* [2006] EWCA Crim 2754, where the Court of Appeal stressed that in historic cases the dangers inherent in such cases required the judge carefully to scrutinise the evidence himself to see whether it is safe to leave to the jury. This scrutiny requires the judge to consider not only the nature and quality of the evidence, but also inconsistencies, either within the evidence of one witness or between a number of witnesses. Clearly, if the judge decides to leave such a case to the jury, the jury should be directed carefully as to the inconsistencies.

CHAPTER 16

ANONYMITY IN SEX CASES AND REPORTING RESTRICTIONS RELATING TO CHILDREN AND YOUNG PERSONS

INTRODUCTION

The provisions of the Youth Justice and Criminal Evidence Act 1999 repealing the **16.03**
provisions on anonymity in the Sexual Offences (Amendment) Act 1976 and
extending those in the Sexual Offences (Amendment) Act 1992 to cover all sex
offences, came into force on October 7, 2004.[1]

ANONYMITY IN SEX CASES

ANONYMITY OF COMPLAINANTS OF ANOTHER SEX OFFENCE

Sections 4 and 5 of the 1976 Act have been repealed by the Youth Justice and **16.08** *et*
Criminal Evidence Act 1999: see para.16.03 above. *seq.*

The 1992 Act has been substantially amended by the Youth Justice and Criminal **16.13**
Evidence Act 1999: see para.16.03 above.

The inclusion in a publication or broadcast of a person's name, address or picture **16.14**
will be "likely to lead" to their identification if there is a real risk, real danger or
real chance that it may lead to their identification: *O'Riordan v DPP*.[2] See further

---

[1] Youth Justice and Criminal Evidence Act 1999 (Commencement No. 10) (England and Wales)
Order 2004 (SI 2004/2428).
[2] [2005] EWHC 1240 (Admin), citing Dame Elizabeth Butler Sloss in *Attorney General v Greater
Manchester Newspapers Ltd*, *Times*, December 7, 2001.

R. (on the application of Gazette Media Co Ltd) v Teesside Crown Court,[3] discussed in para.16.33 below.

16.15   The 1992 Act does not apply to the offences relating to indecent photographs and pseudo-photographs of children contained in the Protection of Children Act 1978 and s.160(1) of the Criminal Justice Act 1988: see *R. (on the application of Gazette Media Co Ltd) v Teesside Crown Court.*[4] For the purpose of those offences, a "child" is defined as a person under 18: see para.8.42 of the main work. Where these offences are charged, an order under s.39 of the Children and Young Persons Act 1933 may be necessary to protect the child or young person concerned.

16.17   The offence under s.5 of the 1992 Act, though one of strict liability, does not offend against Art.10 of the ECHR: *O'Riordan v DPP.*[5]

16.18   The relevant provisions of the 1999 Act came into force on October 7, 2004: see para.16.03 above.

REPORTING RESTRICTIONS RELATING TO CHILDREN AND YOUNG PERSONS

Restrictions on Identification of Child or Young Person by Media: The Current Law

16.29   For the approach to be adopted in cases where s.39 of the Children and Young Persons Act 1933 is inapplicable because the child or young person in question is not "concerned in the proceedings", and no other statutory exception to the principle of open justice applies, see *Re S. (a child) (identification: restriction on publication)*[6] (relating to the sibling of the child to whom the proceedings related).

16.33   An order purportedly made under s.39 that explicitly prohibited the identification of the defendant by name was quashed in *R. (on the application of Gazette Media Co Ltd) v Teesside Crown Court.*[7] The defendants, S and L, were charged on an indictment containing one count of conspiracy to rape and a number of counts under s.1 of the Protection of Children Act 1978. The complainant was S's daughter, who had been the subject of indecent photographs and also an agreement between the defendants to commit further offences against her. While the conspiracy count fell within the scope of the anonymity provisions of the

---

[3] [2005] EWCA Crim 1983; [2006] Crim. L.R. 157.
[4] [2005] EWCA Crim 1983; [2006] Crim. L.R. 157.
[5] Above n.1.
[6] [2004] UKHL 47; [2004] 4 All E.R. 683.
[7] Above n.2.

Sexual Offences (Amendment) Act 1992, the 1978 Act counts did not. The trial judge therefore made an order under s.39, which inter alia prohibited the identification by name of S. Three media companies appealed against the order. The Attorney General submitted on the appeal that the prohibition on the naming of S was necessary in order to give effect to the complainant's respect for private life under Art.8 of the ECHR, and the obligation of the court under s.3 of the Human Rights Act 1998 to read and give effect to primary legislation in a way that is compatible with the Convention. The Court of Appeal rejected this argument, holding that there was no scope in the present case for extending the restriction on freedom of expression (Art.10 of the ECHR) beyond what was provided by s.39 as construed in *Godwin*. Were Art.8 to stand alone, the Attorney's argument would have had greater force. However, it co-existed with the right to freedom of expression, and the balance between the two was struck by the primary legislation. The Court accordingly quashed the order and substituted one made in conventional terms.

It added that it was not axiomatic that reporting that identified S by name, and referred to the complainant as "an 11-year-old schoolgirl", would comply with a proper order under s.39, or avoid a breach of s.1 of the 1992 Act. Offences of the kind in question were often committed by fathers and step-fathers. In this case, the history of photography and the planning of further offences were indicative of a close relationship between the defendant and the complainant. Were a defendant to be named and the complainant described as an 11-year-old schoolgirl, in circumstances in which the defendant had an 11-year-old daughter, it would be at least arguable that the composite picture embraced "particulars calculated to lead to the identification" of the complainant within the meaning of s.39.

RESTRICTIONS ON IDENTIFICATION OF PERSONS UNDER 18 BY MEDIA: THE YOUTH JUSTICE AND CRIMINAL EVIDENCE ACT 1999

Power to restrict reporting of criminal proceedings involving persons under 18

Footnote 77: The reporting restrictions in s.49 of the 1933 Act cease to apply once **16.42** the defendant has attained 18, even if the proceedings continue to be dealt with in the Youth Court by virtue of s.29(1) of the Children and Young Persons Act 1933: *T. v DPP.*[8]

Breach of restrictions or direction

Section 49 of the 1999 Act came into force on October 7, 2004, for the purposes **16.45** of s.46 (reports relating to adult witnesses) and s.47 (restrictions on reporting directions under Ch.I or II) of the 1999 Act.[9]

[8] [2003] EWHC 2408 (Admin); [2005] Crim. L.R. 739.
[9] Youth Justice and Criminal Evidence Act 1999 (Commencement No. 10) (England and Wales) Order 2004 (SI 2004/2428).

Defences

16.46 Section 50 of the 1999 Act came into force on October 7, 2004, for the purposes of s.46 (reports relating to adult witnesses) and s.47 (restrictions on reporting directions under Ch.I or II) of the 1999 Act.[10]

---

[10] Youth Justice and Criminal Evidence Act 1999 (Commencement No. 10) (England and Wales) Order 2004 (SI 2004/2428).

CHAPTER 17

VULNERABLE WITNESSES, "SPECIAL MEASURES" AND RELATED MATTERS

INTRODUCTION

On the difficulty of identifying "vulnerable" witnesses, see M. Burton, R. Evans **17.01** and A. Sanders, *Implementing special measures for vulnerable and intimidated witnesses: The problem of identification* [2006] Crim. L.R. 229.

Speaking Up for Justice

Footnote 8: Section 23 of the Criminal Justice Act 1988 has been repealed and the **17.08** admissibility of previous statements is now governed by ss.114, 116, 120 and 139 of the Criminal Justice Act 2003.

Availability of special measures: pre-recorded cross-examination

Footnote 11: Jane Furniss's letter is superseded by Mark de Pulford's of August **17.09** 3, 2005: see para.17.24 below.

VULNERABLE WITNESSES AND "SPECIAL MEASURES"

Child witnesses

Research by the NSPCC and Victim Support has suggested that child witnesses **17.15** in criminal proceedings receive inadequate levels of support and frequently feel intimidated: see generally Barbara Esam, *Caring for children in court: making a difference for child witnesses* J.P. 2005, 169(15), 271–273.

Adult witnesses

Section 16(1)(b)

17.19 The procedure for applying for special measures is now governed by Pt 29 of the Criminal Procedure Rules 2005, set out in Appendix A to this Supplement. At present, the procedure remains the same as set out in the Crown Court (Special Measures Directions and Directions Prohibiting Cross-Examination) Rules 2002, described in the main work.

Section 17

17.21 Section 23 of the Criminal Justice Act 1988 has been repealed. The admissibility of a fearful witness's statement is now governed by ss.114 and 116(2)(e) of the Criminal Justice Act 2003.

Special Measures and the Defendant

17.22 In *R. (D.) v Camberwell Green Youth Court*,[1] the House of Lords rejected a challenge to the YJCEA 1999 scheme under Article 6 of the ECHR based upon inequality of arms, in so far as the scheme does not apply to defendants. Baroness Hale, with whom the other members of the House agreed, recognised the real difficulties that exist in the Youth Court, where child defendants are often among the most disadvantaged and the least able to give a good account of themselves. However, the answer to these problems was not to deprive the court of the best evidence available from other child witnesses merely because the YJCEA 1999 scheme does not apply to the accused. Rather, the question was what, if anything, the court needs to do to ensure that the defendant is not at a "substantial disadvantage" compared to the prosecution and any other defendants. The defendant is excluded from the statutory scheme because it would be "clearly inappropriate" to apply the whole scheme to him. There are obvious difficulties, said Baroness Hale, about admitting a video-recorded interview as the defendant's evidence-in-chief. For example, who would conduct it, and how? What safeguards could there be against repeated interviews? There are also obvious difficulties in applying binding advance presumptions about how a defendant's evidence should be given, if indeed it is to be given at all, when the defence is ordinarily free to make such decisions in the light of events as they unfold. Baroness Hale therefore preferred to rely upon the "wide and flexible" inherent powers of the courts to ensure that the defendant receives a fair trial, which includes a fair opportunity of giving the best evidence he can.

---

[1] [2005] UKHL 4; [2005] 1 W.L.R. 393; [2005] 2 Cr. App. R. 1; see further para.17.35 below.

The decision in the *Camberwell* case has to some extent been overtaken by events **17.22A** in the shape of s.47 of the Police and Justice Act 2006, which came into force on January 15, 2007.[2] Section 47 inserts a new s.33A into the YJCEA 1999, under which a vulnerable defendant in either the magistrates' court or before the Crown Court may give evidence by live-link. Where the defendant is under 18 at the date of the application, a direction may be made that any oral evidence given by the defendant is given via live-link where this is in the interests of justice and the conditions in s.33A(4) are satisfied. Those conditions are:

"(a) his ability to participate effectively in the proceedings as a witness giving oral evidence in court is compromised by his level of intellectual ability or social functioning, and

(b) use of a live link would enable him to participate more effectively in the proceedings as a witness (whether by improving the quality of his evidence or otherwise)."

In addition, where a defendant has attained the age of 18 at the time of the application, a live-link direction may be given if it is in the interests of justice and the conditions in s.33A(5) are satisfied. Those conditions are:

"(a) he suffers from a mental disorder (within the meaning of the Mental Health Act 1983) or otherwise has a significant impairment of intelligence and social functioning,

(b) he is for that reason unable to participate effectively in the proceedings as a witness giving oral evidence in court, and

(c) use of a live link would enable him to participate more effectively in the proceedings as a witness (whether by improving the quality of his evidence or otherwise)."

The question arises whether the courts have inherent power to allow the use of **17.22B** live-link in cases falling outside the scope of the statutory scheme. In *R. (on the application of S) v Waltham Forest Youth Court*,[3] the Divisional Court held that they do not. Baroness Hale in the *Camberwell* case clearly had some difficulty with this decision, but as the point was not before the House, she left open whether the case had been correctly decided. Then in *Ukpabio*,[4] decided after the coming into force of s.33A, the Court of Appeal declined an invitation to depart from the *Waltham Forest* case in the light of the doubts expressed by Baroness Hale. The Court there upheld the refusal of the trial judge to allow the defendant, who fell outside the statutory scheme, to give evidence by live-link, holding that the scheme as extended to defendants by s.33A is exhaustive of the circumstances in which a live-link may be used for this purpose. The statutory provisions are based on the premise that where they do not apply, evidence should be given by a witness present in court subject to such protective measures (short of live-link) as the court considers appropriate to ensure that the witness is able to give evidence fully and without fear. However, the Court went on to hold that there may well be

---

[2] Police and Justice Act 2006 (Commencement No. 1, Transitional and Savings Provisions) Order 2006 (SI 2006/3364).

[3] [2004] EWHC 715 (Admin).

[4] [2007] EWCA Crim 2108.

circumstances in which it may be appropriate that a defendant, on his own application, should not be present in court for all or part of a trial, provided that he can participate adequately by live-link or in some other way. Accordingly, the trial judge had been wrong to hold that he had no power to accede to the appellant's application to participate in the trial (other than by giving evidence) through live-link. However, having considered the material put before the judge in support of that application, the Court concluded that it could not conceivably have justified the making of the order sought.

17.22C   In conclusion, it appears that Parliament is determined that fewer special measures should be available to young defendants than to other young witnesses. This is so even though there are no practical difficulties in using live-link. For example, the provisions of the Police and Justice Act 2006 do not permit a defendant, who is vulnerable through fear or distress, to give evidence by live-link. Consequently, there remains a concern for a defendant who fears giving evidence in front of his co-defendants.

A live-link direction may be discharged following an application to the court, or by the court of its own motion.[5] However, when a live-link direction has effect, the defendant may only give evidence through the live-link.

It remains the case that a defendant is not eligible for special measures other than the live-link, unless the court uses its inherent powers. It is of concern that in some cases, prosecutors may not be applying for special measures for eligible witnesses for fear that the defendant will succeed in arguing on appeal that the disparity in treatment rendered the trial process unfair. Other jurisdictions are not so restrictive. So in Scotland, all witnesses under the age of 16 are eligible for special measures, with the exception of screens and video-recorded evidence before a Commissioner.[6] In New South Wales, investigative interviews and video recordings of those under 16 can constitute their examination-in-chief if they later face trial, and cross-examination may also be by live-link if the defendant might suffer mental or emotional harm if required to testify in the ordinary way or the facts might be better ascertained over the live-link. Further, in New South Wales, defendants are entitled to be accompanied by a court supporter who is permitted to act as an interpreter in order to assist with any difficulties associated with a disability the defendant may face when given evidence.

It is submitted that the question for any court is whether denying a defendant special measures will deny him a fair trial. In relation to child witnesses, it is important to remember that in order to protect their rights under Art.6 of the ECHR they must be able to participate effectively in the trial. This may provide strong support for an application to the court that a young defendant, or a defendant with cognitive functioning below their natural age, should have the

---

[5] s.33A(6), (7) of the YJCEA 1999.
[6] See the Vulnerable Witnesses (Scotland) Act 2004, s.271F; Ch.8B of Laura Hoyano and Caroline Keenan, *Child Abuse Law & Policy Across Boundaries*, Oxford University Press, 2007.

assistance of an intermediary to ensure their effective participation. The Court should itself consider the appropriateness of appointing an intermediary and using other special measures to cure any abuse of process that might occur in circumstances where the defendant's understanding of the proceedings is limited.

AVAILABILITY

Home Office Circulars 58/2003, 38/2005 and 39/2005 have been replaced by   **17.24** Ministry of Justice Circular 25/06/2007, with a notification letter pursuant to s.18(2) of the YJCEA 1999 dated August 1, 2005. The following Table sets out the position regarding implementation as of September 25, 2007. It should be noted that s.27 (video-recorded evidence-in-chief) is available in the Crown Court for all s.16 witnesses, and is also available in the Crown Court for s.17(4) witnesses when the investigation commenced after September 1, 2007. In the magistrates' courts, s.27 is available for child witnesses in need of special protection.

Appendix 2

YOUTH JUSTICE & CRIMINAL EVIDENCE ACT 1999: SPECIAL MEASURES IMPLEMENTATION (ENGLAND & WALES)

Availability in criminal proceedings (England & Wales) from 1 September 2007 For availability up to 01/09/07 please see table attached to HO circular 39/2005	CROWN COURT		MAGISTRATES' COURT	
	Section 16 witnesses (children & vulnerable adults)	**Section 17** witnesses (intimidated/ fear or distress	**Section 16** witnesses (children & vulnerable adults)	**Section 17** witnesses (intimidated/ fear or distress)
Section 23 *screening witness from accused*	Full availability (note 1)	Full availability (note 1)	Full availability (note 2)	Full availability (note 2)
Section 24 *evidence by live link*	Full availability (note 1)	Full availability (note 1)	Full availability (note 3 & 4)	Full availability (note 4)
Section 25 *evidence given in private*	Full availability (note 1)	Full availability (note 1)	Full availability (note 2)	Full availability (note 2)
Section 26 *removal of wigs and gowns*	Full availability (note 1)	Full availability (note 1)	**Not applicable**	**Not applicable**

Availability in criminal proceedings (England & Wales) from 1 September 2007 For availability up to 01/09/07 please see table attached to HO circular 39/2005	CROWN COURT		MAGISTRATES' COURT	
	Section 16 witnesses (children & vulnerable adults)	**Section 17** witnesses (intimidated/ fear or distress)	**Section 16** witnesses (children & vulnerable adults)	**Section 17** witnesses (intimidated/ fear or distress)
Section 27 video recorded evidence in chief	Full availability (note 1)	Partial availability— for complainants in serious sexual offences (note 9)	Partial availability— for child witnesses in need of special protection only (note 3 and 5)	Not available (note 5)
Section 28 video recorded cross-examination/ re-examination	Not available (note 6)	Not available (note 6)	Not available (note 6)	Not available (note 6)
Section 29 examination through an intermediary	Partial availability— pilot areas (note 7)	**Not applicable**	Partial availability— pilot areas (note 7)	**Not applicable**
Section 30 aids to communication	Full availability (note 1)	*Not applicable*	Full availability (note 8)	*Not applicable*

Note 1: – full availability for these witnesses in these courts since 24/07/02

Note 2: – full availability for these witnesses in these courts since 03/06/04

Note 3: – available for "child witnesses in need of special protection" (defined by section 21 of the 1999 Act) only since 24/07/02

Note 4: – available since 01/09/04 in West London magistrates' court and full availability across magistrates' courts from 03/10/05

Note 5: – no decision on the extension of video-recorded evidence in chief to vulnerable and intimidated witnesses in the magistrates' courts will be taken until we assess the impact of the extension to adult complainants in sex offence cases in the Crown Court

Note 6: – we are currently reviewing the workability of this measure in the context of a review of child evicence.

Note 7: – intermediaries are being piloted in preparation for national roll out (planned 2006/07)— Merseyside pilot went live 23/02/04, Thames Valley 02/10/04, West Midlands 01/11/04 (from 13/09/04 in Black-Country area), Norfolk 01/02/05, S Wales 01/02/05 (Cardiff Crown Court and related magistrates' courts in S Wales), Devon and Cornwall 20/06/05 (Plymouth Crown and magistrates' court), Leicestershire 01/04/07 (Leicester Crown Court and related magistrates' courts) and Derbyshire 30/04/07 (Derby Crown Court and related magistrates' courts).

Note 8: – available in Merseyside since 23/02/04; full availability across magistrates' courts since 03/06/04.

Note 9: – available in England and Wales for complainants in sexual offence cases tried in the Crown Court for investigations commencing on or after 01/09/07—see MoJ circular 25/06/2007

Intermediaries are also being piloted in Merseyside, Thames Valley, West Midlands, Norfolk, South Wales and Devon and Cornwall. It is anticipated that a further eight pilot areas will be designated in late 2007, with national roll out planned for Spring 2008.

INFLEXIBILITY OF THE PROVISIONS FOR CHILD WITNESSES

The House of Lords in the *Camberwell* case held that s.21(5) of the YJCEA 1999   **17.35** does not infringe Art.6 of the ECHR, in so far as it prevents individualised consideration of the necessity for a special measures direction at the stage at which the direction is made.[7] The arguments before the Divisional Court were repeated before the House. Baroness Hale, in an opinion with which the other members of the House agreed, enumerated the benefits that flow from the "primary rule" and said that the court must start from the statutory presumption that there is nothing intrinsically unfair in children giving evidence in accordance with the rule. As for Article 6, nothing in the provisions of the YJCEA 1999 is inconsistent with its principles, because all the evidence is produced at trial in the presence of the accused, who can see and hear it and has every opportunity to challenge it and question the witnesses against him. The only thing missing is a face-to-face confrontation, but that is not something guaranteed by the Convention. In conclusion, the YJCEA scheme enables the best evidence to be put before the court while preserving the essential rights of the accused to know and challenge all the evidence against him. Parliament having decided that the scheme is justified for good policy reasons, the courts are entitled to apply it without the need to show special justification in every case.

Baroness Hale noted that after a live-link direction has been made, the court may give permission under s.24(3) of the Act for the witness to give evidence in some other way, if this appears to be in the interests of justice. The appropriate time to consider these matters will usually be at trial, when the trial judge will be in the best position to consider the matter in the round. Possible circumstances in which permission may be given under s.24(3) are where the live-link equipment is not working properly, or where the child is positively anxious to give evidence in court rather than via the live-link, or where the alleged abuse involved video-recording the witness. Similarly, circumstances may arise in which the court may, in the exercise of its discretion under s.27(2), exclude the video-recorded interview as the child's evidence-in-chief, on the ground that it would not be in the interests of justice to admit it.

DEFENCE WITNESSES

Footnote 58: Criminal Procedure Rule 29.7(10) is to the same effect.   **17.37**

---

[7] *R. (D) v Camberwell Green Youth Court* [2005] UKHL 4; [2005] 1 W.L.R. 393; [2005] 2 Cr. App. R. 1.

TYPES OF SPECIAL MEASURES

17.39   The table at para.17.24 details the available measures as of October 2007.

Screens

17.40   Screens are now available in magistrates' courts. As explained in para.17.35 above, there may be circumstances when a witness would prefer to give evidence from behind a screen rather than via live-link. As has been noted by others, a concomitant of the widespread use of video-link evidence (and appearances by defendants via video-link) is the introduction of large plasma screens into courtrooms, which enable everyone in the room, from Bench to dock to public gallery, to see the person on screen.[8] An additional reassurance to a witness who gives evidence from behind a screen is that they are shielded from the public gaze and, perhaps more importantly, from the defendant. It may also be the case that evidence from a witness who wishes to be in the witness box will be more effective than if they are made to give evidence via live-link. Use of a screen may place the jury in a better position to fully assess the witness's demeanour as they give their evidence. However, one disadvantage to screens is that the defendant is unable to see the witness. The usual course should be for the defendant to see all witnesses unless the circumstances are exceptional.[9] That said, the Privy Council recently held that there had been a fair trial where screens had been used to shield a complainant from the view not only of the defendant, and also, in breach of the mandatory requirements of s.23(2)(b) of the YJCEA 1999, from counsel except when they were directly questioning the complainant. The majority of the Board held that this defect was not such as to require the conviction to be set aside, as it had not prevented the appellant having a fair trial. Lords Brown and Roger dissented, on the ground that it is essential that the defendant's representatives and the prosecution should be in a position to see the witness during the entirety of their evidence.[10] Finally, it was held in *Brown*[11] that the fact that one witness elected to give evidence without screens does not require that all other witnesses do so as well.

Giving Evidence in Private

17.42   The special measure of giving evidence in private is now available in the magistrates' courts.

---

[8] Hoyano and Keenan, *op cit*. n.6, p.637.
[9] Hoyano and Keenan, *op cit*. n.6, p.638.
[10] *Attorney General for the Sovereign Base Areas of Akrotiri and Dhekelia v Steinhoff* [2005] UKPC 31.
[11] [2004] EWCA Crim 1620; [2004] Crim. L.R. 1034.

VIDEO-RECORDED EVIDENCE-IN-CHIEF

This special measure is currently available in the Crown Court for child witnesses   **17.44**
and adult witnesses eligible by virtue of s.16(1)(b). The provision is also available
in the Crown Court for adult complainants of sexual offences (under s.17(4) when
the investigation commenced on or after September 1, 2007. In the magistrates'
courts, video-recorded evidence-in-chief is only available to child witnesses in
need of special protection.

In deciding whether to admit a video-recorded interview as evidence, the starting   **17.47**
point is the strong presumption in the YJCEA 1999 in favour of the use of special
measures, but where there have been breaches of the guidelines for conducting
interviews, the court should ask itself whether a reasonable jury properly directed
could be sure that the witness has given a credible and accurate account on the
video tape, notwithstanding any breaches: *Howard K.*[12] That case concerned an
allegation that the appellant had indecently assaulted his daughter. Three video-
recorded interviews were conducted when the child was six years old, and it was
only in the third that she implicated the appellant. The interviews had been
conducted in breach of the ABE guidelines because the complainant's mother had
been present at them and had participated. At one point, she said to her daughter:
"You have to tell the truth, then we can go." Shortly afterwards, the complainant
gave the evidence that implicated the appellant. In deciding whether to admit that
evidence, the trial judge considered whether the evidence given on the video tape
could be relied upon by reference to other supporting evidence. The Court of
Appeal held that the primary consideration should be the reliability of the video-
recorded evidence itself, which will normally be assessed by reference to the
interview itself, the conditions under which it was held, the age of the child and
the nature and extent of any breach of the guidelines. There might be cases where
other evidence demonstrated that the breaches had not had the effect of
undermining the credibility or accuracy of the video interview. But any reference
to other evidence should be made with considerable caution. In *Howard K.*,
although the judge did not address the appropriate test in terms, it was plain that
he had in fact considered whether the jury could properly rely on the video, and
the Court declined to allow the appeal on that basis.[13] See also *Powell*[14] and *DPP
v R.*,[15] discussed at para.17.94 below.

Corrigendum: The relevant provision is s.139 of the Criminal Justice Act 2003,   **17.51**
which came into force on April 5, 2004.[16]

---

[12] [2006] 2 Cr. App. R. 10, citing *Hanton* [2005] EWCA Crim 2009.
[13] Though it did allow it on another ground.
[14] [2006] 1 Cr. App. R. 31.
[15] [2007] EWHC 1842 (Admin).
[16] Criminal Justice Act 2003 (Commencement No.3 and Transitional Provisions) Order 2004 (SI 2004/829).

Exclusion of video-recorded interview when the witness retracts the contents

17.54   Section 119 of the Criminal Justice Act 2003 came into force on April 4, 2005.[17]

Jury access to video transcripts

17.62   For recent approval of the approach in *Welstead*, see *R. v SW*.[18]

VIDEO-RECORDED CROSS-EXAMINATION AND RE-EXAMINATION (WHERE EXAMINATION-IN-CHIEF IS SO RECORDED)

17.63   For criticism of s.28, see Debbie Cooper, *Pigot unfulfilled: Video-recorded cross-examination under section 28 of the Youth Justice and Criminal Evidence Act 1999* [2005] Crim. L.R. 456.

17.64   Section 23 of the Criminal Justice Act 1988 has been repealed. See now ss.114, 116, 120 and 139 of the Criminal Justice Act 2003. In *Crown Prosecution Service v CE*,[19] it was held that video video evidence given by a complainant of rape and tendered under s.116 of the 2003 Act had been properly excluded by the trial judge on grounds of fairness, where the complainant refused to attend court to be cross-examined through fear which had not been induced by the defendant. The Court of Appeal said that admission of the evidence would have infringed Art.6(3) of the ECHR, and that if the defendant had been convicted on the basis of hearsay evidence which had not been cross-examined, he would have been likely to succeed in an appeal against conviction.

INTERMEDIARIES

17.65   It is anticipated that from October 2007 intermediaries will be available in a further eight designated pilot areas and that the scheme will roll out nationally in Spring 2008. It is submitted that where necessary, applications for intermediaries can be made in a non-pilot area, subject to funding from the Office for Criminal Justice Reform (OCJR).

It should be remembered that the provisions relating to intermediaries are available to all witnesses under the age of 17 and are not limited to witnesses eligible by virtue of s.16(2) of the YJCEA 1999. Consideration should therefore be given as to whether any child would benefit from the assistance of an intermediary.

---

[17] Criminal Justice Act 2003 (Commencement No.8 and Transitional Provisions) Order 2005 (SI 2005/950).
[18] [2004] EWCA Crim 2979.
[19] [2006] EWCA Crim 1410.

The function of an intermediary is to facilitate communication between the questioner and the witness. Their interventions can range from establishing, as early as the ABE video, the types of questions the witness will comprehend, to interpreting the questions asked of a witness during cross-examination at trial. To ensure the effective use of an intermediary, their involvement should be established at the preliminary stages of the investigation. Consequently, as with so many special measures, it is vital that the police are aware of their availability and that both prosecution and defence solicitors are alive to the useful role they may play in the trial process.

The OCJR maintains a register of intermediaries (at the time of writing there are 130) and has issued guidance on their use.[20] The intermediary's initial role is to use their professional skills as speech or language therapists to assess the witness's communication needs. The assessment will consider whether the witness is able to give evidence at all and, if so, what difficulties exist and how they can be overcome. During the ABE interview, the role of the intermediary is to ensure that the interviewer only asks questions that the witness will understand. The intermediary may ask the officer to re-phrase the question, or may themselves establish whether the interviewee has understood what they are being asked. The guidance however makes plain that the intermediary is not a second interviewer.

The intermediary prepares a report for the court detailing the witness's needs. The arrangements as to how the witness will give evidence, the number and timing of breaks, and the type of questions which they will be able to answer should all be established at a pre-trial hearing. The intermediary should attend that hearing with trial counsel. If a pre-trial hearing is not possible, then this exercise should be performed on the first day of the trial. As a general rule, it will be advantageous to explain to the jury the role of the intermediary; in one of the pilot cases, involving a witness with cerebral palsy, the intermediary explained to the jury how the witness would give evidence and the jury were shown the "Bliss" board so they would understand how the answers were being communicated.[21] In less extreme cases, it is envisaged that where all parties have been told and have understood the type of questions that a particular witness can deal with, the intermediary will have a less interventionist role. Where an intermediary is of the view that a witness could not understand or has not understood the question asked, they will ask Counsel to re-phrase the question, and if Counsel is unable to do so satisfactorily, the intermediary will "interpret" the question for the witness.

See generally on intermediaries David Wurtzel, *A new voice in court*, *Counsel Magazine*, December 2005, 20–22; Rebecca Seden, *Intermediaries and s.29 of the Youth Justice and Criminal Evidence Act 1999*, Crim. Law 2006, 159, 3–5; David Wurtzel, *It's about best evidence*, *Counsel Magazine*, August 2007, 8–9.

---

[20] *Procedural Guidelines for practitioners on the intermediary provision (s.29) of the Youth Justice and Criminal Evidence Act 1999* (OCJR, October 2005), which are to be read in conjunction with the *Intermediary procedural guidance manual* (OCJR, October 2005).

[21] David Wurtzel, *Intermediaries: a good thing happens* [2007] 3 *Archbold News* 8.

Procedure for Applying for, or Opposing, Special Measures

17.67 The Rules of Court have been replaced by Pt 29 of the Criminal Procedure Rules 2005, which can be found in Appendix A to this Supplement.[22] Part 29 does not alter the substance or time-limits contained in the previous Rules. An application form is scheduled to the Rules: Pt A must be completed in all cases, while the remainder deals with the additional information required in applications for use of a live-link (Pt B), for an intermediary (Pt C) and for tendering video-recordings as evidence-in-chief (Pt D).

17.68 Footnote 18: See now CPR 29.1(4).

17.69 Footnote 19: See now CPR 29.1(5), (6).
Footnote 20: See now CPR 29.1(7).
Footnote 21: See now CPR 29.1(9).
Footnote 22: See now CPR 29.1(13).

17.70 Footnote 23: See now CPR 29.2(3).
Footnote 24: See now CPR 29.3(1)(b).

17.71 Footnote 25: See now CPR 29.3(1)(a).
Footnote 26: See now CPR 29.3(2)(b). This provision is directory rather than mandatory: *Brown*.[23] The court said that for many special measures, in particular the giving of video-recorded evidence, there are obvious reasons why applications for their use should be made well in advance, but this was much less obvious where (as in *Brown*) the relevant measure is the use of screens. Any significant handicap to the defence arising from a late application would be a matter for the judge to take carefully into account, but the Court was satisfied that there was no handicap arising from the late application in the case before it.
Footnote 27: See now CPR 29.3(3).
Footnote 28: See now CPR 29.3(4).

17.72 Footnote 29: See now CPR 29.4(1).
Footnote 30: See now CPR 29.4(4).
Footnote 31: See now CPR 29.5(1).
Footnote 32: See now CPR 29.5(4).

17.73 Footnote 33: See now CPR 29.6 and 29.7.
Footnote 34: See now CPR 29.6(2), (3).
Footnote 35: See now CPR 29.6(4), (5).

---

[22] And on the Ministry of Justice website.
[23] [2004] EWCA Crim 1620; [2004] Crim. L.R. 1034.

Footnote 36: See now CPR 29.7.	**17.74**
Footnote 37: See now CPR 29.7(2).	
Footnote 38: See now CPR 29.7(3).	
Footnote 40: See now CPR 29.7(7).	**17.76**
Footnote 41: See now CPR 29.7(8).	
Footnote 42: See now CPR 29.7(10).	**17.77**
Footnote 43: See now CPR 29.7(12).	
Footnote 44: See now CPR 29.7(15).	
Footnote 45: See now CPR 29.9.	**17.78**
Footnote 46: See now CPR 29.9.	**17.79**

VULNERABLE WITNESSES: PRACTICAL CONSIDERATIONS

PRE-TRIAL PREPARATION: PRACTICALITIES

The plea and directions hearing ("PDH") is now referred to as the plea and case   **17.88**
management hearing ("PCMH").

COMPETENCE TO GIVE EVIDENCE

COMPETENCE

The test of competence in s.53(3) of the 1999 Act is one of intelligibility, namely   **17.94**
whether the witness can understand the questions asked of him in court and give
answers that the jury can understand: *MacPherson*[24]; *Sed (Ali Dahir)*[25]; *R. v D.*[26]
In *MacPherson*,[27] the Court of Appeal said that where an issue is raised as to the
competence of a witness, in the ordinary way, that issue should be determined
before the witness is sworn, usually as a preliminary issue at the start of a trial.
Where the witness is a child, the court should watch the video-taped interview
with the child and/or ask the child appropriate questions. A young child who can
speak and understand basic English with strangers would be competent. There is
no requirement that the witness should be aware of their status as a witness.
Questions as to the credibility and reliability of the witness's evidence go to

[24] [2005] EWCA Crim 365.
[25] [2005] 2 Cr. App. R. 4.
[26] [2002] 2 Cr. App. R. 36.
[27] *MacPherson*, above n.24.

weight, not competence. In cases where reliance is sought to be placed on a witness's ABE interview as their evidence-in-chief, competence must be established both at the time of the video recording and at the time of trial (otherwise an application could be made to admit the ABE video as a hearsay document pursuant to s.116 CJA 2003).

Whilst initially the question of competence will be determined on a *voire dire,* it may be appropriate to review the witness's competence during and at the conclusion of their evidence: *Powell.*[28] In that case the witness, aged three-and-a-half, had complained to her mother that the appellant had licked her private parts. The witness was not ABE interviewed until nine weeks after the alleged incident. The appellant was charged with indecent assault, and unfortunately the case took some nine months from the girl's initial complaint to reach trial. The trial judge ruled at the outset that the complainant was competent and the issue was not revisited during the course of the trial. On appeal, the Court of Appeal held that the issue of competence should have been reconsidered at the conclusion of the complainant's evidence. The Court was of the view that had this course been taken, the judge would have concluded that the complainant was not a competent witness and so would have withdrawn the case from the jury, because the complainant's answers to questions put in cross-examination were not intelligible in the context of the case. The argument to the contrary, which did not persuade the Court, is that the complainant remained competent during cross-examination and it was for the jury to decide how reliable her answers were.

The Court in *Powell* went on to express concern about the unfortunate length of time that elapsed between the initial complainant, the ABE video and the subsequent trial. It said that it is essential in cases involving very young children that the ABE interview takes place very soon after the event and that the trial (at which the child has to be cross-examined) takes place very soon thereafter.[29] Looking at the case with hindsight, it was "completely unacceptable" that the appellant should have been tried for an offence, proof of which relied on the evidence of a three-and-a-half year old, when the trial did not take place until over nine months had passed from the date of the alleged offence. One might add that it was also wholly unsatisfactory that, by reason of the delay, the child was denied the opportunity to give her best evidence of the incident that led to the charge. Even very young children may be capable of giving reliable evidence, but cases need to be fast-tracked to enable them to do so. Otherwise, there is a serious risk that paedophiles who target very young children will gain de facto immunity from prosecution.

Lack of memory does not equate to incompetence. In *DPP v R,*[30] the defendant and the complainant were aged 13 at the time of the allegation and both were severely mentally handicapped. The defendant was accused of touching the girl indecently. After the initial complaint, the girl was interviewed in accordance with ABE. Whilst it was apparent that she had some disabilities and limitations, she was

[28] [2006] 1 Cr. App. R. 31.
[29] See also the CPS *Policy for Child Witnesses and Victims.*
[30] [2007] EWHC 1842 (Admin).

able to provide an intelligible account of what had occurred. Her video was admitted as her evidence-in-chief. However, at the stage of cross-examination, the girl stated that she could not recall any of the events and could only rely upon what she had said during her video interview. The magistrates held that they could not be sure of the defendant's guilt after concluding that, having failed to recall the relevant events, the complainant was incompetent under s.53 of the 1999 Act; that her video interview was not admissible as hearsay under s.116(2)(b) of the Criminal Justice Act 2003, as her incompetence did not mean she was unfit to give evidence by reason of her mental condition; but that it was in the interests of justice to admit the interview as hearsay evidence under s.114 of the 2003 Act.

The Divisional Court held that the issue of competence has to be addressed both at the time when consideration is given to the admission of the video-recorded interview and throughout the trial, particularly at the cross-examination stage. If by the start of the trial it is clear that a witness is mentally incompetent under s.53, then the court could refuse to admit the video interview under s.27(4) of the 1999 Act on the basis that the witness would not be available for cross-examination.[31] If the video interview had already been adduced in evidence, then s.27(4) did not permit the court to retrospectively to exclude it. The evidence would then have to be assessed as a whole, but given that it could not be tested in cross-examination, the court would probably place little weight on it. As for the ruling that the complainant was incompetent, that had been erroneous, as her problem stemmed from a loss of memory rather than a capacity to understand or provide intelligible answers. However, the fact that she was not incompetent did not mean that her video-recorded evidence was reliable, and it was for the court to assess whether her memory loss prevented her from giving useful evidence. By and large, a witness who is incompetent is likely to be unfit as a witness within s.116(2)(b). Further, even on their erroneous finding that the complainant was incompetent, it had not been necessary for the magistrates to consider s.114 of the 2003 Act. The video interview had already been adduced in evidence pursuant to a perfectly proper special measures direction under s.27 of the 1999 Act. It had not required consideration as hearsay evidence. However, although the video interview was admissible independently of s.114, it was for the trial court to decide whether it should be accepted at face value.

PROHIBITION ON CROSS-EXAMINATION BY THE DEFENDANT IN PERSON

There were concerns that, by virtue of legislative oversight, complainants of sexual **17.97** offences pre-dating the SOA 2003 were denied the protection of ss.34 and 35 of the YJCEA 1999. This has now been resolved by the Court of Appeal in

---

[31] See further *Crown Prosecution Service v CE* [2006] EWCA Crim 1410, above para.17.64.

Cartwright.[32] Notwithstanding the draftsman's error, complainants do enjoy the protections given by YJCEA 1999. See para.18.3.

17.99   *Corrigendum:* s.35(3)(a) of the 1999 Act applies expressly only to offences under Pt 1 of the Sexual Offences Act 2003. But see the discussion at para.17.97, above.

17.101   The procedure to be followed (in the Crown Court and magistrates' courts) where a person is prohibited by s.34 or s.35 from cross-examining in person is now set out Pt 31 of the Criminal Procedure Rules 2005, set out in Appendix A to this Supplement.

[32] November 7, 2007.

CHAPTER 18

RESTRICTIONS ON EVIDENCE OR QUESTIONS ABOUT THE COMPLAINANT'S SEXUAL HISTORY

SECTIONS 41 TO 43 OF THE YOUTH JUSTICE AND CRIMINAL EVIDENCE ACT 1999

COMPARISONS WITH SECTION 2 OF THE SEXUAL OFFENCES (AMENDMENT) ACT 1976

Application to pre-Sexual Offences Act 2003 cases

Section 42(1)(d) of the 1999 Act states that "sexual offence" shall be construed in **18.23** accordance with s.62. As enacted, s.62 referred to offences under the Sexual Offences Act 1956. However, it was amended as from May 1, 2004 by the Sexual Offences Act 2003[1] to provide that "sexual offence" means any offence under Part 1 of the 2003 Act. It seems that in making this change the draftsman overlooked the fact that sexual offences committed before May 1, 2004 will continue to be charged under the old law. The point was taken in *Warner*[2] as to whether a complainant should enjoy the protection of s.41 where the defendant is charged with an offence pre-dating the Sexual Offences Act 2003. H.H. Judge Morrison QC ruled that she should not:

> "Does section 41 of the Youth Justice and Criminal Evidence Act 1999 apply? I
> have . . . considered this at considerable length, and tempted though I am to repair
> the gap left by the failure of the then Secretary of State to make the appropriate
> transitional provisions and/or the parliamentary draftsman in his failure to secure the

---

[1] s.139 and Sch.6.
[2] Birmingham Crown Court, June 5, 2007.

261

position in the wording of the statute, I am not persuaded that it is within the competence of the Crown Court so to do.

Accordingly, and as unhappy a state of jurisprudence as that engenders, I cannot hold that the complainant has the protection offered by section 41. As matters stand, it seems to me that as a matter of plain reading section 41 does not apply to trials after 1st May 2004 unless it relates to an offence contemplated in Part 1 of the Sexual Offences Act 2003. That is an effect of the legislative failure and my reading of *A—Prosecutor's Appeal*.[3] A purposive interpretation seems to me only to be possible when there are opposing or ambiguous constructions or those capable of being so described. Here, there are no such constructions: merely an unhappy vacuum."

Professor David Ormerod[4] has argued that the courts are entitled to fill the gap by adopting a purposive approach to the legislation. The Parliamentary intention is clear, the complainant's Article 8 rights are engaged and the situation can be distinguished from *A—Prosecutor's Appeal* as it concerns procedural and evidential matters rather than the substantive law. The point has now been considered by the Court of Appeal in *Cartwright*.[5] The Court decided that s.41 does apply to "old regime" i.e. pre-Sexual Offences Act 2003 cases.

In *Cartwright* the Court of Appeal resolved this important point of statutory construction in respect of a rape trial which had proceeded upon the common assumption that s.41 applied to offences pre-dating the Sexual Offences Act 2003. The jurisdiction point had not been taken at trial. The alleged offences had taken place before May 1, 2004 when the Sexual Offences Act 2003 came into force, but no complaint had been made until after that date. The appellant submitted that it was perfectly clear from a literal reading that the amendment brought about by the 2003 Act had had the effect of disapplying s.41 in respect of "old regime" pre-2003 Act offences. The Court of Appeal observed that if this submission was right, then something extraordinary had happened. A "minor" or "consequential" amendment, by substituting the meaning of "sexual offences" for the purposes of s.62(1) of the 1999 Act, had brought about absurd consequences. It was necessary to consider whether there was legislative incoherence,[5A] which, based on an analysis of the legislative context and structure, produced a result which contradicted the clear intention of Parliament and defeated its legislative purpose. *R. v A.*[5B] could be distinguished. In that case, correcting the oversight by the draftsman would have effected a radical extension of the substantive law relating to criminal liability. By contrast, s.41 was procedural or evidential, representing further development of a statutory process begun in 1976 by extending the restrictions upon the admissibility of the previous sexual history of complainants in sex cases. There had been an omission by the draftsman, which could easily have been covered by a short saving provision, expressly preserving the protection for old offences. The resulting vacuum was wholly unintended and was contrary to the intention of Parliament. The virtually universally discredited common law

---

[3] [2005] EWCA Crim 2533; [2006] 1 Cr. App. R. 28.
[4] In a lecture to the JSB Serious Sexual Offences Seminar, July 2007.
[5] November 7, 2007.
[5A] *Inco Europe Ltd and others v First Choice Distribution (a firm)* [2000] 1 W.L.R. 586.
[5B] Sometimes referred to as *R. v C* [2005] EWCA Crim 3533.

rules relating to cross-examination in this class of case were not resuscitated merely because of adventitious discrepancy between the date when the offences were committed and the trial. The Court of Appeal stated that, despite its careful reasoning, it was not able to follow the judgment of Judge Morrison in *Warner* and held that s.41 did apply.

"any sexual behaviour"

In *Mukadi*,[6] the Court of Appeal did not find it necessary to decide whether   **18.25** getting into a car with a stranger and exchanging telephone numbers was "sexual behaviour" or not. The Court did, however, comment that "it would have been a possible and a proper inference for the jury to conclude that when C accepted this man's invitation and got into the car what she had in mind was that there might follow some sexual activity". Professor Temkin and her colleagues have noted that this raises the question whether C's purpose should be taken into account as a factor in determining whether ambiguous behaviour is sexual or not.[7] They note that s.78 of the Sexual Offences Act 2003 provides a way of determining whether conduct is "sexual" which might be of use in this context as well.[8] It is submitted that if this test is adopted, the reasonable inference that C's purpose was "sexual" would lead to the inevitable conclusion that her conduct was "sexual".

Where issue was genuineness of diary entries, not "sexual behaviour"

In *Lloyd*,[9] the appellant was convicted of 10 counts of indecent assault against four   **18.25A** young women, who at the time were all working with him at a supermarket where he was a trainee manager. The defence case was that there had been no indecent assaults, that the complainants had fabricated their evidence and that they were acting in collusion with one employee (not a complainant) whose work the appellant had criticised.

In order to rebut the defence of recent fabrication, the prosecution introduced into evidence a diary entry which one of the complainants said she had made on the same day as the assaults, June 12, 2002. The relevant page was put before the jury. The diary entry read: "James abused me (sexual) in cake shop." The defence sought to cross-examine the complainant about an entry for June 14 on the opposite page of the same diary, which had been deleted but which could still be read. It read as follows: "I had 10-inch cock in my mouth today mmm." The complainant stated in a witness statement that the entry had been made by a friend

---

[6] [2003] EWCA Crim 3765; [2004] Crim. L.R. 373.

[7] L. Kelly, J. Temkin, S. Griffiths, *Section 41: an evaluation of new legislation limiting sexual history evidence in rape trials*, Home Office, London (2006).

[8] s.78 provides that penetration, touching or any other activity is sexual if a reasonable person would consider that (a) whatever its circumstances or any person's purpose in relation to it, it is because of its nature sexual, or (b) because of its nature it may be sexual and because of its circumstances or the purpose of any person in relation to it (or both) it is sexual.

[9] [2005] EWCA Crim. 1111.

as a joke and that she had crossed it out when she saw it. In a witness statement, disclosed in the unused material, the friend denied all knowledge of the diary.

The trial judge refused to permit cross-examination on the diary entry for June 14. He ruled that the entry related to "sexual behaviour" and thus cross-examination was prohibited under s.41. Furthermore, such cross-examination would only go to credit, and could not be relevant to the issue of fabrication of the allegations.

The Court of Appeal held that defence counsel's proposed questions in respect of the June 14 diary entry were intended to highlight the potential untruthfulness of the complainant as to the authorship of an entry in the diary, and not to assert that the entry in the diary, although having a sexual content, was true. The proposed cross-examination went to the accuracy and veracity of the pages in the diary as a record. Although the content in relation to June 14 was sexual in nature, the cross-examination would not be about sexual activity. Instead it would have been directed to the disputed explanation for the appearance of the entry in the diary. The cross-examination would have been carried out to show that the complainant's account as to how the entry came to be in her diary was untrue. The trial judge had failed to focus on the real issue of relevance, the genuineness of the diary entry.[10]

Complainant's denial of previous sexual experience

18.25B   The s.41 regime applies in the case of evidence or questions about a complainant's false denial of a previous sexual experience. A complainant's false assertion that she was a virgin at the time of the alleged allegation, when earlier that day she had sexual intercourse with someone other than the accused, relates to her "sexual behaviour."[11] For evidence of false complaints, see para.18.90 below.

Procedure

18.32   See the Criminal Procedure Rules 2005 as amended by the Criminal Procedure (Amendment No. 2) Rules 2006.[12] A wholly new set of rules now governs applications by the defence to introduce evidence or cross-examine a witness about a complainant's sexual behaviour despite the prohibition in s.41 of the 1999 Act. The Court of Appeal has underlined that there should be rigorous compliance with the rules.[13] The rules are as follows:

---

[10] If the complainant had denied stating that a friend had made the entry, the defence would have been entitled to call the friend to contradict her under s.4 of Criminal Procedure Act 1865: see *R. v V* [2006] EWCA Crim 1901.

[11] *R. v S* [2003] All E.R. (D.) 408 (Feb).

[12] SI 2006/2636. In L. Kelly, J. Temkin, and S. Griffiths, *Section 41: an evaluation of new legislation limiting sexual history evidence in rape trials*, Home Office, London (2006), at p.76, the authors recommend that there should be an absolute requirement that all applications be made in writing.

[13] *McKendrick* [2004] EWCA Crim 1393.

"**When this Part applies**
36.1 This part applies in magistrates' courts and in the Crown Court where a defendant wants to—
   (a) introduce evidence; or
   (b) cross-examine a witness
about a complainant's sexual behaviour despite the prohibition in section 41 of the Youth Justice and Criminal Evidence Act 1999.

Application for permission to introduce evidence or cross-examine
36.2 The defendant must apply for permission to do so—
   (a) in writing; and
   (b) not more than 28 days after the prosecutor has complied or purported to comply with section 3 of the Criminal Procedure and Investigations Act 1996 (disclosure by prosecutor).

Content of application
36.3 The application must—
   (a) identify the issue to which the defendant says the complainant's sexual behaviour is relevant;
   (b) give particulars of—
      (i) any evidence that the defendant wants to introduce, and
      (ii) any questions that the defendant wants to ask;
   (c) identify the exception to the prohibition in section 41 of the Youth Justice and Criminal Evidence Act 1999 on which the defendant relies; and
   (d) give the name and date of birth of any witness whose evidence about the complainant's sexual behaviour the defendant wants to introduce.

Service of application
36.4 The defendant must serve the application on the court officer and all other parties.

Reply to application
36.5 A party who wants to make representations about an application under rule 36.2 must—
   (a) do so in writing not more than 14 days after receiving it; and
   (b) serve those representations on the court officer and all other parties.

Application for special measures
36.6 If the court allows an application under rule 36.2 then—
   (a) a party may apply not more than 14 days later for a special measures direction or for the variation of an existing special measures direction; and
   (b) the court may shorten the time for opposing that application.

Court's power to vary requirements under this Part
36.7 The court may shorten or extend (even after it has expired) a time limit under this Part."

It is important to note that whilst the court has the power to vary the time limits or hear an application out of time, there is no power to waive the requirement that the application should be in writing. It follows that even if the issue arises out of time during the trial for good reason, the application must still be in writing.

Section 43(1) of the 1999 Act requires that all such applications are made in private and in the absence of the complainant. If an application is made in public and sexual history evidence has been revealed, a reporting direction under s. 46 cannot be made.

The Position of the Prosecution

18.33   In *Soroya*,[14] a broad forensic attack was made on the impact of s.41 of the 1999 Act and its compatibility with the requirements of Art.6 of the European Convention of Human Rights. It was argued on appeal that the evidence of the complainant's previous sexual history had been wrongly introduced by the prosecution at trial in circumstances that would not have been permitted to the defence. This constituted a breach of the appellant's right to a fair trial, and infringed the requirement that there should be "equality of arms" between prosecution and defence. The prohibitions in s.41 should embrace the prosecution, and, as they do not, the process was unbalanced, adversely to the defendant. The Court of Appeal rejected this argument, holding that s.78 of the Police and Criminal Evidence Act 1984 is perfectly apt to be deployed in an appropriate case where the impact of s.41 might produce an adverse effect upon the fairness of the proceedings. In any event, in this case no such issue arose, and no justified complaint could be made about the admission of the evidence, which was relevant and admissible. The issue of the complainant's sexual experience had only arisen for consideration because, as an integral part of the incident, and to avoid the rape, she made what was admittedly an untruthful claim she was a virgin. It was important evidence bearing on the issue of consent. It explained how the complainant had reacted, and what she had said, to avoid the dreadful incident unfolding.

THE FOUR GATEWAYS AND TWO RESTRICTIONS

The First Gateway—Section 41(3)(A)—Issue Other than Consent

18.38   In *R. v A (No.2)*[15] Lord Hope gave four examples of issues that fall within s.41(3)(a), because evidence is proffered for specific reasons pointing to guilt or innocence as opposed to impermissible generalisations about consent. If there is sufficient evidence to open a particular gateway, the judge must still consider whether the test in s.41(2)(b) is satisfied, i.e. whether exclusion of the evidence might render unsafe a conclusion of the jury on a relevant issue in the case. However, where the evidence relates to a relevant issue in the case, and the criteria for admissibility are established, then, subject to s.41(4), the court lacks any discretion to refuse to admit the evidence, or to limit its admission. Once the criteria for admissibility are established, all the evidence relevant to the issues may be adduced. As Lord Justice Judge put it in *R. v F*[16]:

---

[14] [2006] EWCA Crim 1884.
[15] [2002] 1 A.C. 45 at para.79.
[16] [2005] 2 Cr. App. R. 13.

"It is sometimes loosely suggested that the operation of s.41 involves the exercise of judicial discretion. In reality, the trial judge is making a judgment whether to admit or refuse to admit evidence which is relevant, or asserted by the defence to be relevant. If the evidence is not relevant, on elementary principles, it is not admissible . . . As part of his control over the case, the judge is required to ensure that a complainant is not unnecessarily humiliated or cross-examined with inappropriate aggression, or treated otherwise than with proper courtesy. All that is elementary, but his obligation to see that the complainant's interests are protected throughout the trial process does not prevent him by way of general discretion, to prevent the proper deployment of evidence which falls within the ambit permitted by statute merely because, as here, it comes in a stark uncompromising form."

For the facts of *R. v F*, see para.18.43 below.

(a) the defendant's belief

The effect of the change in the law as to mental element

The scope for evidence of a complainant's sexual history to be relevant to the issue of a defendant's belief that the complainant was consenting has narrowed significantly now that, under the Sexual Offences Act 2003, such a belief has to be reasonable to provide a defence. As Lord Woolf C.J. observed in *Bahadoor*[17]: "Honest belief and reasonable belief are very different things." In *Bahadoor*, the appellant had been charged with indecent assault. It was his contention that he genuinely believed the complainant was consenting because he had seen her earlier that evening in a night club take part in a competition which involved her exposing her breasts and simulating oral sex. The Court felt compelled to conclude that since the appellant's defence was based on honest belief, it was difficult to say that what he contended had taken place on stage could not have been relevant, but it gave the strongest possible hint it would not have been relevant under the new law.   **18.40**

Judicial control under s.41(2)(b)

In any event, the extent to which a complainant may be cross-examined about her previous sexual history for the purposes of the defence of honest belief will be subject at all times to control by the court under s.41(2)(b). For instance, in *Bahadoor*, the Court of Appeal held that the exclusion of the evidence did not render unsafe the conclusion of the jury that the appellant was guilty of the offence of which he was convicted, and the evidence had been properly excluded under s.41(2)(b).   **18.40A**

Relevance of sexual history with third parties to the defence of honest and reasonable belief

Where there is strongly diverging evidence as to what happened, there may be little scope for a defence of belief in consent and evidence of belief may be of marginal relevance to the real issue in the case, which will often be whether the   **18.40B**

[17] [2005] EWCA Crim 396.

complainant or the defendant has given a truthful account. See for instance *Miah and Uddin*,[18] where the Court of Appeal held that the trial judge had been right to refuse the defence permission to call a third man, whom the defence claimed had had consensual sex with the complainant at a party when he had never previously met her, and only a short while after she had performed oral sex on the accused, with whom she had also not previously been sexually involved.

It follows that, quite apart from the repercussions that flow from the stricter test under the Sexual Offences Act 2003, in many trials the defence of belief in consent will not in practice be available. Often there will be no scope on the facts for a separate and different finding on the issue of honest and reasonable belief. The issues of absence of consent and the defendant's reasonable belief in consent will stand or fall together. In Canadian and Californian cases, there is a requirement that there be evidence of equivocal conduct from the complainant—something which could have caused the accused to make a mistake.[19] Jenny McEwan argues that that the judgment in *R. v A (No. 2)* has set courts in England some way along this road. Certainly in cases where the facts are diametrically opposed, there is unlikely to be any scope for a separate defence of reasonableness of purported belief, and in such cases this cannot be used as a basis for admission of evidence of previous sexual history.

A graphic example of where the Court of Appeal felt that the application for leave to cross-examine was ill-conceived can be found in *Harrison*,[20] where the defence wished to cross-examine the complainant on an act of consensual sexual intercourse with a third party three hours earlier. The fact that the complainant had had consensual intercourse three hours before the incident did not go to any belief of the defendant that she had consented. That was precisely the kind of evidence that s.41 was designed to prevent, as it laid the ground for the inadmissible submission that, because the complainant had had consensual sexual intercourse with the third party, she was likely to have had consensual sex with the defendant. The trial judge had refused the application on the basis that it was peripheral evidence, and an attempt to admit evidence already excluded under s.41 by the back door. The Court of Appeal held that this decision was not only right, but had been compelled by s.41.

(b) that the complainant was biased against the accused or had a motive to fabricate the evidence

18.43 *R. v F*[21] it was alleged that the complainant was subjected to systematic sexual abuse and repeatedly raped by the appellant, her step-father, starting when she was

---

[18] [2006] EWCA Crim 1168.

[19] For an illuminating discussion, see Jenny McEwan, *"I Thought She Consented": Defeat of the Rape Shield or the Defence that Shall Not Run?* [2006] Crim. L.R. 969. See also *Esau* [1997] 2 S.C.R. 443 and *The People v Williams* 841 P.2d 961 (1992), for a Canadian and a Californian example of the principle that a defendant cannot plead both defences absent significant evidence of equivocal conduct explaining how it could be that the defendant believed consent existed where it did not.

[20] [2006] EWCA Crim 1543.

[21] [2005] 2 Cr. App. R. 13.

about 7 years old, and continuing throughout her childhood and puberty until she was 16. The appellant denied that any form of sexual activity had taken place during the appellant's childhood or adolescence. It was, however, common ground that they lived together and shared a consensual sexual relationship for four or five years when the complainant was aged between 18 or 19 and 24 years, and the appellant between 30 and 36 years. It was the appellant's case that the complainant had made false allegations motivated by malice following his decision to end the adult relationship. The trial judge had allowed the defence to ask questions about the appellant's adult relationship with the complainant, on the basis that otherwise he would be unable to advance a crucial element of his defence which was that the complaint of childhood abuse was motivated by his action in ending the adult relationship. However, the trial judge refused to allow evidence to be adduced or questions to be asked concerning photographs and video tapes made during the course of the adult relationship. The material showed the complainant posing in a pornographic manner.

The Court of Appeal allowed the appeal. The photographs and video tapes were relevant to (i) whether the complaint of childhood abuse had been motivated by a desire for revenge and (ii) in the light of the critical dispute as to how the adult relationship started and its nature, whether the childhood abuse had occured at all. Where evidence of sexual behaviour relates to a relevant issue in the case, and the criteria for admissibility are established, and it is not caught by s.41(4), the trial judge has no discretion to exclude it or limit its admission because it is in stark uncompromising form such as the pornographic videos. The case illustrates that, whilst due regard must be had to the need to protect the complainant from indignity and from humiliating questions, there may be cases where that protection must give way to some extent if the defence case is to be put properly. However, if the evidence sought to be adduced had only been of minimal relevance, then presumably the judge would have been obliged to exclude it under s.41(2)(b).

(d) especially in the case of young complainants, the detail of their account must have come from some other sexual activity before or after the event which provides an explanation for their knowledge of that activity.

A young complainant's knowledge of sexual terminology

In *R. v A (No. 2)*, Lord Hope provided as an example of an issue which might fall   **18.50** within s.41(3)(a), as an issue which "is not an issue of consent", "(d) especially in the case of young complainants . . . that the detail of their account must have come from some other sexual activity before or after the event which provides an explanation for their knowledge of that activity". In *R. v MF*[22] the Court of Appeal emphasised the word "must" in that example. At trial, the defence had sought leave to cross-examine the complainant as to whether she had told a doctor

[22] [2005] EWCA Crim 3376.

that she had had penile intercourse with a boy from school. This was on the basis that the incident showed she had been sexually active before she had complained to the police about the appellant, and this activity provided a source of knowledge of the explicit details given in her account, other than the alleged acts of the appellant. The trial judge refused the application on the grounds that, being 14, the complainant fell outside the scope of young complainants who, it could be thought, could only have acquired their knowledge of sexual activity through the alleged acts that were the subject matter of the trial. The judge also indicated that the complainant's account to the police went beyond penile intercourse, and that the proposed question could not provide an explanation for her knowledge of the matters she described to them which did not involve any penile penetration. The Court of Appeal upheld the judge's decision and stated that the reasons he had given were "obviously correct". It was "almost inevitable" that a 14-year-old would be able to describe acts of masturbation and sexual intercourse. The defence were rightly denied the opportunity to cross-examine the complainant about what she had told the doctor.

The Second Gateway—Section 41(3)(B)—Consent and Contemporaneity

18.51   In *R. v A (No. 2)* the House of Lords indicated that behaviour that took place more than 24 hours before the event was unlikely to fall within this subsection. Even if it was within 24 hours, simply because the evidence relates to "the sexual behaviour of the complainant . . . alleged to have taken place at or about the same time as the event which is the subject matter of the charge against the accused", it does not necessarily follow that it relates to an issue of consent or that the judge will be satisfied that a refusal of leave might leave unsafe a decision of the jury.[23]

The decision in *Mukadi*[24] has been widely criticised and we submit it should not be followed as an example as to how this subsection should operate. It is out of kilter with the approach adopted in the vast majority of Court of Appeal decisions on s.41. Both Professor Birch[25] and Professor Temkin and her colleagues[26] consider that the trial judge was wholly correct in his ruling refusing leave to cross-examine the complainant about an incident that took place earlier on the same day as the alleged rape.

Professor Ormerod[27] has described the recent cases of *Tilambala*[28] and *R. v M*[29] as striking examples of how s.41 should operate to protect the complainant. In *Tilambala* the appellant was convicted of raping a 19-year-old girl whom he had

[23] *GM v R* [2004] EWCA Crim 1393.
[24] [2003] EWCA Crim 3765.
[25] [2004] Crim. L.R 373, where Professor Birch points out that consent is not a transferable commodity.
[26] *Op cit.* n.12, at p.16.
[27] In a lecture to the JSB Serious Sexual Offences Seminar, July 2007.
[28] [2005] EWCA Crim 2444.
[29] [2006] EWCA Crim 1971.

met in a bar. The defence case was that the complainant had suggested they go to his hostel, whilst the complainant alleged that she had gone to the hostel because the appellant had invited her to tea, and he had raped her at the hostel. At trial, the appellant's counsel had sought leave to ask the complainant's friend about an incident at the bar two days earlier, when the complainant had sought her friend's advice as to whether she should go back to the house of the man with whom she has been dancing. The friend had told her not to be stupid, and she had not gone back with the man. It was submitted that the complainant had given the impression in her statements and her evidence that she was a faithful girlfriend to her boyfriend in Germany, and the evidence was capable of undermining her account. The Court of Appeal took the view that the defence submission was unarguable. Clearly the defence wished to argue, by the admission of this evidence, that the complainant was the sort of a girl who was prepared to go back to the house of a man she met in the bar to engage in sexual activity. This would be an illegitimate line of reasoning, and is clearly precluded by s.41.

In *R. v M*, the appellant was charged with sexual offences against his step-daughter committed when she was aged 13 and 14, when she was a virgin. She made the allegations against him when she was 17. He denied that any abuse had taken place. The defence had wished to ask her about remarks she was supposed to have made (when she was 17) to a boy when having sex with him: it was alleged that she had said it was her "first time". It was argued on the appellant's behalf that the remark went not simply to the complainant's credibility, but to the heart of the allegation of rape. The Court of Appeal gave this argument short shrift. What the complainant had said in a moment of intimacy would not in any way assist the jury in deciding whether the rape had occurred three days earlier.

THE FOURTH GATEWAY—SECTION 41(5)—THE REBUTTAL GATEWAY

In *R. v F*,[30] Judge L.J. noted that s.41(4) does not apply for the purposes of s.41(5), **18.75** unlike the other exceptions to the exclusion. However, even if the proposed questioning does fall within s.41(5), the judge still has to consider the court's overriding duty under s.41(2)(b) and should refuse leave if not satisfied that such a refusal would have the result of rendering unsafe a conclusion of the jury. See further para.18.79 below.

Section 41(5)(b) provides that the questioning by the defence must "go no further than is necessary to enable the evidence adduced by the prosecution to be rebutted or explained." In principle, evidence given by a complainant when being cross-examined may trigger the rebuttal provisions. However, in *Minhas and Haq*[31] the Court of Appeal upheld the trial judge's refusal of leave to allow the defence to put to the complainant that she had a sexually transmitted disease, on the basis of her answers in cross-examination that she would not have taken drugs voluntarily or had sexual intercourse with the defendant.

[30] [2005] EWCA Crim 493. This observation was also made in *Rooney* [2001] EWCA Crim 2844.
[31] [2003] EWCA Crim 135.

18.78   In his commentary on *Beedall*,[32] Neil Kibble has raised the issue of whether in a same-sex rape, the prosecution should be allowed to anticipate or respond to suggestions express or implied that the complainant is homosexual or prepared to engage in homosexual sexual activity by calling evidence that the complainant would never have engaged in such activity. He notes that occasionally the courts have approved of a complainant giving evidence to counter such implications.[33] Once admitted, such evidence would open the rebuttal gateway.[34]

The Court's Overriding Duty under Section 41(2)(B)

18.79   Even if the evidence falls within one of the exceptions, it does not follow that its admission will be automatic. The judge must be satisfied in accordance with s.41(2)(b) that a "refusal of leave might have the result of rendering unsafe a conclusion of the jury or the court on any relevant issue in the case". Professor Temkin has pointed out that there is a clear danger that insufficient heed will be paid to this provision and that evidence which falls within one of the exceptional categories will be admitted even where it is of minimal relevance to the issues in the case.[35]

Even if at the time of the application, the evidence should have been admitted and at that time a refusal of leave might have had the result in rendering the jury's conclusion unsafe, it does not follow that the Court of Appeal will allow an appeal if it considers in the light of all the evidence that the conviction was in fact safe.[36]

The Two Restrictions

The credibility restriction—section 41(4)

18.85   In *R. v F*,[37] the Court of Appeal cited *Martin*[38] in stating that merely because cross-examination may impugn a complainant's credibility, it does not necessarily follow that impugning credibility is its purpose or main purpose. The Court also noted that s.41(4) applies only for the purposes of s.41(3) and not for the purposes of s.41(5).

---

[32] [2007] EWCA Crim 23, discussed para.18.86A, below.

[33] *Amado-Taylor* [2001] EWCA Crim 1898.

[34] See Kramer, *When men are victims: applying rape shield laws to male same-sex rape* (1998) 73 N.Y.U.L.Rev. 293, where it is argued that the prosecution should not be allowed to use past sexual history or orientation evidence to show consent. Kramer claims that the prosecution leading such evidence is unfair to the defendant and may open the door to "humiliating testimony about the victim" being introduced in rebuttal. See *Murphy* (1996) 919 P.2d 191, where the prosecution's emphasis on the complainant having been married and having children to show that he would not consent to same-sex activity led to the introduction of expert evidence to the effect that married men may nevertheless be homosexual. Whilst such expert evidence would not be admissible in this jurisdiction, once evidence of sexual orientation is given, issues in respect of a complainant's family life may become live.

[35] *Op. cit.* n.12.

[36] *Rooney* [2001] EWCA Crim 2844.

[37] [2005] EWCA Crim 493.

[38] [2004] EWCA Crim 916.

The specific instance restriction—section 41(6)

Cases frequently arise where there is medical evidence that the condition of a   **18.86**
young complainant's vagina is consistent with penetration by an object the size of
a penis. The defence is a complete denial of any form of sexual abuse. Defence
counsel wishes to cross-examine the complainant to the effect that she has had
some form of sexual relationship with some other person, so as to provide an
alternative explanation for the complainant's physical condition. Whilst the
gateway under s.41(3)(c) may be opened if the defence have evidence of sexual
behaviour which might provide such an alternative explanation,[39] the question
arises as to whether the defence are precluded from asking any questions in the
absence of evidence of such a specific instance. Is it sufficient to argue that it is the
logical extension of the defendant's case that there has been such a sexual
occurrence involving penetration, even though the details and the timing are not
known? Neil Kibble has argued[40] that s.41(6) should be read as outlawing
questions or evidence as to reputation as well as fishing expeditions, but not the
simple, single question as to whether the physical condition was brought about by
sex with another.

Evidence as to sexual orientation

It is submitted that evidence of sexual orientation is suggestive of sexual activity,   **18.86A**
and should be regarded as subject to s.41 restrictions. Its compass is wider than
evidence of sexual behaviour because it may include marital status and pater-
nity.

There is no difference in substance between questioning a female complainant
about her suggested sexual habits, promiscuity or frequency of casual sexual
engagement, and questioning a male about his suggested homosexuality and casual
homosexual encounters, since in both cases the questions are predicated on the
position that previous consent is evidence of present consent. This would apply
equally to evidence of previous sexual partners or habitual association with places
where homosexual encounters take place. In *Beedall*,[41] the appellant had been
convicted of homosexual rape and associated sexual assaults. At trial, defence
counsel had been refused leave to ask the complainant whether he was homosexual. On appeal, the submission was renewed based on medical findings that
following the rape the complainant did not appear to have suffered any anal trauma

---

[39] *R v A (No. 2)* [2002] 1 A.C. 45 at para.79, *per* Lord Hope.

[40] In a lecture to the JSB Serious Sexual Offences Seminar, July 2007. Kibble criticises the Court
of Appeal in *White* [2004] EWCA Crim 946 for adopting a very narrow reading of s.41(6). Section 41(6)
is simply one of the hurdles that must be negotiated if evidence is to be allowed., and does not have
an added requirement of potential probative force. He concludes that it is wrong to read that
requirement into s.41(6), the purpose of which was to ensure that reputation evidence was no longer
admissible and to put an end to fishing expeditions. See also Kibble, *Judicial perspectives on the operation
of s.41 and the relevance and admissibility of prior sexual history evidence: Four scenarios* [2005] Crim. L.R.
190 at pp.202 *et seq.*, from which it appears that the majority of judges would have allowed the one
question in relation to sexual penetration by a third party, but not any further questions.

[41] [2007] EWCA Crim 23.

and that his anus was unusually lax, capacious and patulous, although the report made it clear that this did not necessarily mean that the complainant had engaged in previous homosexual activity. The Court of Appeal dismissed the appeal, holding that the question was precluded by s.41(6) unless *R. v A (No. 2)* applied. The Court stated that the inconclusive medical evidence, had it been admissible, would have entitled the jury to conclude that the complainant had previous homosexual experience. If he had no interest in men, then on the face of it, he would have been less likely to have consented. Conversely, if he did have a sexual interest in men, it is possible to argue that he was more likely to have consented, although the issue of whether he had actually consented on the occasion in question remained open. However, the purpose of the 1999 Act was to eliminate the perpetuation of that myth, as well as the myth that a promiscuous complainant is less credible.

It followed that the evidence as to sexual orientation was designed to provide a foundation for an illegitimate line of reasoning. If it is possible for there to be a fair trial in the case of the allegedly promiscuous female complainant, it had to be equally possible for there to be a fair trial in relation to a homosexual male complainant. If the Court had held that evidence of sexual orientation was relevant and admissible, it would have led to the argument that a complainant's bisexuality or homosexuality was a proper basis for arguing that he was more likely to be willing to engage in casual sex with another man.

Neil Kibble points out[42] that whilst the decision in *Beedall* broadly reflects the position in the USA,[43] academic literature contains arguments to the contrary. He rephrases the Court's question, whether there is a sufficient distinction between male and female complainants to warrant a different outcome, as follows: "Is there a difference in substance between questions of a female complainant about her sexuality in an opposite-sex rape and questions of a male complainant about his sexuality in a same-sex rape?" He points out that the question of heterosexuality is not usually engaged in opposite-sex rape. In most cases there will be an assumption that the complainant is heterosexual, whereas in same-sex rape, the question of sexual orientation is engaged. Kibble suggests that it is less than clear that the answer to his rephrased question should be a resounding "No", as it was to the Court's actual question.

EVIDENCE THAT THE COMPLAINANT HAS MADE FALSE COMPLAINTS

Application of the principles in the leading case of *R. v RT, R. v MH*[44]

18.90   Where the defence has a proper evidential basis for asserting that a previous allegation of a sexual offence was untrue, then cross-examination genuinely directed towards establishing that a previous false complaint had been made (i.e.

---

[42] Commentary in forthcoming Crim. L.R. (November 2007).
[43] *Hackett* 365 NW 2d 120 (1984) and *Whaley* 1993 WL 167342.
[44] [2002] 1 W.L.R. 632; [2002] Crim. L.R. 73.

that the complainant had lied), rather than being directed towards the sexual behaviour itself, is not prohibited by s.41: *R. v V.*[45]

It is clear from the extended definition of "sexual behaviour" in s.42(1)(c) and the decision in the leading case of *R. v RT, R. v MH*[46] that "sexual behaviour" includes situations where the complainant has been a victim, and accordingly s.41 is engaged. It follows that if the defence wish to ask the complainant questions about alleged previous false complaints, they will need to seek a ruling from the judge that the questions are not excluded by s.41. Following the approach in *R. v RT, R. v MH*, the Court of Appeal emphasised in *R. v E*[47] that the judge is entitled to seek assurances from the defence that it has a proper evidential basis for asserting that the previous statement was made and that it was untrue. If not, the questions would not be about lies but would be about the sexual behaviour of the complainant, and so would be caught by s.41.[48]

Where there is evidence of a previous complaint, a proper evidential basis for asserting that it was untrue may derive, in part, from evidence of the complainant's subsequent refusal to co-operate with the police. In *Shino Garaxo*,[49] the Court of Appeal concluded that the material was such that the judge should have permitted cross-examination regarding the two previous complaints, in that once a proper evidential basis for cross-examination is established, it would be wrong to prevent the defence from asking questions which may permit a jury to draw an inference that the victim has fabricated complaints:

> "It seems to us that the material was such that, depending on answers given by Miss B, the jury could have been satisfied that these two previous allegations were untrue. The reference by Miss B, in the first complaint, to getting a crime reference number for the 'Social' seems to us at least capable of implying an improper motive for making the complaints . . . and the refusal to co-operate with the police, in our judgment, is also capable of providing or founding an inference that the complainant is untruthful, particularly when the complainant was, as the note of her complaint makes clear, under the influence of drugs at the time."

Garaxo is very much a decision on its own facts, and is not an authority for the proposition that an inference that a previous complaint was false can be drawn from the mere fact of withdrawal. In *R. v V*, the Court of Appeal, having been referred to *Garaxo*, expressed the view (*obiter*) that "a failure to co-operate may or may not justify a conclusion that an allegation is false, depending on the circumstances".

Where there is no evidential basis for asserting that the previous complaints were false, it is not open to the advocate to ask the question in the hope of receiving an answer that they were true and to follow that up with a question as

---

[45] [2006] EWCA Crim 1901.

[46] Above n.44. See also *R. v V*, last note.

[47] [2005] Crim. L.R. 227.

[48] The Court pointed out that because none of the later allegations had been investigated, there was no evidence that they were untrue. If the cross-examination elicited assertions by the complainants that their subsequent complaints had been true, then the Court would be faced with the dilemma of either letting those allegations stand unanswered, or descending into factual enquiries with no obvious limit and wholly collateral to the issue in the case.

[49] [2005] EWCA Crim 1170.

to why none had led to charges being pursued. In *Abdelrahman*[50] the Court of Appeal noted that s.41 is not just designed to "preserve the sexual reputation of the complainant, it is to protect her from having to relive previous experiences and ordeals in the witness box save to the extent permitted by that section".

It is important that allegations of previous false allegations should be rigorously scrutinised. The facts of *Stephenson*[51] are instructive. The Court of Appeal in that case concluded that the defence case statement, in which it had been suggested that the complainant had accused every adult male with whom she had had significant contact of abusing her, was "grossly overstated". The suggestion that the complainant had accused her natural father of abusing her was based on a single and subsequently retracted suggestion she made to a counsellor in the course of counselling, where she said, " I don't know, but my father may have abused me." In relation to an old man she was said to have accused of being a paedophile, the complainant had merely repeated, in police interview, gossip that she had heard that the man was a paedophile, but she made no allegation against him whatsoever. The Court of Appeal re-affirmed the principles laid down in *R. v RT, R. v MH*, noting that it is important to register that there have to be grounds for saying that the allegations against other people were false before that line of authority becomes relevant.

Overlap between s.41 and s.100 of the Criminal Justice Act 2003

18.90A An application to cross-examine the complainant on such a basis may require a ruling under s.100 of the Criminal Justice Act 2003, although s.41 is likely to be a more formidable obstacle to overcome. In *R. v V*[52] the trial judge refused leave under s.100 for the defence to adduce evidence of a previous false complaint by the complainant, having concluded that there was no evidential basis for saying that the previous allegations was false. By the time of the trial, however, the defence renewed the application on the basis of further evidence from a witness, which was to the effect that the complainant had told her that the earlier complaint was false.

Deployment of s.4 of the Criminal Procedure Act 1865

18.90B In *R. v V* the judge ruled that s.4 of the Criminal Procedure Act 1865 did not permit the defence to cross-examine the complainant about the previous conversation with the witness, and then, if she denied it, to call the witness to prove the inconsistent statement. The Court of Appeal held that, in the light of the available evidence from the witness, there had been a sufficient evidential basis for asserting that the earlier complaint had been untrue, from which it followed that (i) cross-examination about it had not been prohibited by s.41 and (ii) the test for leave under s.100 of the Criminal Justice Act 2003 had been satisfied. Furthermore, the

---

[50] [2005] EWCA Crim 1367.
[51] [2006] EWCA Crim 2325.
[52] Above n.45.

complainant's denial that she had told the witness that the allegation was false would be a denial "relative to the subject matter of the indictment or proceeding" within the meaning of s.4 of the 1865 Act, and it followed that this was the classic situation for the deployment of s.4 by calling the witness to prove the inconsistent statement. Notwithstanding this, the conviction was upheld as safe in light of all the evidence.

Where an earlier complaint has resulted in an acquittal

The fact that the complainant has made an earlier sexual allegation which resulted **18.90C** in an acquittal is insufficient to make that allegation a false complaint: *R. v BD*[53] In that case the defendant had wished to call the acquitted person. The Court of Appeal also had serious concerns in respect of retrying the earlier allegations.

Position once questioning permitted as to false complaints

Even though s.4 of the Criminal Procedure Act 1865 may be engaged, if **18.90D** questioning is permitted as to false complaints, care must be taken not to allow contradiction of a complainant's denial to become protracted and to lead to an exploration of irrelevant materials: *R. v B (Lee)*.[54]

THE FUTURE OF SECTION 41

There have been a number of academic studies evaluating the operation of s.41 in **18.103** the aftermath of *R. v A (No. 2)*.[55] Writing after his research,[56] Neil Kibble has put forward three options as appearing to merit careful investigation:

(i) Leave the section alone, now that *R. v. A (No. 2)* has introduced a measure of judicial "discretion".

(ii) Add further exceptions to s.41—for example, to provide for motive to fabricate, prior false allegations and evidence of prior sexual history with the defendant.

(iii) Adopt the Canadian "twin myths" model, as amended by the New South Wales Law Reform Commission.

However, Kibble stresses that any reform must first give proper consideration to the primary and fundamental question of judicial discretion and should recognise that a reasonable measure of judicial discretion should be preserved. He states that

---

[53] [2007] EWCA Crim 4.
[54] [2005] EWCA Crim 3146; and see *R. v S* [2003] All E.R. (D.) 408 (Feb).
[55] Neil Kibble, *Judicial Perspectives on Section 41 of the Youth Justice and Criminal Evidence Act 1999*, a research report sponsored by the Criminal Bar Association of England and Wales, jointly funded with the University of Wales, Aberystwyth. Kibble has reproduced much of the report in two articles in the Criminal Law Review: [2005] Crim. L.R. 190, 263.
[56] [2005] Crim. L.R 263, at p.274.

whilst open-ended rules are not the answer, neither are rules which permit only mechanical application and do not permit judges to exercise judgement.

Professor Jennifer Temkin and her colleagues have made a number of recommendations of changes to the legislation in their report produced for the Home Office[57]:

    (i) Both "sexual behaviour" and "sexual experience" should be defined.

    (ii) The embargo on sexual behaviour evidence should also apply to the prosecution, as is the case in some jurisdictions.

    (iii) Consideration should be given to amending and substantially curtailing s.42(1)(b) (the belief in consent exception) to reflect both the Sexual Offences Act 2003 and the fact that it is not generally reasonable to formulate a belief in consent on the basis of past history.

    (iv) A new exception to the rule of exclusion should be inserted into s.41, allowing for evidence of previous or subsequent sexual behaviour with the accused. The exception could have a time limitation.

    (v) There should be a clear statement in the legislation that sexual behaviour evidence is not to be admitted by trial judges other than in the exceptional circumstances set out in the legislation.

The report argues that *R. v A (No. 2)* has engendered uncertainty, and judges tend to interpret it more broadly than was intended. However, it must be remembered that that the introduction of non-discretionary prohibitions may lead the courts to re-introduce a measure of judicial discretion to ensure fair trials where such a prohibition is unworkable. In this jurisdiction, that discretion derives from the strong interpretive obligation to read and give effect to legislation in a way that is compatible with Art.6 of the ECHR. In any event, the scope of *R. v A (No. 2)* should not be exaggerated. The twin myths are illegitimate lines of reasoning. Previous sexual history evidence involving third parties remains admissible only in exceptional circumstances. *R. v A (No. 2)* has not opened the floodgates and heralded a return to old s.2. It is to be noted that in *White*,[58] Laws L.J. giving the judgment of the Court of Appeal made it clear that *R. v A (No. 2)* is not authority for any wider reading of s.41 by force of s.3 of the Human Rights Act in a case where sexual acts of the complainant with men other than the appellant are sought to be adduced than is justified by the application of conventional canons of construction.

Furthermore, the rigorous regime imposed by s.41 demands that those defending in such cases should submit coherent written argument as to why the previous sexual history evidence in question is truly relevant and should spell out in terms the questions that are proposed. Any submission that the court need not look any further than *R. v A (No. 2)* is unlikely to find favour.

In *R. v A (No. 2)*, Lord Steyn observed that "while the statute pursued desirable goals, the methods adopted amounted to legislative overkill." Kibble[59]

---

[57] L. Kelly, J. Temkin, S. Griffiths, *Section 41: an evaluation of new legislation limiting sexual history evidence in rape trials*, Home Office, London (2006), p.76.

[58] [2004] EWCA Crim 946, at para.35.

[59] Kibble, *op cit.* n.55.

notes that this observation mirrors the conclusion reached by the Hon. Mrs. Justice McLachlin (as she then was) in *Seaboyer*[60] when the Supreme Court of Canada was considering whether the then Canadian rape shield provisions infringed the right to a fair trial found in the Canadian Charter of Rights and Freedoms:

> "In achieving its purpose—the abolition of the outmoded, sexist based use of sexual conduct evidence—it overshoots the mark and renders inadmissible evidence which may be essential to the presentation of legitimate defences and hence to a fair trial. In exchange for the elimination of the possibility that the judge and jury may draw illegitimate inferences from the evidence, it exacts as a price the real risk that an innocent person may be convicted. The price is too great in relation to the benefits secured, and cannot be tolerated in a society that does not countenance in any form the conviction of the innocent."

Kibble recommends that the words of Lord Steyn and the Hon. Mrs. Justice McLachlin should be heeded before any further change to s.41 is introduced.

---

[60] (1991) 83 D.L.R. (4th) 193; [1991] 2 S.C.R. 577.

CHAPTER 19

MEDICAL ASPECTS OF SEXUAL ASSAULT

by Dr. Beata Cybulska

INTRODUCTION

Sexual assault has continued to generate considerable attention since the main **19.01** work was published, due not least to an increase in reporting, continuing high attrition and low conviction rates, and controversy around the issue of alcohol consumption and consent. Multi-agency efforts have continued to change the way rape is investigated, prosecuted and managed both forensically and medically with the aim of improving conviction rates.[1]

SEXUAL ASSAULT STATISTICS

Since publication of the main work, there has been a further increase in rape **19.02** allegations against women recorded by the police in England and Wales, to 14,449 in 2005/06.[2] Conviction rates nonetheless remain low, at under 6 per cent in England and Wales and 4 per cent in Scotland, and rape remains under-reported. An Amnesty International report in November 2005 highlighted an ambivalent attitude towards rape among the public.[3] The reality is that the majority of

---

[1] B. Cybulska, *Sexual assault—Key issues*, J.R.S.M., 2007; July, 100: 321–324.

[2] *Recorded crime statistics for England and Wales*, Home Office Statistical Bulletin 19/05 (Vol. 5), London. Interestingly, in 2006, the 3 per cent increase in reporting in women was associated with a 2 per cent decrease among men.

[3] Amnesty International Report, London, November 2005.

complainants know their assailant, most have no injuries on examination and many cases are associated with alcohol consumption.[4] The picture is complicated by high attrition rates, combined with the fact that only 14 per cent of allegations result in criminal proceedings and 9 per cent of allegations are classified as false (the majority of which are among the 16–25 age group).[5]

Consequences of Rape

19.03   The consequences of rape, apart from well-recognized psychological syndromes such as post traumatic stress disorder, include physical injuries, unwanted pregnancy and sexually transmitted infection (STI). Although many people experience psychological symptoms after rape, most recover, and a minority of victims of sexual assault have significant and disabling persistent symptoms that require specialist intervention.[6] The impact on family, partner and children should not be forgotten. Plans for expert witnesses to give evidence in court about psychological trauma suffered by victims have been shelved. Instead, the Government is proposing that the jury be presented with statements about the impact of rape in the form of a leaflet, drawn up by experts and agreed by both the defence and prosecution.[7]

Sexual Assault Referral Centres

19.05   Sexual Assault Referral Centres ("SARCs") are services dedicated to addressing the forensic and aftercare needs of the complainants of sexual violence. The Home Office has promoted this model of service as a gold standard and there are now 15 SARCs in the UK, located mainly in the larger cities. The most well-established are the Juniper Centre in Lancashire, the REECH Centre in Northumbria, the New Pathways in Wales and the three Havens in London (Camberwell, which was set up in 2000, and Paddington and Whitechapel, which were set up in 2004). The Havens cover the entire Metropolitan Police area and offer 24-hour a day cover for forensic examinations within an hour of request, facilities for non-police referrals, psychosocial support to complainants and medical aftercare, including prophylaxis and screening for STIs.[8]

---

[4] A. Abbey, T. Zawacki, P.O. Buck, A. Clinton, P. McAuslan, *Alcohol and Sexual Assault*, Alcohol Health and Research World 2001; 25:43–51.

[5] L. Kelly, J. Lovett, L. Regan, *A Gap or Chasm? Attrition in Reported Rape Cases*, Home Office Research Study 293, London, 2005.

[6] J. Welch and F. Mason, *Rape and sexual assault*, BMJ, 2007; 334: 1154–1158.

[7] *Rape trial trauma plans shelved*, http://news.bbc.co.uk/2/hi/uk_news/7012446.stm.

[8] See *Sexual Assault Referral Centres: Getting Started*, Association of Chief Police Officers, London, 2005, available at http://police.homeoffice.gov.uk/operational-policing/crime-disorder/sexual-offences?version=5; J. Welch, *Medical care following sexual assault: Guidance for Sexual Assault Referral Centres*, Home Office, London, 2005, available at http://police.homeoffice.gov.uk/operational-policing/crime-disorder/sexual-offences?version=5.

Another type of service provision is the non-SARC model, which relies on dedicated forensic physicians, trained and experienced in sexual assault examinations, carrying out forensic examinations of complainants at the request of the police in so called Victim Examination Suites, usually located in police stations.

A survey of SARC and non-SARC settings has highlighted a disproportion in service provision, with non-SARC settings not offering examinations without police involvement, many not having enough doctors to offer a 24-hour service and most not offering screening for STIs.[9]

PROJECT SAPPHIRE

Following the success of the specialist Sapphire Units, dedicated to the investigation of rape in the Metropolitan Police area and using officers specially trained in the Sexual Offences Investigative Technique (SOIT), the Rape Action Plan 2002 put forward recommendations and suggestions for action to the police and the CPS, including the establishment of facilities for forensic examination, training for police officers, specialist prosecutors and special measures for complainants in court.[10] A report published in 2007 following a review of progress against the Rape Action Plan acknowledged considerable the efforts that had been made and identified the many challenges ahead.[11] Further specialist police units have been set up in other parts of the UK alongside specialist CPS prosecutors. **19.06**

In London, one of the successes of the Sapphire Units has been the introduction of the Early Evidence Kit ("EEK"), containing a urine collection container and a mouth swab, which is used by SOITs immediately after meeting the complainant. Use of the EEK facilitates the preservation of some forensic evidence prior to a full forensic medical examination.

FORENSIC EXAMINATION

Forensic Medical Examination ("FME") plays an important role in the collection of DNA evidence, the recording of injuries, immediate medical aftercare and the facilitation of follow-up.[12] Medical needs often include referral to Social Services, Victim Support or a Community Safety Unit. Many complainants require counselling or psychological referral. **19.07**

FME is usually undertaken at the request of the police when the case is reported and the complainant wishes it to be investigated. Another option available in some SARC settings includes FME without police involvement, as a non-police referral where forensic evidence is gathered and samples tested anonymously or stored. In addition, intelligence information is collected and released to the police with

---

[9] M. Pilli. S. Smith, *Facillities for complainant's of sexual assault throughout the United Kingdom*, J. Clin. Forensic Med. 2006; 13: 164–71.

[10] *Rape Action Plan 2002*. Home Office, London, available at *http://www.homeoffice.gov.uk/crime/ sexualoffences/rape_action_plan.html*.

[11] *Without Consent*, CPS and ACPO Report on Rape, available at *http://hmcpsi.gov.uk/reports/ Without_Consent_Therapeutic.pdf*.

[12] B. Cybulska, G. Forster, *Sexual assault—Examination of the victim*, Medicine 2006; 29:7.

consent, anonymously. The non–police option gives the complainant time to consider whether to report the assault to the police without losing valuable forensic evidence. In cases where a match has been found of the anonymously tested sample with the entry on the national DNA database, the police may approach the victim to report and cooperate, particularly if the assailant appears to be a serial attacker.

Forensic Samples and Chain of Evidence

19.12   In 2007, the Faculty of Forensic and Legal Medicine at the Royal College of Physicians, in conjunction with the Forensic Science Service, published detailed guidelines for the collection of forensic specimens in complaints of sexual assault, outlining the method of collection and packaging and the forensic cut-off points for the detection of DNA evidence (seven days in vaginal penetration, up to two days in oral penetration and three days in anal penetration with a penis). Other samples which can be taken include: urine and blood for the presence of alcohol and drugs, skin swabs for body fluids or contact DNA, fingernail swabs or cuttings, hair swabs or cuttings, clothing, sanitary wear, gowns and couch cover.[13] In non-police referrals, samples can initially be stored in the SARC setting if the complainant wishes, or can be tested anonymously. A long-term storage option is also available.[14]

Drug-Facilitated Sexual Assault

19.13   Despite the publicity given to drug-facilitated sexual assault, studies carried out in the UK by the Home Office, the Forensic Science Service and the Police Standards Unit showed that during the period 2000-02, flunitrazepam (Rohypnol) was detected in only one case and gamma hydroxybutyric acid (GHB) in only two cases out of 1014 suspected such assaults.[15] Operation Matisse, which looked at samples taken over 12 months in 2004-05, detected no cases of flunitrazepam and only two of GHB.[16]

In both studies, alcohol was detected in about half of the study sample, either alone or in combination with illicit drugs. Cases in which alcohol was detected were characterised by delayed presentation. Problems with the detection of drugs such as GHB and Rohypnol in body fluids are related to their short elimination times from the body. In urine, for example, these drugs can be detected for up to 12 and 72 hours respectively, with detection times in blood being even shorter. Late presentation due to intoxication with alcohol, confusion, uncertainty and symptoms of hangover complicate matters further. In delayed presentations, it is

---

[13] *Guidelines for the collection of specimens*, Faculty of Forensic and Legal Medicine, April 2007, *http://www.fflm.ac.uk.*

[14] See *http://thehavens.co.uk; http://www.kent.police.uk.*

[15] M. Scott-Ham, F.C. Burton, *Toxicological findings in cases of alleged drug facilitated sexual assault in the United Kingdom over 3-year period,* J. Clin. Forensic Med., 2005; 12:175–186.

[16] *Operation Matisse: Investigating Drug Facilitated Sexual Assault*, Association of Chief Police Officers, November 2006.

possible to look for drugs in hair samples.[17] The report of the Advisory Council on the Misuse of Drugs published in April 2007 put forward a number of recommendations, amongst them public education about drug-facilitated rape and the use of Early Evidence Kits.[18]

INJURIES IN VAGINAL PENETRATION

The Home Office published a useful guide to genital anatomy in 2005.[19] Hymenal findings are often crucial in cases of alleged sexual assault. Interpretation of them depends on whether or not the presentation is acute and whether, for example, the complainant is pre- or post-pubertal. The hymenal tissue changes over time and the opening becomes more elastic. In cases presenting after acute injuries have healed, findings may be normal or there may be scarring, narrowing of the hymen, enlargement of the hymeneal opening and healed partial clefts or transactions.[20] Ano-genital trauma generally heals quickly and often without residual signs, and most children presenting following an allegation of suspected sexual abuse have normal examination findings.[21] Adams *et al* concluded that tears at the posterior fourchette were most common among adolescents following sexual assault and hymenal tears were uncommon even in self-described virginal girls.[22] In addition, there is a wide variation of normal appearances, such that hymenal findings should be interpreted with caution.[23] Examination of findings particularly in adolescent girls is often difficult due to the effects of oestrogenisation. Some authors have recommended the use of foleys catheter as a useful aid in examining the hymen in post-pubertal girls.[24] A comparison of injury patterns in virgin and non-virgin groups of adolescent girls showed that genital and body injuries are not routinely found after an allegation of rape or sexual assault, even when there has been no previous sexual experience. The absence of injury does not exclude the possibility of intercourse, whether with or without consent.[25] The vast majority of adult

19.15

---

[17] P. Kintz, M. Villain, B. Lused, *Testing for the undetectable in Drug-Facilitated Sexual Assault using hair analyzed by tendem mass spectroscopy as evidence*, Ther. Drug Monit. 2004; 26(2): 211–214.

[18] *Drug Facilitated Sexual Assault*, Advisory Council on the Misuse of Drugs, Home Office, April 2007.

[19] M. Volpellier, J. Welch, E. Weston-Price, *Forensic examination following sexual assault: Your questions answered*, Home Office, 2006.

[20] J. Adams, *Approach to the interpretation of medical and laboratory findings in suspected child sexual abuse: A 2005 revision*, APSAC Advisor 2005; 17: 7–12.

[21] J. Adams, K. Harper, S. Knudson, et al., *Examination findings in legally confirmed child sexual abuse: It's normal to be normal*, Pediatrics 1994; 94: 310–317.

[22] J.A. Adams, B. Girardin, D. Faugno, *Adolescent sexual assault. Documentation of injuries using photocolposcopy*, North Amn. Socy. for Pediatr. Adolesc. Gynaeclogy, 2001; Nov: 175–180.

[23] A.H. Heger, L. Ticson, L. Guerra, J. Lister, T. Zaragoza, G. McConnell, M. Morahan, *Appearance of the genitalia of girls selected for non-abuse*, Review of Hymenal Morphology and Non-specific Findings, J. Ped. Adolesc. Gynaecology, 2002 (Feb), Vol 12, (1): 27–35 (9).

[24] Jones et al., Adolescent Foley Catheter Technique for Visualizing Hymenal Injuries in Adolescents, Acad. Emerg. Med. 2003; 10: 1001–1004.

[25] C. White, I. McLean, *Adolescent complainants of sexual assault; injury patterns in virgin and non-virgin groups*, J. Clin. Forensic Med., 2006; Vol 12: 171–180.

female complainants of rape have no injuries on examination[26] and findings of injury can be due to penetration with an object, including the penis, friction and rubbing, which may be consensual or non-consensual, or the presence of vulvo-vaginal infections or skin conditions such as lichen sclerosis or eczema. The likelihood of injury will depend on the presence or absence of adequate lubrication, the degree of force used, length of time, relaxation, resistance, age of the complainant and their body build, sexual experience, vaginal delivery and the existence of a hormonal imbalance, e.g. during the menopause.[27]

Extra-Genital Injuries

19.26   Questions about the ageing of bruises often arise in court. For years, bruises have been aged by the presence of yellow colour in them, indicating that the bruise is 18 hours or more old. Recent research points at individual variations in the perception of yellow, making attempts to age bruises more unreliable.[28] The better view is that, whilst comments may be made about bruises, they cannot be accurately aged.

Forensic Colposcopy

19.28   Colposcopy has become a very useful tool in the assessment and photo-documentation of genital findings of sexual assault, mainly in children. The technique allows observation of the vulvo-vaginal structures under magnification and the making of a video or CD recording of the viewed area. The recording may be used evidentially as well as for training and peer review. Evidential material can be made available to another medical expert for viewing and a second opinion. The Royal College of Paediatrics and Child Health has recommended the use of colposcopy in child abuse cases, particularly in single doctor examinations where a second opinion can be obtained at a later date.

While the use of colposcopy has become standard in child sexual abuse cases, its use in relation to adults remains controversial, particularly as the presence of injuries does not help to distinguish between consensual and non-consensual intercourse. Studies do, however, demonstrate that the use of colposcopy in adults improves the detection of genital trauma, compared with visual examination alone, to a statistically significant degree.[29]

The use of colposcopic evidence in court is controversial, as it raises many concerns amongst the medical profession about the possibility of recorded

---

[26] C. Lincoln, *Genital injury: is it significant? A review of the literature*, Med. Sci. Law, 2001; Vol. 41 No.3: 206–216; L. Bowyer, M. Dalton, *Female victims of rape and their genital injuries*, British J. Obs. and Gynae., 1997; 104 (5): 617–620.

[27] D.J. Templeton, *Sexual assault in postmenopausal women*, J. of Clin. Forensic Med. 2005; 12: 98–00.

[28] V.K. Hughes, P.S. Ellis, N.E.I. Langlois, *The perception of yellow in bruises*, J. Clin. Forensic Med., 2004; 11: 257–259.

[29] L.C. Lenahan, A. Ernst, B. Johnson, *Colposcopy in evaluation of adult sexual assault victims*, Am. J. Emerg. Med., 1998, March; 16 (2): 183–4.

sensitive material being shown in public. Some see this concern as related to political and gender issues, and consider that to offer the option of photo-documentation to adult complainants of sexual assault who have the right to evidence-based medicine does them an injustice.[30] There is general agreement in the medical profession that recorded material should be made available for viewing only by appropriate medical experts.

ASPECTS OF AFTER CARE: SEXUALLY TRANSMITTED INFECTIONS

It is recommended that screening for STIs should take place two weeks after the assault. As the infection may predate the assault, a careful assessment of sexual history and contact tracing (screening and treatment) of sexual partners is essential. Positive STI results can be used as evidence, particularly if detected in individuals not previously sexually active or so-called "inexperienced orifices". In such circumstance, a chain of evidence relating to custody of the samples must be demonstrated. **19.33**

Isolation of *Neisseria gonorrhoeae* is currently the gold standard for the definitive diagnosis of gonorrhoea and for use in medico–legal cases in the UK. Molecular detection methods are increasingly used, but are untested as evidence of infection in a court of law. In one case an isolate of *N. gonorrhoeae* was obtained from a child and an article of clothing from an adult male who was suspected of sexual abuse of the child. Biochemical and immunological tests were used to confirm the isolate as N. gonorrhoeae. Amplification by Polymeraze Chain Reaction (PCR) was used both as further confirmation of the isolate and to detect the presence of gonococcal-specific DNA from the clothing. The relationship of the gonococcal DNA from the child and the adult was investigated using genotyping. Both samples were indistinguishable and shared the same sequence type. This resulted in conviction of the man for sexual assault.[31]

International guidelines state that *Neisseria gonorrhoeae* infection in pre-pubertal children is always, or nearly always, sexually transmitted. Prof. Felicity Goodyear-Smith, in her review of literature on the subject, draws attention to the fact that following identification of *N. gonorrhoea* in 1880 it became recognised that when the infection was introduced into children's institutions, it rapidly spread among pre-pubertal girls. The medical literature records over 40 epidemics involving about 2000 children in Europe and the United States. Communal baths, towels or fabric, rectal thermometers and carers' hands were identified as means of transmission. Sensitive to heat and drying, gonorrhoea may remain viable in pus on cloth for several days. There have been reports of accidental transmissions due to contamination from laboratory samples. Indirect transmission has occurred in epidemics of conjunctivitis in third world rural populations. Infection can spread

[30] P.A.W. Brennan, *The medical and ethical aspects of photography in the sexual assault examination: Why does it offend?*, J. Clin. Forensic Med., 2006; 13: 194–202.
[31] I.M.C. Martin, Ellie Foreman , Vicky Hall , Anne Nesbitt , Greta Forster , Catherine A. Ison, *Non-cultural detection and molecular genotyping of* Neisseria gonorrhoeae *from a piece of clothing*, J. Med. Microbiol. 2007 Apr; 56 (Pt 4): 487–90.

via the contaminated hands of infected careers. Whilst all paediatric cases of gonorrhoea must be taken seriously, including contact-tracing and testing, forensic medical examiners should keep an open mind about possible means of transmission. The author highlights the need for doctors and lawyers to be aware of the large body of literature demonstrating both sexual and non-sexual means of transmission of gonorrhoea in children.[32]

VULNERABLE VICTIMS

19.39   There is a need to recognise and address the particular risks that vulnerable people face following sexual violence. It has been increasingly recognised that many complainants of sexual assault are vulnerable because of their age, particularly at the extremes, with adolescents representing the biggest group. Further, of 240 female complainants of sexual assault over the age of 13 seen at the Haven Whitechapel over a six-month period (September 2004 to February 2005), about 21 per cent gave a history of deliberate self-harm (DSH) and 20 per cent of mental health problems, and 8 per cent had learning difficulties.[33] Many assaults occur as part of domestic violence, with 50 per cent of women and 35 per cent of men experiencing more then one type of intimate violence since the age of 16. Matters are further complicated in relation to certain ethnic minorities, with cultural issues, language barriers and limited knowledge of personal rights having an impact on reporting and attrition rates. Survivors of sexual assault often display psychological sequelae, including elevated rates of suicide ideation/attempts. A prevalence of mental health problems was established in 121 forensic cases seen at the Haven Whitechapel between June and August 2004. Levels of safety and vulnerability are formally assessed prior to complainants leaving the Haven. When mental health problems are identified, additional screening questions are asked, and a flow chart is used that outlines appropriate care pathways. 4 per cent of Haven Whitechapel clients required urgent follow-up and 3 per cent immediate referral to a psychiatric liaison team. There is a high background prevalence of mental health problems and DSH in the study population. These findings have implications for the expansion of the entire SARC network.

MEDICAL EVIDENCE IN COURT

19.40   Giving evidence in court can be a daunting prospect for the doctor. There is a lack of minimum standards in this area, and also no accreditation arrangements, although the need for these has been recognised following certain highly publicised trials. It is important that doctors assist the court by offering an opinion that is objective, impartial, evidence-based and unbiased. There is a lack of a good

---

[32] F. Goodyear-Smith, *What is the evidence for non-sexual transmission of gonorrhoea in children after the neonatal period? A systematic review*, J. of Legal and Forensic Med., 2007 *http://www.science direct.com/jcfm.*

[33] L. Campbell, A. Keegan, B. Cybulska, G. Forster, *Prevalence of mental health problems and deliberate self-harm in complainants of sexual assault*, J. Clin. Forensic Med. 2007; 14: 75–8.

evidence-base in the area of sexual assault and more needs to be done to help physicians support their opinions in court.[34] Increasingly, the need is being recognised for pre-trial discussions between experts with a view to reaching agreement where possible.

[34] G. Norfolk, C. White, *Interpretation of evidence in court—the dangers and pitfalls*, J. Clin. Forensic Med. 2006; 13: 160–1.

289

CHAPTER 20

DNA, LAW AND STATISTICS

by Graham Cooke

INTRODUCTION

The science of DNA has moved on again since the main work was published in   **20.01**
2004. The National DNA Database has also expanded considerably and more
information about how it is working is now available. There have also been
important changes in the rules of expert evidence and of procedure regarding the
giving of expert evidence and the linked duties of disclosure.

DEVELOPMENTS IN DNA TECHNOLOGY

Partial profiles

Scientists have been successful in further increasing their ability to extract DNA   **20.02**
material from tiny or degraded crime samples. However, one side-effect of this
greater power is that the possibility of contamination is increased, because the
process now successfully detects DNA in ever-decreasing fractions of a gram. The
amount of material from which a DNA profile can now be extracted is as little as
a fraction of a nanogram (a billionth of a gram, i.e. one thousandth of a millionth
of a gram). This paucity of DNA material may well result in a partial profile being
produced. Partial profiles may also appear when the DNA sample is extracted
from degraded material. Because of the very sensitive scientific techniques used,
the DNA profile emerging from the analysis may well be a mixed and a partial
profile, in other words a profile to which more than one person has contributed.
The results in such cases are often less than clear-cut and can give rise to genuine
differences of opinion between experts. The results emerge in a computer-
produced graph which shows "peaks" of various heights. These are then
interpreted by the expert into the measurements of the "bits" of DNA in the
sample. The height of a peak is one of the most important factors for an expert in

deciding whether a peak is actually a piece of DNA or not. The issues around "what is a peak and what is not" are not clear-cut and different experts may have different opinions on the question. In any case in which there is a contentious reported "match", it is recommended that copies of these graphs be obtained from the prosecution. The reporting laboratory will have its own internal rules and procedures governing what is a match and what is not, but full disclosure of any possible area of doubt is very important and is now required under the Criminal Procedure Rules.[1] The Forensic Science Service has procedures for conducting an independent check on the reporting scientist's conclusions. Part of its procedure reads[2]:

> "Resolution of a Profile
>
> It is strongly recommended that any annotation of the DNA results and summary sheets is kept to a minimum so that the results can be independently checked by the reviewer. If necessary, notes and any highlighting relating to your interpretation can be made on a separate sheet or on a photocopy of the results."

20.02A In *Bates*,[3] the Court of Appeal thoroughly examined the issues involved in the use of partial profiles. The judgment merits thorough reading by anybody dealing with a "partial profile" case. In terms of admissibility of partial profiles, the Court said:

> "We can see no reason why partial profile DNA evidence should not be admissible provided that the jury are made aware of its inherent limitations and are given a sufficient explanation so as to evaluate it. There may be cases where the match probability in relation to all the samples tested is so great[4] that the judge may consider its probative value to be minimal and decide to exclude the evidence in the exercise of his discretion, but this gives rise to no new decision of principle and can be left for decision on a case by case basis."[5]

Unfortunately, there are two passages in the judgment where the Court committed a form of the "prosecutor's fallacy".[6] The passages do not impugn the decision on the appeal, but do illustrate how easy it is to slip into error, even after thorough argument. The differences between a correct logical statement and a fallacious one are very subtle. This is significant in a trial context where, of course, the DNA evidence is oral unless, unusually, the difficult parts are reduced to writing. The lesson to be drawn from *Bates*, and other examples of fallacious statements about DNA evidence, is that juries (and others) should be positively warned not to slip into a fallacious understanding of the significance of DNA evidence.

---

[1] See Rule 33.3(f), para.20.19 below.
[2] FSS-TS-385(B), para.6.
[3] [2006] EWCA Crim 1395.
[4] i.e. very frequent profiles.
[5] para.32.
[6] paras 10 and 13. For explanation of the "prosecutor's fallacy", see para.20.12(h) of the main work.

Low copy number

"Low copy number" is the name given to a new technique for extracting DNA,   **20.02B**
used generally when other techniques have failed. As with any new technique, its
use in Court may need to be challenged. In mid-2007, one major laboratory was
refusing to use the technique on the basis that it was not satisfied that the
technique is sufficiently reliable. That is enough to sound warning bells about
allowing such evidence to be used without challenge.

ADMISSIBILITY OF DNA EVIDENCE

The hearsay issue and section 127 of the Criminal Justice Act 2003

A practice has grown up over many years for prosecution experts (whether in   **20.18**
relation to DNA or anything else) to rely upon material containing the primary
laboratory findings of fact. These may be results from a laboratory remote from
the expert whose opinion is to be given in court. The "reporting" experts would
frequently give their opinion without the primary underlying facts being proved.
The case law was (and is) quite clear that the expert's opinion was only as good
as the facts on which he relies, which must be put in evidence by an admissible
route. Any challenge to the admissibility of the expert's opinion was often met by
a demand that the defence should admit the relevant "facts", and judges have even
from time-to-time threatened to order costs against a defence advocate for
insisting on proper proof of the underlying facts. None of this area was helpfully
illuminated by the persistent, and erroneous, habit of calling such evidence
"continuity evidence". Continuity of exhibits is an important issue in its own
right. These issues are now addressed by s.127 of Criminal Justice Act 2003, which
provides a procedure by which the judge is in control of the admissibility of such
statements setting out the underlying facts on which an expert reports. The test
for admission is the "interests of justice".

SCIENTIFIC BASIS OF DNA EVIDENCE

Criminal Procedure Rules 2005

Rule 33.2(1) of the Criminal Procedure Rules 2005 provides that an expert must   **20.19**
help the court to achieve the overriding objective by giving objective, unbiased
opinion on matters within his expertise. By Rule 33.3(1), an expert's report
must:

    (a) give details of the expert's qualifications, relevant experience and
           accreditation[7];
    (b) give details of any literature or other information which the expert had
           relied on in making the report;

---

[7] Including any registration with the Council for the Registration of Forensic Practitioners.

(c) contain a statement setting out the substance of all facts given to the expert which are material to the opinions expressed in the report or on which those opinions are based[8];

(d) make clear which of the facts stated in the report are within the expert's own knowledge;

(e) say who carried out any examination, measurement, test or experiment which the expert has used for the report and:

   (i) give the qualifications, relevant experience and accreditation of that person;

   (ii) say whether or not the examination, measurement, test or experiment was carried out under the expert's supervision, and

   (iii) summarise the findings on which the expert relies;

(f) where there is a range of opinion on the matters dealt with in the report:

   (i) summarise the range of opinion, and

   (ii) give reasons for his own opinion[9];

(g) if the expert is not able to give his opinion without qualification, state the qualification;

(h) contain a summary of the conclusions reached;

(i) contain a statement that the expert understands his duty to the court, and has complied and will continue to comply with that duty; and

(j) contain the same declaration of truth as a witness statement.

The Birmingham Database

20.32 The National Database now contains well over three million profiles. Part of this expansion has been caused by the widening of the circumstances in which police are allowed to take and store DNA from people who have come into contact with the criminal justice system. There are controversial aspects to the principles underlying this expansion, which lie outside the scope of this summary.

The DNA Custodian's Annual Report for 2003-04 refers to a project under which some 24,000 DNA suspect profiles, which had been matched with a crime scene sample using the SGM system, were upgraded using the SGM Plus system. The somewhat surprising result was that in 3,600 cases (15 per cent), the SGM "match" with the crime scene sample was found to be a mis-match using SGM Plus.[10] A sample of 100 cases was taken to see if any wrongful convictions had occurred. None had. Nevertheless, it is of concern that there should have been so many cases where what seemed like very powerful DNA evidence of guilt, typically one in several million, was shown on further analysis to be conclusive evidence of innocence. This is not a criticism of the Database or of the underlying DNA evidence, but the results do underline the point that a DNA match (on its own) is

---

[8] See the discussion of s.127 of the Criminal Justice Act 2003 in para.20.18 above.

[9] The "reporting" expert should set out the possibility that another expert may hold a different opinion, even if the reporting expert's opinion is strongly held.

[10] SGM used six markers. SGM Plus uses the same six and then four more.

not as conclusive as many people think it is. Plainly, a full match on SGM Plus is very powerful evidence. This is typically reported as "of the order of 1 in a billion".

The Annual Report for 2005–06 reports that about 12 per cent of all the profiles on the Database are "replicates", i.e. a profile for which a second, matching profile is found under a different name. This amounts to a total of about 345,000 profiles, and it is of concern that so many exist.

These matters are of indirect relevance to trial issues, but they do serve to remind practitioners of the need for great care when dealing with DNA evidence.

CHAPTER 21

DISCLOSURE

by Johannah Cutts

INTRODUCTION

In the main work, a number of problems were identified in relation to applications **21.01**
for disclosure of potentially relevant material held by third parties. In particular,
these related to confusion as to who should make such applications, applications
being made without knowledge of the relevant rules and correct procedure, and
late applications resulting in delayed hearings in the very cases that warrant an
expeditious trial.

    The persistence of these problems, and other problems presented by disclosure
generally, has resulted in the publication of a revised *Code of Practice* under the
Criminal Procedure and Investigations Act 1996 (March 2005)[1]; revised Attorney-
General's Guidelines for prosecution disclosure (also issued in 2005); a *Protocol for
the control and management of unused material in the Crown Court*, issued by the
judiciary in 2006 (the "Disclosure Protocol")[2]; and amendments to the provisions
on disclosure in the Criminal Procedure Rules 2005.[3]

    The introduction of the Criminal Procedure Rules in 1999[4] was designed to
improve the management of Crown Court trials so as to ensure efficiency, decrease
delay and prevent costly and unnecessary hearings. Disclosure nevertheless has
continued resolutely to cause problems in the trial process. As the *Protocol* recognises[5]:

> "Disclosure is one of the most important—as well as one of the most abused—of the
> procedures relating to criminal trials. There needs to be a sea-change in the approach

[1] s.23(1).
[2] To be found at *http://www.hmcourts-service.gov.uk/cms/files/disclosure_protocol.pdf.*
[3] By SI 2007/699, which can be found at *http://www.opsi.gov.uk/si/si2007/20070699.htm.* The
amendments came into force on April 2, 2007.
[4] Crown Court (Miscellaneous Amendments) Rules 1999 (SI 1999/598).
[5] Above n.2, at para.1.

of both judges and the parties to all aspects of the handling of the material which the prosecution do not intend to use as part of their case. For too long, a wide range of serious misunderstandings has existed, both as to the exact ambit of the unused material to which the defence is entitled, and the role to be played by the judge in ensuring that the law is properly applied. All too frequently applications by the parties and decisions by the judges in this area have been based either on misconceptions as to the true nature of the law or a general laxity of approach (no matter how well intentioned). This failure properly to apply the binding provisions as regards disclosure has proved extremely and unnecessarily costly and has obstructed justice. It is, therefore, essential that disclosure obligations are properly discharged—by both the prosecution and the defence—in all criminal proceedings, and the court's careful oversight of this process is an important safeguard against the possibility of miscarriages of justice."

Whilst this criticism relates to disclosure as a whole, third party material is particularly singled out as an area that has caused "some difficulties".[6]

The answer provided by all the above-mentioned documents is for judges to insist on rigid adherence to the rules, both in terms of substance and time. As plea and case management hearings (PCMHs) take on increasing importance at the start of the Crown Court process, counsel, both prosecution and defence, are required to identify issues and the need for disclosure at an early stage of the proceedings. The judge is now required at the PCMH to enquire about disclosure, including whether there is likely to be any application for third party disclosure. He is now to identify who is to make any such application and provide a timetable for them to do so. Sections of new forms specifically cover this area.

There is also new guidance as to how and when to make application for disclosure and attempts have been made to simplify the process. There can be no doubt that all will be expected to know and follow the rules to the letter.

Prosecution Duty to Disclose

21.04   The Disclosure Protocol identifies the three regimes to be followed by the prosecution in relation to disclosure[7]:

- In relation to offences in respect of which the criminal investigation began before April 1, 1997, the common law will apply and the test for disclosure is that set out in *Keane*.[8]
- If the criminal investigation commenced on or after April 1, 1997, but before April 4, 2005, then the Criminal Procedure and Investigation Act 1996 ("CPIA") will apply in its original form, as set out in paras 21.04–21.07 of the main work, with separate tests for disclosure of unused prosecution material at the primary and secondary disclosure stages (the latter following service of a defence statement). The disclosure provisions of the Act are supported by the 1997 edition of the *Code of Practice* issued under s.23(1) of the Act.[9]

[6] Above n.2, at para.52.
[7] Above n.2, at para.10.
[8] [1994] 1 W.L.R. 746.
[9] SI 1997/1033.

- Where the criminal investigation commenced on or after April 4, 2005, the law is set out in the CPIA as amended by Pt V of the Criminal Justice Act 2003. There is then, as set out in the main work, a single test for disclosure of unused material in the hands of the prosecution, and the April 2005 edition of the *Code of Practice* issued under s.23(1) of the CPIA will apply.[10]

Prosecutors are also expected to have regard to the Attorney-General's guidelines on disclosure, most recently published in 2005. Although these do not have the force of law, the Disclosure Protocol requires them to be given "due weight".

Code of Practice 2005

The Disclosure Protocol points out that for the statutory scheme to work properly, **21.04A** investigators and disclosure officers responsible for the gathering, inspection, retention and recording of relevant unused prosecution material must perform their tasks thoroughly, scrupulously and fairly. In this, they must adhere to the appropriate provisions of the CPIA Code of Practice.[11]

An important provision in relation to trials of sexual offences is para.3.6 of the Code, which states that if the officer in charge of the investigation believes that other persons may be in possession of material that may be relevant to the investigation, he should ask the disclosure officer to inform them of the existence of the investigation and to invite them to retain the material in case they receive a request for its disclosure. The disclosure officer should inform the prosecutor that the third person may have such material. However, the officer in charge of the investigation is not required to make speculative enquiries of other persons: there must be some reason to believe that the third person may have relevant material. In practice, it would be sensible for an officer investigating a case where social services have been involved with the complainant or other important witness, to make enquiry of the relevant social services department as to whether records exist and, if so, whether there is likely to be material of relevance within them.

Paragraph 5.1 reminds the investigator that he must retain information obtained in a criminal investigation which may be relevant to the investigation. Material may be copied if the original is to be returned to its owner. This is of particular significance where an officer may have had access to third party documents but not been permitted to retain them.

Paragraph 6.12 requires the disclosure officer to list on a sensitive schedule any material, "the disclosure of which he believes would give rise to a real risk of serious prejudice to an important public interest, and the reason for that belief". This specifically includes material given in confidence, and material supplied to an investigator which relates to a child or young person and which has been generated by a local authority social services department, an Area Child Protection

---

[10] SI 2005/985.
[11] Above n.2, at para.13.

Committee or other party contacted by an investigator during the investigation and material relating to the private life of a witness (this must include medical records).

The judge's duty to enforce the statutory scheme

21.04B　　The Disclosure Protocol notes the time limit of 70 days from the time that cases are sent to the Crown Court for the service of sufficient evidence to amount to a prima facie case.[12] Paragraph 21 recognizes that the time limit does not specifically apply to unused prosecution material, but notes that the court will need to consider at the preliminary hearing whether it is practicable for the prosecution to comply with primary or initial disclosure at the same time as service of such papers, or whether disclosure ought to take place after a certain interval but before the PCMH. The Protocol also seeks to ensure that any foreseeable difficulties relating to disclosure are notified to the court early by stating that it would be helpful for the prosecution advocate to make these clear at the magistrates' court or at the preliminary hearing. If that is not possible, the prosecutor should notify the defence and court as soon as such difficulties arise. The judge can and should then set a realistic timetable from the outset.[13]

At the PCMH, all advocates, prosecution and defence, must be fully instructed about any difficulties there may be in complying with their respective disclosure obligations and be in a position to put forward a reasonable timetable for resolution of them.

It is not just the prosecution who must adhere to the rules on disclosure. Paragraph 37 of the Protocol requires a "complete change in the culture" on defence case statements. The defence must serve the defence case statement by the due date and judges must then examine it with care to ensure that it complies with the formalities required by the CPIA.

The Protocol states that it is vital the prosecution are mindful of their continuing duty of disclosure, and they must particularly review disclosure in the light of issues identified in the defence case statement. The judge should set a date by which any application by the defence for disclosure under s.8 of the CPIA (if there is to be one) should be made.[14]

Public interest immunity

21.08　　Rules made under the CPIA setting out the procedure by which applications for disclosure of material held by third parties are to be made were amended by the Criminal Procedure (Amendment) Rules 2007.[15]

---

[12] Crime and Disorder Act 1998 (Service of Prosecution Evidence) Regulations 2005.
[13] paras 23–27.
[14] para.43.
[15] Above n.3.

MATERIAL IN THE HANDS OF THIRD PARTIES

Documents held by the civil court

The procedure governing applications to the civil court for material which forms **21.25** part of family proceedings has been amended by Rule 10.20A of the Family Proceedings (Amendment No. 4) Rules 2005.[16] Rule 10.20A supersedes Rule 4.23 of the Family Proceedings Rules 1991. It provides:

> "(2) For the purposes of the law relating to contempt of court, information relating to the proceedings (whether or not contained in a document filed with the court) may be communicated:
> (a) Where the court gives permission;
> (b) Subject to any direction of the court, in accordance with paragraphs (3) or (4) of this rule[17]; or
> (c) Where the communication is to
>   (i)   a party,
>   (ii) the legal representative of a party,
>   (iii) a professional legal advisor,
>   (iv) an officer of the service or a Welsh family proceedings officer,
>   (v)   the welfare officer,
>   (vi) the Legal Services Commission,
>   (vii) an expert whose instruction by a party has been authorised by the court, or
>   (viii) a professional acting in furtherance of the protection of children."

It can be seen that Rule 10.20A differs from Rule 4.23 in a number of respects:

Information relating to the proceedings (whether or not contained in a document filed with the court)

Rule 4.23 related to disclosure of documents held by the court. Rule 10.20A **21.25A** widens this to "information relating to the proceedings (whether or not contained in a document filed with the court)". This change in wording was considered in *Reading Borough Council v D. (Angela) and others (Chief Constable intervening)*,[18] in which Sumner J. held that the 2005 Rules do not alter the previous situation in which a distinction was made between information which comes into the possession of a local authority or another party prior to or during family court proceedings, and documents filed with the court during those proceedings. Nor do the new rules affect the position of preparatory documents held by a local authority which contain information but which are not on the court file. They remain confidential and subject to public interest immunity. Disclosure of the information in those documents to the police (as happened in this case) remains permissible and is to be encouraged in appropriate cases. As in the past, that

---

[16] SI 2005/1976, which came into force on October 31, 2005.

[17] These paragraphs set out who may communicate information relating to the proceedings or the text or summary of the whole or part of a judgment given in the proceedings, to whom they may communicate it and for what purpose.

[18] [2006] EWHC 1465 (Fam); [2007] 1 All E.R. 293.

disclosure does not remove their confidentiality.[19] The 2005 Rules merely make clear that there is no need to obtain the court's permission if information which a local authority, for instance, wishes to pass on to the police is already in a document filed with the family court.

In that case, the local authority started care proceedings with the parents as respondents. A social worker subsequently handed five documents to a police officer. These comprised two medical reports on injuries sustained by one of the children and their causation (these were already on the court file), an undated and unsigned statement from the mother blaming the father for the injuries, a signed statement from the father, prepared for the care proceedings in which he accepted being violent to the mother but denying causing the injuries (these were destined for the court file but had not yet reached it), and a later unsigned and undated statement from the father in which he withdrew a confession of responsibility for the child's injuries, stating that he had confessed under pressure from the mother and maternal grandmother. Sumner J. held that the 2005 Rules permitted the communication of the information contained in all of the documents to a child protection officer, whether the documents were filed with the court or not. Even copying the documents on the court file was permissible, but the Rules establish:

> "the difference between information and documents. Once the police have information from a local authority in the form of a document, they can use it for child protection purposes. However it is confidential and the document (as compared to the information within it) cannot otherwise be used without the court's express permission. This applies both to documents not filed with the court e.g. social services records because they are confidential.[20] It also applies to documents filed with the court because only the court can authorise their use."[21]

The police will therefore still require the permission of the civil court before they can disclose to any other party or use in the course of a criminal trial a document that comes into their hands in this way. The court made clear that if an application by the police to use such documents is unopposed, the application could be considered on paper and without the need for a hearing. This is subject to the court subsequently requiring an oral hearing if such appears advisable.[22]

Parties to whom disclosure can be made without the need for permission of the court

21.25B   Rule 10.20A(2) introduces two new categories of such persons:

---

[19] The information remains confidential but, once known to the police, it is subject to the CPIA disclosure regime. If the provider of the material wishes to assert public interest immunity to prevent disclosure, then he or she is entitled to do so prior to disclosure. If the prosecution considers that its duty under the CPIA requires disclosure of the information to be made, it should notify the third party of that fact prior to disclosure and a PII hearing should be arranged for the third party to argue the matter. See para.54 of Attorney General's Guidelines 2005.

[20] Although not stated, it is unlikely that the learned judge meant that parties to criminal proceedings need to go to the civil court for disclosure of social services records prepared prior to the care proceedings. Disclosure of these will remain the province of the criminal trial judge.

[21] Above n.18, at para.70.

[22] At para.90.

(a) A professional legal advisor

Sub-paragraph (5) defines this as "a barrister or a solicitor, solicitor's employee or other authorised litigator (as defined in the Courts and Legal Services Act 1990) who is providing advice to a party but is not instructed to represent that party in the proceedings."

At first sight this appears to include the representatives of a defendant in a criminal trial where that defendant is also a party in family proceedings. Such a development would have been welcome, as a defendant could have disclosed documents from the family proceedings to his legal team in the criminal proceedings for those representatives to decide whether they wanted to make use of them in the criminal trial. If so, they could then have made application to the civil court. However, Sumner J. in *Reading Borough Council v D. (Angela) and others*[23] held otherwise. Instead, "a professional legal advisor" covers a party to the family proceedings seeking legal advice from a lawyer to assist *in those proceedings*. "The language is not apt to cover advice to someone who is or may become a defendant in criminal proceedings rather than a party."

Sumner J. gave guidance on how a defence lawyer wishing to obtain the court's permission to disclosure should make that application. This could be a straightforward application through another party (presumably the defendant himself would qualify) subject to:

a. notification being given in writing to all parties;
b. the application identifying the documents concerned and being supported by a letter from the defence lawyer;
c. the court reserving the right to hear argument directly from the defence lawyer.[24]

(b) A professional acting in furtherance of the protection of children

Sub-paragraph (5) defines this term to include:

a. an officer of a local authority exercising child protection functions,
b. a police officer who is—
  i. exercising powers under s.46 of the Act of 1989; or
  ii. serving in a child protection unit or a paedophile unit of a police force;
c. any professional person attending a child protection conference or review in relation to a child who is the subject of the proceedings to which the information relates; or
d. an officer of the NSPCC.

---

[23] At para.94.
[24] At para.96. This is directed specifically towards the defence. It must be possible for the CPS also to make application for disclosure in writing in these terms, although this will probably have to be a separate application as it is unlikely that they can make application through an existing party to the proceedings. It may be important for the prosecution to notify all parties following the Divisional Court decision in *R. (TB) v The Combined Court at Stafford* [2006] EWHC 1645 (Admin) (see below). This will have the effect of the defendant in criminal proceedings being able to argue for disclosure to the prosecution of material held by the civil court.

The inclusion of a child protection officer in the category of persons who can receive information relating to family proceedings does not alter the existing position on exchange of information, repeatedly emphasised by the Court of Appeal prior to the commencement of this rule.[25]

Rule 10.20A(3) is in the form of a table entitled "Communication of information without permission of the court". This sets out who can disclose certain information, to whom they can disclose it and for what purpose. The two most relevant to criminal trials of sexual offences are:

    a.   Any party to the family proceedings can disclose the text or summary of the whole or part of a judgment given in the proceedings to a police officer for the purposes of a criminal investigation;

    b.   Any party or person lawfully in receipt of information[26] can disclose a text or summary of the whole or part of a judgment given in the proceedings to a member of the Crown Prosecution Service for the purpose of enabling the CPS to discharge its functions under any enactment.[27]

Sumner J. made clear in *Reading Borough Council v D. (Angela) and others*[28] that the 2005 Rules do not change the existing case law on the circumstances when court documents should or should not be disclosed. The case law on this, set out in the main work, will thus still apply. They do widen the group of those to whom information in those documents can be given by including the police in their child protection role, and also allow judgments to be disclosed to certain specified groups, including the police if it is for a criminal investigation.

Documents not held by the civil court

21.50   As has already been noted, the Disclosure Protocol recognised that "the disclosure of unused material that has been gathered or generated by a third party is an area of the law that has caused some difficulties . . . This is because there is no specific procedure for the disclosure of material held by third parties in criminal proceedings, although the procedure under s.2 of the Criminal Procedure (Attendance of Witnesses) Act 1965 . . . is often used in order to effect such disclosure."[29]

Section 2 of the Criminal Procedure (Attendance of Witnesses) Act 1965 remains the vehicle by which applications for third party disclosure are made. The procedure by which to make them has been changed by the Criminal Procedure

---

[25] See e.g. *In re G. (A Minor) (Social Worker: Disclosure)* [1996] 1 W.L.R. 1407 (para.21.27 of the main work).

[26] This would include a police officer.

[27] This would permit e.g. a local authority in receipt of such material to disclose it to the CPS in order for the latter to discharge any obligations under the CPIA. If the CPS then required access to further documentation from the family proceedings, they would have to apply for the family court's permission under Rule 10.20A(2)(a).

[28] Above n.18, at 32.

[29] Disclosure Protocol, para.52. Paras 54–62 set out a procedure, that is largely followed in the Criminal Procedure (Amendment) Rules 2007.

(Amendment) Rules 2007.[30] These include a "new part 28 (witness summonses, warrants and orders)" which, according to the *Guide for Court Users, Staff and Practitioners*[31] "revises and simplifies the rules about applications for witnesses to give evidence or produce documents for use in evidence."

The procedure, set out in Rule 28, is as follows:

Application for summons, warrant or order: general rules

28.3—(1) A party who wants the court to issue a witness summons, warrant or order must apply as soon as practicable after becoming aware of the grounds for doing so.

(2) The party applying must—
  (a) identify the proposed witness;
  (b) explain—
      (i) what evidence the proposed witness can give or produce,
      (ii) why it is likely to be material evidence, and
      (iii) why it would be in the interests of justice to issue a summons, order or warrant as appropriate.

Written application: form and service

28.4-(1) An application in writing under rule 28.3 must be in the form set out in the Practice Direction,[32] containing the same declaration of truth as a witness statement.

(2) The party applying must serve the application—
  (a) in every case, on the court officer and as directed by the court; and
  (b) as required by rule 28.5, if that rule applies.

Application for summons to produce a document, etc.: special rules

28.5-(1) This rule applies to an application under rule 28.3 for a witness summons requiring the proposed witness—
  (a) to produce in evidence a document or thing; or
  (b) to give evidence about information apparently held in confidence, that relates to another person.

(2) The application must be in writing in the form required by rule 28.4.

(3) The party applying must serve the application—
  (a) on the proposed witness, unless the court otherwise directs; and
  (b) on one or more of the following, if the court so directs—
      (i) a person to whom the proposed evidence relates,[33]
      (ii) another party.

(4) The court must not issue a witness summons where this rule applies unless—
  (a) everyone served with the application has had at least 14 days in which to make representations about whether there should be a hearing of the application before the summons is issued; and
  (b) the court is satisfied that it has been able to take adequate account of the duties and rights, including rights of confidentiality, of the proposed witness and of any person to whom the proposed evidence relates.

---

[30] Above n.3 at Sch.3.

[31] Prepared by the Secretariat to the Criminal Procedure Rule Committee and to be found on the Ministry of Justice Website at *http://www.justice.gov.uk/criminal/procrules_fin/index.htm.*

[32] To be found at HMCS website, *http://www.hmcourts-service.gov.uk/cms/pds.htm.* This contains the actual form to be completed by any applicant.

[33] This and the following paragraph were inserted into the rules as a result of the Divisional Court's decision in *R. (TB) v The Combined Court at Stafford,* above n.24. For full discussion of the import of this ruling see below.

Rule 28.6 provides for the person in receipt of the summons to object to production of the material sought on the grounds that it is not likely to be material evidence or, if it is, the duties or rights, including rights of confidentiality, of the proposed witness or of any person to whom the document or thing relates outweigh the reasons for issuing a summons. The court may require the proposed witness to make the material available for the objection to be assessed, and may invite the proposed witness or any person to whom the document or thing relates or his representative to help the court assess the objection.

21.50A It can be seen that an applicant for disclosure of third party material must still satisfy the court that the document itself is likely to be material evidence. As mentioned in the main work, the most obvious way of doing this is to argue that the document sought would be admissible as a business record pursuant to s.117 of the Criminal Justice Act 2003. The amendments to the Rules do, however, change the existing position in two important respects.

First, the applicant must now set out why it would be in the interests of justice to issue a summons, order or warrant.[34] It is submitted that this must involve in part the applicant setting out the reasons why the material sought is of importance to his case, and thus ensures that applications are properly considered and not a "fishing expedition". Whilst this may appear at first sight to be an additional hurdle for the applicant, this requirement is in fact more likely to assist proper applicants in obtaining the disclosure they seek. If the application is properly made and the material sought of importance to the person making it, then the judge is likely to find that it is in the interests of justice to issue the summons and may be more likely to find in favour of the applicant when considering the material in question.

Secondly, the rules introduce a new requirement, where the material sought relates to another person, for the court to consider whether that person should be given notice of the application and an opportunity to make representations about disclosure.[35] There is also a specific requirement under rule 28.5(4)(b) for the court to be satisfied that it has been able to take adequate account of the duties and rights, including rights of confidentiality, of any person to whom the information relates before issuing the witness summons.

This change in the Rules was brought about by the Divisional Court's decision in *R. (TB) v The Combined Court at Stafford*,[36] in which the court considered the Art.8 ECHR rights of a person whose records were sought, and stressed the need for the Criminal Procedure Rule Committee to amend the rules to ensure that these rights are taken into account in every application for third party disclosure.

As mentioned in para.21.81 of the main work, any disclosure of confidential records of bodies such as social services, medical practitioners and counsellors must infringe the right to respect for the private life of the person concerned,

[34] Rule 28.3(2)(b)(iii).
[35] Rules 28.5(3)(b)(i) and 28.6(3)(b).
[36] [2006] EWHC 1645 (Admin).

afforded by Art.8 of the ECHR. In deciding the question of disclosure, judges were therefore required to consider the right protected by Art.8 before the decision in the *Stafford* case. This was recognised in the Disclosure Protocol:

> "Victims do not waive the confidentiality of their medical records, or their right to privacy under article 8 of the ECHR, by the mere fact of making a complaint against the accused. Judges should be alert to balance the rights of victims against the real and proven needs of the defence. The court, as a public authority, must ensure that any interference with the article 8 rights of those entitled to privacy is in accordance with the law and necessary in pursuit of a legitimate public interest."[37]

There was thus recognition that the Art.8 rights of the person whose records were sought featured in any judicial decision on disclosure. But prior to the *Stafford* case, there was no suggestion that the person whose rights would be infringed by disclosure of the material should be given notice of the application and afforded the opportunity to make representations to the court. The Divisional Court had no hesitation in holding that this should occur.

The *Stafford* case concerned TB, a 14-year-old girl making sexual allegations. She **21.50B** had been receiving psychiatric treatment and had attempted suicide by overdose on three separate occasions. The defence wanted access to her medical and hospital records on the grounds that a history of self-harm and mental illness might undermine her credibility as a witness. Application was made in the usual way. The NHS Trust resisted disclosure and a hearing took place, following which the judge ordered disclosure of 23 pages of her psychiatric records. The Trust informed the Official Solicitor, who asked the judge to state a case for the consideration of the High Court. The judicial review claim form sought a declaration that TB was entitled to service of the application for disclosure and to make representations as to what order should be made.

The Court held that TB undoubtedly had a right of privacy in relation to her medical records within Art.8 of the ECHR. The confidentiality of her records belonged to her, not to the Trust. It was insufficient for the interests of TB to have been represented by the Trust. As a public authority, the Crown Court had to act in a way compatible with a Convention right and, if it was to consider ordering disclosure of TB's medical records, it had to balance TB's right of privacy and confidentiality and the defendant's right to have his defence informed by the content of her medical records. Although at that time the Criminal Procedure Rules did not expressly oblige the court to give notice of an application for a witness summons to a person in TB's position, the overriding objective (that criminal cases are dealt with justly[38]) required it:

> "The court was being invited to trample on TB's rights of privacy and confidentiality. TB was both a witness and a victim of alleged crime. The court was obliged to respect her interests and these were some of them."[39]

---

[37] para.62.
[38] Rule 1.1 Criminal Procedure Rules 2005.
[39] Above, n.36 at para.22.

Article 8 requires that the decision making process is fair and affords due respect to the interests it protects. The process must be such as to secure that the views of those whose rights are in issue are made known and duly taken into account:

> "What has to be determined is whether, having regard to the particular circumstances of the case and notably the serious nature of the decisions to be taken, the person whose rights are in issue has been involved in the decision making process seen as a whole, to a degree sufficient to provide them with the requisite protection of their interests. If they have not there will be a failure to respect their family life and privacy and the interference resulting from the decision will not be capable of being regarded as 'necessary' within the meaning of Article 8."[40]

The Court held that, in TB's case, procedural fairness in the light of Art.8 undoubtedly required that she should have been given notice of the application for the witness summons. Since the Rules did not require this of the applicant, the requirement was on the court as a public authority. In this case the court acted unlawfully and in infringement of her Convention rights.

The Court "cautiously confined" its decision to the specific facts of the case and drew attention to the fact that the Rule Committee was likely to amend Rule 28. May L.J. plainly wanted the Committee to address a number of potential difficulties. He invited them to address which person or class of person with Art.8 rights in respect of documents should be given notice. It was clear that a child victim of alleged sexual abuse who is to be a prosecution witness should be given notice of an application for disclosure of her medical and psychiatric records. He could not see why this would not also apply to adult witnesses in the same position. He raised queries with regard to education and social services records.

21.50C The new rules address some of May L.J.'s questions in stating that it is for the judge to decide whether or not a particular person should be given notice of an application and the chance to make representations.[41] They fail, however, to provide any answer to the question of which class of person with Art.8 rights in respect of documents should be given notice or opportunity. They are silent on this, leaving everything to the discretion of the judge.

What is clear is that every judge to whom application is made will have to consider the position of the person whose records are sought. Until other cases are brought to the appellate courts, the only guidance is provided by the *Stafford* case. It would seem that in every case where medical records are sought and voluntary disclosure refused a court is likely to require the person whose records they are to be told of the application and given a chance to make representations. It is difficult to see that those who are the subject of social services and education records should not also be afforded this opportunity.

This raises very difficult issues. Under these Rules, the applicant is required to make a written application stating what he wants and why he wants it. Disclosure of that application to the witness he wishes to cross-examine will alert that witness

---

[40] Above, n.36 at para.23.
[41] Rules 28.5(3)(b) and 28.6(3)(b).

to the issues likely to be raised at trial. Advocates will have to consider carefully whether or not they want to take that course.

Medical records are one thing, social services records something else entirely. There must be a real concern that social workers and other professionals will be unwilling to write unpalatable assessments in records for fear that they will be disclosed to the person they have written about.

Consideration as to who should be served with notice of the application will have to be given at an early stage of the proceedings. This could become potentially complicated in cases with multiple complainants.

There is also a very real practical problem. Someone in TB's position, aged 14 at the time of the application, clearly cannot represent herself at any hearing. The question of disclosure is complex and she would need representation. There is currently no provision for financial assistance for those such as TB. To invite TB to make representations and yet give her no legal assistance to do so is to deny her a proper opportunity to argue her case.

It will be of interest to see how these rules operate in practice. Until more guidance is available practitioners and judges will have to approach each case on its individual facts and merits.

The duty to obtain third party records in a criminal trial

The main work identified the existence of confusion and dissent amongst   **21.71** practitioners as to which party should seek disclosure from third parties in criminal cases. Assistance has now been given in the Disclosure Protocol[42] and amended Attorney-General's Guidelines.[43]

Attorney-General's Guidelines 2005

Paragraph 51 of the Attorney-General's Guidelines on Disclosure changes the   **21.72** wording and, it is submitted, the emphasis of its predecessor.[44] It provides:

> "There may be cases where the investigator, disclosure officer or prosecutor believes that a third party (for example, a local authority, a social services department, a hospital, a doctor, a school, a provider of forensic services) has material or information which might be relevant to the prosecution case. In such cases, if the information might reasonably be considered capable of undermining the prosecution case or of assisting the case for the accused prosecutors should take what steps they regard as appropriate in the particular case to obtain it."

It is thus still for the prosecution to consider whether the third party holds relevant material. The Guidelines now underline that if the prosecutor believes that the third party has such material and that material might assist the defence, he "should" take appropriate steps to obtain it. This wording seems to afford a lesser "margin of consideration"[45] to the prosecutor than the wording of the old para.30.

---

[42] Above n.2.
[43] Attorney-General's Guidelines 2005.
[44] para.30 of the Attorney-General's Guidelines 2000.
[45] As described in *Alibhai* [2004] EWCA Crim 681.

The 2005 Guidelines follow their predecessor in stating that, if the prosecutor seeks access to third party material but the third party declines to allow access to it, the matter cannot be left and the prosecutor must apply for a witness summons if the requirements of s.2 of the Criminal Procedure (Attendance of Witnesses) Act 1965 are met.[46]

Importantly, para.54 deals with the position when material originally from a third party comes into the possession of the prosecution. As explained in the main work, this material falls to be disclosed under the more liberal test for prosecution disclosure set out the CPIA. Paragraph 54 of the Guidelines states that consultation with the other agency should take place before disclosure is made. This is because there may be public interest reasons which justify withholding disclosure and which would require the issue of disclosure of the information to be placed before the court.

This is an area which often causes confusion. It is submitted that the prosecution should not argue any matter of PII before the court, but instead should notify the original holder of the material that disclosure will be made unless they wish to claim PII. If they do, a hearing can then take place for resolution of the issues.

The court's "careful oversight" of disclosure obligations[47]

21.72A The Disclosure Protocol requires judges to manage the disclosure process. It states that:

- Where issues are raised in relation to allegedly relevant third party material, the judge must ascertain whether inquiries with the third party are likely to be appropriate and, if so, identify who is going to make the request, what material is to be sought, from whom the material is to be sought and within what time scale must the matter be resolved.[48]

- The judge should consider what action would be appropriate in the light of the third party failing or refusing to comply with a request, including inviting the defence to make the request on its own behalf and, if necessary, to make an application for a witness summons. A timetable should be laid down and any failure to comply with it must immediately be referred back to the court for further directions. A hearing will not always be necessary.[49]

---

[46] para.52.

[47] The requirement set out in para.1 of the Disclosure Protocol is "an important safeguard against the possibility of miscarriages of justice".

[48] para.56.

[49] para.57. This is of importance. Cases involving complex issues of third party disclosure often result in a larger number of "mention" hearings than usual. This is so that the Court can keep an eye on the position, as it is required to do. On the other hand, recent changes to payments for advocates brought about by the Carter Review do not allow for large numbers of mention hearings. Indeed, practitioners are told that they are to be discouraged. Thought may need to be given to resolution of these issues informally between counsel where possible, and review by the judge of the position at least initially without a hearing.

- Where the prosecution do not consider it appropriate to seek such a summons the defence should consider doing so where they are of the view (notwithstanding the prosecution assessment) that the third party may hold material which might undermine the prosecution case or assist that of the defendant and the material would be likely to be "material evidence". The defence should not sit back and expect the prosecution to make the running. The judge at the PCMH should specifically enquire whether any such application is to be made by the defence and set out a clear timetable. The objectionable practice of defence applications being made in the few days before trial must end.[50]
- It is recognised that a number of Crown Court Centres have developed local protocols, usually in respect of sexual offences and material held by social services and health and education authorities. These "often provide an excellent and sensible way to identify relevant material that might assist the defence or undermine the prosecution.[51]
- The court must be alive to Art.8 rights of the person whose records are sought.[52]

The Protocol concludes:

"The public rightly expects that the delays and failures which have been present in some cases in the past where there has been scant adherence to sound disclosure principles will be eradicated by observation of this Protocol. The new regime under the Criminal Justice Act and the Criminal Procedure Rules gives judges the power to change the culture in which such cases are tried. It is now the duty of every judge actively to manage disclosure issues in every case. The judge must seize the initiative and drive the case along towards an efficient, effective and timely resolution, having regard to the overriding objective of the Criminal Procedure Rules (Part1). In this way the interests of justice will be better served and public confidence in the criminal justice system will be increased."[53]

CONCLUSION

21.94 It can be seen that since the main work was published in 2004, there have been real and practical changes in the procedure for obtaining disclosure. These are relatively new and it remains to be seen how they will operate in practice. It cannot be doubted, however, that at last there is a real will to improve the efficiency of applications, to have matters resolved well ahead of the trial date and thus to

---

[50] para.58. This is again important. New PCMH forms require these matters to be aired at that hearing. It is submitted that the more desirable route is for the prosecution and defence to liaise with a view to agreeing what is required from third parties, following which the prosecution can make application for the information they and the defence seek.

[51] para.61. In consequence of the Disclosure Protocol, the Criminal Procedure (Amendment) Rules 2007 and new PCMH forms, many courts have refined existing procedures. Although local differences remain, there is some movement towards a unified approach. This is to be welcomed.

[52] para.62. The Disclosure Protocol was drafted before the *Stafford* case (above n.24) and the Criminal Procedure (Amendment) Rules 2007. It is submitted that once any application is made, the judge should at that point decide who should have service of it. This will almost certainly require a hearing for representations by the parties to be heard.

[53] para.63.

eradicate delay. It is to be hoped that improved judicial management of this issue will also eradicate the practice of social services files, produced by the local authority, sitting in the Court office awaiting the selection of the "trial judge" and not being considered until the day of trial.

Practitioners must also play their part. The rules and procedure for obtaining third party material are clearer than they have ever been. Advocates must be alive to potential issues of third party material and be in a position to assist the court in setting realistic timetables at an early stage of the proceedings. This creates more work at the start of a case, but in these times when counsel are required to "own" their cases, it at least ensures that trials take place on the date they are fixed. It remains for the Crown Court listing officers to undergo their own cultural change and recognise that, where counsel has advised on disclosure, there is a compelling argument for fixing a case for counsel's convenience.

21.95   See now the model protocol on the exchange of information in the investigation and prosecution of child abuse cases, developed by the Crown Prosecution Service, Association of Chief Police Officers, Local Government Association of England and Association of Directors of Social Services. The protocol provides a framework within which the CPS, the police and local authority social services and education departments can co-operate to share information in child protection investigations for the purpose of criminal prosecutions. The signatories to the protocol encourage Chief Crown Prosecutors, Chief Officers of Police and Chief Executives of Local Authorities to adopt it in their area, tailored as necessary to suit local circumstances. However, some local authorities have declined to adopt the protocol: see generally on the protocol's shortcomings Alastair G. Perkins and Elizabeth Tomlinson, *Disclosure of social services documents into criminal proceedings* Fam. Law 2005, 35(Oct), 806–813.

CHAPTER 22

SENTENCING OF SEX OFFENDERS

AUTOMATIC LIFE SENTENCES

"EXCEPTIONAL CIRCUMSTANCES"

A recent example of the approach of the Court of Appeal to automatic life **22.53**
sentences is provided by *R. v PH.*[1] The appellant was released on licence from a
six year sentence of imprisonment for firearms offences in March 2004. In June
2004, he went to his former girlfriend's home and raped her twice. Present in the
house at the time of the rapes was C, the five-year-old daughter of the victim and
the appellant. The firearms offences which resulted in the six year sentence from
which he had been released in March 2004 arose from police being called to a
dispute between the appellant and the same complainant. The appellant was in his
car and behaved in an abusive and uncooperative way to officers who attended.
One of the officers drew a baton, so the appellant took out a handgun, pointed it
at the officer and pulled the trigger. The gun was broken and did not fire. The
appellant had been sentenced on the basis that he was aware that the gun was
unable to fire. The offences revealed the appellant's dominant and aggressive
attitude to women and his inability to control himself, given that the offences took
place when he knew that he was on licence from a six year sentence and his five-
year-old daughter was present in the house. The sentencing judge had been right
to find that there were no exceptional circumstances which justified him not
imposing an automatic life sentence.

[1] [2006] EWCA Crim 2394.

SENTENCES TO BE IMPOSED ON SEX OFFENDERS

Sentences under ss.224 to 229 of the CJA 2003

22.64 The problems of interpretation and practical application of the provisions relating to imprisonment for public protection ("IPP") contained in ss.224 to 229 of the CJA 2003 have required a good deal of attention from the Court of Appeal. The well-known case of *Lang*[2] provided invaluable initial guidance. Giving the judgement of the Court, the then Vice President, Rose L.J., set out a number of principles that sentencing judges should have regard to in applying the scheme set out in ss.224 to 229.

First, when a sentencer is assessing whether a "significant risk" exists, he should take the following factors into account[3]:

> "(i) The risk identified must be significant. This is a higher threshold than mere possibility of occurrence and in our view can be taken to mean (as in the Oxford Dictionary) 'noteworthy, of considerable amount or importance.'
>
> (ii) In assessing the risk of further offences being committed, the sentencer should take into account the nature and circumstances of the current offence; the offender's history of offending including not just the kind of offence but its circumstances and the sentence passed, details of which the prosecution must have available, and, whether the offending demonstrates any pattern; social and economic factors in relation to the offender including accommodation, employ-ability, education, associates, relationships and drug or alcohol abuse; and the offender's thinking, attitude towards offending and supervision and emotional state. Information in relation to these matters will most readily, though not exclusively, come from antecedents and pre-sentence probation and medical reports. The Guide for sentence for public protection issued in June 2005 for the National Probation Service affords valuable guidance for probation officers. The guidance in relation to assessment of dangerousness in paragraph 5 is compatible with the terms of this judgment. The sentencer will be guided, but not bound by, the assessment of risk in such reports. A sentencer who contemplates differing from the assessment in such a report should give both counsel the opportunity of addressing the point.
>
> (iii) If the foreseen specified offence is serious, there will clearly be some cases, though not by any means all, in which there may be a significant risk of serious harm. For example, robbery is a serious offence. But it can be committed in a wide variety of ways many of which do not give rise to a significant risk of serious harm. Sentencers must therefore guard against assuming there is a significant risk of serious harm merely because the foreseen specified offence is serious. A pre-sentence report should usually be obtained before any sentence is passed which is based on significant risk of serious harm. In a small number of cases, where the circumstances of the current offence or the history of the offender suggest mental abnormality on his part, a medical report may be necessary before risk can properly be assessed.
>
> (iv) If the foreseen specified offence is not serious, there will be comparatively few cases in which a risk of serious harm will properly be regarded as significant. The

---

[2] [2005] EWCA Crim 2864; [2006] 1 W.L.R. 2509; [2006] 2 All E.R. 410; [2006] 2 Cr. App. R. (S) 3; [2006] Crim. L.R. 174.

[3] At para.17.

huge variety of offences in Schedule 15, includes many which, in themselves, are not suggestive of serious harm. Repetitive violent or sexual offending at a relatively low level without serious harm does not of itself give rise to a significant risk of serious harm in the future. There may, in such cases, be some risk of future victims being more adversely affected than past victims but this, of itself, does not give rise to significant risk of serious harm.

(v) In relation to the rebuttable assumption to which section 229(3) gives rise, the court is accorded a discretion if, in the light of information about the current offence, the offender and his previous offences, it would be unreasonable to conclude that there is a significant risk. The exercise of such a discretion is, historically, at the very heart of judicial sentencing and the language of the statute indicates that judges are expected, albeit starting from the assumption, to exercise their ability to reach a reasonable conclusion in the light of the information before them. It is to be noted that the assumption will be rebutted, if at all, as an exercise of judgment: the statute includes no reference to the burden or standard of proof. As we have indicated above, it will usually be unreasonable to conclude that the assumption applies unless information about the offences, pattern of behaviour and offender show a significant risk of serious harm from further offences.

(vi) In relation to offenders under 18 and adults with no relevant previous convictions at the time the specified offence was committed, the court's discretion under section 229(2) is not constrained by any initial assumption such as, under section 229(3), applies to adults with previous convictions. It is still necessary, when sentencing young offenders, to bear in mind that, within a shorter time than adults, they may change and develop. This and their level of maturity may be highly pertinent when assessing what their future conduct may be and whether it may give rise to significant risk of serious harm.

(vii) In relation to a particularly young offender, an indeterminate sentence may be inappropriate even where a serious offence has been committed and there is a significant risk of serious harm from further offences (see for example, *R. v. D.* [2005] EWCA Crim 2282).

(viii) It cannot have been Parliament's intention, in a statute dealing with the liberty of the subject, to require the imposition of indeterminate sentences for the commission of relatively minor offences. On the contrary, Parliament's repeatedly expressed intention is to protect the public from serious harm (compare the reasoning of the Court in relation to automatic life sentences in *R. v. Offen* [2001] 2 Cr.App.R.(S.) 44, paragraphs 96 to 99).

(ix) Sentencers should usually, and in accordance with section 174(1)(a) of the Criminal Justice Act 2003 give reasons for all their conclusions: in particular, that there is or is not a significant risk of further offences or serious harm; where the assumption under section 229(3) arises for making or not making the assumption which the statute requires unless this would be unreasonable; and for not imposing an extended sentence under sections 227 and 228. Sentencers should, in giving reasons, briefly identify the information which they have taken into account."

Secondly, the risk to be assessed is to "members of the public" and that seemed to the Court to be an all-embracing term. It is wider than "others" which would exclude the offender himself, and the Court saw no need to construe the term so as to exclude any particular group such as prison officers or staff at mental hospitals.

Thirdly, when offenders are to be sentenced for several offences, only some of which are specified, the court which imposes an indeterminate sentence under s.225 or s.226 or an extended sentence under s.227 or s.228 for the principal offences, should generally impose a shorter concurrent sentence for the other offences. In the case of a specified offence where there is a risk of serious harm, the sentence for such other offence must be an extended sentence where the principal offence is a serious offence (s.227(2)). It will not usually be appropriate to impose consecutive extended sentences, whether the principal offence is serious or merely specified.[4]

Fourthly, care should be taken to ensure that a continuing offence which, as initially indicted, straddled April 4, 2005 (the date on which the scheme under ss.224 to 229 came into force) is indicted, if necessary by amendment, so that sentence can properly be passed by reference to the new and/or old regime as appropriate.[5]

Finally, the Court advised that if, in relation to a dangerous offender, the requirements of the Mental Health Act 1983 are satisfied, the Court can dispose of the case under those provisions.

22.64A Subsequently, in *Johnson*,[6] the Court amplified the guidance and clarified some of the potential areas of misunderstanding in *Lang*. In prefacing the judgement of the Court, Sir Igor Judge P. cautioned against according *Lang* near statutory status. He observed:

> "Invaluable understanding of this complicated piece of legislation was provided in *R. v. Lang and others* [2006] 1W.L.R. 2509 in the illuminating judgment given by Rose L.J., the Vice President of the Court of Appeal Criminal Division. Perhaps the fact that the judgment was given in his customary clear and trenchant terms by one of the pre-eminent criminal judges of this generation has led practitioners to conclude, and certainly for some of them to advance arguments which proceed, as if every word of the judgment should be treated as statute. Indeed that was precisely how one counsel

---

[4] See para.22.67 below for further examination of the issues relating to consecutive sentences which include a sentence under ss.224 to 229.

[5] In *Robert Michael S. and others* [2007] EWCA Crim 1622, the Court of Appeal re-emphasised this guidance and gave advice to sentencing judges as to the appropriate course to take when faced with a count in an indictment which spanned the commencement date. Judge L.J. said (at paras 11–12):

> "We do not necessarily conclude that that is a final and comprehensive list of the relevant invitations but the analysis demonstrates how wide-ranging this problem may be. The end result, in our judgment, is that in cases where the count in the indictment spans the commencement date, the court should not impose any of the penalties created in sections 224 to 229 of the 2003 Act, unless satisfied that at least one relevant offence occurred after 4th April 2005. Once it is so satisfied, then the mere fact that the count was framed so that it spanned that date does not preclude such a sentence if it would otherwise be appropriate or mandated. We should perhaps add that, even if it is not open to the court to impose any of the dangerous offender penalties, because it is unsure whether the offence was committed before or after 4th April, if a qualifying offence or offences is committed after that date, then offences committed before the date may have some bearing on the assessment of dangerousness and, of course, on the determination of the minimum term. These offences do not cease to be relevant because the dangerous offender sentencing provisions do not apply directly to them. We have two further comments: some care needs to be taken with the drafting of the appropriate counts in an indictment. Where it can realistically and sensibly be done, the indictments should be drafted to reflect the significance of 4th April 2005. Where it is difficult to produce an indictment in that form, then the judge, considering all the evidence should make whatever findings are appropriate in the light of the evidence and give reasons for his conclusions, in particular, if in such a case the offence is found, on analysis of the evidence, to have taken place after 4th April."

[6] [2006] EWCA Crim 2486; [2007] 1 W.L.R. 585; [2007] 1 Cr. App. R.(S.) 112.

appearing before us did describe it, treating the judgment as synonymous with the statute with which the judgment was concerned. However, and unsurprisingly, Rose L.J. himself emphasised that the judgment represented 'an attempt to summarise the approach to sentencing which the Act requires and to give guidance as to its meaning'. He warned against treating it as if it were a 'substitute for looking at the Act's provisions'.[7]

The Court went on to address a number of specific issues relating to the exercise of the power to impose sentences of IPP under ss.224 to 229, in particular the assessment of dangerousness, and gave the following guidance[8]:

"(i) Just as the absence of previous convictions does not preclude a finding of dangerousness, the existence of previous convictions for specified offences does not compel such a finding. There is a presumption that it does so, which may be rebutted.

(ii) If a finding of dangerousness can be made against an offender without previous specified convictions, it also follows that previous offences, not in fact specified for the purposes of section 229, are not disqualified from consideration. Thus, for example, as indeed the statute recognises, a pattern of minor previous offences of gradually escalating seriousness may be significant. In other words, it is not right, as many of the submissions made to us suggested, that unless the previous offences were specified offences they were irrelevant.

(iii) Where the facts of the instant offence, or indeed any specified offences for the purposes of section 229(3) are examined, it may emerge that no harm actually occurred. That may be advantageous to the offender, and some of the cases examined in *Lang* exemplify the point. Another such example is *R. v. Isa* [2006] Crim.L.R. 356. On the other hand the absence of harm may be entirely fortuitous. A victim cowering away from an armed assailant may avoid direct physical injury or serious psychological harm. Faced with such a case, the sentencer considering dangerousness may wish to reflect, for example, on the likely response of the offender if his victim, instead of surrendering, resolutely defended himself. It does not automatically follow from the absence of actual harm caused by the offender to date, that the risk that he will cause serious harm in the future is negligible.

Nothing in the decision in *R. v. Shaffi* [2006] EWCA Crim 418, which was relied on before us, suggests the contrary. Giving the judgment of the court, at paragraph 11, Sir Richard Curtis summarised the various submissions made on behalf of the appellant. One of them was that the appellant's previous convictions demonstrated that although the appellant was carrying a knife and a screwdriver in two of the cases, no harm was actually occasioned. The court accepted the force of the overall submission made by counsel that the sentencer was wrong to find that there was a risk of *serious* harm, and the court was unable to find significant evidence of such harm caused during the commission of the appellant's previous offences. However the conclusion represented a finding of fact in the particular case. *Shaffi* is not authority for the proposition that as a matter of law offences which did not result in harm to the victim should be treated as irrelevant. Indeed if that is what *Shaffi* decided, it would, in effect, have re-written the statute.

(iv) We considered arguments based on the inadequacy, suggestibility, or vulnerability of the offender, and how these and similar characteristics may bear on dangerousness. Such characteristics may serve to mitigate the offender's culpability. In the final analysis however they may also serve to produce or reinforce the conclusion

---

[7] At para.2.
[8] At para.10.

that the offender is dangerous. In one of the instant cases it was suggested that the sentence was wrong because an inadequate offender had suffered what was described as an 'aberrant moment'. But, as experience shows, aberrant moments may be productive of catastrophe. The sentencer is right to be alert to such risks of aberrant moments in the future, and their consequences.

(v) In *Lang*, Rose L.J. suggested that the prosecution should be in a position to describe the facts of previous specified offences. This is plainly desirable (see also *Isa*), but this is not always practicable. There is no reason why the prosecution's failure to comply with this good practice, even when it can and should, should either make an adjournment obligatory, or indeed preclude the imposition of the sentence, when appropriate. In any such case, counsel for the defendant should be in a position to explain the circumstances, on the basis of his instructions. If the Crown is not in a position to challenge those instructions, then the court may proceed on the information it has. Equally, there are some situations in which the sentence imposed by the court dealing with earlier specified offences may enable the sentencer to draw inferences about its seriousness, or otherwise. In short, failure to comply with best practice on this point should be discouraged, but it does not normally preclude the imposition of the sentence.

(vi) The effect of the 2003 Act, and *Lang*, has been examined in a number of cases. It is not obligatory for the sentencer to spell out all the details of the earlier specified offences. To the extent that a judge is minded to rely upon a disputed fact in reaching a finding of dangerousness, he should not rely on that fact unless the dispute can fairly be resolved adversely to the defendant. In the end, the requirement is that the sentencing remarks should explain the reasoning which has led the sentencer to the conclusion."

The President also emphasised that the Court of Appeal will not normally interfere with conclusions reached by a sentencer who has accurately identified the relevant principles, and applied his mind to the relevant facts. The Court could not too strongly emphasise that the question to be addressed in the Court of Appeal is not whether it is possible to discover some words used by the sentencer which may be inconsistent with the precise language used in *Lang*, or indeed some failure on his part to deploy identical language to that used in *Lang*, but whether the imposition of the sentence was manifestly excessive or wrong in principle. Notwithstanding the labyrinthine provisions of ss.224 to 229, and the guidance offered by *Lang*, those essential principles are not affected.

In *Fulton*,[9] a division of the Court of Appeal presided over by the then Vice-President, Rose L.J., explained that a sentence under the scheme of ss.224 to 229 of the CJA 2003 will be wrong in principle if the Court concludes, on reviewing all the material before it, that there is no sufficient basis for a finding that there was a risk of serious harm to the public. The Court overturned the sentence of IPP imposed on the appellant.[10]

---

[9] [2006] EWCA Crim 960; [2007] 1 Cr. App. R.(S.) 5.
[10] For further examples of the Court of Appeal overturning a sentence of IPP, see *McGowan* [2006] EWCA Crim 620; *Sinton* [2007] EWCA Crim 2115; *King* [2007] EWCA Crim 1515; *Roberts (Ricki)* [2007] EWCA Crim 1465; *Xhelollari* [2007] EWCA Crim 2052; and *Barwell* [2007] EWCA Crim 2561. For instances of the Court upholding sentences of IPP, see *Manir* [2006] EWCA Crim 2188; [2007] 1 Cr. App. R.(S.) 94; *Greaves* [2006] EWCA Crim 641; [2006] 2 Cr. App. R.(S.) 89; *Lordan* [2007] EWCA Crim 2136; *Alison* [2007] EWCA Crim 1808; *Pocock* [2007] EWCA Crim 2133; and *Goldspink* [2007] EWCA Crim 1904.

In *McCormack*,[10A] the Court of Appeal stressed that a sentence of IPP was akin to a sentence of life imprisonment and that care must be taken when considering imposing such a sentence. M had pleaded guilty to an offence of rape. The complainant had woken up to find M, with whose girlfriendshe shared a house, havingsexual intercourse with her. She hit out at him and he immediatelystopped and moved away from her.Both parties had been drinking heavily throughout the evening. M initially denied that any sexual contact had taken place, then admitted that sexual contact had occurred but claimed that it had been consensual. Finally, M admitted the rape in a letter written to the complainant before trial. When sentencing, the judge expressed his assessment of M's dangerousness in the following terms:

> "Because you had already been convicted of affray and assault with intent to resist arrest when you committed this offence, I am required by law to assume there is a significant risk to the public of serious personal injury caused by you committing further offences specified in schedule 15. I do not consider that it would be unreasonable to conclude that there is such a risk.
>
> In reaching that conclusion, I have considered the nature and circumstances of your current and previous offences and in particular the involvement of excessive consumption of alcohol, not only in this offence, but in the offence of affray. I have also considered what I know about you, particularly what is contained in the pre-sentence report, where the author comes to the conclusion that you do pass the threshold of dangerousness and that there is a significant risk of serious harm; I agree."

The Court of Appeal discovered that very little was known by the sentencing judge about the previous convictions for affray and assault with intent to resist arrest. The prosecution had been unable to provide him with any details of the offences.M's account of the offences, on which the Court consequently had to proceed, was that they were of a minor nature involving no injuries to any person. In addition, the Court was highly critical of the pre-sentence report on which the judge relied, describing it astroubling for a number of reasons. Inoverturning the sentence of IPP and substituting a determinate sentence of four years and three months, the Court observed:

> "The judge's explanation of his reasons for passing the sentence that he did was brief. A succinct statement of reasons for reaching his conclusion might have been adequate if the pre-sentence report on which he relied had itself explained the necessary reasoning, but it did not.
>
> A sentence of imprisonment for public protection is in substance akin to a sentence of life imprisonment. There may be circumstances where it is so obvious from the facts that the dangerousness criteria are made out that a judge need say little more, but this was not such a case. If an indeterminate sentence was to be passed in this case, it required careful thought and careful explanation. We are troubled that in this case that was not given to it. The previous offences, of which the judge knew next to nothing, do not suggest that the criteria of dangerousness were met. The sexual offence, although grave, was isolated and would not of itself suggest that the criteria of dangerousness were met. The personal opinions of the probation officer are lacking in a clear factual foundation and lacking also in a full analysis of relevant matters,

[10A] [2007] EWCA Crim 2223.

including the remorse shown by the appellant and the facts of the previous offences.

In these circumstances, we conclude that the judge was wrong to hold that theappellant should have been held to satisfy the criteria of dangerousness by virtue of the statutory presumption. On the contrary, on the material before us it appears to us unreasonable to have drawn the conclusion. If there is a message from this case, it is that cases of this kind require much more close attention before a sentence of this kind is imposed."

The need for a pre-sentence report

22.64B In most cases where a sentencer is considering a sentence of IPP, he should secure a pre-sentence report. In *Attorney-General's Reference (No. 145 of 2006)*,[11] Pitchers J, giving the judgment of a Court presided over by Lord Phillips L.C.J., said:

> "The sentencing court has an obligation under section 156(3) of the Act to obtain a report before considering this issue unless it is of the opinion that it is unnecessary to do so. At each extreme of the spectrum of sexual offending, it may be that the answer to the question of risk is so clear that no report need be obtained. However, in most cases the court will need help from the Probation Service who use such risk assessment tools as OASYS and Risk Matrix 2000 which can provide valuable help to the sentencer in taking this crucial sentencing decision."[12]

In *Kulah*,[13] the Court of Appeal overturned a sentence of IPP when inappropriate use of the *Goodyear*[14] procedure meant that the appellant had been sentenced without a pre-sentence report and thus without any proper risk assessment as to dangerousness being carried out. The Court said that it was not necessarily inappropriate to seek or to give a *Goodyear* indication merely because a defendant is charged with a specified offence, but there may be dangers in undertaking such a course and it is necessary to warn of them. Any court giving a *Goodyear* indication when an assessment of future risk had still to be carried out should make the following clear:

> "(a) The offence (or one or more of them) is a specified offence listed in Schedule 15, Criminal Justice Act, 2003, bringing into operation the 'dangerous offender' provisions contained in Part 12, Chapter 5 of that Act.
> (b) The information and materials necessary to undertake the assessment of future risk which is required by those provisions are not available and that that assessment remains to be conducted.
> (c) If the defendant is later assessed as 'dangerous', the sentences mandated by the provisions—an indeterminate or extended sentence—will be imposed.

---

[11] [2007] EWCA Crim 692.

[12] See para.18 of transcript of *AG's ref No. 145 of 2006 ibid.* The importance of securing a pre-sentence report in most cases where dangerousness was being assessed was also re-emphasised in *Considine; Davies* [2007] EWCA Crim 1166; [2007] Crim. L.R. 824.

[13] [2007] EWCA Crim 1701.

[14] [2005] EWCA Crim 888; [2005] 3 All ER 117; [2005] Crim. L.R. 659.

(d) If the defendant is not later assessed as 'dangerous', the indication relates in the ordinary way to the maximum determinate sentence which will be imposed.

(e) If the offender is later assessed as 'dangerous', the indication can only relate to the notional determinate term which will be used in the calculation of the minimum specified period the offender would have to serve before he may apply to the Parole Board to direct his release; or, in a case where an extended sentence is the only lawful option, it will relate to the appropriate custodial term within the extended sentence (that is, the indication does not encompass the length of any extension period during which the offender will be on licence following his release). It must be remembered that where an extended sentence is imposed on any offender, the appropriate custodial term cannot be less that 12 months (subsections 227(3)(b); 228(3)(b)).

(f) If an indeterminate sentence is mandated by the provisions, the actual amount of time the offender will spend in custody is not within the control of the sentencing judge, only its minimum."

The use of untried allegations

A sentencing judge is not entitled to reach a finding of guilt in relation to a contested but untried allegation so as to justify the imposition of a sentence of IPP. In *Farrar*,[15] the 22-year-old appellant had abducted a boy of six and taken him back to his home in May 2005. Once there, he put a pillowcase over the boy's head and bounced him up and down on his knee whilst he masturbated. He pleaded guilty to the abduction and sexual assault of the boy. Psychiatric, psychological and pre-sentence reports were prepared for the purposes of sentence. He was found by the psychologist to have an overall IQ rating of 74, he pretended to the psychiatrist that he could not remember the offences and the pre-sentence report prepared on him concluded that he posed a very high risk of physical and psychological sexual harm to young boys. The author of the pre-sentence report had discovered that there had been a number of reports to the local *VISOR* team of predatory males approaching young boys, including one in August 2004 involving a seven-year-old boy. The appellant had admitted involvement in each of the incidents but had denied any ill intent. From the outset, the sentencing judge had in mind the possibility of a sentence of IPP, but the prospect troubled him because the appellant had no previous convictions of any kind. Section 229(2) of the CJA 2003 sets out express statutory guidance by which the process of assessment of dangerousness should be governed when an offender is either under 18 or has no previous convictions. Under s.229(2), when assessing dangerousness the court "must take into account all such information as is available to it about the nature and circumstances of the offence" and "may take into account any information which is before it about any pattern of behaviour of which the offence forms part". The sentencing judge therefore decided to hear evidence about the August 2004 incident and determine where the truth lay to the criminal standard. He found against the appellant and concluded that his conduct was prompted by a sexual

22.64C

[15] [2006] EWCA Crim 3261; [2007] 2 Cr. App. R.(S) 35.

motive. The judge then treated the incident as information about a pattern of behaviour of which the offence formed part under s.229(2)(b) of the CJA 2003, and noted the appellant's continuing interest in contact with children as relevant information about him under s.229(2)(c) of the same Act. He concluded that there was a high risk of the repetition of specified sexual offences against children and that the risk was of serious harm. He therefore sentenced the appellant to IPP. The Court of Appeal quashed and considered afresh the sentence of IPP, as it was not open to the sentencing judge to find in the way that he did that the appellant had committed the assault in August 2004. The Court observed:

> "14. . . . the law was not in doubt before the enactment of the Criminal Justice Act 2003:
>> 'A defendant is not to be convicted of any offence with which he is charged unless and until his guilt is proved. Such guilt may be proved by his own admission or (on indictment) by the verdict of a jury. He may be sentenced only for an offence proved against him (by admission or verdict) or which he has admitted and asked the court to take into consideration when passing sentence: see *Anderson* [1978] A.C. 94. If, as we think, these are basic principles underlying the administration of the criminal law, it is not easy to see how a defendant can lawfully be punished for offences for which he has not been indicted and which he has denied or declined to admit.' *Per* Lord Bingham C.J. in *Canavan* [1998] 1 Cr.App.R.(S.) 243 at 245–246.
>
> 15. Nothing in the 2003 Act expressly overrides that principle, unlike section 17 (yet to be in force) of the Domestic Violence, Crime and Victims Act 2004. Does section 229(2)(b) do so impliedly? It will only do so if there is a necessary implication to that effect: 'a necessary implication is one which necessarily follows from the express provisions of the statute construed in their context. It distinguishes between what it would have been sensible or reasonable for Parliament to have included or what Parliament would, if it had thought about it, probably have included and what it is clear that the express language of the statute shows that the statute must have included. A necessary implication is a matter of express language and logic not interpretation.' *Per* Lord Hobhouse of Woodborough in *R. (on the application of Morgan Grenfell and Co Ltd) v. Special Commissioner of Income Tax* [2003] 1 A.C. 563 at paragraph 45.
>
> 16. Or, as Lord Nicholls put it in *B (a minor) v. DPP* [2000] 2 A.C. 428 at 464:
>> ' . . . 'necessary implication' connotes an implication which is compellingly clear.'
>
> 17. It is neither a matter of express language and logic, nor is it compellingly clear, that section 229(2)(b) has the effect of permitting a judge alone to decide that a defendant is guilty of a discrete offence unconnected with that for which he is to be sentenced. A 'pattern of behaviour' constituted by discrete offences can just as well be established by conviction by a jury or magistrates' court of the offences as by the finding of a judge alone. Hence, 'language and logic' do not require the implication. Further, it is not 'compellingly clear' that Parliament can be taken to have intended to deprive a defendant of the right to a trial by judge and jury or magistrates' court of a discrete offence by implication.
>
> 18. Accordingly, we hold that it was wrong in principle for the judge to undertake the exercise, and make the finding, that he did in relation to the August 2004 incident.
>
> 19. The principle must not be taken too far. As the court in *Canavan* recognised, full account can be taken of 'acts done in the course of committing that offence or offences even when such acts might have been separately charged'. In the specific case of sexual offences against children, evidence about the offences charged may demonstrate a pattern of behaviour before their commission which includes other criminal conduct,

for example conduct which is an offence contrary to sections 14 or 15 of the Sexual Offences Act 2003. Such conduct is clearly part of 'a pattern of behaviour of which the offence forms part'. Nor, in our view, would a judge who had presided over a trial of a defendant charged with a sexual offence at which evidence of similar conduct was given, and must have been accepted by a jury, whether in relation to the same or another complainant, be prevented from taking such behaviour into account under section 229(2)(b). The judge who sentenced Z (see [2003] All E.R. 385) could not realistically have been expected to treat his offence of rape as an isolated incident.

20. In his sentencing remarks, the judge made it clear that it was his finding about the incident in August 2004 which led him to conclude that the statutory criteria for a sentence of imprisonment for public protection were satisfied. Because the means by which he reached that decision was flawed, we must review it afresh."

On considering the case afresh, the Court was in receipt of new information relating to the appellant secured for the purposes of the appeal hearing and was able legitimately to impose a sentence of IPP.[16] The new material which they were able to take into account included a psychiatric report prepared for the purposes of the appeal which revealed that the offender admitted having sexual feelings for the boy he assaulted in the August 2004 incident.

In *Considine; Davies*,[17] a five-judge Court of Appeal presided over by Sir Igor Judge P. stressed that *Farrar* clearly did not decide that, absent a conviction, the court making the decision as to dangerousness is precluded from considering evidence of previous misconduct which would amount to a criminal offence. The "information" which can be taken into account for the purposes of s.229(2) is not restricted to "evidence", nor the offender's previous convictions or a pattern of behaviour established by them. Instead, as a matter of statutory construction, relevant information bearing on the assessment of dangerousness may take the form of material adverse to the offender which is not substantiated or proved by criminal convictions. In fact, ultimately in *Farrar* the Court of Appeal had taken into account material directly related to the August 2004 incident which was contained in the fresh psychiatric report. The Court observed that it was therefore difficult to see how evidence admitted under the bad character provisions of the CJA 2003 for consideration by the jury determining the defendant's guilt could be ignored for the purposes of the assessment under s.229. If such evidence is relevant and admissible as to guilt then it may plainly provide "information" for a dangerousness assessment. If such evidence would have been admissible for the bad character purposes of the CJA 2003, the defendant could not legitimately circumvent its deployment in the course of a dangerousness assessment by pleading guilty. Equally, if a judge excluded bad character evidence on the basis of lack of relevance or the unfairness which would ensue if it were admitted, the same conclusion would follow. The Court accepted the submissions of the then Attorney General, Lord Goldsmith, that there can be no logical reason for

---

[16] See para.24.12 below for an example of the Court of Appeal imposing a SOPO by the same process after quashing the original SOPO made by the sentencing judge.

[17] [2007] EWCA Crim 1166; [2007] Crim. L.R. 824.

distinguishing between formal evidence, adduced before a jury, and evidence or information which comes before the court through some different route.[18]

The Court stated, following *Johnson*,[19] that when a judge is reaching a conclusion as to dangerousness which is adverse to the defendant, he should not rely on a disputed fact unless it could be resolved "fairly" to the offender. The Court cited an example of unfairness as being when a defendant was undercharged (notwithstanding the availability of evidence to prosecute him for a more serious offence) on the basis that, if convicted of the less serious offence, the court could then be supplied by the prosecution with all the "information" relating to the more serious offence. If the defendant was then treated as if he had been convicted of that offence, that would be unfair to him because he might effectively be convicted in the course of the sentencing process without due process. However, the Court deliberately declined to lay down any hard and fast rules as to how a court should approach the resolution of disputed facts when making the necessary dangerousness risk assessment. The Court was of the view that, in reality, there will be very few cases in which a fair analysis of the information in the prosecution papers, the events at any trial, the judicial assessment of the defendant's character and personality,[20] the mitigation material presented to the court on behalf of the defendant, the pre-sentence report and any psychiatric or psychological reports should not provide the judge with sufficient information for his task in relation to s.229.

Consecutive sentences involving a sentence of imprisonment under ss.224 to 229 of the CJA 2003

22.64D   The Court of Appeal has issued substantial guidance to sentencing judges as to the practice to be followed when consecutive sentences are to be passed which include one of the sentences under ss.224 to 229 of the CJA 2003. In *O'Brien and others*[21] the Court was faced with two related questions: first, "Can a sentence of IPP be ordered to run consecutively to another sentence of IPP?" and, second, "If a defendant has offended whilst on licence and the court wishes to order a defendant to serve the remaining period of a previous sentence of imprisonment pursuant to section 116 of the PCCSA 2003 and is also sentencing the defendant to s sentence of IPP, how may that he achieved?". In giving the judgment of the Court, Hooper L.J. gave the following detailed explanation of the relevant principles required to answer those questions:

---

[18] The Court entertained reservations as to whether the full ambit of the principle in *Canavan* applied to the assessment of dangerousness under s.229. What *Farrar*, in keeping with *Canavan*, prohibits is the introduction of a hybrid arrangement of an effective conviction of a serious criminal offence after trial by judge alone in the course of a sentencing decision. The Court explained that a *Newton* hearing is not an acceptable form of trial for a criminal offence. It is a precondition to a *Newton* hearing that the defendant admits guilt and so it is inappropriate to use a *Newton* hearing to decide whether the offender has committed a similar offence to those before the court when assessing dangerousness.

[19] Above n.6.

[20] The Court observed that this is always a critical feature in the assessment.

[21] [2006] EWCA Crim 1741; [2007] 1 W.L.R. 833; [2007] 1 Cr. App. R.(S.) 75.

"**The general principles**
58. We were taken through the statutory provisions relevant to indeterminate sentences and it is agreed that there is no provision which forbids the imposition of consecutive indeterminate sentences or the imposition of an indeterminate sentence consecutive to another period of imprisonment. The situation has not changed since the decision in *Jones* [1962] Cr.App.R.129. Ashworth J giving the judgment of the Court of Criminal Appeal said: (pages 148–149)

'There remains the question of sentence. The learned judge in passing sentence said:

"You have been found guilty now of two crimes, evil to a degree beyond all adjectives, and it is proper that you should serve your sentence for the first crime and that neither as a matter of fact nor of appearance should it cease to be operative. In these circumstances, I pass upon you the sentence according to statute that you can be sentenced to imprisonment for life and for the protection of the public I think firstly that it should be a sentence to commence upon the expiration of your existing sentence and secondly that it would be lamentable indeed if upon the second sentence you did not serve a far longer time than upon the first."

It was contended before us that the form of the sentence was wrong in principle in that it amounted to a 'sentence of life imprisonment less the unremitted portion of the sentence of fourteen years.' Further, it was contended that the learned judge was in error in supposing that if the sentence of life imprisonment were made to take effect at once, the sentence of fourteen years would merge with it and for practical purposes cease to operate.

We were assisted on this point by the Attorney-General as *amicus curiae*, and he assured us that the two sentences would not merge, if the life sentence were made concurrent, and that the sentence of fourteen years would not be affected in any way. According to him, there was no practical difference whatever between a life sentence made concurrent and one made consecutive, but he submitted the view that it is undesirable to make the life sentence consecutive since it achieves no practical result.

We have no doubt that the learned judge had power to make the life sentence consecutive to the earlier sentence of fourteen years, but we accept the Attorney-General's submission that a consecutive sentence is undesirable. Since the practical result would be the same in any event, we see no reason to allow the appeal against sentence, and it is dismissed.

We would only add that our attention was called to several unreported judgment of this court in regard to life sentences. It is, in our view, difficult to reconcile all the observations contained in those judgments, but on the present occasion there is no need to attempt the task.'

59. We share the view expressed in that case that it is undesirable to impose consecutive indeterminate sentences or order an indeterminate sentence to be served consecutively to another period of imprisonment. Common sense suggests that a sentence of life imprisonment or of IPP starts immediately on its imposition. Given the difficulties that may be encountered already in determining when a prisoner must be released or is eligible for parole, it seems to us to be much easier not to compound those difficulties by making indeterminate sentences consecutive to other sentences or periods in custody.

60. We are supported in our conclusion by a passage in *Lang and others* where the Vice President said (in paragraph 20) that it 'will not usually be appropriate to impose consecutive extended sentences'. (See also *S.* [2005] EWCA Crim 3616, paragraph 30.)

61. We shall consider first the following situation: but for the undesirability of making indeterminate sentences consecutive to other terms, the judge would want the period

before which the defendant will become eligible for parole to be consecutive to an existing sentence or to follow a period imposed under section 116 of the Powers of Criminal Courts (Sentencing) Act (return to prison where offence committed during original sentence). How does the judge ensure that the sentence includes the balance of the existing sentence or the section 116 period?

62. The judge should increase the notional determinate term to reflect that balance or that period. The authority for so doing is *Haywood* [2000] 2 Cr.App.R.(S.) 418. The appellant had been sentenced to 8 years' imprisonment for robbery etc and two days after being sentenced he attacked a prison officer. He pleaded guilty to wounding with intent (section 18). The Recorder of Liverpool sentenced him to life imprisonment, as he was obliged to do and specified: 'the part to be served by reference to the period the appellant would have had to serve if the Recorder had imposed seven years' imprisonment consecutive, as he would have done but for section 2 [automatic life sentence].'

63. The Recorder started with a term of 15 years and halved it and then (wrongly as the Court of Appeal said) reduced that period by the time spent in custody on remand (the appellant had never been in custody anyway for the robbery).

64. In the words of Lord Bingham C.J. (pages 432–433):

'In our judgment the Recorder took a logical and obviously sensible step . . . This result is in no way unjust to the appellant who on any showing deserves a measure of punishment for this serious offence, and who clearly presents a continuing risk of danger to the public. We consider that the course which the Recorder adopted promotes the public policy underlying the Act and it furthermore avoided the obvious anomaly which would have arisen had the submissions of counsel been accepted.'

65. If the Recorder had set the notional determinate term to reflect only the section 18 offence, then, in Lord Bingham's words, 'virtually nothing' would have been added to the sentence which the appellant was already serving, a result which Lord Bingham described as 'obviously absurd' (page 422). The principle in *Haywood* was cited with approval by the Vice President in *Szczerba* [2002] EWCA Crim 440, paragraph 33; [2002] 2 Cr.App.R.(S.) 86, at page 387. The statutory provision in *Haywood* equivalent to what is now section 82A of the Powers of Criminal Courts (Sentencing) Act 2000 . . . was section 28 of the Crime (Sentences) Act 1997. Given that the two provisions are very similar, the principles laid down in *Haywood* would also apply to section 82A.

66. In *Szczerba* the Vice President said (paragraph 33):

'There are, however, circumstances in which more than half may well be appropriate. Dr Thomas identified two examples. In *Hayward* [2000] 2 Cr.App.R.(S.) 418 a life sentence was imposed on a serving prisoner for an offence committed in prison. In such a case the term specified can appropriately be fixed to end at a date after that on which the defendant would have been eligible for release on licence from his original sentence. This may involve identifying a proportion of the notional determinate term up to two-thirds. Another example is where a life sentence is imposed on a defendant for an offence committed during licensed release from an earlier sentence, who is therefore susceptible to return to custody under section 116 of the Powers of Criminal Courts (Sentencing) Act 2000. In such a case the specified period could properly be increased above one-half, to reflect the fact that a specified period cannot be ordered to run consecutively to any other sentence.'

67. On our reading of *Haywood* the Recorder achieved the desired objective by increasing the notional determinate term and not by dividing that term by (up to) two thirds rather than by a half to reach the minimum term. We think that increasing the notional determinate sentence is the better way. Indeed, for cases to which section 244

of the Criminal Justice Act 2003 applies . . . the notional determinate sentence should be divided by half to arrive at the specified minimum term.

68. In our view any section 116 period should be treated in the same way, that is by adding it to the notional determinate term which the judge would otherwise have set. As we understand it, a section 116 period attracts the early release provisions. A defendant sentenced to three years imprisonment to be served following a one year section 116 period will be released after two years. By adding the period to the notional determinate term and then halving it, the prisoner is in the same position as he would have been if the judge had passed a determinate term of the same length as the notional determinate term and made it consecutive to the section 116 period.

69. There is one more practical problem which we should address. Assume that a judge is imposing concurrent indeterminate sentences for two or more offences with corresponding concurrent minimum terms. Assume that, if he had not passed indeterminate sentences he would have passed determinate custodial sentences for those offences consecutive to each other. How does he reflect in the notional determinate term the totality of the offending? The answer is, we believe, either to choose the same notional determinate term for all of the offences or take the most serious and make the notional determinate term reflect the totality of the offending. We return to the *O'Brien* case. The notional determinate term for the robbery should reflect the need to punish both the assault with intent to rob and the robbery. That is why we increased the notional determinate sentence for the robbery in his case. This is in accordance with section 82A(3)(a) of the Powers of Criminal Courts (Sentencing) Act 2000 . . .

70. Finally we wish to say something about appeals. Given our view that it is not unlawful but merely undesirable to make consecutive indeterminate sentences or to make them consecutive to some other term or period of imprisonment, permission to appeal should not normally be granted on this ground only. Our reason for saying this is that if an appeal succeeds on this point only, then it is unlikely that the length of time which the prisoner will have to serve before being eligible for parole will be altered. In such circumstances there would be no practical point in giving permission to appeal."

O'Brien has since been followed in a number of cases dealing with the practical **22.64E** problems associated with sentences under ss.224 to 229. In *Brown*,[22] the Court of Appeal considered problems associated with the imposition of consecutive extended sentences and the imposition of an extended sentence along with a consecutive determinate sentence. Whilst the court has the power to pass either combination of sentences, difficulty might arise in both situations because of the terms of s.247 of the CJA 2003. That section dictates that a prisoner serving an extended sentence must be released as soon as he has served half of the custodial term of the sentence and the Parole Board has directed his release, being satisfied that it is no longer necessary for the protection of the public that he be confined. If consecutive extended sentences are imposed then considerable problems are created in determining the application of the appropriate licence period once the custodial element has been served. If a determinate sentence was made consecutive to an extended sentence it may be difficult to determine when the custodial element of the extended term ends and the determinate sentence began. The Court therefore advised that consecutive extended sentences and the imposition of

---

[22] [2006] EWCA Crim 1996; [2007] 1 Cr. App. R.(S.) 77.

a determinate sentence consecutive to an extended sentence are, in general terms, not appropriate and should be avoided. The Court could see no reason to suggest that such problems would arise if an extended sentence were made consecutive to a determinate sentence. Similarly, concurrent extended sentences would not cause such problems, nor would an extended sentence concurrent to a determinate sentence cause insuperable difficulties. However, in the latter case a concurrent determinate sentence longer than the custodial element of the extended sentence might well have the effect of subsuming the extended licence period and thus defeating the object of the extended sentence. It is thus sensible to avoid such a combination of sentences.

22.64F   In *R. v C and others*,[23] the Court of Appeal was again dealing with extended sentences, but its judgment applies equally to sentences of imprisonment for life and IPP. In giving the judgment of the Court, the Vice-President, Latham L.J., stated:

> "In summary, our conclusions as to the practice to be adopted in dealing with consecutive and concurrent sentences in this complex area of sentencing are as follows:
> a. There is nothing unlawful about the imposition of a concurrent or consecutive sentence within either regimes relating to extended sentences, and indeed, as explained by Hooper L.J. in *R. v O'Brien et al* [2006] EWCA Crim 1741, where sentences of life imprisonment or imprisonment for public protection are imposed under chapter 5, this court will not interfere where extended or indeterminate sentences were justified, unless the practical result is manifestly excessive, or for some reason gives rise to real problems of administration.
> b. Nonetheless, judges should try to avoid consecutive sentences if that is at all possible and adjust the custodial term or minimum period within concurrent sentences to reflect the overall criminality if that is possible within other sentencing constraints.
> c. If consecutive sentences are considered appropriate, as in the example that we have already given, or necessary, if one or more of those sentences are determinate sentences, the determinate sentences should be imposed first, and the extended sentence or sentences expressed to be consecutive.
> d. In shaping the overall sentence, judges should remember that there is no obligation for the sentences to be expressed in historical date order. There is nothing wrong with stating that the sentence for the first offence in point of time should be served consecutively to a sentence or sentences imposed for any later offence or offences."

22.64G   In *Ashes*[24] the Court of Appeal gave yet more guidance in this difficult field. It answered three questions concerned with the imposition of sentences of IPP and determinate sentences. The first ("Issue A") was how, under the existing legislation, a court should set a minimum term when imposing a sentence of IPP where it is imposed upon a prisoner who is already subject to and serving an existing custodial term. The second ("Issue B") was how the court should

---

[23] [2007] EWCA Crim 680; [2007] 3 All E.R. 735; *Times*, May 9, 2007.
[24] [2007] EWCA Crim 1848.

approach as a matter of principle imposing a sentence of imprisonment upon someone who is already serving a sentence of IPP and whether in the circumstances some adjustment, if it is otherwise permissible, may be made to the term which he is destined to serve before release may be considered. The third ("Issue C") was how in such circumstances, if it is permissible to do either the first or second as a matter of principle, the court should approach the time spent in custody. So far as Issue A is concerned, in the light of *O'Brien* and *R. v C*, the court should try to impose a term for the sentence for public protection which is concurrent with the existing determinate sentence but which also takes account of:

(a) the period still then remaining to be *served* under the existing determinate term and that should be the period of the sentence still to be served but then halved to take account of the automatic release provisions for determinate sentences;

(b) the appropriate *additional* period as the *sentence* for the offence in respect of which the court was minded to impose a term of IPP, which should then be halved; and

(c) the need to ensure that the total of the sentences imposed under paragraphs (a) and (b) above does not offend the principle of totality.

The Court also stressed that the sentencing judge should bear in mind that the period imposed in the sentence for public protection is the period which the offender *must* serve before he or she is considered for parole, and that means that the constituent period to be taken into account for ascertaining the determinate sentence at stage (a) above is the period remaining to be *served* (which is now one-half of the sentence) rather than the total sentence imposed.

So far as Issue B is concerned, the Court (echoing the concerns expressed in *Brown* and *R. v C.*) observed that, in the ordinary way, in cases in which the appropriate sentence would be a consecutive sentence to the sentence of IPP, there is a serious problem because a sentencing judge considering imposing such a sentence does not know when the existing sentence of IPP will expire as he or she cannot predict when the Parole Board will agree to release the offender. The Court also recognised the further difficulty that, even if the offender might be safe for release at the end of the sentence for public protection, there is no guarantee that he or she will also be safe to be released at the end of any consecutive determinate sentence. Thus problems arise, first, as to how to shape a sentence which would overcome this difficulty, and, secondly, in ascertaining the date when the sentence of IPP ends and when the determinate sentence starts. The Court suggested that there are three possible approaches depending on the circumstances:

(a) if the subsequent offence is one for which a sentence of IPP is available, then the sentencing judge could pass a new sentence of IPP so as to take account of not only the balance yet to be served of the existing minimum term but also the principle of totality;

(b) if the offence with which the sentence is concerned is "associated" with the offence of which the sentence of IPP was passed, one other option might be to adjust the minimum term of the sentence of IPP to reflect the criminality of that extra offence but to give no separate sentence for the new offence (see s.226(1) of the 2003 Act); or

(c) the judge could order that the determinate sentence be served first and the sentence for IPP be served consecutively but *only* if he was dealing with them on the same occasion.

The Court also expressed a provisional view that when dealing on a subsequent occasion with a further offence, the sentencing court should impose an appropriate concurrent sentence, be it determinate, indeterminate or extended, depending on the circumstances. In any event the Parole Board would be able to take into consideration the subsequent offence in determining whether to release the offender. The case before it did not require a concluded decision on that issue and the Court considered that it would be more appropriate to await a case in which that issue is a live point.

So far as Issue C is concerned, the answer to the question depends on whether the offender was in custody because he was serving an existing sentence when he is sentenced for the second offence. If he was, then his time in custody will not be deducted for the purpose of the second sentence, while if he was in custody but not because he was serving an existing sentence, then this time will be deducted from his sentence.[25]

22.64H Where an offender is convicted on two counts of an indictment, the first of which requires a sentence of IPP and the second of which requires an extended sentence, the sentencing court must impose the extended sentence and not order "no separate penalty" on the second count, deeming the criminality to have been covered by the sentence of IPP on the first count. There has to be both a sentence of IPP and an extended sentence, no matter how artificial and cumbersome that may be for the prison service.[26]

EXTENDED SENTENCES

22.72 Extended sentences may only be passed on adults who have committed specified offences for which the maximum sentence is less than 10 years' imprisonment. The scope for their use in respect of adult sex offending has therefore been dramatically reduced since the implementation of the CJA 2003. In effect, such

---

[25] The Court analysed the provisions of s.240 of the CJA 2003 and the Remand in Custody (Effect of Concurrent and Consecutive Sentences of Imprisonment) Rules 2005 in reaching that conclusion.

[26] *Younas* [2007] EWCA Crim 1676.

sentences are now confined to use in relation to the offences included in ss.30 to 41 of the Sexual Offences Act 2003.[27]

A further restriction on the use of extended sentences is that, by virtue of s.227(3)(b) of the CJA 2003, the minimum period of the custodial term is 12 months. Thus, in circumstances where a short period of custody followed by a longer period of licence might be appropriate, that option is no longer open to sentencers.

It is thus arguable that the scheme under ss.224 to 229 of the CJA 2003 has removed a valuable weapon from the armoury of sentencing judges.[28]

So far as youths are concerned, by virtue of s.226(3) of the CJA 2003, a sentencing court may (in circumstances where a sentence of IPP would have to be imposed on an adult) pass an extended sentence unless it is of the opinion that it would not be adequate for the purposes of protecting the public. The vast majority of extended sentences imposed in respect of sex offending will therefore be passed on youths.

Where an offender has crossed the relevant age threshold between the commission of the offence and the date of conviction, the starting point for the sentencing court is how that particular defendant would have been sentenced at the date of the offence following a plea of guilty.[29]

It is sometimes appropriate to pass a non-custodial sentence upon a youth where the appropriate sentence in respect of an adult would have been of an immediate custodial nature.[30]

In *Bullen*[31] the appellant pleaded guilty to an offence of indecent exposure   **22.72A** contrary to s.66 of the Sexual Offences Act 2003. The sentencing judge passes an extended sentence of three years (which was comprised of a custodial sentence of nine months' imprisonment and an extended period of licence of 27 months), which was varied on appeal to one of 21 months (being comprised of nine months' imprisonment and an extension period of 12 months) as the maximum sentence for the s.66 offence is two years' imprisonment.

---

[27] In *The Queen on the Application of Crown Prosecution Service v The Crown Court at Guildford* [2007] EWHC 1798 (Admin), the CPS sought to challenge by way of judicial review the passing of an extended sentence for an offence of rape. The sentence was obviously wrong in principle and the first avenue of recourse should have been to seek to have the case referred as unduly lenient by the Attorney General. That option was not available, as the relevant time period for making such a reference had elapsed. The Administrative Court. presided over by Lord Phillips L.C.J., ruled that the issue was a matter relating to trial on indictment under s.29(3) of the Supreme Court Act 1981 and thus the court had no jurisdiction to quash the sentence passed.

[28] In *Farrar*, above n.15, the Court of Appeal observed that the case before it would have been appropriately disposed of by way of an extended sentence under sentencing powers which pre-dated the CJA 2003.

[29] *R. v R* [2006] EWCA 3184, applying *Ghafoor* [2002] EWCA Crim 1857; [2003] 1 Cr. App. R.(S.) 84. See also *Robson* [2006] EWCA Crim 1414; [2007] 1 All E.R. 506; [2007] 1 Cr. App. R.(S.) 54.

[30] *Attorney-General's Reference (No. 96 of 2006)* [2006] EWCA Crim 3251; [2007] 2 Cr. App. R.(S.) 30.

[31] [2006] EWCA Crim 1801.

22.72B   In *S and others*[32] the Court of Appeal reached the tentative conclusion that an extension period under s.227 or s.228 of the CJA 2003 begins to run at the end of the custodial period determined by the court, and not on the date of release on licence. That is so whether or not part of the custodial period is "served" on licence. The Court reached that view for three main reasons. First, it seems to be the natural reading of the sections. Secondly, it avoids the absurdity that, where the custodial period is substantial, the passing of a short extension period will reduce the period on licence. For example, if the custodial term is one of five years and the extension period two years, then if the offender was released on licence at the halfway point and the extension period begins to run, the whole sentence would be over after four and a half years. That would be a shorter period than if the offender was simply sentenced to a conventional term of five years' imprisonment where the licence would run until the whole five years had elapsed. Thirdly, there is no reason to suppose that Parliament intended to change the concept of the previous legislation, namely that the extended period added to any initial licence period. Instead, the contrary appeared to be the case.

DISQUALIFICATION FROM WORKING WITH CHILDREN

22.77   In *R. v G*,[33] the Court of Appeal dismissed an appeal against an order disqualifying the appellant from working with children. He had been convicted under s.1 of the Child Abduction Act 1984 of abducting his son and appealed against the disqualification order relying on Arts 3, 7 and 8 of the ECHR. The Court held that the imposition of the order did not amount to degrading treatment within the meaning of Art.3, as it did not humiliate or debase an individual by showing a lack of respect for or diminishing his human dignity, nor did it arouse feelings of fear, anguish or inferiority capable of breaking an individual's moral and physical resistance. Article 7 was not engaged as the order was preventative rather than punitive. As for Art.8, a disqualifying order would not affect the appellant's employability any more than his conviction for abduction, resulting in 18 months' imprisonment, and two further convictions for assault occasioning actual bodily harm and criminal damage both committed against the boy's mother. Article 8 was not therefore engaged, but even if it were, the order was in accordance with domestic law and was necessary for the prevention of disorder or crime and the protection of the morals, rights and freedom of children.

An offender cannot be disqualified from working with children under s.28 of the 2000 Act following conviction for child abduction, contrary to s.2 of the Child Abduction Act 1984, as that offence is not an "offence against a child" within the meaning of the 2000 Act: *Prime (Roy Vincent)*.[34]

---

[32] [2005] EWCA Crim 3616.
[33] [2005] EWCA Crim 1300; [2006] 1 Cr. App. R.(S.) 30.
[34] [2004] EWCA Crim 2009; [2005] 1 Cr. App. R.(S.) 45.

In the case of an extended sentence passed under s.85 of the PCC(S)A 2000, the whole extended sentence and not simply its custodial element is to be taken into account in determining whether the sentence is a "qualifying sentence" within the meaning of s.30(1) of the 2000 Act: *Wiles.*[35]

---

[35] [2004] 2 Cr. App. R. 88. The Court of Appeal held that the conflicting decision of the Court in *Graham S.* [2001] 1 Cr. App. R.(S.) 97 had been wrongly decided *per incuriam.*

CHAPTER 23

NOTIFICATION AND NOTIFICATION ORDERS

INTRODUCTION

For regulations made under s.86, see the Sexual Offences Act 2003 (Travel   **23.04**
Notification Requirements) Regulations 2004 (SI 2004/1220) and the Sexual
Offences Act 2003 (Travel Notification Requirements) (Scotland) Regulations
2004 (SSI 2004/205).

NOTIFICATION

Qualifying offenders

In *Forbes*,[1] the Court of Appeal (Civil Division) rejected an argument that the   **23.07**
imposition of notification requirements upon a person convicted of an offence
contrary to s.170(2)(b) of the Customs and Excise Management Act 1979 relating
to the importation of child pornography was incompatible with Art.8 of the
ECHR. The fact that for the offence to be made out it was only necessary to show
that the defendant believed that the goods being imported were prohibited, and
did not require any knowledge or belief on his part that they contained
pornographic images of children, did not mean that the notification requirements
were either too broad or disproportionate. The Court emphasised that it is entirely
appropriate that people directly involved in the sexual exploitation of children
should be subject to notification requirements. That applies to persons who
deliberately import child pornography into this jurisdiction, but equally applies to
those who deliberately import prohibited goods either careless or heedless as to the

---
[1] [2006] EWCA Civ 962.

risk that those goods might contain child pornography. In giving the judgement of the Court, Sir Igor Judge P. cited with approval the following dictum of Kerr J. in *An application by Kevin Gallagher for Judicial Review*[2] when rejecting an argument that the automatic imposition of the notification requirements of the Sex Offenders Act 1997 infringed the applicant's Article 8 rights:

> "It is inevitable that a scheme which applies to sex offenders generally will bear more heavily on some individuals than others. But to be viable the scheme must contain general provisions that will be universally applied to all who come within its purview. The proportionality of the reporting requirements must be examined principally in relation to its general effect. The particular impact that it has on individuals must be of secondary importance . . . The automatic nature of the notification requirements is in my judgment a necessary and reasonable element of the scheme. Its purpose is to ensure that the police are aware of the whereabouts of all serious sex offenders. This knowledge is of obvious assistance in the detection of offenders and the prevention of crime."

23.08   In *Longworth*,[3] the House of Lords confirmed that a person conditionally discharged for an offence to which the Sex Offenders Act 1997 applies (in contrast to a person conditionally discharged for an offence to which the Sexual Offences Act 2003 applies) is not susceptible to the imposition of notification requirements. In doing so, the House reversed the controversial decision to the contrary of the Court of Appeal.[4]

The notification period

23.10   The entry in the Table relating to a person sentenced to imprisonment for life or for a term of 30 months or more has been amended to include a person sentenced to imprisonment for public protection under s.225 of the Criminal Justice Act 2003: s.57(1) of the Violent Crime Reduction Act 2006, which came into force on February 12, 2007.[5]

23.13   In the case of an extended sentence passed under s.85 of the PCC(S)A 2000, the length of the notification period is determined by the length of the whole extended sentence and not simply its custodial element: *Wiles*.[6]

When a young offender is made to subject to a detention and training order, the length of the notification period is not determined by the whole of the duration of the order (including the supervision element), but instead simply by reference to the detention and training period.[7]

---

[2] [2003] NIQB 26.
[3] [2006] UKHL 1; [2006] Crim. L.R. 553.
[4] *Longworth* [2004] EWCA Crim 2145; [2004] All E.R. (D.) 439 (Jul).
[5] SI 2007/74.
[6] [2004] 2 Cr. App. R. 88. The Court of Appeal held that the conflicting decision of the Court in *Graham S.* [2001] 1 Cr. App. R.(S.) 97 had been wrongly decided *per incuriam*.
[7] *Slocombe* [2006] 1 Cr. App. R. 33.

Notification requirements

For criticism of the notification scheme for enabling notified persons to evade its 23.18
impact by repeatedly moving, see Alisdair Gillespie, *Registering the loopholes*, NLJ
2007 (Jan), 52–53.

There is now provision for the police to enter and search a notified person's home 23.27
address under a warrant issued by a justice of the peace: s.96B of the 2003 Act,
inserted by the Violent Crime Reduction Act 2006, s.58, with effect from May 31,
2007. Section 96A makes similar provision relating to Scotland.

Footnote 10: The 2004 Regulations were revoked and replaced by the Sexual 23.28
Offences Act 2003 (Prescribed Police Stations) Regulations 2005 (SI 2005/210).
For Scotland, see the Sexual Offences Act 2003 (Prescribed Police Stations)
(Scotland) Regulations 2004 (SSI 2004/137), as amended by SSIs 2004/370,
2005/9, 2005/156 and 2007/72.

Offences relating to notification

An offence of failing to comply with notification requirements will be aggravated 23.31
if the offender has attempted to evade the requirements and to avoid being
checked by the authorities. In *Adams*,[8] the appellant had pleaded guilty to failing
to notify a change of address, failing to notify a change of name and obtaining a
pecuniary advantage by deception by obtaining employment. He was required to
comply with notification requirements as a result of convictions for indecent
assault on young boys and possession of indecent images of young boys. Following
his release from the custodial term he served for those offences, he had registered
his address as being in Manchester. On a routine check of the address by police
officers, it was discovered that he had left the address without leaving a forwarding
address or notifying any change of address to the authorities. The police then
commenced enquiries as to his whereabouts and he was found in a flat in Brighton.
He had changed his name from "Daniel Paul Gregory" to "Christopher Adams"
and was working as a fairground ride attendant. He had obtained that employment
by not disclosing his previous convictions. He was sentenced to two years'
imprisonment for the offence of failing to notify a change of address, two years
consecutive for failing to notify his change of name and a further six months
consecutive to the first two terms for obtaining a pecuniary advantage by
deception. He appealed against that sentence on the grounds, first, that the first
two terms should not have been consecutive to each other and, secondly, that the
totality was manifestly excessive. In the course of argument, the Court of Appeal
was referred to the case of *Wilcox*[9] where the appellant was subject to notification
requirements and a further requirement that, although he was running a business

---

[8] [2003] EWCA Crim 3231; [2004] 2 Cr. App. R.(S.) 15.
[9] [2003] 1 Cr. App. R.(S.) 43. See para.24.16 of the main work.

providing an inflatable aeroplane for children's parties, he should not remain at the parties whilst they were ongoing. He breached the latter requirement on a number of occasions and was sentenced to two years' imprisonment, which was reduced to a term of 12 months on appeal. The Court regarded the offending in *Adams* as far more serious than that in *Wilcox*. Wilcox had not changed his name or address and could be checked by the authorities when appropriate. By contrast, Adams had made a determined effort to avoid the registration requirements and avoid being checked by the authorities. The Court held that there was nothing wrong in principle with consecutive sentences for the first two offences as they were different in nature and occurred at different times. However, the sentence of two years' imprisonment for the offence of failing to notify a change of address was reduced to 12 months, as the totality of four-and-a-half years was manifestly excessive. The appeal was therefore allowed to the extent that the total sentence was reduced to one of three-and-a-half years.

Repeated failure to comply with notification requirements will also aggravate such an offence. In *Clarke*,[10] the appellant had failed to comply with notification requirements to which he was subject on six previous occasions between 2003 and 2005 and had been variously sentenced to custodial terms ranging between two and six months' imprisonment. When imposing a sentence of two years' imprisonment for a further breach, the Recorder said that it called for a sharp increase in the custodial term. On appeal against that sentence, the Court of Appeal agreed with the Recorder's conclusion as to the necessity for a sharp increase in the custodial term, but in the light of the appellant's early plea and his voluntary surrender to a police station to admit that he was in breach of the notification requirements, the appropriate custodial term was one of 15 months.[11]

---

[10] [2006] EWCA Crim 491.

[11] See also *Bowman* [2005] EWCA Crim 3612; [2006] 2 Cr. App. R.(S.) 40; *R. v B (David* [2005] EWCA Crim 158; [2005] 2 Cr. App. R.(S.) 65; and *Jordan* [2007] EWCA Crim 1729.

CHAPTER 24

SEXUAL OFFENCES PREVENTION ORDERS, FOREIGN TRAVEL ORDERS AND RISK OF SEXUAL HARM ORDERS

SEXUAL OFFENCES PREVENTION ORDERS

In *Richards*,[1] the Court of Appeal held that a custodial sentence within the scheme   **24.09**
created by ss.224 to 229 of the CJA 2003 (that is to say imprisonment for life,
imprisonment for public protection or an extended sentence) is not a prerequisite
or concomitant to a SOPO. The point had been the subject of debate[2] centring on
the meaning of "serious harm" in the Criminal Justice Act 2003 and "serious
sexual harm" in the Sexual Offences Act 2003. It was argued that if a sentencing
judge did not find that an offender posed a risk of "serious harm" to the public
within the meaning of s.229 of the CJA 2003 (and therefore a sentence under the
scheme of ss.224 to 229 was not warranted), he was precluded from making an
order under s.104 of the SOA 2003, as a SOPO may only be made when the court
is satisfied that it is necessary for the purpose of protecting the public or any
particular members of the public from "serious sexual harm" from the offender.
The underlying basis of that argument was that the two tests were materially
indistinguishable, because the definitions of "serious harm" in s.224(3) of the CJA
2003 ("death or serious personal injury, whether physical or psychological") and
of "serious sexual harm" in s.106(3) of the SOA 2003 ("serious physical or
psychological harm") were very similar, and it was difficult to see why "serious
harm" in the CJA 2003 should not include "serious sexual harm". In giving the
judgment of the Court in *Richards*, where the basis of the appeal was that a SOPO

---

[1] [2006] EWCA Crim 2519; and see *Rampley* [2006] EWCA Crim 2203.
[2] See commentary on *Isa* by Dr Thomas at [2007] Crim. L.R. 356; Alasdair Gillespie, *Dangerousness: Variations on a theme by Thomas* [2006] Crim. L.R. 828; and commentary on *Rampley* by Dr Thomas at [2007] Crim. L.R. 84.

should not have made when an extended sentence had not been imposed, Sir Igor Judge P. described the argument as formidable.[3] Nevertheless, there was sufficient to distinguish the two schemes and demonstrate their disconnection so as to enable the Court to reject the argument. First, the CJA 2003 and the SOA 2003 had been enacted on the same day (November 20, 2003), and if the appellant's argument was correct, the consequence would be that the Act which created the power in the court to make a SOPO was limited or controlled by a provision in a different Act, enacted on the same day and silent about its intended effect on the new power. Secondly, the scheme in ss.224 to 229 is concerned with "dangerousness" and does not contemplate a non-custodial sentence, whereas a SOPO may be made where there is no question of a custodial sentence. The making of a SOPO is not governed by dangerousness. Thirdly, there are a number of terminological differences between the two Acts. As one example, a SOPO is concerned with the protection of the public from serious physical or psychological harm, but not encompassing the risk of death, which is part of the definition in s.224(3) of the CJA 2003. In conclusion, the two schemes were intended to be and are distinct. The Court made it clear that, whilst the instant appeal was concerned with extended sentences, its judgment applied equally to sentences of life imprisonment and imprisonment for public protection imposed under the CJA 2003.[4]

24.09A Schedules 3 and 5 to the 2003 Act were amended by the Sexual offences Act 2003 (Amendment of Schs 3 and 5) Order 2007,[5] which came into force on February 18, 2007. The Order:

(a) inserts into Sch.3 the offences under ss.48–50 of the 2003 Act, where the offender was 18 or over or is sentenced to at least 12 months' imprisonment, and

(b) removes those offences from Sch.5, and inserts into that Schedule the offence of outraging public decency and offences under ss.1 and 9(1)(a) of the Theft Act 1968 (theft and burglary), ss.1 and 2 of the Child Abduction Act 1984 (child abduction), s.2 of the Protection from Harassment Act 1997 (harassment), s.85(3) and (4) of the Postal Services Act 2000 (prohibition on sending certain articles by post) and s.127(1) of the Communications Act 2003 (improper use of pubic electronic communications network).

24.12 SOPOs made since the implementation of the SOA 2003 have varied greatly in their scope. Challenges to the appropriateness or otherwise of conditions included

---

[3] Above n.1, at para.22.
[4] The basis, if not the effect, of this judgment is the subject of further criticism by Dr Thomas in a commentary at [2007] Crim. L.R. 173.
[5] SI 2007/296.

in a SOPO have been dealt with by the Court of Appeal on a case-by-case basis, with some finding at least partial success[6] and others being roundly dismissed.[7]

In *Collard*,[8] a Court presided over by the then Vice-President, Rose, L.J., and dealing with a case involving a restraint order under s.5A of the Sex Offenders Act 1997, approved the earlier case of *Halloren*.[9] The two cases establish, first, that it is a matter of discretion for the court whether to make an order. Secondly, before the court can exercise its discretion to make such an order, it must be satisfied that it is necessary in order to protect the public in general or any particular member of the public from serious harm. Thirdly, there must be material on which the court can reach the conclusion that an order is necessary to protect the public from serious sexual harm. Subsequently, the Court of Appeal has followed *Collard* and *Halloren* in relation to SOPOs, stressing the importance of the third stipulation in those cases and allowing appeals against elements of SOPOs on account of a lack of evidence to support their necessity.

In *Kyle Rogers*,[10] the Court allowed an appeal in respect of a condition in a SOPO of five years' duration that the appellant was not to have anyone aged under 16 in his home or any other residence in which he was staying temporarily unless the child was accompanied by an adult. In 2006, when the victim was aged 15 and the appellant was some four years older, he had touched her on the breasts and vagina. He repeated the behaviour on a number of occasions until she made a complaint to a church elder. The appellant, who was of previous good character, was arrested, admitted the offences and pleaded guilty. A pre-sentence report concluded that he was not a predatory sex offender nor was he at imminent risk of re-offending. The sentencing judge remarked that he thought the SOPO condition in question was appropriate because the appellant had "apparently not grasped the reality of what [he had] done". The Court of Appeal, explicitly following *Collard* and *Halloren*, emphasised the requirement of evidence of the necessity for a SOPO condition, and stated that it did not consider that "not grasping the realities" is a wholly fair basis for an order of the kind in question. The order had to be necessary and proportionate and, in the instant case, the statutory test was not met.[11]

---

[6] See *Demidoff* [2006] EWCA Crim 1017; *Oakley* [2005] EWCA Crim 2644; *Ardener* [2006] EWCA Crim 2103; [2007] 1 Cr. App. R.(S.) 92; *Thomas* [2006] EWCA Crim 1697.

[7] See *Wilson* [2006] EWCA Crim 505 for a good example of a wide-ranging SOPO being upheld. See also *Whitton* [2006] EWCA Crim 3229; [2007] 2 Cr. App. R.(S.) 15, where a SOPO was upheld in respect of a 43 year old man who had pleaded guilty to a number of offences of intentional exposure contrary to s.66 of the SOA 2003.

[8] [2004] EWCA Crim 1164.

[9] [2004] 2 Cr. App. R.(S.) 57.

[10] [2007] EWCA Crim 1870.

[11] In giving the judgment of the Court, Sir Richard Curtis highlighted the case-by-case approach to such appeals by emphasising that the decision was made on the facts of the case in front of the Court and stressing that: "It is not intended, and should not be misused, for establishing some more general proposition applicable to other cases. Experience shows, particularly in matters of this kind, that much turns on the precise facts and interpretation by the court of them in these difficult cases" (para.18).

Similarly, in *Badiei (Ali)*[12] the Court of Appeal ruled that a condition in a SOPO that prevented the appellant engaging in any work or organised leisure activity with a child under the age of 16 was not justified by any evidence. The appellant had pleaded guilty to making indecent photographs or pseudo-photographs of a child following his arrest during the course of Operation Ore. The photographs, which were numerous, included 33 at level 4. The appellant was a 45-year-old married man of previous good character with no children. The SOPO made as part of the sentence in his case prohibited him, first, from downloading material from the internet save for lawful employment or study and, secondly, from engaging in any work or organised leisure activity with a child under the age of 16. In setting aside the second element of the SOPO, the Court of Appeal observed:

> "In this case, although it is plain that harm can be done to groups of people from the taking, viewing or distributing of child pornography, that aspect has been covered by other provisions which have been made, including the restriction on the use of the internet . . . The restriction on organised leisure or working with children would only be justified if the evidence showed that that was necessary to prevent harm which arose from direct contact between the appellant and children. There is no evidence at all which suggests that the appellant is a danger through contact in that way. Therefore there was no justification for the making of that order."[13]

24.12A If a sentencing judge includes a condition in a SOPO following an erroneous exercise of the powers in s.104 of the SOA 2003, the Court of Appeal may nonetheless exercise those powers afresh and make such a condition. In *R. v D*,[14] the appellant pleaded guilty to eight offences committed against his daughter over the period when she was aged between 10 and 13. The offences, which were sample counts, comprised three indecent assaults, two attempted rapes, two offences of sexual activity with a child and one of assault by penetration. The appellant was sentenced to six years' imprisonment and made subject to a SOPO which, inter alia, prohibited the appellant from approaching, seeking to approach or communicating directly or indirectly with either his daughter or his son. The appellant challenged the part of the SOPO which prohibited any sort of contact or attempted contact with his son, on the basis that the conditions for making that part of the order were not fulfilled. The sentencing judge had not carried out the necessary risk assessment and there had been no evidence before him which justified the imposition of the condition as being necessary to prevent serious physical or psychological harm to the son. The Court of Appeal agreed with the appellant's submission that the judge had erroneously exercised his powers under s.104. Nevertheless, it was able to exercise those powers afresh with the benefit of further information it had received for the purposes of the hearing. In the light of that information, the Court was able to conclude that the requirements for the making of an order in respect of the son were fulfilled, and consequently it made

---

[12] [2005] EWCA Crim 970, followed in *Andrew* [2006] EWCA Crim 1297.
[13] At para.13.
[14] [2006] 2 Cr. App. R.(S.) 32.

such an order. On a separate point, the Court of Appeal also observed that where a court is considering making a SOPO to prevent abuse within the family, particularly of a sibling of the abused person, it may be desirable to draft the order in terms that provide a link with the court's family jurisdiction. A SOPO will often lack the flexibility to meet the constantly changing needs of a child such as, for example, the child developing a wish to have contact with the parent. In the instant case, the order made by the Court of Appeal was therefore to the effect that the appellant should not communicate or seek to communicate with the son without the order of a judge exercising jurisdiction under the Children Act 1989.[15]

In addition to the cases cited in footnotes 29–31, see *Fenton*,[16] in which the Court **24.16** of Appeal gave general guidance on sentencing for breach of a sex offender order.

In *Williams (Christopher)*,[17] the Court of Appeal quashed a total sentence of 10 years' imprisonment imposed in 2006 in respect of six counts of breach of a SOPO and substituted a total sentence of five years' imprisonment. The appellant had been convicted in 1991 of taking a child without lawful authority and false imprisonment and had been sentenced to a total of seven years' imprisonment. In 1998, he was convicted of taking a child without lawful authority and indecent assault on a male under the age of 16, and was sentenced to a total of eight years' imprisonment. In 2002 he was released on licence. He was recalled to prison in August 2003 following a breach of a licence condition requiring him to stay out of Edmonton and Enfield. He was then re-released on July 8, 2005, having been made the subject of a SOPO in June 2005, before his release. A condition of the order was that he was not to "carry out any lengthy and sustained observations on children outside of his home address". Police officers kept him under surveillance following his release and he was arrested on August 2, 2005 in respect of seven allegations of following children. The matters proceeded to trial and the appellant was convicted by the jury on six counts relating to the breach of his SOPO and acquitted on another count. The sentencing judge recognised that the offence of breaching a SOPO was not a specified offence within Sch.15 to the CJA 2003, so that the appellant could not be sentenced under the scheme contained in ss.224 to 229 of that Act. But he went on to observe that it is self-evident that some persons who have committed offences which are not specified offences may nevertheless constitute a significant risk of causing serious harm to the public by the commission of further offences. The appellant was one such person: he would pose a very grave risk to young boys when he was released into the community. The judge viewed the appellant as having an uncontrolled compulsion which made it almost inevitable that, given the opportunity, he would re-offend, and his offending would be of a very serious kind. The judge concluded that, in view of the appellant's history and his own assessment of him, he was sure that justice

---

[15] This suggested practice appears to have been followed in *Ardener*, above n.5.

[16] [2006] EWCA Crim 2156; [2007] 1 Cr. App. R.(S.) 97.

[17] [2007] EWCA Crim 1951.

demanded that public protection must be the overwhelmingly dominant consideration in the sentencing process. He therefore passed consecutive sentences of imprisonment totalling 10 years. The Court of Appeal agreed with every word of the judge's observations and said that it may be that the question of whether the statute should be amended to add the offence in question to the list in Sch.15 should be looked at carefully. It seemed to the Court that, if the offence had been specified, a sentence of IPP would likely have been appropriate. Nevertheless, the Court concluded that the sentence of 10 years, where the appellant had not touched the children, was far too long. That order of determinate sentence is routinely passed for very serious offences involving actual sexual contact, of which there was none in the instant case. The Court therefore substituted a total sentence of five years' imprisonment.

RISK OF SEXUAL HARM ORDERS

24.32   The offence provision (s.128 of the 2003 Act) will be extended in due course to cover contraventions of RSHOs and interim RSHOs made in Scotland under s.2 or s.5 of the Protection of Children and Prevention of Sexual Offences (Scotland) Act 2005: the Violent Crime Reduction Act 2006, s.56(2), which is not in force at the date of writing.

24.33   Section 129 of the 2003 Act will be extended in due course to cover convictions under s.7 of the Protection of Children and Prevention of Sexual Offences (Scotland) Act 2005 (contravention of RSHOs and interim RSHOs in Scotland): the Violent Crime Reduction Act 2006, s.56(3), which is not in force at the date of writing.

Appendix A

CRIMINAL PROCEDURE RULES

Part 29—Special measures directions
Part 31—Restriction on cross-examination by a defendant acting in person
Part 34—Hearsay evidence
Part 36—Evidence about a complainant's sexual behaviour

Part 29

29.1 Application for special measures directions

(1) An application by a party in criminal proceedings for a magistrates' court or the Crown Court to give a special measures direction under section 19 of the Youth Justice and Criminal Evidence Act 1999 must be made in writing in the form set out in the Practice Direction.

(2) If the application is for a special measures direction—

    (a) enabling a witness to give evidence by means of a live link, the information sought in Part B of that form must be provided;

    (b) providing for any examination of a witness to be conducted through an intermediary, the information sought in Part C of that form must be provided; or

    (c) enabling a video recording of an interview of a witness to be admitted as evidence in chief of the witness, the information sought in Part D of that form must be provided.

(3) The application under paragraph (1) above must be sent to the court officer and at the same time a copy thereof must be sent by the applicant to every other party to the proceedings.

(4) The court officer must receive the application—

    (a) in the case of an application to a youth court, within 28 days of the date on which the defendant first appears or is brought before the court in connection with the offence;

    (b) in the case of an application to a magistrates' court, within 14 days of the defendant indicating his intention to plead not guilty to any

345

charge brought against him and in relation to which a special measures direction may be sought; and

(c) in the case of an application to the Crown Court, within 28 days of

   (i) the committal of the defendant, or

   (ii) the consent to the preferment of a bill of indictment in relation to the case, or

   (iii) the service of a notice of transfer under section 53 of the Criminal Justice Act 1991 (2), or

   (iv) where a person is sent for trial under section 51 of the Crime and Disorder Act 1998 (3), the service of copies of the documents containing the evidence on which the charge or charges are based under paragraph 1 of Schedule 3 to that Act, or

   (v) the service of a Notice of Appeal from a decision of a youth court or a magistrates' court.

(5) A party to whom an application is sent in accordance with paragraph (3) may oppose the application for a special measures direction in respect of any, or any particular, measure available in relation to the witness, whether or not the question whether the witness is eligible for assistance by virtue of section 16 or 17 of the 1999 Act is in issue.

(6) A party who wishes to oppose the application must, within 14 days of the date the application was served on him, notify the applicant and the court officer, as the case may be, in writing of his opposition and give reasons for it.

(7) Paragraphs (5) and (6) do not apply in respect of an application for a special measures direction enabling a child witness in need of special protection to give evidence by means of a live link if the opposition is that the special measures direction is not likely to maximise the quality of the witness's evidence.

(8) In order to comply with paragraph (6)—

(a) a party must in the written notification state whether he—

   (i) disputes that the witness is eligible for assistance by virtue of section 16 or 17 of the 1999 Act,

   (ii) disputes that any of the special measures available would be likely to improve the quality of evidence given by the witness or that such measures (or a combination of them) would be likely to maximise the quality of that evidence, and

   (iii) opposes the granting of a special measures direction; and

(b) where the application relates to the admission of a video recording, a party who receives a recording must provide the information required by rule 29.7(7) below.

(9) Except where notice is received in accordance with paragraph (6), the court (including, in the case of an application to a magistrates' court, a single justice of the peace) may—

(a) determine the application in favour of the applicant without a hearing; or

(b) direct a hearing.

(10) Where a party to the proceedings notifies the court in accordance with paragraph (6) of his opposition to the application, the justices' clerk or the Crown Court must direct a hearing of the application.

(11) Where a hearing of the application is to take place in accordance with paragraph (9) or (10) above, the court officer shall notify each party to the proceedings of the time and place of the hearing.

(12) A party notified in accordance with paragraph (11) may be present at the hearing and be heard.

(13) The court officer must, within 3 days of the decision of the court in relation to an application under paragraph (1) being made, notify all the parties of the decision, and if the application was made for a direction enabling a video recording of an interview of a witness to be admitted as evidence in chief of that witness, the notification must state whether the whole or specified parts only of the video recording or recordings disclosed are to be admitted in evidence.

(14) In this Part:

"an intermediary" has the same meaning as in section 29 of the 1999 Act; and

"child witness in need of protection" shall be construed in accordance with section 21(1) of the 1999 Act.

29.2 Application for an extension of time

(1) An application may be made in writing for the period of 14 days or, as the case may be, 28 days specified in rule 29.1(4) to be extended.

(2) The application may be made either before or after that period has expired.

(3) The application must be accompanied by a statement setting out the reasons why the applicant is or was unable to make the application within that period and a copy of the application and the statement must be sent to every other party to the proceedings.

(4) An application for an extension of time under this rule shall be determined by a single justice of the peace or a judge of the Crown Court without a hearing unless the justice or the judge otherwise directs.

(5) The court officer shall notify all the parties of the court's decision.

29.3 Late applications

(1) Notwithstanding the requirements of rule 29.1—

(a) an application may be made for a special measures direction orally at the trial; or

(b) a magistrates' court or the Crown Court may of its own motion raise the issue whether a special measures direction should be given.

(2) Where an application is made in accordance with paragraph (1)(a)—

(a) the applicant must state the reasons for the late application; and

(b) the court must be satisfied that the applicant was unable to make the application in accordance with rule 29.1.

(3) The court shall determine before making a special measures direction—

(a) whether to allow other parties to the proceedings to make representations on the question;

(b) the time allowed for making such representations (if any); and

(c) whether the question should be determined following a hearing at which the parties to the proceedings may be heard.

(4) Paragraphs (2) and (3) do not apply in respect of an application made orally at the trial for a special measures direction—

(a) enabling a child witness in need of special protection to give evidence by means of a live link; or

(b) enabling a video recording of such a child to be admitted as evidence in chief of the witness,

if the opposition is that the special measures direction will not maximise the quality of the witness's evidence.

29.4 Discharge or variation of a special measures direction

(1) An application to a magistrates' court or the Crown Court to discharge or vary a special measures direction under section 20(2) of the Youth Justice and Criminal Evidence Act 1999 must be in writing and each material change of circumstances which the applicant alleges has occurred since the direction was made must be set out.

(2) An application under paragraph (1) must be sent to the court officer as soon as reasonably practicable after the change of circumstances occurs.

(3) The applicant must also send copies of the application to each party to the proceedings at the same time as the application is sent to the court officer.

(4) A party to whom an application is sent in accordance with paragraph (3) may oppose the application on the ground that it discloses no material change of circumstances.

(5) Rule 29.1(6) to (13) shall apply to an application to discharge or vary a special measures direction as it applies to an application for a direction.

29.5 Renewal application following a material change of circumstances

(1) Where an application for a special measures direction has been refused by a magistrates' court or the Crown Court, the application may only be renewed ("renewal application") where there has been a material change of circumstances since the court refused the application.

348

(2) The applicant must—

    (a) identify in the renewal application each material change of circumstances which is alleged to have occurred; and

    (b) send the renewal application to the court officer as soon as reasonably practicable after the change occurs.

(3) The applicant must also send copies of the renewal application to each of the parties to the proceedings at the same time as the application is sent to the court officer.

(4) A party to whom the renewal application is sent in accordance with paragraph (3) above may oppose the application on the ground that it discloses no material change of circumstances.

(5) Rules 29.1(6) to (13), 29.6 and 29.7 apply to a renewal application as they apply to the application which was refused.

29.6 Application for special measures direction for witness to give evidence by means of a live television link

(1) Where the application for a special measures direction is made, in accordance with rule 29.1(2)(a), for a witness to give evidence by means of a live link, the following provisions of this rule shall also apply.

(2) A party who seeks to oppose an application for a child witness to give evidence by means of a live link must, in order to comply with rule 29.1(5), state why in his view the giving of a special measures direction would not be likely to maximise the quality of the witness's evidence.

(3) However, paragraph (2) does not apply in relation to a child witness in need of special protection.

(4) Where a special measures direction is made enabling a witness to give evidence by means of a live link, the witness shall be accompanied at the live link only by persons acceptable to the court.

(5) If the special measures directions combine provisions for a witness to give evidence by means of a live link with provision for the examination of the witness to be conducted through an intermediary, the witness shall be accompanied at the live link only by—

    (a) the intermediary; and

    (b) such other persons as may be acceptable to the court.

29.7 Video recording of testimony from witnesses

(1) Where an application is made to a magistrates' court or the Crown Court for a special measures direction enabling a video recording of an interview of a witness to be admitted as evidence in chief of the witness, the following provisions of this rule shall also apply.

(2) The application made in accordance with rule 29.1(1) must be accompanied by the video recording which it is proposed to tender in evidence and must include—

    (a) the name of the defendant and the offence to be charged;

(b) the name and date of birth of the witness in respect of whom the application is made;

(c) the date on which the video recording was made;

(d) a statement as to whether, and if so at what point in the video recording, an oath was administered to, or a solemn declaration made by, the witness;

(e) a statement that, in the opinion of the applicant, either—

    (i) the witness is available for cross-examination, or

    (ii) the witness is not available for cross-examination and the parties have agreed that there is no need for the witness to be so available;

(f) a statement of the circumstances in which the video recording was made which complies with paragraph (4) of this rule; and

(g) the date on which the video recording was disclosed to the other party or parties.

(3) Where it is proposed to tender part only of a video recording of an interview with the witness, the application must specify that part and be accompanied by a video recording of the entire interview, including those parts which it is not proposed to tender in evidence, and by a statement of the circumstances in which the video recording of the entire interview was made which complies with paragraph (4) of this rule.

(4) The statement of the circumstances in which the video recording was made referred to in paragraphs (2)(f) and (3) of this rule shall include the following information, except in so far as it is contained in the recording itself—

(a) the times at which the recording commenced and finished, including details of interruptions;

(b) the location at which the recording was made and the usual function of the premises;

(c) in relation to each person present at any point during, or immediately before, the recording—

    (i) their name, age and occupation,

    (ii) the time for which each person was present, and

    (iii) the relationship, if any, of each person to the witness and to the defendant;

(d) in relation to the equipment used for the recording—

    (i) a description of the equipment,

    (ii) the number of cameras used,

    (iii) whether the cameras were fixed or mobile,

    (iv) the number and location of the microphones,

    (v) the video format used; and

    (vi) whether it offered single or multiple recording facilities and, if so, which were used; and

(e) the location of the mastertape if the video recording is a copy and details of when and by whom the copy was made.

(5) If the special measures directions enabling a video recording of an interview of a witness to be admitted as evidence in chief of the witness with provision for the examination of the witness to be conducted through an intermediary, the information to be provided under paragraph (4)(c) shall be the same as that for other persons present at the recording but with the addition of details of the declaration made by the intermediary under rule 29.9.

(6) If the special measures directions enabling a video recording of an interview of a witness to be admitted as evidence in chief of the witness with provision for the witness, in accordance with section 30 of the Youth Justice and Criminal Evidence Act 1999, to be provided with a device as an aid to communication during the video recording of the interview the information to be included under paragraph (4)(d) shall include also details of any such device used for the purposes of recording.

(7) A party who receives a recording under paragraph (2) must within 14 days of its receipt, notify the applicant and the court officer, in writing—

    (a) whether he objects to the admission under section 27 of the 1999 Act of any part of the video recording or recordings disclosed, giving his reasons why it would not be in the interests of justice for the recording or any part of it to be admitted;

    (b) whether he would agree to the admission of part of the video recording or recordings and, if so, which part or parts; and

    (c) whether he wishes to be represented at any hearing of the application.

(8) A party who seeks to oppose an application for a special measures direction enabling a video recording of an interview of a child witness to be admitted as evidence in chief of the witness must, in order to comply with rule 29.1(6), state why in his view the giving of a special measures direction would not be likely to maximise the quality of the witness's evidence.

(9) However, paragraph (8) does not apply if the witness is a child witness in need of special protection.

(10) Notwithstanding the provisions of rule 29.1 and this rule, any video recording which the defendant proposes to tender in evidence need not be sent to the prosecution until the close of the prosecution case at the trial.

(11) The court may determine an application by the defendant to tender in evidence a video recording even though the recording has not, in accordance with paragraph (10), been served upon the prosecution.

(12) Where a video recording which is the subject of a special measures direction is sent to the prosecution after the direction has been made, the prosecutor may apply to the court for the direction to be varied or discharged.

(13) An application under paragraph (12) may be made orally to the court.

(14) A prosecutor who makes an application under paragraph (12) must state—

(a) why he objects to the admission under section 27 of the 1999 Act of any part of the video recording or recordings disclosed, giving his reasons why it would not be in the interests of justice for the recording or any part of it to be admitted; and

(b) whether he would agree to the admission of part of the video recording or recordings and, if so, which part or parts.

(15) The court must, before determining the application—

(a) direct a hearing of the application; and

(b) allow all the parties to the proceedings to be present and be heard on the application.

(16) The court officer must notify all parties to the proceedings of the decision of the court as soon as may be reasonable after the decision is given.

(17) Any decision varying a special measures direction must state whether the whole or specified parts of the video recording or recordings subject to the application are to be admitted in evidence.

29.8 Expert evidence in connection with special measures directions

Any party to proceedings in a magistrates' court or the Crown Court who proposes to adduce expert evidence (whether of fact or opinion) in connection with an application or renewal application for, or for varying or discharging, a special measures direction must, not less than 14 days before the date set for the trial to begin—

(a) furnish the other party or parties and the court with a statement in writing of any finding or opinion which he proposes to adduce by way of such evidence and notify the expert of this disclosure; and

(b) where a request is made to him in that behalf by any other party to those proceedings, provide that party also with a copy of (or if it appears to the party proposing to adduce the evidence to be more practicable, a reasonable opportunity to examine) the record of any observation, test, calculation or other procedure on which such finding or opinion is based and any document or other thing or substance in respect of which any such procedure has been carried out.

29.9 Intermediaries

The declaration required to be made by an intermediary in accordance with section 29(5) of the Youth Justice and Criminal Evidence Act 1999 shall be in the following form:

> "I solemnly, sincerely and truly declare that I will well and faithfully communicate questions and answers and make true explanation of all matters and things as shall be required of me according to the best of my skill and understanding."

Part 31

31.1 Restrictions on cross-examination of witness

(1) This rule and rules 31.2 and 31.3 apply where an accused is prevented from cross-examining a witness in person by virtue of section 34, 35 or 36 of the Youth Justice and Criminal Evidence Act 1999.

(2) The court shall explain to the accused as early in the proceedings as is reasonably practicable that he—

    (a) is prevented from cross-examining a witness in person; and

    (b) should arrange for a legal representative to act for him for the purpose of cross-examining the witness.

(3) The accused shall notify the court officer within 7 days of the court giving its explanation, or within such other period as the court may in any particular case allow, of the action, if any, he has taken.

(4) Where he has arranged for a legal representative to act for him, the notification shall include details of the name and address of the representative.

(5) The notification shall be in writing.

(6) The court officer shall notify all other parties to the proceedings of the name and address of the person, if any, appointed to act for the accused.

(7) Where the court gives its explanation under paragraph (2) to the accused either within 7 days of the day set for the commencement of any hearing at which a witness in respect of whom a prohibition under section 34, 35 or 36 of the 1999 Act applies may be cross-examined or after such a hearing has commenced, the period of 7 days shall be reduced in accordance with any directions issued by the court.

(8) Where at the end of the period of 7 days or such other period as the court has allowed, the court has received no notification from the accused it may grant the accused an extension of time, whether on its own motion or on the application of the accused.

(9) Before granting an extension of time, the court may hold a hearing at which all parties to the proceedings may attend and be heard.

(10) Any extension of time shall be of such period as the court considers appropriate in the circumstances of the case.

(11) The decision of the court as to whether to grant the accused an extension of time shall be notified to all parties to the proceedings by the court officer.

31.2 Appointment of legal representative

(1) Where the court decides, in accordance with section 38(4) of the Youth Justice and Criminal Evidence Act 1999, to appoint a qualified legal representative, the court officer shall notify all parties to the proceedings of the name and address of the representative.

(2) An appointment made by the court under section 38(4) of the 1999 Act shall, except to such extent as the court may in any particular case determine, terminate at the conclusion of the cross-examination of the witness or witnesses in respect of whom a prohibition under section 34, 35 or 36 of the 1999 Act applies.

31.3 Appointment arranged by the accused

(1) The accused may arrange for the qualified legal representative, appointed by the court under section 38(4) of the Youth Justice and Criminal Evidence Act 1999, to be appointed to act for him for the purpose of cross-examining any witness in respect of whom a prohibition under section 34, 35 or 36 of the 1999 Act applies.

(2) Where such an appointment is made—

   (a) both the accused and the qualified legal representative appointed shall notify the court of the appointment; and

   (b) the qualified legal representative shall, from the time of his appointment, act for the accused as though the arrangement had been made under section 38(2)(a) of the 1999 Act and shall cease to be the representative of the court under section 38(4).

(3) Where the court receives notification of the appointment either from the qualified legal representative or from the accused but not from both, the court shall investigate whether the appointment has been made, and if it concludes that the appointment has not been made, paragraph (2)(b) shall not apply.

(4) An accused may, notwithstanding an appointment by the court under section 38(4) of the 1999 Act, arrange for a legal representative to act for him for the purpose of cross-examining any witness in respect of whom a prohibition under section 34, 35 or 36 of the 1999 Act applies.

(5) Where the accused arranges for, or informs the court of his intention to arrange for, a legal representative to act for him, he shall notify the court, within such period as the court may allow, of the name and address of any person appointed to act for him.

(6) Where the court is notified within the time allowed that such an appointment has been made, any qualified legal representative appointed by the court in accordance with section 38(4) of the 1999 Act shall be discharged.

(7) The court officer shall, as soon as reasonably practicable after the court receives notification of an appointment under this rule or, where paragraph (3) applies, after the court is satisfied that the appointment has been made, notify all the parties to the proceedings—

   (a) that the appointment has been made;

   (b) where paragraph (4) applies, of the name and address of the person appointed; and

(c) that the person appointed by the court under section 38(4) of the 1999 Act has been discharged or has ceased to act for the court.

31.4 Prohibition on cross-examination of witness

(1) An application by the prosecutor for the court to give a direction under section 36 of the Youth Justice and Criminal Evidence Act 1999 in relation to any witness must be sent to the court officer and at the same time a copy thereof must be sent by the applicant to every other party to the proceedings.

(2) In his application the prosecutor must state why, in his opinion—

    (a) the evidence given by the witness is likely to be diminished if cross-examination is undertaken by the accused in person;

    (b) the evidence would be improved if a direction were given under section 36(2) of the 1999 Act; and

    (c) it would not be contrary to the interests of justice to give such a direction.

(3) On receipt of the application the court officer must refer it—

    (a) if the trial has started, to the court of trial; or

    (b) if the trial has not started when the application is received—

        (i) to the judge or court designated to conduct the trial, or

        (ii) if no judge or court has been designated for that purpose, to such judge or court designated for the purposes of hearing that application.

(4) Where a copy of the application is received by a party to the proceedings more than 14 days before the date set for the trial to begin, that party may make observations in writing on the application to the court officer, but any such observations must be made within 14 days of the receipt of the application and be copied to the other parties to the proceedings.

(5) A party to whom an application is sent in accordance with paragraph (1) who wishes to oppose the application must give his reasons for doing so to the court officer and the other parties to the proceedings.

(6) Those reasons must be notified—

    (a) within 14 days of the date the application was served on him, if that date is more than 14 days before the date set for the trial to begin;

    (b) if the trial has begun, in accordance with any directions issued by the court; or

    (c) if neither paragraph (6)(a) nor (b) applies, before the date set for the trial to begin.

(7) Where the application made in accordance with paragraph (1) is made before the date set for the trial to begin and—

    (a) is not contested by any party to the proceedings, the court may determine the application without a hearing;

    (b) is contested by a party to the proceedings, the court must direct a hearing of the application.

(8) Where the application is made after the trial has begun—
    (a) the application may be made orally; and
    (b) the court may give such directions as it considers appropriate to deal with the application.

(9) Where a hearing of the application is to take place, the court officer shall notify each party to the proceedings of the time and place of the hearing.

(10) A party notified in accordance with paragraph (9) may be present at the hearing and be heard.

(11) The court officer must, as soon as possible after the determination of an application made in accordance with paragraph (1), give notice of the decision and the reasons for it to all the parties to the proceedings.

(12) A person making an oral application under paragraph (8)(a) must—
    (a) give reasons why the application was not made before the trial commenced; and
    (b) provide the court with the information set out in paragraph (2).

Part 34

34.1 When this applies

This Part applies in a magistrates' court and in the Crown Court where a party wants to introduce evidence on one or more of the grounds set out in section 114(1)(d), section 116, section 117 and section 121 of the Criminal Justice Act 2003, and in this Part that evidence is called "hearsay evidence".

34.2 Notice of hearsay evidence

The party who wants to introduce hearsay evidence must give notice in the form set out in the Practice Direction to the court officer and all other parties.

34.3 When the prosecutor must give notice of hearsay evidence

The prosecutor must give notice of hearsay evidence—
    (a) in a magistrates' court, at the same time as he complies or purports to comply with section 3 of the Criminal Procedure and Investigations Act 1996 (disclosure by prosecutor); or
    (b) in the Crown Court, not more than 14 days after—
        (i) the committal of the defendant, or
        (ii) the consent to the preferment of a bill of indictment in relation to the case, or
        (iii) the service of a notice of transfer under section 4 of the Criminal Justice Act 1987 (serious fraud cases) or under section 53 of the Criminal Justice Act 1991 (certain cases involving children), or

(iv) where a person is sent for trial under section 51 of the Crime and Disorder Act 1998 (indictable-only offences sent for trial), the service of copies of the documents containing the evidence on which the charge or charges are based under paragraph 1 of Schedule 3 to the 1998 Act.

34.4 When a defendant must give notice of hearsay evidence

A defendant must give notice of hearsay evidence not more than 14 days after the prosecutor has complied with or purported to comply with section 3 of the Criminal Procedure and Investigations Act 1996 (disclosure by prosecutor).

34.5 Opposing the introduction of hearsay evidence

A party who receives a notice of hearsay evidence may oppose it by giving notice within 14 days in the form set out in the Practice Direction to the court officer and all other parties.

34.6 [Revoked]

34.7 Court's power to vary requirements under this Part

The court may—
(a) dispense with the requirement to give notice of hearsay evidence;
(b) allow notice to be given in a different form, or orally; or
(c) shorten a time limit or extend it (even after it has expired).

34.8 Waiving the requirement to give a notice of hearsay evidence

A party entitled to receive a notice of hearsay evidence may waive his entitlement by so informing the court and the party who would have given the notice.

Part 36

36.1 When this Part applies

This Part applies in magistrates' courts and in the Crown Court where a defendant wants to—
(a) introduce evidence; or
(b) cross-examine a witness
about a complainant's sexual behaviour despite the prohibition in section 41 of the Youth Justice and Criminal Evidence Act 1999.

36.2 Application for permission to introduce evidence or cross-examine

The defendant must apply for permission to do so—
(a) in writing; and

357

(b) not more than 28 days after the prosecutor has complied or purported to comply with section 3 of the Criminal Procedure and Investigations Act 1996(5) (disclosure by prosecutor).

36.3 Content of application

The application must—
- (a) identify the issue to which the defendant says the complainant's sexual behaviour is relevant;
- (b) give particulars of—
    - (i) any evidence that the defendant wants to introduce, and
    - (ii) any questions that the defendant wants to ask;
- (c) identify the exception to the prohibition in section 41 of the Youth Justice and Criminal Evidence Act 1999 on which the defendant relies; and
- (d) give the name and date of birth of any witness whose evidence about the complainant's sexual behaviour the defendant wants to introduce.

36.4 Service of application

The defendant must serve the application on the court officer and all other parties.

36.5 Reply to application

A party who wants to make representations about an application under rule 36.2 must—
- (a) do so in writing not more than 14 days after receiving it; and
- (b) serve those representations on the court officer and all other parties.

36.6 Application for special measures

If the court allows an application under rule 36.2 then—
- (a) a party may apply not more than 14 days later for a special measures direction or for the variation of an existing special measures direction; and
- (b) the court may shorten the time for opposing that application.

36.7 Court's power to vary requirements under this Part

The court may shorten or extend (even after it has expired) a time limit under this Part.

Appendix B

MEMORANDUM OF UNDERSTANDING BETWEEN CROWN PROSECUTION SERVICE (CPS) AND THE ASSOCIATION OF CHIEF POLICE OFFICERS (ACPO) CONCERNING SECTION 46 SEXUAL OFFENCES ACT 2003

1. Introduction
2. Purpose of the Memorandum
3. Principles
4. Factors to be taken into account
5. Specific agreements
6. The Internet Watch Foundation (IWF)

Introduction

The aim of this memorandum is to help clarify the position of those professionally involved in the management, operation or use of electronic communications networks and services who may face jeopardy for criminal offences so that they will be re-assured of protection where they are acting to combat the creation and distribution of images of child abuse. This memorandum has been created within the context of child protection, which will always take primacy.

The Protection of Children Act 1978 (the 1978 Act) prohibits at Section 1(1)(a) the "taking or making" of an indecent photograph or pseudo-photograph of a child. Making includes the situation where a person downloads an image from the Internet, or otherwise creates an electronic copy of a file containing such a photograph or pseudo-photograph. To be an offence, such "making" must be a deliberate and intentional act, with knowledge that the image made was, or was likely to be, an indecent photograph or pseudo-photograph of a child (*R v Smith and Jayson, 7th March 2002*). So a person accidentally finding such an image already has a defence to that act of making. However, in some cases, it may still be necessary for that person, or others (for example a person to whom the accidental find is reported), to knowingly "make" another copy of the photograph or pseudo-photograph in order that it will be reported to the authorities, and clearly it is desirable that they should be able to do so without fear of prosecution.

The Sexual Offences Act 2003 includes at section 46 an amendment to the 1978 Act of creating a defence to a charge of "making". A defence is available where a person "making" such a photograph or pseudo-photograph can prove that it was necessary to do so for the purposes of the prevention, detection or investigation of crime, or for the purposes of criminal proceedings.

This reverse burden is intended to allow those people who need to be able to identify and act to deal with such images to do so. It also presents a significant obstacle to would-be abusers and those who exploit the potential of technology to gain access to paedophilic material for unprofessional (or personal) reasons.

It is important, therefore, to protect people whose legitimate duties expose them by necessity to potentially illegal material, so that they are able to report it with confidence to the appropriate authorities, whether that be the police or the Internet Watch Foundation (IWF). It is also important that people who report such material indirectly, for example through an ISP abuse team or an internal escalation process, also benefit from this protection. The key is that the purpose of the act of making a copy is clear, and not a veil for abusive behaviour.

Purpose of the Memorandum of Understanding

Any person who falls within its provisions can claim the benefit of the defence, and have that claim tested by the authorities. However, many people working in all sorts of industries may be called upon to respond professionally to the presence of indecent photographs/ pseudo photographs, and this memorandum seeks specifically to give further reassurance to those people. It provides guidance to organisations and those whose work involves them in the discovery or reporting of indecent images of children in electronic communications media, in order to create the right balance between protecting children and effective investigation of offences. The Police Service and industry have worked hard to create an excellent working partnership between themselves and interested organisations. The fight against this kind of crime would be damaged if people wishing to report such images felt they could not do so for fear of prosecution.

This memorandum therefore sets out, briefly, the major factors that the police and CPS consider will be relevant to a decision on how to proceed in a particular case. It focuses on the new defence to "making" but inevitably there are links to the existing offences of distribution and possession of such indecent photographs, and their associated defences. In general, if the handling of a particular photograph or pseudo-photograph satisfies the tests set out below, it is highly unlikely that it would be in the public interests to embark on a prosecution.

General Principles

- The Police Service retain primary responsibility for investigation in this area
- CPS retain primary responsibility for decisions relating to prosecution
- The police service relies on the support and cooperation of service providers and others involved in working with computers and electronic

communications services and systems. Those working in this field deserve clarification of the agreed approach between ACPO and CPS in relation to possible legal consequences of investigative actions

- Individuals or organisations who accidentally discover criminal activity or to whom such activity is reported require protection from the risk of prosecution where, in order to report it, they make a copy.
- Society requires this protection to be appropriate and controlled in order to protect children from future or continuing abuse and to bring to justice those responsible.
- Vigilantism is not merely unnecessary it is unhelpful: anyone taking it upon themselves to seek out or investigate this kind of material where there is no legitimate duty to do so will be liable to prosecution.
- People with a legitimate role in knowingly investigating suspect images in order that they should be reported should be able to do so without fear.

Major factors to be taken into account

Whilst the facts of each case will be different the issues below identify when protection will be offered. The factors below indicate what may have been the intentions of individuals when they "made" a particular indecent photograph or pseudo-photograph.

It is the combination of all the circumstances that will guide investigation and prosecution decisions. Where the authorities are satisfied that the facts indicate that the intention of the "making" was genuinely to prevent, investigate, or detect crime under the 1978 Act a prosecution would not be pursued, because the defence would apply.

Generally, large and complex organisations involved in reporting of this kind of abusive image would be expected to have more formal guidance, setting out how suspect or illegal images should be dealt with, than smaller organisations. For an individual in a large organisation to be sure that they, individually, can benefit from the defence, they must have confidence that the internal systems of the organisation will show that they have not abused their position in relation to the image, and that the system as a whole was acting for the purposes set out. An individual in a smaller organisation may not need formal written procedures, but will still need to be able to show what was done, and that what was done is justified in pursuit of the purposes set out.

Where the "making" was genuinely carried out and reported in a timely manner by the person acting in their legitimate professional capacity, with the right intentions, the exception under section 46 of the Sexual Offences Act 2003 will apply and there will therefore be insufficient evidence to prosecute. If in exceptional circumstances the section 46 defence did not apply to someone who was nevertheless operating in a legitimate professional capacity, it may still not be in the public interest to prosecute.

The section 46 defence would not apply where there was other evidence that the person was abusing their position with the intention of "making".

Factors affecting the decision whether to accept a claim that "making" was covered by the new defence:

1. The way the indecent photograph or pseudo-photograph was discovered or made

Those knowingly making abusive images will need to demonstrate that they have some identified role or duty, as a result of which they needed to respond to a complaint, or investigate the abuse of a computer or other electronic communications system, or otherwise access particular data, and that they "made" the images in the course of that duty.

2. The speed with which the indecent photograph or pseudo-photograph was reported, and who it was reported to

"Making" of an abusive image which is genuinely for the purposes of investigation, detection or prevention of crime will at some point result in a report to the relevant authorities, and will always be with the intention that such a report should be made. While this will not always be a direct referral, since investigation of a suspect image in a large organisation may involve more than one staff member, the timing of the report, bearing in mind the particular circumstances, would be material in deciding whether prosecutions would be in the public interest. Each staff member in such an organisation is responsible only for their own actions and good faith, and can benefit from the defence if those meet the requirements of this memorandum. The authorities will need to be satisfied that any delay was reasonable, and that failure to report was not intended to prevent or hinder effective investigation of an offence.

3. The handling and storage of the indecent photograph or pseudo-photograph was appropriate and secure

What is done with an image in addition to "making" and reporting it will also be relevant to consideration of the applicability of the defence: physical mishandling or electronic misuse of an image, for example by irrelevant distribution or unnecessary personal storage, may raise questions about the motivation for the "making" resulting in investigation and possibly prosecution. On the other hand, handling involving demonstrable restriction of access to the image(s), and secure storage by the "maker", for example, maybe evidence in support of the applicability of the defence.

4. Copying of photographs or pseudo-photographs must be the minimum to achieve the objective and be appropriate

Investigation should not involve making more images, or more copies of each image, than is needed in all the circumstances: an individual reporting an image seen on a site, for example, does not need to examine the rest of the site or similar sites. What is necessary will depend, amongst other things, on the purpose. For example, where the intent is simply to report an internet site to establish whether illegal material truly is present, relatively little is necessary, and doing more should be avoided. Where, on the other hand, there is a need to store very transitory data in order to report apparently illegal material, more extensive action is likely to be justified. A responsible person, acting in a legitimate professional capacity to secure evidence, may, as part of the preparation of a report on suspect images, take reasonable steps to preserve that data relevant to the discovery, including disc images, audit and log files, archives, mailboxes and the like. What is reasonable will depend on all the circumstances including the nature of the communications medium concerned. Where the action is proportionate and necessary it will not be in the public interest to prosecute.

5. Individuals should be expected to have acted reasonably

A prosecution is likely where there is evidence that the individual has deliberately flouted procedural safeguards, taken on an unnecessary self-appointed role as an investigator as cover for abuse, or otherwise gone out of their way to seek out indecent images for inappropriate reason.

Specific Agreements and Advice

Sometimes electronic communications providers -or others -handling considerable traffic or offering particular services may seek further guidance, for example in seeking endorsement in advance that internal processes would when followed result in indecent images being handled acceptably. Specific written authorities to undertake particular work in support of the legislation can be given by officers acting on behalf of a chief officer (ACPO). This will give additional certainty to individuals and organisations who are likely to need, frequently, to "make" indecent photograph or pseudo-photograph and, provided the conditions were adhered to, such activities would not be subject to a criminal investigation as it would not be in the public interest to prosecute.

These authorities might specify people, departments or organisations (such as IWF) to handle material specific to an individual investigation or for a wider remit.

The authority will outline that it is given subject to it being

- For the purpose of preventing / detecting / investigating an offence under the 1978 Act or;
- For the purposes of preventing another from committing or continuing to commit an offence in connection with indecent images or;
- To prevent the image being concealed, lost, altered or destroyed AND to preserve evidence

An individual or body wilfully acting outside such guidance once it has been offered could not expect to benefit from it.

Similarly, even at an individual level, shortcomings may sometimes be identified in the way a particular abusive image has been identified or handled. Though not subject of a prosecution, this may mean that advice is offered by investigating officers on future conduct. Ignoring such advice would be a relevant factor in prosecution decisions as to sufficiency of evidence and public interest should the issue arise again.

Role of the IWF

The IWF is funded by service providers, mobile network operators, software and hardware manufacturers and other associated partners. It is supported by the Police and CPS and works in partnership with the Government to provide a 'hotline' for individuals or organisations to report potentially illegal content and then to assess and judge that material on behalf of UK law enforcement agencies. It also exists to assist service providers to avoid abuse of their systems by distributors of child abuse content and to support law enforcement officers, at home and abroad, to detect and prosecute offenders. Reports made to the IWF in line with its procedures will be accepted as a report to a relevant authority.

If potentially illegal content is hosted in the UK the IWF will work with the relevant service provider and British police agency to have the content 'taken down' and assist as necessary to have the offender(s) responsible for distributing the offending content detected.

In cases where the potentially illegal content is hosted outside the UK, the IWF will work in partnership with hotlines across the world and various Law Enforcement bodies at home and abroad to have the content investigated.

For the avoidance of doubt, the IWF assesses and traces potentially illegal child abuse content if it is judged to contravene UK law irrespective of where the content originated.

Service Providers and Police Agencies are provided with a dedicated and streamlined "internet" reporting mechanism to the IWF.

Members of the public who are exposed to indecent images of children can report their exposure by either, telephone, mobile, fax or preferably through an 'Internet hotline' at *http://www.iwf.org.uk*

Each Police force will have a single point of contact with service providers. Information on how to report crime is available on police websites *http://www.police.uk*.

A GUIDE TO PROSECUTING AND DEFENDING CASES INVOLVING SEXUAL OFFENCES
by Patricia Lees

PROSECUTING

1. DRAFTING INDICTMENTS

Para C.02:

(iii) The Criminal Procedure Amendment Rules 2007[1] have brought about an important change to the rule against particularising a series of like offences within a single count meaning that it is no longer essential for a count to relate to a single act. Part 14 of the Criminal Procedure Rules as amended applies to all cases sent, transferred or committed to the Crown Court on or after April 2, 2007. New Rule 14.2(2) is a revision of what is often called the "rule against duplicity". It allows a prosecutor in certain circumstances to bring a single charge against a defendant even though that includes more than one incident of the offence alleged. This means a change in the way an indictment can be drafted in order to reflect a continuing course of conduct. Instead of the old rule of charging a series of counts, dividing up both the time-frame and type of assault, it is now proper to charge one count covering a period over which a number of offences have occurred. It is suggested, however, that this should be limited to counts reflecting periods of 12 months or similar, rather than a number of years, and so it may not in fact affect the way in which such indictments are often drafted, i.e. as covering a period of a calendar year for each type of assault.

Prosecutors should note that it is still necessary to draft separate counts to reflect each type of assault, in order for the jury to differentiate between the types of assault alleged and for the sentencer properly to reflect gravity and criminality

---

[1] SI 2007/699.

in the total sentence. Consideration must still be given as to whether this is the correct approach in each particular case. It is most likely to be appropriate when a complainant cannot differentiate between many occasions over a period of time, making a broad allegation without detail of, for example, several years of regular and repeated acts. But it is unlikely to be appropriate where for example there are differences within the evidence creating the possibility of different verdicts dependant upon dates or other factors. See para.15.67.

(iv) When pleading offences under the Sexual Offences Act 2003 which fall within the child or familial categories, prosecutors should consider the advantages and disadvantages of undertaking to prove more elements. Thus, a sexual touching by a defendant under 18 will often attract higher maximum penalties if the child or familial sections are not used. Further, they will by definition be easier to prove. For example, an allegation of sexual touching by a boy aged 17 on a complainant aged 12 will attract a maximum of 14 years if pleaded under s.7 (sexual assault) as opposed to 5 years (even if the assault were penetrative) under s.13.

(vi) It is now clear that applications for severance where there are allegations of rape which straddle the legislative changes affecting the law in relation to belief in consent will be rarely, if ever, appropriate. See para.15.67B.

2. DISCLOSURE

Para C.04:

(iii) It will be important for the judge to be made aware of the implications of the ruling of the Divisional Court in *R. (TB) v The Combined Court at Stafford*,[2] setting out the right of the complainant (or, by inference, any witness) to be able to make representations in respect of personal records is established and rules of procedure set down. It may be, ultimately, that the overriding principle of the need for a fair trial requiring disclosure has its own consequences for a trial but that cannot obviate the need for adherence to the procedure which should be adopted.

3. SIMILAR FACT

Para C.05:

Applications to admit such material as evidence of bad character are now regularly made under the provisions of the Criminal Justice Act 2003. It is important for the rules in relation to timing to be adhered to particularly in sex cases where a complainant waiting to give evidence should not be required to re-attend at some

---

[2] [2006] EWHC 1645 (Admin).

later date because of inefficiency. See para.15.40A. Remember that the underlying facts of a conviction or previous allegation need to be either agreed or capable of being properly proved. It is usually much more effective to call a previous complainant live than read a witness statement, even if it is agreed. See paras 15.40B, 15.67.

5. DELAY

Para C.06:

(ii) *R. v. B.*[3] has not been regularly followed in the Court of Appeal; it very much turns on its own facts, i.e. a very old case involving a single complainant without any supporting evidence.

9. SPECIAL MEASURES

Para C.10:

(iv) For cases investigated on or after September 1, 2007, the provisions allowing for the use as evidence-in-chief of an adult witness's Achieving Best Evidence video are now in force. This means that an adult complainant can give evidence in the same way as a child, though of course this may not always be the most desirable course; a concern about the jury's proper assessment of a witness may then arise. One solution which allows for a witness's video to be played, having the advantage of capturing the allegation at an early stage after complaint and not requiring the witness to repeat it at least in chief, is for the witness then to come into court to be cross-examined (this can of course be done using a screen).

(v) The pilot scheme for examination through an intermediary has now ended; as of September 1, 2007, the facility is available throughout the jurisdiction. The purpose is of course to assist communication and not circumvent questions which may shed light on the truth, and so asking the trial judge to set some ground rules is likely to assist. It is also a good idea to speak to the intermediary before the witness gives evidence in order to find out how best to communicate with the witness yourself; the intermediary should only intervene if he or she perceives a difficulty has arisen for the witness in either understanding the question or communicating the answer. You should receive disclosure notes of a pre-trial meeting between the witness and the intermediary.

(vi) The use of witness profiling is possible, but not yet as widely available as intermediaries; this may be a question of training and funding. A witness profile is created after meetings between the profiler and the witness (including

---

[3] [2003] 2 Cr. App. R. 13.

defendants), which provides all parties with information which should be followed in order to ensure that a vulnerable witness is able to communicate and give evidence as fully as possible. In order to seek assistance in cases which may require a witness profile, Geraldine Monaghan and Mark Pathak of Liverpool City Council should be the first port of call for prosecution or defence as they have put in place a model scheme. A concern which might need to be addressed is the issue of disclosure; care needs to be taken during the creation of the profile to ensure that the evidence is not discussed during meetings between profiler and witness.

14. NON-DEFENDANT'S BAD CHARACTER

Para C.14:

Note the apparent lacuna in the application of s.41 to "old regime" cases which pre-date May 1, 2004 has now been held by the Court of Appeal not to exist.[3A] See para.18.23.

NEW 15A. EVIDENCE OF BAD CHARACTER AND SIMILAR FACT EVIDENCE

C.15A:

Bad character and hearsay applications under the Criminal Justice Act 2003 are all potentially relevant to historic abuse cases, no matter how old. Bad character may be relevant even if it post-dates the offence(s).

1. *Prosecutors*: Should have regard to what it is you consider may be admissible *and* how it is proposed it will be placed before the jury. Do not assume that either the police or Crown Prosecution Service have always checked whether there are concurrent proceedings. It will be rare that the defence or the trial judge will simply accept evidence of a conviction let alone an acquittal as being sufficient. At the least the papers of the previous/other case will need to be seen. In an acquittal case (see *R. v Z.*[4]), check to see if the earlier complainant is prepared to go through giving evidence again, as will invariably be required. See para.15.40B.
2. *Defenders*: Should request the underlying facts on which the application is based, in statement form preferably. If a crime report is provided and gives sufficiency of information, instructions need to be taken to see if it is accepted (was there an agreed and accepted basis of plea upon which the defendant was previously sentenced). If the facts are not accepted

---

[3A] *Cartwright* Court of Appeal November 7, 2007.
[4] [2000] 2 A.C. 483.

and cannot be proved in an admissible form, they should not go before the jury,[5] although this does not necessarily mean that the conviction itself will be excluded.

3. *Both parties should adhere to the time constraints placed upon them for such applications*; judges will often refuse an application on the basis it is out of time. See para.15.40A.

16. SENTENCING

Para C.18

(ii) The "dangerousness" provisions of the CJA 2003 governing such sentences are now in force. The Court of Appeal has repeated that bothj counsel must be in a position to assist judges as to their powers. See *Reynolds*[5A] where the Court of Appeal had to deal with a number of cases where judges had passed extended sentences upon adults convicted of serious specificed offences. The judges did not have the power to pass extented sentences in respect of "serious specified" offences where the offender is 18 or over.

DEFENDING

1. DELAY

Para C.20:

When considering whether to make an application to stay the proceedings as an abuse of process on the grounds of delay, the principles to be applied are now set out in *Stephen Pauls*.[6] Note the procedure to be followed for making such an application as set out in the current Practice Direction.[7]

The decision in *Smolenski*[8] has meant that unless a case is exceptional, the best time for applying for a stay is after the evidence of the complainant has been called. In practice, *Smolenski* has had the dual effect of both reducing outset-of-trial applications and emasculating those that take place after the evidence.

---

[5] *Humphris* [2005] EWCA 2030.
[5A] [2007] 2 Cr. App. R. (S) 87. See also *Cain* [2007] 2 Cr. App. R. (S) 25 (p.135) LCJ.
[6] [2006] EWCA Crim 756, para.21.
[7] (Criminal Proceedings, Consolidation) [2002] 1 W.L.R. 2970, para.IV.36.1–5.
[8] [2004] EWCA Crim 127.

2. DISCLOSURE

Para C.21:

See Para C.04 (iii) above.

4. APPROPRIATE MEASURES

Para C.22:

Note that the use of intermediaries and witness profiling is now widely available. If these would assist a vulnerable defendant an application similar to one for any other special measure in the interests of justice may be made. See para C.10 above.

NEW 6A. EXPERT EVIDENCE

Para C.24A:

Note the recent authorities in respect of cases involving very young children which raise the question of childhood amnesia. In *R. v H. (J.R.),*[9] the Court of Appeal admitted evidence from a psychologist and expert in the field of memory formation and development. However, there is an important caveat, in that such evidence is only likely to be helpful in the most unusual cases of child abuse and normally the ability of a witness to remember events will, in the absence of special consideration, be well within the experience of jurors. In *Snell and Wilson,*[10] involving the same expert witness, the Court of Appeal said that "save where there is evidence of mental disability or learning difficulties, attempts to persuade the court to admit such evidence should be scrutinised with great care".

8. RESTRICTIONS ON EVIDENCE OF PREVIOUS SEXUAL HISTORY

Para C.26:

Note the application of s.41 to cases which pre-date May 1, 2004: see para.18.23.

---

[9] [2006] 1 Cr. App. R. 10.
[10] [2006] EWCA Crim 1404.

INDEX